I C

Wenham, Mass.

PALEARCTIC

b

f

g

ORIENTAL

k

OPIAN

C

Faunal Regions of the World

The black letters refer to the region codes used in this book

By the same author

WORDS FOR BIRDS:

A Lexicon of North American Birds with Biographical Notes

Checklist of the
WORLD'S BIRDS

A complete list of the species, with names,
authorities and areas of distribution

EDWARD S. GRUSON
with the assistance of
RICHARD A. FORSTER

QUADRANGLE/THE NEW YORK TIMES BOOK CO.

For my mother, Edith Black Gruson, and my father, the late Harry Gruson

First published 1976 by William Collins Sons & Co. Ltd.
Copyright © 1976 by Edward S. Gruson.
All rights reserved, including the right to reproduce this book
or portions thereof in any form.
For information, address:
Quadrangle/The New York Times Book Co.,
10 East 53 Street,
New York, New York 10022.
Manufactured in the United States of America.

Library of Congress Catalog Card Number: 72-85239

International Standard Book Number: 0-8129-0296-3

Contents

vii

Introduction

This is a book for 'listers' and 'tickers'.

The book offers a static view of bird speciation; a snapshot of the birds of the world which cannot take into account the evolution of avian species. For this reason the book is more like Boucard's *Catalogus Avium*, published in 1876 or Sharpe's *Handbook of the Genera and Species of Birds*, published in the decade between 1899 and 1909 than Peters' *Checklist of the Birds of the World*.

Peters' *Checklist* is the standard, authoritative reference for the professional biologist. Thirteen of the projected fifteen volumes have been published. Not only are the species of birds and their ranges given, but in addition, all of the subspecies for each species are treated and it is for this reason that it is a primary tool for the taxonomist and systematist. In only two volumes are English names for the species of birds provided. Indeed, the editors comment on the controversy that even this gesture generated among the audience to whom the series is directed.

Ornithological literature includes a number of one-volume surveys of the families of birds of the world. Austin and Singer's *Birds of the World*, Fisher & Peterson's *The World of Birds*, and Gilliard's *Living Birds of the World* are the three most frequently seen. Each has a particular point of view but each treats the Class Aves at the family level. Within each family, species are discussed; but none can be what they do not set out to be, a complete listing of the species. Edited by John Gooders, a nine-volume *Birds of the World* was published recently, in parts-form, in England. Although a notable achievement in ornithological journalism, it lacks the authority of Peters. In addition, while it lists most of the species of birds it remains incomplete from this point of view. For example, among the Monarch Flycatchers, the genus *Monarcha* is described as consisting of thirty-six species but only one is listed. Among the Sylvinae the genus *Apalis* is described as consisting of sixteen species but only one is made explicit.

It is the purpose of this book to provide as complete a listing of the species of birds of the world as possible, to give the scientific name and an English common name for each of the species, to provide a source to which the reader is referred if more information about the species is wanted and to give a gross idea of its range. The last two pieces of information are provided in code form. The source codes will be found on page 193 and the region codes are on the endpapers.

THE AVIFAUNAL REGIONS

The earth's surface, land and water, has been divided by zoogeographers into five major faunal regions. These are shown on the map on the endpapers of this book. Overlapping zones of transition between these regions are shown and, for convenience sake, some avifaunal regions are futher subdivided.

The Holarctic Avifaunal Region has been subdivided into the Nearctic and Palearctic regions. The Neotropical Avifaunal Region has been subdivided into South America, The Caribbean or West Indies and Central American regions. The Ethiopian Avifaunal Region distinguishes only between the African land mass south of the Sahara and the Madagascan regions. The Oriental Avifaunal Region has been subdivided into the Indo-Pakistani subcontinental area, South-east Asia to the Wallace line between Bali and Lombok and Southern China. The Australasian Avifaunal Region includes New Guinea and surrounding islands, Australia and New Zealand, and the islands of the Pacific Ocean.

Conceptually, regions are most frequently thought of as referring to an area of land and water. To most zoogeographers faunal regions allude to a communality of species and families of living organisms. In a sense then the regions are best thought of as in a dynamic state although these representations on maps suggest a static situation.

THE SOURCES

For each of the avifaunal regions and subregions standard reference works were assembled if they were available. From these reference works lists were made, edited for duplications and a final tally is presented in this book. These sources may be found on page 193.

Not all the avifaunal regions have been equally well studied; nor do all taxonomists agree with one another!

For the Palearctic Avifaunal Region, Vaurie's *Birds of the Palearctic Fauna* was used. This was supplemented by *The A.O.U. Checklist of North American Birds* and recent addenda to that volume.

For the Neotropical Avifaunal Region, de Schauenzee's *Guide to the Birds of South America*, Eisenmann's *Species of Middle American Birds* and Bond's *Birds of the West Indies* were used.

For the Ethiopian Region, C. B. N. White's revision was supplemented by the work of Hall and Moreau. Rand's book on Madagascar was the source of the list for that subregion.

The Oriental Avifaunal Region was a more difficult challenge to overcome. Ripley's *Synopsis* took care of the Indo-Pakistani subcontinent. Smythie's books cover Borneo and Burma and Delacour's book accounted for Malaya. Other parts of this region were treated in greater or lesser reliability in a host of articles. For example, the birds of the Celebes have not been treated comprehensively since Stressemann's articles of 1939 and 1940. It was a matter of luck that galleys of Ben King's *Field Guide to the Birds of South-East Asia* were made available. (This book, now published, is the first one-volume treatment of this subregion.)

The Australasian Region was even more difficult. The *Official Checklist of the Birds of Australia* is out of date, although New Zealand has a new one. In the main, the paper by Mayr and Serventy (1944) and the CSIRO publication were used for Australian species. New Guinea is covered in Gilliard and Rand's book. The offshore islands were covered by searching the literature.

The islands of the Pacific Ocean were covered by starting with Myer's *Birds of the South west Pacific* and then searching the literature for treatments of the avifauna of specific islands. A double check for endemic species was made by using Greenway's *Extinct and Vanishing Birds of the World* as well as the list of *Extinct and Endangered Birds and Mammals of the World* contained in Fisher's *Wildlife Crisis*.

ORGANIZATION

The sequence of families and genera follows Peters very closely. For the convenience of the non-professional user it was decided to list the sequence of species within genera alphabetically. There is at least some intellectual support for this somewhat unusual treatment. Moreau (1960), in his review of the Ploceidae, concludes:

> What is this order of genera really worth? Being unable to
> indicate evolutionary radiation, a linear order cannot reflect
> any concept of the phylogeny of the group; it obscures the
> fact that the biological gaps between the genera are of
> extremely unequal extent; ... In other words, an attempt at a
> logical or phylogenetic order is hopelessly prejudiced. I
> prefer the alternative of an arbitrary, alphabetical order;
> and that is what will be offered in the summary.

These are brave, almost revolutionary, words. What concerned Moreau about the sequence of genera is at least equally valid about the sequence of species.

Mayr (1965), the Nestor of systematists, has written a rebuttal of Moreau's despair. He presents cogent arguments for the necessity of 'placing species into natural groups' and goes on to say that this 'does not permit the intellectually lazy solution of an alphabetical sequence'. Further on he notes that as field and chemical studies are increasingly used in making taxonomic decisions, alphabetical orderings would prevent the results of these studies being compared with the results of morphological studies. He does point out that taxonomy 'cannot abandon the endeavour to improve its theories, its classifications. Yet this brings it at once into immediate conflict with one of the functions of classification, ease of reference'.

Since a vast majority of the users of this book will not be involved in, or perhaps even aware of, the problems of taxonomy, the list is arranged to maximize the 'ease of reference'.

I have tried to avoid making taxonomic or systematic judgements, I am not competent to do so. Where conflicts occur I have tried to resolve them 'reasonably' and have used footnotes extensively. The footnotes are not intended to provide direction to the literature but to indicate the decision made and to at least permit the user to know what has happened. When species have been 'lumped' I usually use the phrase 'Includes ...' to denote which species have been relegated to subspecific rank. When a genus has been 'lumped', the footnote, beginning with 'Replaces ...' lists the name of the genus or genera that have been dropped.

A NOTE ON NAMES

When the binomial classification of animal species was introduced Latin was the universal language of science. The gender of the generic and specific constituents of the binomial matched. Over the years, as taxonomic revision has gone on, this matching has in many cases been neglected. It would be a nicety if it could be revived by an official body.

With regard to the English common names a pleasant disorder reigns. There are 'Rock Wrens' in the United States and New Zealand. Their only common characteristic is their name. Who is to change? Birdwatchers in New Zealand or the United States? The American Ornithologists' Union or The Ornithological Society of New Zealand? Should all species in the Genus *Alcippe* be called 'Tit-babblers', 'Quaker Babblers' or 'Nun Babblers'? Can they or can they not be mixed? And who is to decide? It would seem especially inappropriate at this time for an American to be telling an English-speaking birder from another country what to call the birds of that country. In developing this list alternative names for species were commonly found. The choice of one over another was relatively arbitrary. Some were chosen for euphony or charm and others were chosen because they seemed more apt. When no common name for a species was found as neutral a one as possible was made-up—with three exceptions—when the author thought of one, and friends of two, irresistible puns.

ACKNOWLEDGEMENTS

Many people helped in the preparation of this book.

Peter Alden, James Baird, Paul Miliotis, Robert Smart and Bruce Sorrie were all encouraging and helpful especially with the choice of common names and with proof-reading.

Raymond A. Paynter of the Museum of Comparative Zoology at Harvard University was extremely generous with his time and material from his unique personal library. I am equally grateful for his tact in not discouraging me from continuing this project.

Mrs Ruth Hill, the Librarian of the Museum of Comparative Zoology, and her staff were ever helpful and I wish to acknowledge my gratitude to them.

C. J. O. Harrison very kindly reviewed the manuscript and corrected errors, great and small. Those that remain are, of course, my responsibility.

E.S.G.
Concord, Massachusetts

Scientific Name	Common Name	Source Codes	Region Codes

STRUTHIONIDAE · OSTRICH 1 species recorded

Scientific Name	Common Name	Source Codes	Region Codes
Struthio camelus	Ostrich	2 8	b c

RHEIDAE · RHEAS 2 species recorded

Scientific Name	Common Name	Source Codes	Region Codes
Rhea americana	Greater Rhea	6	d
Pteroicnemia pennata	Lesser Rhea	6	d

CASUARIIDAE · CASSOWARIES 3 species recorded

Scientific Name	Common Name	Source Codes	Region Codes
Casuarius bennetti	Dwarf Cassowary	35 38	j k
Casuarius casuarius	Australian Cassowary	35 36	i j
Casuarius unappendiculatus	Single-wattled Cassowary	35	j

DROMAIIDAE · EMU 1 species recorded

Scientific Name	Common Name	Source Codes	Region Codes
Dromaius novaehollandiae	Emu	36	i

APTERYGIDAE · KIWIS 3 species recorded

Scientific Name	Common Name	Source Codes	Region Codes
Apteryx australis	Brown Kiwi	37	i
Apteryx haasti	Great Spotted Kiwi	37	i
Apteryx oweni	Little Spotted Kiwi	37	i

TINAMIDAE · TINAMOUS 46 species recorded

Scientific Name	Common Name	Source Codes	Region Codes
Tinamus guttatus	White-throated Tinamou	6	d
Tinamus major	Great Tinamou	4 6	d e
Tinamus osgoodi	Black Tinamou	6	d
Tinamus solitarius	Solitary Tinamou	6	d
Tinamus tao	Gray Tinamou	6	d
Nothocercus bonapartei	Highland Tinamou	4 6	d e
Nothocercus julius	Tawny-breasted Tinamou	6	d
Nothocercus nigrocapillus	Hooded Tinamou	6	d
Crypturellus atrocapillus	Red-legged Tinamou	6	d
Crypturellus bartletti	Bartlett's Tinamou	6	d
Crypturellus boucardi	Slaty-breasted Tinamou	4 6	d e
Crypturellus brevirostris	Rusty Tinamou	6	d
Crypturellus casiquiare	Barred Tinamou	6	d
Crypturellus cinereus	Cinereous Tinamou	6	d
Crypturellus cinnamomeus	Rufescent Tinamou	4 6	d e
Crypturellus duidae	Gray-legged Tinamou	6	d
Crypturellus kerriae	Choco Tinamou	6	d
Crypturellus noctivagus	Yellow-legged Tinamou	6	d
Crypturellus obsoletus	Brown Tinamou	6	d
Crypturellus parvirostris	Small-billed Tinamou	6	d
Crypturellus ptaritepui	Tepui Tinamou	6	d

Scientific Name	Common Name	Source Codes	Region Codes

TINAMIDAE · TINAMOUS *contd.*

Scientific Name	Common Name	Source Codes	Region Codes
Crypturellus saltuarius	Magdalena Tinamou	6	d
Crypturellus soui	Little Tinamou	4 6	d e
Crypturellus strigulosus	Brazilian Tinamou	6	d
Crypturellus tataupa	Tataupa Tinamou	6	d
Crypturellus transfasciatus	Pale-browed Tinamou	6	d
Crypturellus undulatus	Undulated Tinamou	6	d
Crypturellus variegatus	Variegated Tinamou	6	d
Rhynchotus rufescens	Red-winged Tinamou	6	d
Nothoprocta cinerascens	Brushland Tinamou	6	d
Nothoprocta curvirostris	Curve-billed Tinamou	6	d
Nothoprocta kalinowski	Kalinowski's Tinamou	6	d
Nothoprocta ornata	Ornate Tinamou	6	d
Nothoprocta pentlandii	Andean Tinamou	6	d
Nothoprocta perdicaria	Chilean Tinamou	6	d
Nothoprocta taczanowskii	Taczanowski's Tinamou	6	d
Nothura boraquira	White-bellied Nothura	6	d
Nothura chacoensis	Chaco Nothura	6	d
Nothura darwinii	Darwin's Nothura	6	d
Nothura maculosa	Spotted Nothura	6	d
Nothura minor	Lesser Nothura	6	d
Taoniscus nanus	Dwarf Tinamou	6	d
Eudromia elegans	Elegant Crested-Tinamou	6	d
Eudromia formosa	Quebracho Crested-Tinamou	6	d
Tinamotis ingoufi	Patagonian Tinamou	6	d
Tinamotis pentlandii	Puna Tinamou	6	d

SPHENISCIDAE · PENGUINS 16 species recorded

Scientific Name	Common Name	Source Codes	Region Codes
Pygoscelis adeliae	Adelie Penguin	36	i
Pygoscelis antarctica	Chinstrap Penguin	36	i
Pygoscelis papua	Gentoo Penguin	6 36 37	d i
Aptenodytes forsteri	Emperor Penguin	6	d
Aptenodytes patagonicus	King Penguin	6 36 37	d i
Eudyptes chrysolophus[1]	Macaroni Penguin	6 36 37	d i
Eudyptes crestatus	Rockhopper Penguin	6 8 36 37	c d i
Eudyptes pachyrhynchus	Fiordland-crested Penguin	36 37	i
Eudyptes sclateri	Erect-crested Penguin	36 37	i
Megadyptes antipodes	Yellow-eyed Penguin	37	i
Eudyptula albosignata	White-flippered Penguin	37	i
Eudyptula minor	Little Blue Penguin	36 37	i
Spheniscus demersus	Jackass Penguin	8	c
Spheniscus humboldti	Humboldt Penguin	6	d
Spheniscus magellanicus	Magellanic Penguin	6	d
Spheniscus mendiculus	Galapagos Penguin	46	d

GAVIIDAE · LOONS 4 species recorded

Scientific Name	Common Name	Source Codes	Region Codes
Gavia adamsii	Yellow-billed Loon	2 3 16	a b g
Gavia arctica[1]	Arctic Loon	2 3 4 15 16	a b e f g
Gavia immer	Common Loon	2 3 4	a b e
Gavia stellata	Red-throated Loon	2 3 4 15 16 55	a b e f g

2

Scientific Name	Common Name	Source Codes	Region Codes

PODICIPEDIDAE · GREBES 19 species recorded

Scientific Name	Common Name	Source Codes	Region Codes
Podiceps auritus	Horned Grebe	2 3 16	a b g
Podiceps cristatus	Great-crested Grebe	2 8 15 16 18 36 55	b c f g i
Podiceps dominicus	Least Grebe	3 5 6	a d
Podiceps grisegena	Red-necked Grebe	2 3 16 55	a b g
Podiceps major	Great Grebe	6	d
Podiceps nigricollis	Black-necked Grebe	6 8	a b c d e f g h
Podiceps novaehollandiae	Black-throated Little Grebe	35 36 38	i j k
Podiceps occipitalis	Silvery Grebe	6	d
Podiceps pelzelnii	Madagascar Little Grebe	10	c
Podiceps poliocephalus	Hoary-headed Grebe	36	i
Podiceps rolland	White-tufted Grebe	6	d
Podiceps ruficollis	Little Grebe	2 8 10 15 16 18 21 22 35 38 55	b c f g h j k c
Podiceps rufolaratus	Delacour's Little Grebe	10	
Podiceps rufopectus	New Zealand Dabchick	37	i
Podiceps taczanowskii	Puna Grebe	6	d
Aechmophorus occidentalis	Western Grebe	3 4	a e
Centropelma micropterum	Short-winged Grebe	6	d
Podilymbus gigas	Atitlan Grebe	4 53	e
Podilymbus podiceps	Pied-billed Grebe	3 4 5 6	a d e

DIOMEDEIDAE · ALBATROSSES 13 species recorded

Scientific Name	Common Name	Source Codes	Region Codes
Diomedea albatrus	Short-tailed Albatross	2 3 4 16 38 53	b e g k
Diomedea bulleri	Buller's Albatross	6 36 37	d i
Diomedea cauta	White-capped Albatross	3 6 8 36 37	c d i k
Diomedea chlororhynchos	Yellow-nosed Albatross	3 6 8 36 37	c d i k
Diomedea chrysostoma	Gray-headed Albatross	4 6 8 36 37	c d e i
Diomedea epomophora	Royal Albatross	6 36 37 38	d i k
Diomedea exulans	Wandering Albatross	4 6 8 36 37 38	c d e l k
Diomedea fusca	Sooty Albatross	6 8 36	c d i
Diomedea immutabilis	Laysan Albatross	2 3 4 38	a b e k
Diomedea irrorata	Galapagos Albatross	4 6	d e
Diomedea melanophris	Black-browed Albatross	3 6 8 36 37	c d i k
Diomedea nigripes	Black-footed Albatross	2 3 4 16 38	a b c g k
Diomedea palpebrata	Light-mantled Sooty Albatross	6 8 36 37	c d i

PROCELLARIIDAE · SHEARWATERS, FULMARS, PETRELS 53 species recorded

Scientific Name	Common Name	Source Codes	Region Codes
Macronectes giganteus	Giant Fulmar	6 8 10 36 37	c d i
Daption capenses	Cape Petrel	3 6 8 15 36 37	a c d f i
Fulmarus glacialis	Northern Fulmar	2 3 4 16	a b e g
Fulmarus glacialoides	Silver-gray Fulmar	6 8 36 37	c d e i
Halobaena caerulea	Blue Petrel	6 8 36 37	c d i
Pachyptila belcheri	Slender-billed Prion	6 8 36 37	c d i
Pachyptila desolata	Dove Prion	6 8 36 37	c d i
Pachyptila forsteri[1]	Broad-billed Prion	8 10 36 37	c i
Pachyptila turtur[2]	Fairy Prion	8 35 36 37	c i j
Thalassoica antarctica	Antarctic Petrel	6 36	d i

3

Scientific Name	Common Name	Source Codes	Region Codes
PROCELLARIIDAE · SHEARWATERS, FULMARS, PETRELS contd.			
Adamastor cinereus	Gray Petrel	3 6 36	a d i
Procellaria aequinoctialis	White-chinned Petrel	6 36 37	d i
Procellaria parkinsoni[3]	Parkinson's Petrel	6 36 37	d i
Puffinus assimilis	Little Shearwater	2 3 6 8 36 37 38	a b c d i k
Puffinus bulleri	Gray-backed Shearwater	3 6	a d
Puffinus carneipes	Flesh-footed Shearwater	3 8 15 36 37	a c f i
Puffinus creatopus	Pink-footed Shearwater	3 4 6	a d e
Puffinus diomedea	Cory's Shearwater	2 3 6 8 36 37	a b c d i
Puffinus gravis	Greater Shearwater	3 6 8	a c d
Puffinus griseus	Sooty Shearwater	3 4 6 8 16 36 37 38	a c d e g i k
Puffinus heinrothi	Heinroth's Shearwater	38	k
Puffinus leucomelas[4]	White-faced Shearwater	16 21 22 25 38 55	b f g h j k
Puffinus lherminieri	Audubon's Shearwater	3 38	a d e f k
Puffinus nativitatis	Black Shearwater	3 4 38	e k
Puffinus pacificus	Wedge-tailed Shearwater	2 3 4 6 8 10 15 16 22 36 37 38	b c d e f g h i k
Puffinus puffinus[5,6]	Manx Shearwater	2 3 4 6 8 36	a b c d e i
Puffinus tenuirostris	Short-tailed Shearwater	3 4 15 36 37 38	a e f i k
Pterodroma alba	Phoenix Petrel	37 38	i k
Pterodroma arminjoniana[7]	Trinidade Petrel	3 36	a c i k
Pterodroma axillaris	Chatham Island Petrel	37	i
Pterodroma baraui	Reunion Petrel	49	c
Pterodroma brevirostris	Kerguelen Petrel	36 37	i
Pterodroma cahow	Bermuda Petrel	3 53	a
Pterodroma cookii	Cook's Petrel	3 4 6 36 37	a d e i
Pterodroma externa[8]	White-necked Petrel	4 6	d e
Pterodroma hasitata	Black-capped Petrel	3 5 6 53	a d e
Pterodroma hypoleuca[9]	Bonin Petrel	2 38	b i k
Pterodroma incerta	Hooded Petrel	6	c d
Pterodroma inexpectata	Scaled Petrel	3 36 37	a i
Pterodroma lessonii	White-headed Petrel	6 36 37	d i
Pterodroma leucoptera	Stout-billed Gadfly Petrel	3 16 36 37 38	a e i k
Pterodroma longirostris	Stejneger's Petrel	37	i
Pterodroma macroptera	Gray-faced Petrel	6 36 37	c d i
Pterodroma mollis	Soft-plumaged Petrel	2 6 36	b c d i
Pterdroma neglecta[10]	Kermadec Petrel	4 36 37 38	e i k
Pterodroma phaeopygia	Dark-rumped Petrel	3 4 6	d e k
Pterodroma rostrata	Tahiti Petrel	16 38	e k
Pterodroma solandri	Solander's Petrel	37	i
Pterodroma ultima	Murphy's Petrel	45	k
Pagodroma nivea	Snow Petrel	36	i
Bulweria bulwerii[11]	Bulwer's Petrel	2 3 15 16 21 36 38 55	b f g h i k
Bulweria fallax	Jouanin's Petrel	8	c
Bulweria macgillivrayi	MacGillivray's Petrel	38	k

HYDROBATIDAE · STORM-PETRELS 20 species recorded

Scientific Name	Common Name	Source Codes	Region Codes
Oceanites gracilis[1]	White-vented Storm-Petrel	4 6	d e
Oceanites oceanicus	Wilson's Storm-Petrel	3 4 5 6 8 10 15 36 37 38 55	a c d e f i k
Pelagodroma marina	White-faced Storm-Petrel	2 3 4 6 8 36 37 38	a b c d e i k

Scientific Name	Common Name	Source Codes	Region Codes

HYDROBATIDAE · STORM-PETRELS contd

Scientific Name	Common Name	Source Codes	Region Codes
Fregetta grallaria	White-bellied Storm-Petrel	3 6 8 36 38	a c d i k
Fregetta tropica	Black-bellied Storm-Petrel	6 8 10 15 36 37 38	c d f i k
Garrodia nereis	Grey-backed Storm-Petrel	6 36 37	d i
Nesofregetta albigularis[2]	White-throated Storm-Petrel	38	k
Hydrobates pelagicus	Storm-Petrel	2 8	b c
Oceanodroma castro[3]	Harcourt's Storm-Petrel	2 3 4 6 8	a b c d e
Oceanodroma furcata	Fork-tailed Storm-Petrel	2 3	a b
Oceanodroma homochroa	Ashy Storm-Petrel	3 4	a e
Oceanodroma hornbyi	Ringed Storm-Petrel	6	d
Oceanodroma leucorhoa	Leach's Storm-Petrel	2 3 4 5 6 8 15 16 36 37	a b c d e f g i
Oceanodroma markhami	Sooty Storm-Petrel	3 4 6	a d e
Oceanodroma matsudairae	Matsudaira's Storm-Petrel	2 36	b i
Oceanodroma melania	Black Storm-Petrel	3 4 6	a d e
Oceanodroma monorhis	Swinhoe's Storm-Petrel	2 16 21 36 55	b g h i
Oceanodroma tethys	Galapagos Storm-Petrel	3 4 6	a d e
Oceanodroma tristrami	Tristram's Petrel	2	b
Halocyptena microsoma	Least Storm-Petrel	3 4 6	a d e

PELECANOIDIDAE · DIVING-PETRELS   4 species recorded

Scientific Name	Common Name	Source Codes	Region Codes
Pelecanoides garnotii	Peruvian Diving-Petrel	6	d
Pelecanoides georgicus	South Georgian Diving-Petrel	36 37	i
Pelecanoides magellani	Magellanic Diving-Petrel	6	d
Pelecanoides urinatrix	Subantarctic Diving-Petrel	6 36 37	d i

PHAETHONTIDAE · TROPICBIRDS   3 species recorded

Scientific Name	Common Name	Source Codes	Region Codes
Phaethon aethereus	Red-billed Tropicbird	2 3 4 5 6 8 10 15 16 55	a b c d e f g
Phaethon lepturus	White-tailed Tropicbird	3 4 5 6 8 10 15 16 35 36 38	a c d e f g i j k
Phaethon rubricauda	Red-tailed Tropicbird	2 4 6 8 10 15 16 36 37 38	b c d e f g i k

PELECANIDAE · PELICANS   7 species recorded

Scientific Name	Common Name	Source Codes	Region Codes
Pelecanus conspicillatus	Australian Pelican	35 36	i j
Pelecanus crispus[1]	Dalmatian Pelican	2 15 18 22	b f g
Pelecanus erythrorhynchoss	American White Pelican	3 4 5	a e
Pelecanus occidentalis	Brown Pelican	3 4 5 6	a
Pelecanus onocrotalus	European White Pelican	2 8 15 22 55	b c f h
Pelecanus philippensis	Spot-billed Pelican	16 19 22 55	g h
Pelecanus rufescens	Pink-backed Pelican	8	c

SULIDAE · BOOBIES   7 species recorded

Scientific Name	Common Name	Source Codes	Region Codes
Sula abbotti	Abbot's Booby	36 53	i
Sula bassana[1]	Gannet	2 3 4 8	a b c e
Sula dactylatra	Blue-faced Booby	3 4 5 6 8 15 21 22 35 36 37 38 55	a c d e f h i j k

5

Scientific Name	Common Name	Source Codes	Region Codes
SULIDAE · BOOBIES contd.			
Sula leucogaster	Brown Booby	2 3 4 5 6 8 10 15 16 21 22 35 36 37 38 55	a b c d e f g h i j k
Sula nebouxii	Blue-footed Booby	3 4 6	a d e
Sula sula	Red-footed Booby	3 4 5 6 10 15 16 21 35 36 38 55	a c d e f g h i j k
Sula variegata	Peruvian Booby	6	d

PHALACROCORACIDAE · CORMORANTS   30 species recorded

Scientific Name	Common Name	Source Codes	Region Codes
Nannopterum harrisi	Galapagos Flightless Cormorant	46	
Phalacrocorax africanus	Reed Cormorant	2 8 10	b c
Phalacrocorax albiventer	King Cormorant	6 36 37	d i
Phalacrocorax aristotelis	Shag	2	b
Phalacrocorax atriceps	Blue-eyed Cormorant	6 36	d i
Phalacrocorax auritus	Double-crested Cormorant	3 4 5	a e
Phalacrocorax bougainvillii	Guanay Cormorant	4 6	d e
Phalacrocorax campbelli	Campbell Island Shag	37	i
Phalacrocorax capensis	Cape Cormorant	8	c
Phalacrocorax capillatus[1]	Temminck's Cormorant	2	b
Phalacrocorax carbo	Great Cormorant	2 3 8 15 16 18 19 21 22 35 36 37 55	a b c f g h i j
Phalacrocorax carunculatus	New Zealand King Shag	37 53	i
Phalacrocorax colensoi	Auckland Island Shag	37	i
Phalacrocorax coronatus	Crowned Cormorant	8	c
Phalacrocorax fuscescens	Black-faced Cormorant	36	i
Phalacrocorax fuscicollis	Indian Shag	15 18 55	f g
Phalacrocorax gaimardi	Red-legged Cormorant	6	d
Phalacrocorax magellanicus	Rock Cormorant	6	d
Phalacrocorax melanoleucos	Little Pied Cormorant	19 35 36 37 38	h i j k
Phalacrocorax neglectus	Bank Cormorant	8	c
Phalacrocorax niger[2]	Pygmy Cormorant	15 16 55	f g
Phalacrocorax nigrogularis	Socotra Cormorant	2	b
Phalacrocorax olivaceus	Neotropic Cormorant	3 4 5 6	a d e
Phalacrocorax pelagicus	Pelagic Cormorant	2 3 4 16 55	a b e g
Phalacrocorax penicillatus	Brandt's Cormorant	3 4	a e
Phalacrocorax punctatus	Spotted Shag	37	i
Phalacrocorax pygmaeus	Little Cormorant	2 18 19 21	b h
Phalacrocorax sulcirostris	Little Black Cormorant	19 21 35 36 37	g h i j
Phalacrocorax urile	Red-faced Cormorant	2 3 16	a b g
Phalacrocorax varius	Pied Cormorant	36 37	i

ANHINGIDAE · ANHINGAS   4 species recorded

Scientific Name	Common Name	Source Codes	Region Codes
Anhinga anhinga[1]	Anhinga	3 4 5 6 18 21 22 55	a d e g h
Anhinga melanogaster	Asian Darter	56	g h
Anhinga novaehollandiae	Australian Darter	56	j
Anhinga rufa	African Darter	56	e

Scientific Name	Common Name	Source Codes	Region Codes

FREGATIDAE · FRIGATEBIRDS 5 species recorded

Fregata andrewsi	Christmas Island Frigatebird	15 21 36 55	f g h i
Fregata aquila	Ascension Island Frigatebird		
Fregata ariel	Lesser Frigatebird	3 8 10 15 16 21 22 35 36 38 55	a c f g h i j k
Fregata magnificens	Magnificent Frigatebird	2 3 4 5 6 8	a b c d e
Fregata minor	Greater Frigatebird	3 4 8 10 15 16 21 22 35 36 37 38 55	c e f g h i j k

ARDEIDAE · HERONS, BITTERNS 62 species recorded

Ardea cinerea[1]	Gray Heron	2 3 8 10 15 16 18 19 21 22 55	a b c f g h
Ardea cocoi	Cocoi Heron	4 6	d e
Ardea goliath	Goliath Heron	2 8 10 15	b c f
Ardea herodias[2]	Great Blue Heron	3 4 5 6	a d e
Ardea humbloti	Madagascar Heron	10	c
Ardea imperialis	Great White-bellied Heron	15 18 55	f g
Ardea melanocephala	Black-headed Heron	8	c
Ardea novaehollandiae	White-faced Heron	35 36 37 38	i j k
Ardea pacifica	White-necked Heron	36 37	i
Ardea picata	Pied Heron	35 36	i j
Ardea purpurea	Purple Heron	2 8 10 15 16 18 19 21 22 55	b c f g h
Ardea sumatrana	Dusky-gray Heron	18 19 21 22 35 36 55	g h i j
Butorides rufiventris	Rufous-bellied Heron	8	c
Butorides striatus	Striated Heron	2 4 6 8 10 15 16 18 19 21 22 35 38 55	b c d e f g h i j k
Butorides virescens	Green Heron	3 4 5 6	a d c
Ardeola bacchus	Chinese Pond-Heron	2 15 16 18 19 21 55	b f g h
Ardeola grayii[3]	Indian Pond-Heron	2 15 18 55	b f h
Ardeola idae	Madagascar Squacco Heron	8 10	c
Ardeola ralloides	Squacco Heron	2 8 10	b c
Ardeola speciosa	Javanese Pond-Heron	18 19 21 55	g h
Bubulcus ibis	Cattle Egret	2 3 4 5 6 8 10 15 16 18 19 21 22 35 36	a b c d e f g h i j
Egretta alba[4]	Great Egret	2 3 5 8 10 15 16 18 19 21 22 35 36 37 55	a b c d e f g h i j
Egretta ardesiaca	Black Heron	8 10	c
Egretta caerulea[4]	Little Blue Heron	3 4 5 6	a d e
Egretta dimorpha	Mascarene Reef Heron	10	c
Egretta eulophotes	Chinese Egret	2 16 19 21 36 53 55	b g h i
Egretta garzetta	Little Egret	2 3 8 15 16 18 19 21 22 35 36 37 55	a b c f g h i j
Egretta gularis	Western Reef Heron	2 14 15	b c f
Egretta intermedia	Intermediate Egret	2 8 15 16 18 19 21 22 35 36 55	b c f g h i j

Scientific Name	Common Name	Source Codes	Region Codes

ARDEIDAE · HERONS, BITTERNS *contd.*

Scientific Name	Common Name	Source Codes	Region Codes
Egretta rufescens[4]	Reddish Egret	3 4 5 6	a d e
Egretta sacra	Eastern Reef Heron	2 15 16 18 19 21 22 35 36 37 38 55	a b c f g h i j k
Egretta thula	Snowy Egret	3 4 5 6	a d e
Egretta tricolor	Louisiana Heron	3 4 5 6	a d e
Agamia agami	Chestnut-bellied Heron	4 6	d e
Pilherodius pileatus	Capped Heron	4 6	d e
Syrigma sibilatrix	Whistling Heron	6	d
Cochlearius cochlearius	Boat-billed Heron	4 6	d e
Nycticorax caledonicus	Rufous Night-Heron	2 19 21 22 35 36 37 38	b h i j k
Nycticorax leuconotus	White-backed Night-Heron	8	c
Nycticorax magnifica	Magnificent Night-Heron	16	g
Nycticorax nyctocorax	Black-crowned Night-Heron	2 3 4 5 6 8 10 15 16 18 19 21 22 55	a b c d e f g h
Nycticorax violaceus[5]	Yellow-crowned Night-Heron	3 4 5 6	a d e
Gorsachius goisagi	Japanese Night-Heron	2 16 22	b g h
Gorsachius melanolophus	Tiger Bittern	15 16 18 19 21 22 55	f g h
Zonerodius heliosylus	Forest Bittern	35	j
Tigrisoma fasciatum[6]	Fasciated Tiger-Heron	6	d
Tigrisoma leucolophus	African Tiger-Heron	8	c
Tigrisoma lineatum	Rufescent Tiger-Heron	4 6	d e
Tigrisoma mexicanum	Bare-throated Tiger-Heron	6	d e
Zebrilus undulatus	Zigzag Heron	6	d
Ixobrychus cinnamomeus	Cinnamon Bittern	2 15 16 18 19 21 22 55	b f g h
Ixobrychus eurhythmus	Schrenck's Little Bittern	2 16 18 19 21 22 55	b g h
Ixobrychus exilis	Least Bittern	3 4 5 6	a d e
Ixobrychus involucris	Stripe-backed Bittern	6	d
Ixobrychus minutus	Little Bittern	2 8 10 15 16 36 37	b c f g i
Ixobrychus sinensis	Chinese Little Bittern	2 15 16 18 19 21 22 35 36 38 55	b f g h i j k
Ixobrychus sturmii	Dwarf Bittern	8	c
Botaurus lentiginosus	American Bittern	3 4 5	a d
Botaurus pinnatus	Pinnated Bittern	4 6	d e
Botaurus poiciloptilus	Australian Bittern	36 37 38	i k
Botaurus stellaris	Eurasian Bittern	2 8 15 16 18 19 22 55	b c f g h
Dupetor flavicollis	Black Bittern	15 16 18 19 21 22 35 36 38 55	f g h i j k

BALAENICIPITIDAE · WHALE-HEADED STORK 1 species recorded

Scientific Name	Common Name	Source Codes	Region Codes
Balaeniceps rex	Whale-headed Stork	8	c

SCOPIDAE · HAMMERHEAD STORK 1 species recorded

Scientific Name	Common Name	Source Codes	Region Codes
Scopus umbretta	Hammerhead Stork	8 10	c

Scientific Name	Common Name	Source Codes	Region Codes

CICONIIDAE · STORKS 17 species recorded

Scientific Name	Common Name	Source Codes	Region Codes
Mycteria americana	Wood Stork	3 4 5 6	a d e
Ibis cinereus	Milky Stork	19 55	g h
Ibis ibis	Yellow-billed Stork	8 10	c
Ibis leucocephalus	Painted Stork	15 16 18 19 55	f g h
Anastomus lamelligerus	African Open-bill Stork	8 10	c
Anastomus oscitans	Asian Open-bill Stork	15 18 55	f g
Ciconia abdimii	White-bellied Stork	8	c
Ciconia ciconia[1]	White Stork	2 8 15 19 21 55	b c f g h
Ciconia episcopus[2]	White-necked Stork	8 15 18 19 22 55	c f h
Ciconia nigra	Black Stork	2 8 15 16 18 55	b c f g
Euxenura maguari	Maguari Stork	6	d
Xenorhynchus asiaticus	Black-necked Stork	15 18 35 36 55	f g i j
Ephippiorhynchus senegalensis	Saddle-bill Stork	8	c d e
Jabiru mycteria	Jabiru	6	e
Leptoptilos crumeniferus	Marabou	8	c
Leptoptilos dubius	Greater Adjutant Stork	15 18 55	f g
Leptoptilos javanicus	Lesser Adjutant Stork	15 16 18 21 55	f g h

THRESKIORNITHIDAE · IBISES, SPOONBILLS 31 species recorded

Scientific Name	Common Name	Source Codes	Region Codes
Threskiornis aethiopica	Sacred Ibis	2 8 10 16 18 19 38 55	b c g h k
Threskiornis melanocephala[1]	Oriental Ibis	15 21	b f h
Threskiornis molucca	Australian White Ibis	35 36 37	i j
Threskiornis spinicollis[2]	Straw-necked Ibis	35 36	i j
Pseudibis davisoni[3]	Davison's Ibis	16	g
Pseudibis gigantea[4]	Giant Ibis	53 55	f g
Pseudibis papillosa	Black Ibis	15 18 19 21 55	f g h
Geronticus calvus	Bald Ibis	8	c
Geronticus eremita[5]	Hermit Ibis	2 8	b c
Nipponia nippon	Japanese Crested Ibis	2 16 53	b g
Bostrychia carunculata[6]	Wattled Ibis	8	c
Bostrychia hagedash	Hadada Ibis	8	c
Bostrychia olivacea	Olive Ibis	8	c
Bostrychia rara	Spotted-breasted Ibis	8	c
Harpiprion caerulescens	Plumbeous Ibis	6	d
Theristicus caudatus	Buff-necked Ibis	4 6	d e
Mesembrinibis cayennensis	Green Ibis	4 6	d e
Phimosus infuscatus	Bare-faced Ibis	6	d
Eudocimus albus[7]	White Ibis	3 4 5 6	a d e
Eudocimus ruber	Scarlet Ibis	3 4 6	a d e
Cercibis oxycerca	Sharp-tailed Ibis	6	d
Plegadis chihi	White-faced Ibis	3 4 6	a d e
Plegadis falcinellus	Glossy Ibis	2 3 4 5 8 10 15 16 18 19 21 22 35 36 37 55	a b c e f g h i j
Plegadis ridgwayi[8]	Puna Ibis	6	d
Lophotibis cristata	Crested Wood Ibis	10	c
Platalea ajaja[9]	Roseate Spoonbill	3 4 5 6	a d e
Platalea alba	African Spoonbill	8 10	c
Platalea flavipes	Yellow-billed Spoonbill	36	i
Platalea leucorodia	White Spoonbill	2 3 8 15 16 18 19 21 38 55	a b c f g h k

Scientific Name	Common Name	Source Codes	Region Codes
THRESKIORNITHIDAE · IBISES, SPOONBILLS *contd.*			
Platalea minor	Black-faced Spoonbill	2 16 22 55	b g h
Platalea regia	Royal Spoonbill	35 36 37	i j

PHOENICOPTERIDAE · FLAMINGOS 4 species recorded

Scientific Name	Common Name	Source Codes	Region Codes
Phoeniconaias minor	Lesser Flamingo	8 10 15	c f
Phoenicopterus ruber[1]	Greater Flamingo	2 3 4 5 6 8 10 15 55	a b c d e f g
Phoenicoparrus andinus	Andean Flamingo	6	d
Phoenicoparrus jamesi	James Flamingo	6	d

ANHIMIDAE · SCREAMERS 3 species recorded

Scientific Name	Common Name	Source Codes	Region Codes
Anhima cornuta	Horned Screamer	6	d
Chauna chavaria	Northern Screamer	6	d
Chauna torquata	Southern Screamer	6	d

ANATIDAE · DUCKS, GEESE, SWANS 146 species recorded

Scientific Name	Common Name	Source Codes	Region Codes
Anseranas semipalmata	Magpie Goose	35 36	i j
Dendrocygna arborea	West Indian Tree Duck	3 5	a e
Dendrocygna arcuata	Whistling Tree Duck	19 21 22 35 36 38	h i j k
Dendrocygna autumnalis	Black-bellied Tree Duck	3 4 5 6	a d e
Dendrocygna bicolor	Fulvous Tree Duck	3 4 5 6 8 10 15 18 55	a c d e f
Dendrocygna eytoni	Plumed Whistling Duck	35 36 37	i j
Dendrocygna guttata	Spotted Whistling Duck	22 35	h j
Dendrocygna javanica	Lesser Whistling Duck	15 16 18 19 21 55	f g h
Dendrocygna viduata	White-faced Tree Duck	4 6 8 10	c d e
Coscoroba coscoroba	Coscoroba Swan	6	d
Cygnus atratus	Black Swan	36 37	i
Cygnus columbianus[1]	Whistling Swan	2 3 4 15 16	a b e f g
Cygnus cygnus[2]	Whooper Swan	2 3 4 15 16	a b f g
Cygnus melancoryphus	Black-necked Swan	6	d
Cygnus olor	Mute Swan	2 3 8 15 16 36 37	a b c f g i
Anser albifrons[3]	White-fronted Goose	2 3 4 8 15 16 18 55	a b c e f g
Anser anser	Graylag Goose	2 15 16 18 55	b f g
Anser caerulescens[4]	Snow Goose	2 3 4 15 16	a b e f g
Anser canagicus	Emperor Goose	2 3	a b
Anser cygnoides	Swan Goose	2 16	b g
Anser erythropus	Lesser White-fronted Goose	2 15 16	b f g
Anser fabalis	Bean Goose	2 3 15 16 18 55	a b f g
Anser indicus	Bar-headed Goose	2 15 16 18 55	b f g
Anser rossii	Ross's Goose	3 4	a c
Branta bernicla	Brant	2 3 4 16	a b e g
Branta canadensis	Canada Goose	2 3 4 37	a b e i
Branta leucopsis	Barnacle Goose	2 3	a b
Branta ruficollis	Red-breasted Goose	2 15	b f
Branta sandvicensis	Hawaiian Goose	3 53	k

10

Scientific Name	Common Name	Source Codes	Region Codes
ANATIDAE · DUCKS, GEESE, SWANS *contd.*			
Cereopsis novaehollandiae	Cape Barren Goose	36 37	i
Chloephaga hybrida	Kelp Goose	6	d
Chloephaga melanoptera	Andean Goose	6	d
Chloephaga picta	Upland Goose	6	d
Chloephaga poliocephala	Ashy-headed Goose	6	d
Chloephaga rubidiceps	Ruddy-headed Goose	6	d
Cyanochen cyanoptera	Blue-winged Goose	8	c
Neochen jubata	Orinoco Goose	6	d
Alopochen aegyptiaca	Egyptian Goose	2 8 16	b c g
Tadorna cana	African Sheld Duck	8	c
Tadorna cristata	Crested Sheld Duck	2 53	b
Tadorna ferruginea[5]	Ruddy Sheld Duck	2 3 8 15 16 18 55	a b c f g
Tadorna radjah	White-headed Sheld Duck	35 36	i j
Tadorna tadorna	Sheld Duck	2 3 15 16 18 22 55	a b f g h
Tadorna tadornoides	Mountain Duck	36	i
Tadorna variegata	Paradise Duck	37	i
Lophonetta specularioides	Crested Duck	6	d
Tachyeres brachypterus	Falkland Island Flightless Steamer Duck		
Tachyeres patachonicus	Flying Steamer Duck	6	d
Tachyeres pteneres	Flightless Steamer Duck	6	d
Anas acuta[6]	Pintail	2 3 4 5 6 8 15 16 18 19 21 22 55	a b c d e f g h
Anas americana	American Wigeon	3 4 5 6	a d e
Anas angustirostris	Marbled Teal	2 15	b f
Anas bahamensis	White-cheeked Pintail	3 5 6	a d e
Anas bernieri	Madagascar Teal	10	c
Anas capensis	Cape Widgeon	8	c
Anas castanea[7]	Chestnut Teal	36	i
Anas clypeata	Northern Shoveler	2 3 4 5 6 8 15 16 18 19 21 22 36 55	a b c d e f g h i
Anas crecca	Green-winged Teal	2 3 4 5 8 15 16 18 19 22 55	a b c f g h
Anas cyanoptera	Cinnamon Teal	3 4 6	a d e
Anas discors	Blue-winged Teal	3 4 5 6	a d e
Anas erythrorhynchos	Red-billed Duck	8 10	c
Anas falcata	Falcated Teal	2 3 15 16 18 55	a b f g
Anas flavirostris	Speckled Teal	6	d
Anas formosa	Baikal Teal	2 3 15 16 55	a b f g
Anas georgica	Yellow-billed Pintail	6 8	c d
Anas gibberifrons	Gray Teal	15 18 19 35 36 37 38 55	f g h i j k
Anas hottentota[8]	Hottentot Teal	8 10	c
Anas leucophrys	Ringed Teal	6	d
Anas luzonica	Luzon Duck	23	h
Anas melleri	Meller's Duck	10	c
Anas penelope	Eurasian Wigeon	2 3 4 8 15 16 18 19 21 22 35 55	a b c e f g h j
Anas platalea	Red Shoveler	6	d
Anas platyrhynchos[9]	Mallard	2 3 4 5 8 15 16 18 19 21 36 37 55	a b c e f g h i
Anas poecilorhyncha	Spotbill Duck	2 15 16 18 19 22 55	b f g h

Scientific Name	Common Name	Source Codes	Region Codes
ANATIDAE · DUCKS, GEESE, SWANS *contd.*			
Anas querquedula	Garganey	2 8 15 16 18 19 21 22 35 36 55	b c f g h i j
Anas rhynchotis	Blue-winged Shoveler	36 37 38	i k
Anas rubripes	Black Duck	3	a
Anas sibilatrix	Southern Wigeon	6	d
Anas smithii	Smith's Shoveler	8	c
Anas sparsa	African Black Duck	8	c
Anas specularis	Spectacled Duck	6	d
Anas strepera	Gadwall	2 3 4 5 8 15 16 18 55	a b c e f g
Anas superciliosa	Australian Gray Duck	35 36 37 38	i j k
Anas undulata	African Yellowbill	8	c
Anas versicolor[10]	Silver Teal	6	d
Anas waigiuensis	Salvadori's Teal	35	j
Rhodonessa caryophyllacea	Pink-headed Duck	15 18 55	f g
Malacorhynchus membranaceus	Pink-eared Duck	36	i
Hymenolaimus malacorhynchos	Blue Duck	37	i
Merganetta armata	Torrent Duck	6	d
Stictonetta naevosa	Freckled Duck	36	i
Polysticta stelleri	Steller's Eider	2 3 16	a b g
Somateria fischeri[11]	Spectacled Eider	2 3	a b
Somateria mollissima	Common Eider	2 3	a b
Somateria spectabilis	King Eider	2 3	a b
Aythya affinis	Lesser Scaup	3 4 5 6	a d e
Aythya americana	Redhead	3 4 5	a e
Aythya australis	Australian Pochard	19 35 36 37 38	h i j k
Aythya baeri	Baer's Pochard	2 3 15 16 55	a b f g
Aythya collaris	Ring-necked Duck	3 4 5	a e
Aythya ferina	Common Pochard	2 3 8 15 16 18 22 55	a b c f g h
Aythya fuligula	Tufted Duck	2 3 8 15 16 18 19 21 22 55	a b c f g h
Aythya innotata[12]	Madagascar Pochard	10	c
Aythya marila	Greater Scaup	2 3 4 15 16 18 22 55	a b e f g h
Aythya novaeseelandiae	New Zealand Scaup	37	i
Aythya nyroca	White-eyed Pochard	2 8 15 16 18 55	b c f g
Aythya valisineria	Canvasback	3 4 5	a e
Netta erythrophthalma	Southern Pochard	6 8	c d
Netta peposaca	Rosy-billed Pochard	6	d
Netta rufina	Red-crested Pochard	2 15 16 18 55	b f g
Chenonetta jubata	Maned Goose	36 37	i
Amazonetta brasiliensis	Brazilian Duck	6	d
Aix galericulata	Mandarin Duck	2 15 16 18 55	b f g
Aix sponsa	Wood Duck	3 4 5	a e
Nettapus auritus	African Pygmy Goose	8 10	c
Nettapus coromandelianus	Cotton Pygmy Goose	2 16 21 35 36 55	b f g h i j
Nettapus pulchellus	Green Pygmy Goose	35 36	i j
Sarkidiornis melanotos[13]	Knob-billed Goose	6 8 10 15 16 18 55	c d f g
Cairina moschata	Muscovy Duck	4 6	d e
Cairina scutulata	White-winged Wood Duck	15 18 19 55	f g h
Plectropterus gambensis	Spur-winged Goose	8	c
Pteronetta hartlaubii	Hartlaub's Goose	8	c
Melanitta fusca[14]	White-winged Scoter	2 3 4 16	a b e g
Melanitta nigra	Black Scoter	2 3 4 16	a b e g
Melanitta perspicillata	Surf Scoter	3 4	a e

12

Scientific Name	Common Name	Source Codes	Region Codes
ANATIDAE · DUCKS, GEESE, SWANS *contd.*			
Histrionicus histrionicus	Harlequin Duck	2 3 16	a b g
Clangula hyemalis	Oldsquaw	2 3 15 16	a b f g
Bucephala albeola	Bufflehead	3 4	a e
Bucephala clangula	Common Goldeneye	2 3 4 15 16 18 55	a b e f g
Bucephala islandica	Barrow's Goldeneye	2 3	a b
Mergus albellus[15]	Smew	2 3 15 16 18 55	a b f g
Mergus australis	Auckland Island Merganser	37	i
Mergus cucullatus	Hooded Merganser	3 4 5	a e
Mergus merganser	Common Merganser	2 3 4 15 16 18 55	a b e f g
Mergus octosetaceus	Brazilian Merganser	6	d
Mergus serrator	Red-breasted Merganser	2 3 4 5 15 16 55	a b e f g
Mergus squamatus	Chinese Merganser	2 55	b g.
Oxyura australis	Blue-billed Duck	36	i
Oxyura dominica	Masked Duck	3 4 5 6	a d e
Oxyura jamaicensis	Ruddy Duck	3 4 5 6	a d e
Oxyura leucocephala	White-headed Duck	2 15	b f
Oxyura maccoa	Maccoa Duck	8	c
Oxyura vittata	Lake Duck	6	d
Thalassornis leuconotus	White-backed Duck	8 10	c
Biziura lobata	Musk Duck	36	i
Heteronetta atricapilla	Black-headed Duck	6	d

CATHARTIDAE · NEW WORLD VULTURES   7 species recorded

Scientific Name	Common Name	Source Codes	Region Codes
Cathartes aura	Turkey Vulture	3 4 5 6	a d e
Cathartes burrovianus	Lesser Yellow-headed Vulture	4 6	d e
Cathartes melambrotus	Greater Yellow-headed Vulture	6	d
Coragyps atratus	Black Vulture	3 4 6	a d e
Sarcorhamphus papa	King Vulture	3 4 6	a d e
Vultur californianus[1]	California Condor	3 4 53	a e
Vultur gryphus	Andean Condor	6	d

SAGITTARIIDAE · SECRETARY BIRD   1 species recorded

Scientific Name	Common Name	Source Codes	Region Codes
Sagittarius serpentarius	Secretary Bird	8	c

ACCIPITRIDAE · HAWKS, OLD WORLD VULTURES, HARRIERS   211 species recorded

Scientific Name	Common Name	Source Codes	Region Codes
Spilornis holospilus	Philippine Serpent Eagle	24	h
Aviceda cuculoides	African Cuckoo-Falcon	8	c
Aviceda jerdoni	Brown-crested Lizard Hawk	15 16 18 19 21 22 55	f g h
Aviceda leuphotes	Black-crested Lizard Hawk	15 16 18 55	f g h
Aviceda madagascariensis	Madagascar Cuckoo-Falcon	10	c
Aviceda subcristata	Crested Lizard Hawk	35 36 38	i j k
Leptodon cayanensis	Gray-headed Kite	4 6	d e
Chondrohierax uncinatus	Hook-billed Kite	4 5 6	d e

Scientific Name	Common Name	Source Codes	Region Codes
ACCIPITRIDAE · HAWKS etc. contd.			
Henicopernis infuscata	Black Honey Buzzard	50	j
Henicopernis longicauda	Long-tailed Buzzard	35	i
Pernis apivorus	Honey Buzzard	2 8	b c
Pernis celebensis	Barred Honey Buzzard	22	h
Pernis ptilorhynchus	Crested Honey Buzzard	2 15 16 18 19 21 22 55	b f g h
Elanoides forficatus	Swallow-tailed Kite	3 4 5 6	a d e
Macheiramphus alcinus	Bat Hawk	8 10 18 19 21 35 55	c g h j
Gampsonyx swainsonii	Pearl Kite	4 6	d e
Elanus caeruleus[1]	Black-winged Kite	2 8 15 16 18 19 21 22 35 55	b c f g h j
Elanus leucurus	White-tailed Kite	3 4 6	a d e
Elanus notatus	Black-shouldered Kite	36	i
Elanus riocourii	African Swallow-tailed Kite	8	c
Elanus scriptus	Letter-winged Kite	36	i
Rostrhamus hamatus[2]	Slender-billed Kite	6	d
Rostrhamus sociabilis	Snail Kite	3 4 5 6	a d e
Harpagus bidentatus	Double-toothed Kite	4 6	d e
Harpagus diodon	Rufous-thighed Kite	6	d
Ictinia mississippiensis	Mississippi Kite	3 4 6	a d e
Ictinia plumbea	Plumbeous Kite	4 6	d e
Lophoictinia isura	Square-tailed Kite	36	i
Hamirostra melanosternon	Black-breasted Buzzard	36	i
Milvus migrans	Black Kite	2 8 10 15 16 18 19 21 35 36 55	b c f g h i j
Milvus milvus	Red Kite	2 15	b f
Haliastur indus	Brahminy Kite	15 16 18 19 21 22 35 36 38 55	f g h i j k
Haliastur sphenurus	Whistling Kite	35 36 38	i j k
Haliaeetus albicilla	White-Tailed Eagle	2 3 16 55	a b g
Haliaeetus leucocephalus	Bald Eagle	2 3	a b
Haliaeetus leucogaster	White-bellied Sea Eagle	15 16 18 35 36 55	f g h i j k
Haliaeetus leucoryphus	Pallas' Sea Eagle	2 15 16 18 55	b f g
Haliaeetus pelagicus	Steller's Sea Eagle	2 3 16	a b g
Haliaeetus sanfordi	Sanford's Eagle	38	k
Haliaeetus vocifer	African Fish Eagle	8 10	c
Haliaeetus vociferoides	Madagascar Fish Eagle	10	c
Ichthyophaga ichthyaetus	Gray-headed Fishing Eagle	15 18 19 21 22	f h
Ichthyophaga nana	Lesser Fishing Eagle	15 16 18 19 21 55	f g h
Gypohierax angolensis	Palm-nut Vulture	8	c
Neophron monachus[3]	Hooded Vulture	8	c
Neophron percnopterus	Egyptian Vulture	2 8 15 18 55	b c f g
Gypaetus barbatus	Bearded Vulture	2 8 15 16 53	b c f g
Gyps bengalensis[4]	Indian White-backed Vulture	2 8 15 16 18 55	b c f g
Gyps coprotheres	Cape Vulture	8	c
Gyps fulvus	Griffon Vulture	2 8 15 16	b c f g
Gyps himalayensis	Himalayan Griffon	2 15	b f
Gyps indicus	Long-billed Vulture	15 18 55	f g
Gyps ruppellii	Ruppell's Griffon	8	c
Sarcogyps calvus	Indian Black Vulture	15 16 18 55	f g
Aegypius monachus	European Black Vulture	2 8 15 16 18 55	b c f g
Aegypius tracheliotus[5]	Lappet-faced Vulture	2 8	b c
Trigonoceps occipitalis	White-headed Vulture	8	c
Circaetus cinerascens	Smaller Banded Snake Eagle	8	c
Circaetus cinereus	Snake Eagle	8	c
Circaetus fasciolatus	Southern Banded Snake Eagle	8	c

14

Scientific Name	Common Name	Source Codes	Region Codes

ACCIPITRIDAE · HAWKS *etc. contd.*

Scientific Name	Common Name	Source Codes	Region Codes
Circaetus gallicus[6]	Short-toed Eagle	2　8 15 16 19 55	b　c　f　g　h
Terathopius ecaudatus	Bateleur	8	c
Spilornis cheela	Crested Serpent Eagle	15 16 18 19 21 22 55	f　g　h
Spilornis rufipectus	Celebes Serpent Eagle	29	h
Dryotriorchis spectabilis	Congo Snake Eagle	8	c
Eutriorchis astur	Madagascar Serpent Eagle	10	c
Polyboroides radiatus[7]	African Harrier-Hawk	8　10	c
Geranospiza caerulescens	Crane Hawk	6	d
Circus aeruginosus[8]	Marsh Harrier	2　8 10 15 16　8 19 21 22 35 36 38 55	b　c　f　g　h　i　j k
Circus assimilis	Spotted Harrier	36	i
Circus buffoni	Long-winged Harrier	6	d
Circus cinereus	Cinereous Harrier	6	d
Circus cyaneus	Marsh Hawk	2　3　4　5　6 15 18 21 55	a　d　e　f　g　h
Circus macrourus	Pallid Harrier	2　8 15 16 18 55	b　c　f　g　h
Circus maurus	Black Harrier	8	c
Circus melanoleucus	Pied Harrier	2 15 16 18 19 21 22 55	b　f　g　h
Circus pygargus	Montagu's Harrier	2　8 15 16 55	b　c　f　g
Melierax canorus	Pale Chanting Goshawk	8	c
Melierax gabar	Gabar Goshawk	8	c
Melierax metabates	Chanting Goshawk	2　8	b　c
Melierax poliopterus	Gray Chanting Goshawk	8	c
Megatriorchis doriae	Doria's Hawk	35	j
Erythrotriorchis radiatus	Red Goshawk	36	i
Accipiter albogularis	Pied Hawk	38	k
Accipiter badius[9]	Shikra	2　8 15 16 18 19 55	b　c　f　g　h
Accipiter bicolor	Bicolored Hawk	4　6	d　e
Accipiter brachyurus	New Britain Sparrow-Hawk	34	j
Accipiter brevipes	Levant Sparrow-Hawk	2　8	b　c
Accipiter buergersi	Buerger's Goshawk	35	j
Accipiter castanilius	Chestnut-flanked Goshawk	8	c
Accipiter cirrocephalus[10]	Collared Sparrow-Hawk	35 36	i　j
Accipiter collaris	Semicollared Hawk	6	d
Accipiter cooperii	Cooper's Hawk	3　4	a　e
Accipiter eichhorni[11]	Imitator Hawk	38	k
Accipiter erythropus	Red-thighed Sparrow-Hawk	8	c
Accipiter fasciatus	Brown Goshawk	35 36 38	i　j　k
Accipiter francesii	Madagascar Goshawk	10	c
Accipiter gentilis	Goshawk	2　3　4 15 16 18 55	a　b　e　f　g
Accipiter griseiceps	Celebes Crested Goshawk	29	h
Accipiter gularis	Japanese Sparrow-Hawk	2 21 55	b　g　h
Accipiter gundlachi	Gundlach's Hawk	5	e
Accipiter haplochrous	White-bellied Hawk	38	k
Accipiter henicogrammus	Gray's Goshawk	31	h　j
Accipiter hensti	Henst's Goshawk	10	c
Accipiter luteoschistaceus	Blue-and-Gray Sparrow-Hawk	34	j
Accipiter madagascariensis	Madagascar Sparrow-Hawk	10	c
Accipiter melanochlamys	Black-mantled Goshawk	35	j
Accipiter melanoleucus	Great Sparrow-Hawk	8	c
Accipiter meyerianus	Meyer's Goshawk	35 38	j　k
Accipiter minullus	African Little Sparrow-Hawk	8	c

15

Scientific Name	Common Name	Source Codes	Region Codes
ACCIPITRIDAE · HAWKS etc. contd.			
Accipiter nisus	Sparrow-Hawk	2 8 15 16 18 19 21	b c f g h
Accipiter novaehollandiae[12]	Gray Goshawk	5 36 38	i j k
Accipiter ovampensis	Ovampo Sparrow-Hawk	8	c
Accipiter poliocephalus	New Guinea Gray-headed Goshawk	35	j
Accipiter poliogaster	Gray-bellied Hawk	6	d
Accipiter princeps	New Britain Gray-headed Goshawk	34	j
Accipiter rhodogaster[13]	Vinous-breasted Sparrow-Hawk	31	h j
Accipiter rufitorques	Fiji Goshawk	38	k
Accipiter rufiventris	Rufous-breasted Sparrow-Hawk	8	c
Accipiter soloensis	Chinese Sparrow-Hawk	2 15 16 18 19 21 22 35 55	b f g h j
Accipiter striatus	Sharp-shinned Hawk	3 4 5 6	a d e
Accipiter superciliosus	Tiny Hawk	4 6	d e
Accipiter tachiro	African Goshawk	8	c
Accipiter toussenelii	Vinous-chested Goshawk	8	c
Accipiter trinotatus	Spot-tailed Accipiter	29	h
Accipiter trivirgatus	Crested Goshawk	15 16 18 19 21 22 55	f g h
Accipiter virgatus	Besra Sparrow-Hawk	2 15 16 18 19 21 22 55	b f g h
Urotriorchis macrourus	African Long-tailed Hawk	8	c
Butastur indicus	Gray-faced Buzzard-Eagle	2 16 18 19 21 22 35 36 55	b g h i j
Butastur liventer	Rufous-winged Buzzard-Eagle	18 19	h
Butastur rufipennis	Grasshopper Buzzard	8	c
Butastur teesa	White-eyed Buzzard-Eagle	2 15 16 18 55	b f g h
Kaupifalco monogrammicus	Lizard Buzzard	8	c
Leucopternis albicollis	White Hawk	4 6	d e
Leucopternis kuhli	White-browed Hawk	6	d
Leucopternis lacernulata	White-necked Hawk	6	d
Leucopternis melanops	Black-faced Hawk	6	d
Leucopternis occidentalis	Gray-backed Hawk	6	d
Leucopternis plumbea	Plumbeous Hawk	4 6	d e
Leucopternis polionota	Mantled Hawk	6	d
Leucopternis princeps	Barred Hawk	4 6	d e
Leucopternis schistacea	Slate-colored Hawk	6	d
Leucopternis semiplumbea	Semiplumbeous Hawk	4 6	d e
Buteogallus aequinoctialis	Rufous Crab Hawk	6	d
Buteogallus anthracinus	Black Hawk	3 4 5 6	a d e
Buteogallus urubitinga	Great Black Hawk	4 6	d e
Harpyhaliaetus coronatus	Crowned Eagle	6	d
Harpyhaliaetus solitarius	Solitary Eagle	4 6	d e
Heterospizias meridionalis	Savanna Hawk	4 6	d e
Busarellus nigricollis	Black-collared Hawk	4 6	d e
Geranoaetus melanoleucus	Black-chested Buzzard-Eagle	6	d
Parabuteo unicinctus	Harris's Hawk	3 4 6	a d e
Buteo albicaudatus	White-tailed Hawk	3 4 6	a d e
Buteo albonotatus	Zone-tailed Hawk	3 4 6	a d e
Buteo auguralis	African Red-tailed Buzzard	8	c
Buteo brachypterus	Madagascar Buzzard	10	c
Buteo brachyurus	Short-tailed Hawk	3 4 6	a d e
Buteo buteo	Common Buzzard	2 8 15 16 18 19 55	b c f g h

16

Scientific Name	Common Name	Source Codes	Region Codes

ACCIPITRIDAE · HAWKS *etc. contd.*

Scientific Name	Common Name	Source Codes	Region Codes
Buteo galapagoensis	Galapagos Hawk	53	d
Buteo hemilasius	Upland Buzzard	2 15 16	b f g
Buteo jamaicensis	Red-tailed Hawk	3 4 5	a e
Buteo lagopus	Rough-legged Hawk	2 3 16 55	a b g
Buteo leucorrhous	White-rumped Hawk	6	d
Buteo lineatus	Red-shouldered Hawk	3 4	a e
Buteo magnirostris	Roadside Hawk	4 6	d e
Buteo nitidus	Gray Hawk	3 4 6	a d e
Buteo oreophilus	African Mountain Buzzard	8	c
Buteo platypterus	Broad-winged Hawk	3 4 5 6	a d e
Buteo poecilochrous	Variable Hawk	6	d
Buteo polyosoma	Red-backed Hawk	6	d
Buteo regalis	Ferruginous Hawk	3 4	a e
Buteo ridgwayi	Ridgway's Hawk	5	e
Buteo rufinus	Long-legged Buzzard	2 8 15 16 18 55	b c f g
Buteo rufofuscus	Augur Buzzard	8	c
Buteo solitarius	Hawaiian Hawk	3 53	k
Buteo swainsoni	Swainson's Hawk	3 4 6	a d e
Buteo ventralis	Rufous-tailed Hawk	6	d
Morphnus guianensis	Crested Eagle	4 6	d e
Harpia harpyia	Harpy-Eagle	4 6	d e
Harpyopsis novaeguineae	New Guinea Harpy-Eagle	35	j
Pithecophaga jefferyi	Monkey-eating Eagle	22 53	h
Ictinaetus malayensis	Black Eagle	15 16 18 19 21 55	f g h
Aquila audax[14]	Wedge-tailed Eagle	15 35 36	i j
Aquila chrysaetos	Golden Eagle	2 3 4 15 16 55	a b e f g
Aquila clanga	Spotted Eagle	2 8 15 16 18 55	b c f g
Aquila gurneyi	Gurney's Eagle	35 50	j
Aquila heliaca	Imperial Eagle	2 8 15 16 55	b c f g
Aquila pomarina[15]	Lesser Spotted Eagle	2 8 15 18 55	b c f g
Aquila rapax[16]	Tawny Eagle	8 15 16 18 55	c f g
Aquila verreauxii	Verreaux's Eagle	2 8	b c
Aquila wahlbergi	Wahlberg's Eagle	8	c
Hieraaetus dubius	Ayre's Hawk-Eagle	8	c
Hieraaetus fasciatus	Bonelli's Eagle	2 8 15 16 18 55	b c f g
Hieraaetus kienerii	Rufous-bellied Hawk-Eagle	15 16 18 19 21 22 55	f g h
Hieraaetus morphnoides	Little Eagle	35 36	i j
Hieraaetus pennatus	Booted Eagle	2 8 15 16 18 55	b c f g
Spizastur melanoleucus	Black-and-White Hawk-Eagle	4 6	d e
Lophaetus occipitalis	Long-crested Eagle	8	c
Spizaetus africanus	Cassin's Hawk-Eagle	8	c
Spizaetus alboniger	Blyth's Hawk-Eagle	19 21 55	g h
Spizaetus bartelsi	Java Hawk-Eagle	50	h
Spizaetus cirrhatus[17]	Crested Hawk-Eagle	15 18 19 21 22 55	f h
Spizaetus lanceolatus	Celebes Hawk-Eagle	31	h j
Spizaetus nanus	Small Hawk-Eagle	18 19 21 55	g h
Spizaetus nipalensis	Hodgson's Hawk-Eagle	2 15 16 18 55	b f g
Spizaetus ornatus	Ornate Hawk-Eagle	4 6	d e
Spizaetus philippensis	Philippine Hawk-Eagle	19 22	h
Spizaetus tyrannus	Black Hawk-Eagle	4 6	d e
Stephanoaetus coronatus	Crowned Eagle	8	c
Oroaetus isidori	Black-and-Chestnut Eagle	6	d
Polemaetus bellicosus	Martial Eagle	8	c

Scientific Name	Common Name	Source Codes	Region Codes

PANDIONIDAE · OSPREY   1 species recorded

| *Pandion haliaetus* | Osprey | 2 3 4 5 6 15
19 21 22 35 36 38
55 | a b c d e f g
h i j k |

FALCONIDAE · FALCONS, CARACARAS   61 species recorded

Daptrius americanus	Red-throated Caracara	4 6	d e
Daptrius ater	Black Caracara	6	d
Phalcoboenus albogularis	White-throated Caracara	6	d
Phalcoboenus australis	Striated Caracara	6	d
Phalcoboenus carunculatus	Carunculated Caracara	6	d
Phalcoboenus megalopterus	Mountain Caracara	6	d
Polyborus plancus[1]	Crested Caracara	3 4 5 6	a d e
Milvago chimachima	Yellow-headed Caracara	4 6	d e
Milvago chimango	Chimango Caracara	6	d
Herpetotheres cachinnans	Laughing Falcon	4 6	d e
Micrastur buckleyi	Buckley's Forest-Falcon	6	d
Micrastur mirandollei	Slaty-backed Forest-Falcon	4 6	d e
Micrastur plumbeus	Plumbeous Forest-Falcon	6	d
Micrastur ruficollis	Barred Forest-Falcon	4 6	d e
Micrastur semitorquatus	Collared Forest-Falcon	4 6	d e
Spiziapteryx circumcinctus	Spot-winged Falconet	6	d
Polihierax insignis[2]	Feilden's Falconet	18 55	g
Polihierax semitorquatus	African Pygmy Falcon	8	c
Microhierax caerulescens	Red-thighed Falconet	15 18 21 55	f g h
Microhierax erythrogonys	Philippine Falconet	22	h
Microhierax fringillarius	Black-legged Falconet	19 55	g h
Microhierax latifrons[3]	White-fronted Falconet	21	h
Microhierax melanoleucos	Pied Falconet	15 16 55	f g
Falco alopex	Fox Kestrel	8	c
Falco araea	Seychelles Kestrel	53	
Falco ardosiaceus	Gray Kestrel	8	c
Falco berigora	Brown Falcon	35 36	i j
Falco biarmicus[4]	Lanner Falcon	2 8 15	b c f
Falco cenchroides	Nankeen Kestrel	36 37	i j
Falco cherrug[5]	Saker Falcon	2 8 16 55	b c g
Falco chicquera	Red-headed Falcon	2 8 15	b c f
Falco columbarius	Merlin	2 3 4 5 6 8 15 16 55	a b c d e f g
Falco concolor	Sooty Falcon	2 8 10 15	b c f
Falco cuvieri	African Hobby	8	c
Falco deiroleucus	Orange-breasted Falcon	4 6	d e
Falco dickinsoni	Dickinson's Kestrel	8	c
Falco eleonorae	Eleonora's Falcon	2 8 10	b c
Falco fasciinucha	Taita Falcon	8	c
Falco femoralis	Aplomado Falcon	3 4 6	a d e
Falco hypoleucus	Gray Falcon	36	i
Falco jugger	Laggar Falcon	2 18 55	b g
Falco kreyenborgi	Pallid Falcon	6	d
Falco longipennis	Little Falcon	35 36	i j
Falco mexicanus	Prairie Falcon	3 4	a e
Falco moluccensis	Spotted Kestrel	21	h

18

Scientific Name	Common Name	Source Codes	Region Codes

FALCONIDAE · FALCONS, CARACARAS *contd.*

Scientific Name	Common Name	Source Codes	Region Codes
Falco naumanni	Lesser Kestrel	2 8 15 16 18 55	b c f g
Falco newtoni	Madagascar Kestrel	10	c
Falco novaeseelandiae	New Zealand Falcon	37	i
Falco pelegrinoides	Barbary Falcon	8	c
Falco peregrinus	Peregrine Falcon	2 4 6 8 15 16 18 21 22 35 36 38 55	a b c d e f g h i j k
Falco punctatus	Mauritius Kestrel	53	
Falco rufigularis[6]	Bat Falcon	4 6	d e
Falco rupicoloides	Greater Kestrel	8	c
Falco rusticolus	Gyrfalcon	2 3 16	a b g
Falco severus	Oriental Hobby	15 16 18 19 21 22 35 38 55	f g h j k
Falco sparverius	American Kestrel	3 4 5 6	a d e
Falco subbuteo	Hobby	2 8 15 16 18 55	b c f g
Falco subniger	Black Falcon	36	i
Falco tinnunculus	Common Kestrel	2 3 8 15 16 18 19 21 22 55	a b c f g h
Falco vespertinus[7]	Red-footed Falcon	2 8 15 16 55	b c f g
Falco zoniventris	Madagascar Banded Kestrel	10	c

MEGAPODIIDAE · MEGAPODES 12 species recorded

Scientific Name	Common Name	Source Codes	Region Codes
Megapodius freycinet[1]	Common Scrub Hen	15 19 21 22 36 38	f h i j k
Megapodius laperouse	Marianas Scrub Hen	38 53	k
Megapodius pritchardi	Polynesian Scrub Hen	38 53	k
Megapodius wallacei[2]	Moluccas Scrub Hen	35	h i
Leipoa ocellata	Mallee Fowl	36	i
Alectura lathami	Brush Turkey	36	i
Talegalla cuvieri	Red-billed Brush Turkey	35	j
Talegalla fuscirostris	Black-billed Brush Turkey	35	j
Talegalla jobiensis	Brown-collared Brush Turkey	35	j
Aepypodius arfakianus	Wattled Brush Turkey	35	j
Aepypodius bruijnii	Bruijn's Brush Turkey	35	j
Macrocephalon maleo	Maleo Fowl	27	h

CRACIDAE · CURASSOWS, GUANS, CHACHALACAS 44 species recorded

Scientific Name	Common Name	Source Codes	Region Codes
Ortalis canicollis	Chaco Chachalaca	6	d
Ortalis cinereiceps[1]	Grey-headed Chachalaca	60	d e
Ortalis erythroptera	Rufous-headed Chachalaca	6	d
Ortalis garrula	Chestnut-winged Chachalaca	4 6	d e
Ortalis leucogastra[2]	White-bellied Chachalaca	60	d
Ortalis motmot[3]	Little Chachalaca	6	d
Ortalis ruficauda	Rufous-vented Chachalaca	5 6	d e
Ortalis poliocephala[4]	West Mexican Chachalaca	60	e
Ortalis vetula	Plain Chachalaca	3 4	a e
Penelope albipennis	White-winged Guan	6	d
Penelope barbata[5]	Bearded Guan	60	d
Penelope argyrotis	Band-tailed Guan	6	d
Penelope dabbenei	Red-faced Guan	6	d

19

Scientific Name	Common Name	Source Codes	Region Codes
CRACIDAE · CURASSOWS, GUANS, CHACHALACAS contd.		6	d
Penelope jacquacu	Spix's Guan	6	d
Penelope jacucaca	White-browed Guan	6	d
Penelope marail	Marail Guan	6	d
Penelope montagnii	Andean Guan	6	d
Penelope obscura	Dusky-legged Guan	6	d
Penelope ochrogaster	Chestnut-bellied Guan	6	d
Penelope ortoni	Baudo Guan	6	d
Penelope perspicax[6]	Cauca Guan	60	d
Penelope pileata	White-crested Guan	6	d
Penelope purpurascens	Crested Guan	4 6	d e
Penelope superciliaris	Rusty-margined Guan	6	d
Aburria aburri	Wattled Guan	6	d
Aburria jacutinga[7]	Black-fronted Piping Guan	6	d
Aburria pipile[8]	Common Piping Guan	6	d
Chamaepetes goudotii	Sickle-winged Guan	6	d
Chamaepetes unicolor	Black Guan	4	e
Penelopina nigra	Black Chachalaca	4	e
Oreophasis derbianus	Horned Guan	4 53	e
Nothocrax urumutum	Nocturnal Curassow	6	d
Crax alberti	Blue-billed Curassow	6	d
Crax alector	Black Curassow	6	d
Crax blumenbachii	Red-billed Curassow	6	d
Crax daubentoni	Yellow-knobbed Curassow	6	d
Crax fasciolata	Bare-faced Curassow	6	d
Crax globulosa	Wattled Curassow	6	d
Crax mitu	Razor-billed Curassow	6	d
Crax pauxi	Helmeted Curassow	6	d
Crax rubra	Great Curassow	4 6	d e
Crax salvini	Salvin's Curassow	6	d
Crax tomentosa	Lesser Razor-billed Curassow	6	d
Crax unicornis	Horned Curassow	6	d

TETRAONIDAE · GROUSE   16 species recorded

Scientific Name	Common Name	Source Codes	Region Codes
Tetrao parvirostris	Black-billed Capercaillie	2	b
Tetrao urogallus	Capercaillie	2 16	b g
Lyrurus mlokosiewiczi	Caucasian Blackcock	2	b
Lyrurus tetrix	Black Grouse	2 16	b g
Lagopus lagopus	Willow Ptarmigan	2 3 16	a b g
Lagopus leucurus	White-tailed Ptarmigan	3	a
Lagopus mutus	Rock Ptarmigan	2 3	a b
Dendrogapus canadensis[1]	Spruce Grouse	3	a
Dendrogapus falcipennis	Siberian Spruce Grouse	2 16	b g
Dendrogapus obscurus	Blue Grouse	3	a
Bonasa bonasia[2]	Hazel Grouse	2 16	b g
Bonasa sewerzowi	Severtzov's Hazel Grouse	2 16	b g
Bonasa umbellus	Ruffed Grouse	3	a
Tympanuchus cupido[3]	Prairie Chicken	3 53	a
Tympanuchus phasianellus[4]	Sharp-tailed Grouse	3	a
Centrocercus urophasianus	Sage Grouse	3	a

PHASIANIDAE · QUAILS, PHEASANTS, PEACOCKS   183 species recorded

Scientific Name	Common Name	Source Codes	Region Codes
Dendrortyx barbatus	Bearded Wood-Partridge	4	e
Dendrortyx leucophrys	Buffy-crowned Wood-Partridge	4	e

20

Scientific Name	Common Name	Source Codes	Region Codes

PHASIANIDAE · QUAILS, PEASANTS, PEACOCKS *contd.*

Scientific Name	Common Name	Source Codes	Region Codes
Dendrortyx macroura	Long-tailed Wood-Partridge	4	e
Oreortyx pictus	Mountain Quail	3 4	a e
Callipepla squamata	Scaled Quail	3 4	a e
Lophortyx californicus	California Quail	3 4 36 37	a e i k
Lophortyx douglasii	Elegant Quail	4	e
Lophortyx gambelii	Gambel's Quail	3 4	a e
Philortyx fasciatus	Banded Quail	4	e
Colinus cristatus[1]	Crested Bobwhite	4 6	d e
Colinus nigrogularis[2]	Black-throated Bobwhite	4	e
Colinus virginianus	Bobwhite	3 4 5	a e
Odontophorus atrifrons	Black-fronted Wood-Quail	6	d
Odontophorus balliviani	Stripe-faced Wood-Quail	6	d
Odontophorus capueira	Spot-winged Wood-Quail	6	d
Odontophorus columbianus	Venezuelan Wood-Quail	6	d
Odontophorus dialeucos	Black-crowned Wood-Quail	49	e
Odontophorus erythrops	Rufous-fronted Wood-Quail	4 6	d e
Odontophorus gujanensis	Marbled Wood-Quail	4 6	d e
Odontophorus guttatus	Spotted Wood-Quail	4	e
Odontophorus hyperythrus	Chestnut Wood-Quail	6	d
Odontophorus leucolaemus	White-throated Wood-Quail	4	e
Odontophorus melanonotus	Dark-backed Wood-Quail	6	d
Odontophorus speciosus	Rufous-breasted Wood-Quail	6	d
Odontophorus stellatus	Starred Wood-Quail	6	d
Odontophorus strophium	Gorgeted Wood-Quail	6	d
Dactylortyx thoracicus	Singing Quail	4	e
Cyrtonyx montezumae	Montezuma Quail	3 4	a e
Cyrtonyx ocellatus	Ocellated Quail	4	e
Rhynchortyx cinctus	Tawny-faced Quail	4 6	d e
Lerwa lerwa	Snow Partridge	2 15 16	b f g
Ammoperdix griseogularis	See-see Partridge	2 15	b t
Ammoperdix heyi	Sand Partridge	2 8	b c
Tetraogallus altaicus	Altai Snowcock	2	b
Tetraogallus caspius	Caspian Snowcock	2	b
Tetraogallus caucasicus	Caucasian Snowcock	2	b
Tetraogallus himalayensis	Himalayan Snowcock	2 15 16	b f g
Tetraogallus tibetanus	Tibetan Snowcock	2 15 16	b f g
Tetraophasis obscurus	Verreaux's Monal Partridge	2 16	b g
Tetraophasis szechenyii	Szechenyi's Monal Partridge	2 15 16	b f g
Alectoris barbara	Barbary Partridge	2	b
Alectoris chukar	Chukar Partridge	2 37	b i
Alectoris graeca	Rock Partridge	2 3 15 16	a b f g
Alectoris magna	Przhevalski's Rock Partridge	2	b
Alectoris melanocephala	Arabian Chukor	8	c
Alectoris rufa	Red-legged Partridge	2	b
Anurophasis monorthonyx	Snow Mountain Quail	35	j
Francolinus adspersus	Red-billed Francolin	8	c
Francolinus afer	Bare-throated Francolin	8	c
Francolinus africanus	Graywing	8	c
Francolinus ahantensis	Ahanta Francolin	8	c
Francolinus albogularis	White-throated Francolin	8	c
Francolinus bicalcaratus	Double-spurred Francolin	2 8	b c
Francolinus camerunensis	Cameroon Mountain Francolin	8	c
Francolinus capensis	Cape Francolin	8	c
Francolinus castaneicollis	Chestnut-naped Francolin	8	c
Francolinus clappertoni	Clapperton's Francolin	8	c
Francolinus coqui	Coqui Francolin	8	c
Francolinus erckelii	Erckel's Francolin	3 8	c k

21

Scientific Name	Common Name	Source Codes	Region Codes

PHASIANIDAE · QUAILS, PHEASANTS, PEACOCKS *contd.*

Scientific Name	Common Name	Source Codes	Region Codes
Francolinus finschi	Finsch's Francolin	8	c
Francolinus francolinus	Black Partridge	2 15	b f
Francolinus griseostriatus	Gray-striped Francolin	8	c
Francolinus gularis	Swamp Partridge	15	f
Francolinus hartlaubi	Hartlaub's Francolin	8	c
Francolinus harwoodi	Harwood's Francolin	8	c
Francolinus hildebrandti	Hildebrandt's Francolin	8	c
Francolinus icterorhynchus	Yellow-billed Francolin	8	c
Francolinus jacksoni	Jackson's Francolin	8	c
Francolinus lathami	Latham's Francolin	8	c
Francolinus leucoscepus	Yellow-necked Francolin	8	c
Francolinus levaillantii	Red-winged Francolin	8	c
Francolinus levalliantoides	Archer's Graywing	8	c
Francolinus nahani	Nahani Francolin	8	c
Francolinus natalensis	Natal Francolin	8	c
Francolinus nobilis	Ruanda Francolin	8	c
Francolinus ochrogaster[3]	Pale-bellied Francolin	8	c
Francolinus pictus	Painted Partridge	15	f
Francolinus pintadeanus	Chinese Francolin	15 16 18 22 55	f g h
Francolinus pondicerianus	Gray Francolin	2 15	a f
Francolinus psilolaemus	Montane Francolin	8	c
Francolinus rufopictus	Painted Francolin	8	c
Francolinus schlegelii	Schlegel's Banded Francolin	8	c
Francolinus sephaena	Crested Francolin	8	c
Francolinus shelleyi	Shelley's Francolin	8	c
Francolinus squamatus	Scaly Francolin	8	c
Francolinus streptophorus	Ring-necked Francolin	8	c
Francolinus swainsonii	Swainson's Francolin	8	c
Francolinus swierstrai	Swierstra's Francolin	8	c
Perdix dauuricae	Daurian Partridge	2	b g h
Perdix hodgsoniae	Tibetan Partridge	2 15 16	b f g
Perdix perdix	Gray Partridge	2 3 16	a b g
Rhizothera longirostris	Long-billed Wood-Partridge	18 19 21 55	g h
Margaroperdix madagascariensis	Madagascar Partridge	10	c
Melanoperdix nigra	Black Wood-Partridge	19 21 55	g h
Coturnix chinensis[4]	Blue Quail	8 15 16 18 19 21 22 55	c f g h
Coturnix coromandelica	Black-breasted Quail	15 18 55	f g
Coturnix coturnix	Common Quail	2 3 8 10 15 16 18 22	b c f g h k
Coturnix delegorguei	Harlequin Quail	8 10	c
Coturnix japonica[5]	Japanese Quail	2 55	b
Coturnix novaezealandiae	New Zealand Quail	37	i
Coturnix pectoralis	Pectoral Quail	3 36	i k
Synoicus ypsilophorus	Brown Quail	35 36 37	i j
Perdicula asiatica[6]	Jungle Bush-Quail	15	f
Perdicula erythrorhyncha	Painted Bush-Quail	15	f
Perdicula manipurensis	Manipur Bush-Quail	15	f
Arborophila ardens	Hainan Hill-Partridge	16	g
Arborophila atrogularis	White-cheeked Hill-Partridge	15 18 55	f g
Arborophila brunneopectus	Brown-breasted Hill-Partridge	18 19 55	g h
Arborophila cambodiana	Chestnut-headed Tree-Partridge	55	g
Arborophila charltoni	Chestnut-breasted Tree-Partridge	18 19 21 55	h
Arborophila chloropus[7]	Green-legged Hill-Partridge	18	g

22

Scientific Name	Common Name	Source Codes	Region Codes
PHASIANIDAE · QUAILS, PHEASANTS, PEACOCKS *contd.*			
Arborophila crudigularis	Formosan Hill-Partridge	16	g
Arborophila davidi	David's Tree-Partridge	55	g
Arborophila gingica	Rickett's Hill-Partridge	16	g
Arborophila hyperythra	Red-breasted Tree-Partridge	19 21	h
Arborophila javanica	Chestnut-bellied Tree-Partridge	16 19	g h
Arborophila mandellii	Red-breasted Hill-Partridge	15	f
Arborophila merlini	Annamese Hill-Partridge	55	h
Arborophila orientalis	Sumatran Hill-Partridge	47	h
Arborophila rubrirostris	Red-billed Tree-Partridge	19	h
Arborophila rufipectus	Boulton's Hill-Partridge	2	b
Arborophila rufogularis	Rufous-throated Hill-Partridge	15 16 18 55	f g
Arborophila torqueola	Common Hill-Partridge	2 15 16 18 55	b f g
Caloperdix oculea	Ferruginous Wood-Partridge	18 19 21 55	g h
Haematortyx sanguiniceps	Crimson-headed Wood-Partridge	19 21	h
Rollulus roulroul	Crested Wood-Partridge	18 19 21 55	g h
Ptilopachus petrosus	Stone-Partridge	8	c
Bambusicola fytchii	Bamboo-Partridge	15 16 18 55	f g
Bambusicola thoracica	Formosan Bamboo-Partridge	16	g
Galloperdix bicalcarata	Ceylon Spurfowl	15	f
Galloperdix lunulata	Painted Spurfowl	15	f
Galloperdix spadicea	Red Spurfowl	15	f
Ophrysia superciliosa	Indian Mountain-Quail	15	f
Ithaginis cruentus	Blood Pheasant	2 15 16 18 55	b f g
Tragopan blythii	Blyth's Tragopan	15 18 53 55	f g h
Tragopan caboti	Cabot's Tragopan	16 53	g
Tragopan melanocephalus	Western Tragopan	2 15 16 53	b f g
Tragopan satyra	Satyr Tragopan	2 15 16	b f g
Tragopan temminckii	Temminck's Tragopan	2 15 16 18 55	b f g
Lophophorus impejanus	Himalayan Monal Pheasant	2 15 16 55	b f g
Lophophorus lhuysii	Chinese Monal Pheasant	2 16 53	b g
Lophophorus sclateri	Sclater's Monal Pheasant	2 15 16 18 53 55	b f g
Crossoptilon auritum	Blue Eared-Pheasant	2 16	b g
Crossoptilon crossoptilon	White Eared-Pheasant	2 15 16 53	b f g
Crossoptilon mantchuricum	Brown Eared-Pheasant	2 16 53	b g
Lophura bulweri[8]	Bulwer's Pheasant	21	h
Lophura diardi	Siamese Fireback Pheasant	55	g
Lophura edwardsi	Edwards's Pheasant	53 55	g
Lophura erythrophthalma	Crestless Fireback Pheasant	19 21 55	g h
Lophura ignita[9]	Crested Fireback Pheasant	18 19 21 55	g h
Lophura imperialis	Imperial Pheasant	53 55	g
Lophura inornata	Salvadori's Pheasant	19	h
Lophura leucomelana	Kalij Pheasant	2 15 16 18 55	b f g
Lophura nycthemera	Silver Pheasant	16 18 55	g
Lophura swinhoei	Swinhoe's Pheasant	53	
Gallus gallus	Red Junglefowl	3 15 16 18 19 22 38 55	f g h k
Gallus lafayettii	Ceylon Junglefowl	15	f
Gallus sonneratii	Gray Junglefowl	15	f
Gallus varius	Green Junglefowl	19	h
Pucrasia macrolopha	Koklass Pheasant	2 15 16	b f g
Catreus wallichii	Cheer Pheasant	15	f
Phasianus colchicus	Ring-necked Pheasant	2 3 16 18 36 37 55	a b g h i k
Phasianus versicolor	Green Pheasant	2 3	b k
Syrmaticus ellioti	Elliot's Pheasant	16 53	g

23

Scientific Name	Common Name	Source Codes	Region Codes

PHASIANIDAE · QUAILS, PHEASANTS, PEACOCKS contd.

Scientific Name	Common Name	Source Codes	Region Codes
Syrmaticus humiae	Mrs. Hume's Pheasant	15 16 18 53 55	f g
Syrmaticus mikado	Mikado Pheasant	16 53	g
Syrmaticus reevesii	Reeves's Pheasant	2 3 16	b g k
Syrmaticus soemmerringii	Copper Pheasant	2 3	b k
Chrysolophus amherstiae	Lady Amherst's Pheasant	2 16 18 55	b g
Chrysolophus pictus	Golden Pheasant	2	b
Polyplectron bicalcaratum	Peacock-Pheasant	15 16 18 55	f g
Polyplectron inopinatum	Bronze-tailed Peacock-Pheasant	19 53	h
Polyplectron emphanum	Palawan Peacock-Pheasant	22	h
Polyplectron germaini	Germain's Peacock-Pheasant	55	g
Polyplectron chalcurus	Rothschild's Peacock-Pheasant	19	h
Polyplectron malacense[10]	Malay Peacock-Pheasant	18 19 21 55	g h
Rheinardia ocellata	Crested Argus	19 55	g h
Argusianus argus	Great Argus	18 19 21 55	g h
Pavo cristatus	Peafowl	3 15 36	f i k
Pavo muticus	Green Peafowl	15 16 18 19 55	f g h
Afropavo congensis	Congo Peafowl	8	c

NUMIDIDAE · GUINEAFOWL   8 species recorded

Scientific Name	Common Name	Source Codes	Region Codes
Agelastes meleagrides	White-breasted Guineafowl	8	c
Agelastes niger	Black Guineafowl	8	c
Numida meleagris	Helmet Guineafowl	2 3 5 8 10	a b c e k
Numida reichenowi[1]	Reichenow's Guineafowl	8	c
Guttera edouardi	Crested Guineafowl	8	c
Guttera plumifera	Plumed Guineafowl	8	c
Guttera pucherani	Kenya Crested Guineafowl	8	c
Acryllium vulturinum	Vulturine Guineafowl	8	c

MELEAGRIDIDAE · TURKEYS   2 species recorded

Scientific Name	Common Name	Source Codes	Region Codes
Meleagris gallopavo	Turkey	3 4	a e
Agriocharis ocellata	Ocellated Turkey	4	e

OPISTHOCOMIDAE · HOATZIN   1 species recorded

Scientific Name	Common Name	Source Codes	Region Codes
Opisthocomus hoazin	Hoatzin	6	d

MESITORNITHIDAE · MESITES, MONIA   3 species recorded

Scientific Name	Common Name	Source Codes	Region Codes
Mesoenas unicolor	Brown Mesite	10	c
Mesoenas variegata	White-breasted Mesite	10	c
Monias benschi	Bensch's Monia	10	c

TURNICIDAE · BUSTARD-QUAIL, BUTTON-QUAILS   15 species recorded

Scientific Name	Common Name	Source Codes	Region Codes
Turnix castanota	Chestnut-backed Button-Quail	36	i
Turnix everetti	Everett's Button-Quail	32	j
Turnix hottentotta	Hottentot Button-Quail	8	c

Scientific Name	Common Name	Source Codes	Region Codes

TURNICIDAE · BUSTARD-QUAIL, BUTTON-QUAILS *contd.*

Scientific Name	Common Name	Source Codes	Region Codes
Turnix maculosa	Red-backed Button-Quail	35 36 38	i j k
Turnix melanogaster	Black-breasted Button-Quail	36	i
Turnix nigricollis	Madagascar Button-Quail	10	c
Turnix ocellata	Spotted Button-Quail	22	h
Turnix powelli	Powell's Button-Quail	33	j
Turnix pyrrhothorax	Red-chested Button-Quail	36	i
Turnix suscitator	Bustard-Quail	2 15 16 18 19 22 55	b f g h
Turnix sylvatica	Little Button-Quail	2 8 15 16 18 19 22 55	b c f g h
Turnix tanki	Yellow-legged Button-Quail	2 15 16 18 55	b f g
Turnix varia	Painted Button-Quail	3 36 38	i k
Turnix velox	Little Quail	36	i
Ortyxelos meiffrenii	Quail Plover	8	c

PEDIONOMIDAE · PLAINS WANDERER   1 species recorded

Scientific Name	Common Name	Source Codes	Region Codes
Pedionomus torquatus	Plains Wanderer	36	i

GRUIDAE · CRANES   14 species recorded

Scientific Name	Common Name	Source Codes	Region Codes
Grus americana	Whooping Crane	3 4 53	a e
Grus antigone	Sarus Crane	15 16 18 19 22 36 55	f g h i
Grus canadensis	Sandhill Crane	2 3 4 5 53	a b e
Grus carunculatus[1]	Wattled Crane	8	c
Grus grus	Crane	2 3 8 15 16 18 55	a b c f g
Grus japonensis	Japanese Crane	2 16 53	b g
Grus leucogeranus	Siberian White Crane	2 15 16	b f g
Grus monacha	Hooded Crane	2 15 16	b f g
Grus nigricollis	Black-necked Crane	2 15 16 55	b f g
Grus rubicunda	Brolga	35 36	i j
Grus vipio	White-naped Crane	2 16	b g
Anthropoides paradisea	Blue Crane	8	c
Anthropoides virgo	Demoiselle Crane	2 8 15 16 18 55	b c f g
Balearica pavonina	Crowned Crane	8	c

ARAMIDAE · LIMPKIN   1 species recorded

Scientific Name	Common Name	Source Codes	Region Codes
Aramus guarauna	Limpkin	3 4 5 6	a d e

PSOPHIIDAE · TRUMPETERS   3 species recorded

Scientific Name	Common Name	Source Codes	Region Codes
Psophia crepitans	Gray-winged Trumpeter	6	d
Psophia leucoptera	Pale-winged Trumpeter	6	d
Psophia viridis	Dark-winged Trumpeter	6	d

RALLIDAE · RAILS, COOTS, GALLINULES   124 species recorded

Scientific Name	Common Name	Source Codes	Region Codes
Rallus antarcticus	Austral Rail	6	d
Rallus aquaticus	Water Rail	2 3 15 16 18 21 55	a b f g h

Scientific Name	Common Name	Source Codes	Region Codes
RALLIDAE · RAILS, COOTS, GALLINULES contd.			
Rallus caerulescens	Kaffir Rail	8	c
Rallus elegans	King Rail	3 4 5	a e
Rallus limicola	Virginia Rail	3 4 6	a d e
Rallus longirostris	Clapper Rail	3 4 5 6	a d e
Rallus maculatus	Spotted Rail	6	d e
Rallus madagascariensis	Madagascar Rail	10	c
Rallus nigricans	Blackish Rail	6	d
Rallus owstoni	Guam Rail	38	k
Rallus pectoralis	Lewin's Water Rail	36 37	i
Rallus philippensis	Banded Land-Rail	22 35 36 37 38	h i j k
Rallus rougetii	Rouget's Rail	8	c
Rallus sanguinolentus	Plumbeous Rail	6	d
Rallus semiplumbeus	Bogota Rail	6	d
Rallus striatus	Blue-breasted Banded Rail	15 16 18 19 21 22 55	f g h
Rallus torquatus	Barred Rail	22 35	h j
Rallus wetmorei	Plain-flanked Rail	6	d
Atlantisia rogersi	Inaccessible Island Flightless Rail		
Tricholimnas sylvestris[1]	Lord Howe Wood-Rail	36	i k
Dryolimnas cuvieri	White-throated Rail	10	c
Amaurolimnas concolor	Uniform Crake	4 6	d e
Rallina canningi	Andaman Banded-Crake	15	f
Rallina eurizonoides	Banded-Crake	15 16 18 19 22 55	f g h
Rallina fasciata	Red-legged Banded-Crake	15 16 19 21 22 36 38 55	f g h i k
Rallina tricolor	Red-necked Rail	35 36	i j
Rallicula forbesi[2]	Forbes's Chestnut-Rail	35	j
Rallicula leucospila	White-striped Chestnut-Rail	35	j
Rallicula mayri[2]	Mayr's Chestnut-Rail	35	j
Rallicula rubra	Chestnut-Rail	35	j
Cyanolimnas cerverai	Zapata Rail	5 53	e
Aramides axillaris	Rufous-necked Wood-Rail	4 6	d e
Aramides cajanea	Gray-necked Wood-Rail	4 6	d e
Aramides calopterus	Red-winged Wood-Rail	6	d
Aramides mangle	Little Wood-Rail	6	d
Aramides saracura	Slaty-breasted Wood-Rail	6	d
Aramides wolfi	Brown Wood-Rail	6	d
Aramides ypecaha	Giant Wood-Rail	6	d
Aramidopsis plateni	Platen's Celebes' Rail	27	h
Nesoclopeus woodfordi[3]	Woodford's Rail	38	k
Gymnocrex plumbeiventris	Bare-eyed Rail	35	j
Gymnocrex rosenbergii	Rosenberg's Rail	27	h
Edithornis sylvestris	San Cristobal Mountain-Rail	38	h
Gallirallus australis	Weka	36 37	i
Habropteryx insignis	New Britain Rail	31	j
Habroptila wallacii	Halmahera Rail	31	j
Megacrex inepta	New Guinea Flightless Rail	35	j
Eulabeornis castaneoventris	Chestnut-bellied Rail	35 36	i j
Himantornis haematopus	Stripe-browed Crake	8	c
Canirallus kioloides[4]	Madagascar Gray-throated Rail	10	c
Canirallus oculeus	Gray-throated Rail	8	c
Crex crex	Corncrake	2 3 8 15 16 36	a b c f g i
Crex egregia[5]	African Crake	8	c
Anurolimnas castaneiceps	Chestnut-headed Crake	6	d
Limnocorax flavirostra	African Black Crake	8	c

26

Scientific Name	Common Name	Source Codes	Region Codes
RALLIDAE · RAILS, COOTS, GALLINULES *contd.*			
Porzana albicollis	Ash-throated Crake	6	d
Porzana bicolor	Elwes's Crake	15 16 18 55	f g
Porzana carolina	Sora	3 4 5 6	a d e
Porzana cinerea	Ashy Crake	2 36 55	b g h i
Porzana exquisita	Swinhoe's Yellow Rail	2	b
Porzana flaviventer	Yellow-breasted Crake	4 5 6	d e
Porzana fluminea	Australian Spotted Crake	36	i
Porzana fusca	Ruddy-breasted Crake	2 16 18 19 21 22 36 55	b f g h i
Porzana marginalis	Striped Crake	2 8	b c
Porzana parva	Little Crake	2 8 15 16	b c f g
Porzana paykullii	Band-bellied Crake	2 16 19 21 22 55	b g h
Porzana porzana	Spotted Crake	2 3 8 15 16 18 55	a b c f g
Porzana pusilla	Baillon's Crake	2 8 10 15 16 18 19 21 22 35 36 37 55	b c f g h i j
Porzana tabuensis	Sooty Rail	22 35 36 37 38	h i j k
Nesophylax ater	Henderson Island Rail	45	k
Laterallus exilis	Gray-breasted Crake	4 6	d e
Laterallus fasciatus	Black-banded Crake	6	d
Laterallus jamaicensis	Black Rail	3 4 5 6	a d e
Laterallus leucopyrrhus	Red-and-White Crake	6	d
Laterallus levraudi	Rusty-flanked Crake	6	d
Laterallus melanophaius[6]	Rufous-sided Crake	4 6	d e
Laterallus ruber	Ruddy Crake	4	e
Laterallus spilonotus	Galapagos Rail	46	d
Laterallus spilopterus	Dot-winged Crake	6	d
Laterallus viridis	Russet-crowned Crake	6	d
Laterallus xenopterus[7]	Rufous-faced Crake	6	d
Micropygia schomburgkii	Ocellated Crake	6	d
Coturnicops notata	Speckled Crake	6	d
Coturnicops noveboracensis	Yellow Rail	3 4 16	a e g
Neocrex erythrops	Paint-billed Crake	6	d
Sarothrura affinis	Chestnut-tailed Crake	8	c
Sarothrura ayresi	White-winged Crake	8	c
Sarothrura bohmi	Bohm's Crake	8	c
Sarothrura elegans	Buff-spotted Crake	8	c
Sarothrura insularis	Madagascar Crake	10	c
Sarothrura lugens[8]	Chestnut-headed Crake	8	c
Sarothrura pulchra	White-spotted Crake	8	c
Sarothrura rufa	Red-chested Crake	8	c
Sarothrura watersi	Waters's Crake	10	c
Poliolimnas cinereus	White-browed Rail	19 21 22 35 38	h j k
Porphyriops melanops	Spot-flanked Gallinule	6	d
Tribonyx mortierii	Tasmanian Waterhen	36	i
Tribonyx ventralis	Black-tailed Waterhen	36 37	i
Amaurornis akool	Brown Crake	15 16 18 55	f g
Amaurornis isabellina	Celebes Water-Hen	27	h
Amaurornis olivaceus	Bush-Hen	22 35 36 38	h i j k
Amaurornis olivieri	Olivier's Rail	10	c
Amaurornis phoenicurus	White-breasted Water-Hen	15 16 18 19 21 22 55	f g h
Gallicrex cinerea	Water Cock	2 15 16 18 19 21 22 55	b f g h
Gallinula angulata	Lesser Moorhen	8	c

Scientific Name	Common Name	Source Codes	Region Codes

RALLIDAE · RAILS, COOTS, GALLINULES contd.

Scientific Name	Common Name	Source Codes	Region Codes
Gallinula chloropus	Gray Moorhen	2 3 4 5 6 8 10 15 16 18 19 21 22 38 55	a b c d e f g h k
Gallinula tenebrosa	Dusky Moorhen	35 36	h i j
Porphyriornis nesiotis	Tristan Rail	11	c
Porphyrula alleni	Allen's Gallinule	8 10	c
Porphyrula flavirostris	Azure Gallinule	6	d
Porphyrula martinica	Purple Gallinule	3 4 5 6 8	a c d e
Porphyrio albus	New Britain Gallinule	34	j
Porphyrio porphyrio[9]	Purple Swamp Hen	2 8 15 16 18 19 21 22 35 36 38 55	b c f g h i j k
Notornis mantelli[10]	Takahe	37 53	i
Fulica americana[11]	American Coot	3 4 5 6	a d e
Fulica armillata	Red-gartered Coot	6	d
Fulica atra	Coot	2 3 8 15 16 18 19 21 22 35 36 37 55	a b c f g h i j
Fulica caribaea	Caribbean Coot	5 6	d e
Fulica cornuta	Horned Coot	6	d
Fulica cristata	Crested Coot	2 8 10	b e
Fulica gigantea	Giant Coot	6	d
Fulica leucoptera	White-winged Coot	6	d
Fulica rufifrons	Red-fronted Coot	6	d

HELIORNITHIDAE · SUNGREBE, FINFOOTS   3 species recorded

Scientific Name	Common Name	Source Codes	Region Codes
Podica senegalensis	Finfoot	8	c
Heliopais personata	Masked Finfoot	15 18 19 55	f g h
Heliornis fulica	Sungrebe	4 6	d e

RHYNOCHETIDAE · KAGU   1 species recorded

Scientific Name	Common Name	Source Codes	Region Codes
Rhynochetos jubatus	Kagu	38 53	k

EURYPYGIDAE · SUNBITTERN   1 species recorded

Scientific Name	Common Name	Source Codes	Region Codes
Eurypyga helias	Sunbittern	4 6	d e

CARIAMIDAE · SERIEMAS   2 species recorded

Scientific Name	Common Name	Source Codes	Region Codes
Cariama cristata	Red-legged Seriema	6	d
Chunga burmeisteri	Black-legged Seriema	6	d

OTIDIDAE · BUSTARDS   21 species recorded

Scientific Name	Common Name	Source Codes	Region Codes
Otis tarda	Great Bustard	2 15 16 18	b f g
Otis tetrax	Little Bustard	2 15 16	b f g
Neotis denhami	Denham's Bustard	8	c

Scientific Name	Common Name	Source Codes	Region Codes

OTIDIDAE · BUSTARDS contd.

Scientific Name	Common Name	Source Codes	Region Codes
Neotis heuglinii	Heuglin's Bustard	8	c
Neotis ludwigii	Ludwig's Bustard	8	c
Neotis nuba	Nubian Bustard	8	c
Ardeotis arabs	Great Arabian Bustard	2 8	b c
Ardeotis australis[1]	Australian Bustard	2 8	b c
Ardeotis kori	Kori Bustard	8	c
Ardeotis nigriceps	Great Indian Bustard	15 53	f
Chlamydotis undulata	Houbara Bustard	2 8 15 16	b c f g
Eupodotis afra	Little Black Bustard	8	c
Eupodotis bengalensis	Bengal Florican	15 55	f g
Eupodotis caerulescens	Blue Bustard	8	c
Eupodotis hartlaubii	Hartlaub's Bustard	8	c
Eupodotis humilis	Somali Black-throated Bustard	8	c
Eupodotis melanogaster	Black-bellied Bustard	8	c
Eupodotis ruficrista[2]	Crested Bustard	8	c
Eupodotis senegalensis	Senegal Bustard	8	c
Eupodotis vigorsi[3]	Black-throated Bustard	8	c
Sypheotides indica	Lesser Florican	15	f

JACANIDAE · JACANAS 7 species recorded

Scientific Name	Common Name	Source Codes	Region Codes
Microparra capensis	Smaller Jacana	8	c
Actophilornis africana	African Jacana	8	c
Actophilornis albinucha	Madagascar Jacana	10	c
Irediparra gallinacea	Comb-crested Jacana	19 21 22 35	h i j
Hydrophasianus chirurgus	Pheasant-tailed Jacana	2 15 16 18 19 21 22 55	b f g h
Metopidius indicus	Bronze-winged Jacana	15 18 19 55	f g h
Jacana spinosa[1]	American Jacana	3 4 5 6	a d e

ROSTRATULIDAE · PAINTED SNIPE 2 species recorded

Scientific Name	Common Name	Source Codes	Region Codes
Rostratula benghalensis	Painted Snipe	2 8 10 15 16 18 19 21 22 36 55	b c f g h i
Nycticryphes semicollaris	South American Painted Snipe	6	d

HAEMATOPODIDAE · OYSTERCATCHERS 6 species recorded

Scientific Name	Common Name	Source Codes	Region Codes
Haematopus ater	Blackish Oystercatcher	6	d
Haematopus bachmani	Black Oystercatcher	3 4	a e
Haematopus fuliginosus	Sooty Oystercatcher	37	i
Haematopus leucopodus	Magellanic Oystercatcher	6	d
Haematopus ostralegus[1]	Oystercatcher	2 3 5 8 15 16 18 35 36 55	a b c e f g i j
Haematopus palliatus	American Oystercatcher	3 4 6	a d e

CHARADRIIDAE · PLOVERS, DOTTERELS 62 species recorded

Scientific Name	Common Name	Source Codes	Region Codes
Vanellus albiceps	White-headed Plover	8	c
Vanellus armatus	Blacksmith Plover	8	c
Vanellus chilensis	Southern Lapwing	6	d e

Scientific Name	Common Name	Source Codes	Region Codes
CHARADRIIDAE · PLOVERS, DOTTERELS contd.			
Vanellus cinereus	Gray-headed Lapwing	2 15 16 55	b f g h
Vanellus coronatus	Crowned Lapwing	8	c
Vanellus crassirostris	Long-toed Lapwing	8	c
Vanellus gregarius	Sociable Lapwing	2 8 15	b c f
Vanellus indicus	Red-wattled Lapwing	2 15 16 18 19 55	b f g h
Vanellus leucurus	White-tailed Lapwing	2 8 15	b c f
Vanellus lugubris	Senegal Plover	8	c
Vanellus malabaricus	Yellow-wattled Lapwing	15	f
Vanellus melanocephalus	Spot-breasted Plover	8	c
Vanellus melanopterus	Black-winged Plover	8	c
Vanellus miles	Masked Plover	35 36	i j
Vanellus novahollandiae	Australian Spur-winged Plover	36	i j
Vanellus resplendens	Andean Lapwing	6	d
Vanellus senegallus	Wattled Plover	8	c
Vanellus spinosus	Spur-winged Lapwing	2 8 15 16 18 37 55	b c f g i
Vanellus superciliosus	Brown-chested Plover	8	c
Vanellus tectus	Black-headed Plover	8	c
Vanellus tricolor	Banded Plover	36	h i
Vanellus vanellus	Lapwing	2 3 8 15 16 18	a b c f g h
Hoploxypterus cayanus	Pied Plover	4 6	d e
Pluvialis apricaria	Eurasian Golden Plover	2 3 15	a b f j
Pluvialis dominica	American Golden Plover	3 4 5 6 8 15 16 18 19 21 22 35 36 37 38	a c d e f g h i j k
Pluvialis squatarola	Black-bellied Plover	2 3 4 5 6 8 15 16 18 19 21 22 36 37 38 55	a b c d e f g h i j k
Charadrius alexandrinus	Snowy Plover	2 3 4 5 6 8 15 16 18 19 21 22 36 38 55	a b c d e f g h i k
Charadrius alticola	Puna Plover	6	d
Charadrius asiaticus	Caspian Plover	2 8 15 16 19 21 22 35 36 38	b c f g h i j k
Charadrius bicinctus	Banded Dotterel	36 37	i
Charadrius cinctus[1]	Red-kneed Dotterel	36	i
Charadrius collaris	Collared Plover	4 5 6 35	d e j
Charadrius cucullatus	Hooded Dotterel	36	i
Charadrius dubius	Little Ringed Plover	2 8 15 16 18 19 21 22 35 38 55	b c f g h j k
Charadrius falklandicus	Two-banded Plover	6	d
Charadrius forbesi	Forbes's Banded Plover	8	c
Charadrius hiaticula	Ringed Plover	2 3 8 10 15 16 18 36 55	a b c f g h i
Charadrius leschenaultii	Greater Sand Plover	2 8 10 15 16 18 19 21 22 35 36 37 38 55	b c f g h i j k
Charadrius marginatus[2]	White-fronted Sand Plover	8 10	c
Charadrius melanops	Black-fronted Plover	15 36 37	f i
Charadrius melodus	Piping Plover	3 4 5	a e
Charadrius mongolus	Mongolian Plover	2 3 8 10 15 16 18 19 21 22 35 36 37 38 55	a b c f g h i j k
Charadrius montana[3]	Mountain Plover	3 4	a e
Charadrius novaeseelandiae	New Zealand Shore Plover	37 53	i
Charadrius obscurus[4]	Red-breasted Dotterel	37	i
Charadrius pallidus	Chestnut-banded Sand Plover	8	c

Scientific Name	Common Name	Source Codes	Region Codes

CHARADRIIDAE · PLOVERS, DOTTERELS *contd.*

Scientific Name	Common Name	Source Codes	Region Codes
Charadrius pecuarius	Kittlitz's Plover	2 8 10	b c
Charadrius peroni	Malay Plover	19 21 22 55	g h
Charadrius placidus	Long-billed Ringed Plover	2 15 18 55	b f g h
Charadrius ruficapillus	Red-capped Dotterel	37	i
Charadrius semipalmatus	Semipalmated Plover	3 4 5 6	a d e
Charadrius thoracicus	Black-banded Sand Plover	10	c
Charadrius tricollaris	Three-banded Plover	8 10	c
Charadrius veredus[5]	Oriental Plover	2 37 55	b g i
Charadrius vociferus	Killdeer	3 4 5 6	a d e
Charadrius wilsonia	Wilson's Plover	3 4 5 6	a d e
Oreopholus ruficollis	Tawny-throated Dotterel	6	d
Eudromias morinellus	Dotterel	2 3 16	a b g
Zonibyx modestus	Rufous-chested Dotterel	6	d
Anarhynchus frontalis	Wrybill	37	i
Pluvianellus socialis	Magellanic Plover	6	d
Phegornis mitchellii	Diademed Sandpiper-Plover	6	d

SCOLOPACIDAE · SNIPE, WOODCOCK, SANDPIPERS 81 species recorded

Scientific Name	Common Name	Source Codes	Region Codes
Bartramia longicauda	Upland Sandpiper	3 4 5 6 36	a d e i
Numenius americanus	Long-billed Curlew	3 4 5	a e
Numenius arquata	Eurasian Curlew	2 3 8 10 15 16 18 19 21 22 36 55	a b c f g h i
Numenius borealis	Eskimo Curlew	3 4 6 16 53	a d e g
Numenius madagascariensis	Far Eastern Curlew	2 16 19 21 22 35 36 37 38 55	b g h i j k
Numenius minutus	Little Curlew	2 19 21 22 35 36 37 55	b g h i j
Numenius phaeopus	Whimbrel	2 3 4 5 6 8 10 15 16 18 21 22 35 36 38 55	a b c d e f g h i j k
Numenius tahitiensis	Bristle-thighed Curlew	3 38	a k
Numenius tenuirostris	Slender-billed Curlew	2	b
Limosa fedoa	Marbled Godwit	3 4 5 6	a d e
Limosa haemastica	Hudsonian Godwit	3 4 5 6 37 53	a d e i
Limosa lapponica	Bar-tailed Godwit	2 3 8 10 15 16 19 21 22 35 36 37 38 55	a b c f g h i j k
Limosa limosa	Black-tailed Godwit	2 3 8 15 16 18 19 21 22 35 36 38 55	a b c f g h i j k
Tringa brevipes	Gray-tailed Tattler	2 36 37 55	a b g i
Tringa cancellatus	Tuamotu Sandpiper	54	k
Tringa cinereus	Terek Sandpiper	2 8 10 15 16 18 19 21 22 35 36 37 38 55	b c f g h i j k
Tringa erythropus	Spotted Redshank	2 8 15 16 18 55	b c f g h
Tringa flavipes	Lesser Yellowlegs	3 4 5 6	a d e
Tringa glareola	Wood Sandpiper	2 3 8 15 16 18 19 21 22 35 36 38 55	a b c f g h i j k
Tringa guttifer	Spotted Greenshank	2 15 16 18 19 21 22 55	b f g h
Tringa hypoleucos	Common Sandpiper	2 8 10 15 16 19 21 36 55	b c f g h i j k

Scientific Name	Common Name	Source Codes	Region Codes

SCOLOPACIDAE · SNIPE, WOODCOCK, SANDPIPERS *contd.*

Scientific Name	Common Name	Source Codes	Region Codes
Tringa incana	Wandering Tattler	2 16 36 37	a b d e g h i j k
Tringa macularia[1]	Spotted Sandpiper	3 4 5 6	a d e
Tringa melanoleuca	Greater Yellowlegs	3 4 5 6 37	a d e i
Tringa nebularia	Greenshank	2 8 10 15 16 18 19 21 22 35 36 37 38 55	b c f g h i j k
Tringa ochropus	Green Sandpiper	2 8 10 15 16 18 19 21 22 55	b c f g h
Tringa solitaria	Solitary Sandpiper	3 4 5 6 8	a c d e
Tringa stagnatilis	Marsh Sandpiper	2 8 15 16 18 19 21 22 35 36 37 55	b c f g h i j
Tringa totanus	Redshank	2 3 8 15 16 18 19 21 22 36 55	a b c f g h i
Catoptrophorus semipalmatus	Willet	3 4 5 6	a d e
Gallinago andina[2]	Puna Snipe	6	d
Gallinago gallinago	Common Snipe	2 3 4 5 6 8 16 18 19 22 55	a b c d e f g h
Gallinago hardwickii	Japanese Snipe	2 16 35 36 37	b g i j
Gallinago imperialis	Banded Snipe	6	d
Gallinago macrodactyla	Madagascar Snipe	10	c
Gallinago media	Great Snipe	2 8 15 55	b c f g
Gallinago megala	Swinhoe's Snipe	2 15 16 18 19 21 22 35 36 38 55	b f g h i j k
Gallinago nemoricola	Wood Snipe	2 15 16 18 55	b f g
Gallinago nigripennis	African Snipe	8	c
Gallinago nobilis	Noble Snipe	6	d
Gallinago solitaria	Solitary Snipe	2 15 16 18	b f g h
Gallinago stenura	Pintail Snipe	2 8 18 19 22 55	b c f g h
Gallinago stricklandii	Cordilleran Snipe	6	d
Gallinago undulata	Giant Snipe	6	d
Arenaria interpres	Ruddy Turnstone	3 4 5 6 8 15 16 19 21 22 35 36 37 38 55	a b c d e f g h i j k
Arenaria melanocephala	Black Turnstone	3 4	a e
Limnodromus griseus	Short-billed Dowitcher	3 4 5 6 18 19 21	a d e g h
Limnodromus scolopaceus	Long-billed Dowitcher	2 3 4 6	a b d e
Limnodromus semipalmatus	Asian Dowitcher	2 15 16 22 55	b f g h
Coenocorypha aucklandica	Sub-Antarctic Snipe	37	i
Scolopax celebensis	Celebes Woodcock	27	h
Scolopax minor[3]	American Woodcock	3	a
Scolopax mira	Amami Woodcock	2	b
Scolopax rochussenii	Obi Woodcock	31	g
Scolopax rusticola	Eurasian Woodcock	2 3 15 16 18 19 22 55	a b f g h
Scolopax saturata	East Indian Woodcock	19 35	h j
Lymnocryptes minimus	Jack Snipe	2 3 18 22 55	a b c f g h
Aphriza virgata	Surfbird	3 6	a d e
Calidris acuminata	Sharp-tailed Sandpiper	2 15 16 18 36 37 38 55	a b f g h i j k
Calidris alba[4]	Sanderling	2 3 4 5 6 8 10 15 16 18 21 35 36 37 38 55	a b c d e f g h i j k
Calidris alpinus	Dunlin	2 3 4 8 15 16 19 36 55	a b c e f g h i
Calidris bairdii	Baird's Sandpiper	2 3 4 6 8 36	a b c d e i

32

Scientific Name	Common Name	Source Codes	Region Codes

SCOLOPACIDAE · SNIPE, WOODCOCK, SANDPIPERS *contd.*

Scientific Name	Common Name	Source Codes	Region Codes
Calidris canutus	Red Knot	2 3 4 5 6 8 / 15 16 18 19 21 35 / 36 37 55	a b c d e f g / i j
Calidris ferruginea	Curlew Sandpiper	2 3 8 10 16 18 / 19 21 22 35 36 37 / 55	a b c f g h i j
Calidris fuscicollis	White-rumped Sandpiper	3 4 5 6	a d e
Calidris maritima	Purple Sandpiper	2 3	a b
Calidris mauri	Western Sandpiper	2 3 4 5 6 36	a b d e i
Calidris melanotos	Pectoral Sandpiper	2 3 4 5 6 8 / 36 37 38	a b c d e i k
Calidris minuta	Little Stint	2 8 10 15 18 19 / 22 38 55	b c f g h k
Calidris minutilla	Least Sandpiper	2 3 4 5 6 15 / 16 18 19 21 36 38	a b d e f g h / i k
Calidris ptilocnemis	Rock Sandpiper	2 3	a b
Calidris pusilla	Semipalmated Sandpiper	3 4 5 6	a d e
Calidris ruficollis	Rufous-necked Sandpiper	2 3 8 15 16 21 / 35 36 37 55	a b c f g h i j
Calidris subminuta	Long-toed Stint	22 55	g h
Calidris temminckii	Temminck's Stint	2 8 15 16 18 19 / 21 22 55	b c f g h
Calidris tenuirostris	Great Knot	2 3 15 16 21 35 / 36 55	a b f g h i j
Eurynorhynchus pygmeus	Spoon-billed Sandpiper	2 3 15 16 18 55	a b f g
Limicola falcinellus	Broad-billed Sandpiper	2 8 15 16 18 19 / 21 22 35 36 37 55	b c f g h i j
Micropalama himantopus	Stilt Sandpiper	3 4 5 6	a d e
Tryngites subruficollis	Buff-breasted Sandpiper	3 4 5 6 36	a d e i
Philomachus pugnax	Ruff	2 3 5 8 15 16 / 18 19 21 22 36 55	a b c e f g h i

RECURVIROSTRIDAE · AVOCETS, STILTS 7 species recorded

Scientific Name	Common Name	Source Codes	Region Codes
Ibidorhyncha struthersii	Ibis-bill	2 15 16 18	b f g
Himantopus himantopus[1]	Black-winged Stilt	2 3 5 6 8 10 / 15 16 18 19 21 22 / 35 36 38 55	a b c d e f g / h i j k
Cladorhynchus leucocephalus	Banded Stilt	36	i
Recurvirostra americana[2]	American Avocet	3 4	a e
Recurvirostra andina	Andean Avocet	6	d
Recurvirostra avosetta	Avocet	2 8 10 15 16 18 / 55	b c f g
Recurvirostra novaehollandiae[3]	Red-necked Avocet	36 37	i

PHALAROPODIDAE · PHALAROPES 3 species recorded

Scientific Name	Common Name	Source Codes	Region Codes
Phalaropus fulicarius	Red Phalarope	2 3 4 6 8 15 / 16 36 37	a b c d e f g i
Phalaropus lobatus	Northern Phalarope	2 3 4 6 8 15 / 16 19 21 22 35 36 / 37 38 55	a b c d e f g / h i j k
Phalaropus tricolor	Wilson's Phalarope	3 4 6 36	a d e i

Scientific Name	Common Name	Source Codes	Region Codes

DROMADIDAE · CRAB PLOVER 1 species recorded

Dromas ardeola	Crab Plover	2 8 10 15	b c f

BURHINIDAE · THICK-KNEES 9 species recorded

Burhinus bistriatus	Double-striped Thick-Knee	4 5 6	d e
Burhinus capensis	Spotted Thick-Knee	2 8	b c
Burhinus magnirostris	Southern Stone-Curlew	36	i
Burhinus oedicnemus	Stone-Curlew	2 8 15 18 55	b c f
Burhinus senegalensis	Senegal Thick-Knee	2 8	b c
Burhinus superciliaris	Peruvian Thick-Knee	6	d
Burhinus vermiculatus	Water Thick-Knee	8	c
Esacus magnirostris	Beach Stone-Curlew	35 36	i j
Esacus recurvirostris	Great Stone-Curlew	15 16 18 19 21 22 38	f g h k

GLAREOLIDAE · PRATINCOLES, COURSERS 17 species recorded

Pluvianus aegyptius	Egyptian Plover	2 8	b c
Cursorius africanus[1]	Two-banded Courser	8	c
Cursorius bitorquatus	Jerdon's Courser	15	f
Cursorius chalcopterus	Violet-tipped Courser	8	c
Cursorius cinctus	Heuglin's Courser	8	c
Cursorius coromandelicus	Indian Courser	15	f
Cursorius cursor	Cream-coloured Courser	2 8 15	b c f
Cursorius temminckii	Temminck's Courser	8	c
Peltohyas australis	Australian Dotterel	36	i
Glareola cinerea	Gray Pratincole	8	c
Glareola isabella[2]	Long-legged Pratincole	19 21 35 36	h i j
Glareola lactea	Little Pratincole	2 15 18 55	b f g h
Glareola maldivarum[3]	Eastern Collared Pratincole	2 35 37 55	b g i j
Glareola nordmanni	Black-winged Pratincole	2 8	b c
Glareola nuchalis	White-collared Pratincole	8	c
Glareola ocularis	Madagascar Pratincole	8 10	c
Glareola pratincola	Collared Pratincole	2 8 15 16 18 19 21 22 36	b c f g h i

THINOCORIDAE · SEEDSNIPE 4 species recorded

Attagis gayi	Rufous-bellied Seedsnipe	6	d
Attagis malouinus	White-bellied Seedsnipe	6	d
Thinocorus orbignyianus	Gray-breasted Seedsnipe	6	d
Thinocorus rumicivorus	Least Seedsnipe	6	d

CHIONIDIDAE · SHEATHBILLS 2 species recorded

Chionis alba	Snowy Sheathbill	6	d
Chionis minor	Black-faced Sheathbill	36	i

34

Scientific Name	Common Name	Source Codes	Region Codes

STERCORARIIDAE · SKUAS, JAEGERS 5 species recorded

Scientific Name	Common Name	Source Codes	Region Codes
Stercorarius longicaudus	Long-tailed Jaeger	2 3 4 6 36	a b d e i
Stercorarius parasiticus	Parasitic Jaeger	2 3 4 5 6 8 10 15 36 37	a b c d e f i
Stercorarius pomarinus	Pomarine Jaeger	2 3 4 6 8 15 18 36 37 55	a b c d e f g h i
Stercorarius skua	Great Skua	2 3 4 6 8 10 15 36 37	a b c d e f i
Stercorarius maccormicki	MacCormick's Skua	37 58	i

LARIDAE · GULLS, TERNS 86 species recorded

Scientific Name	Common Name	Source Codes	Region Codes
Larus argentatus[1]	Herring Gull	2 3 4 5 8 15 16 22 55	a b c e f g h
Larus atricilla	Laughing Gull	3 4 5 6	a d e
Larus audouinii	Audouin's Gull	2 53	b
Larus belcheri	Band-tailed Gull	6	d
Larus brevirostris	Red-legged Kittiwake	2 3	a b
Larus brunnicephalus	Brown-headed Gull	2 15 16 18 55	b f g
Larus bulleri	Black-billed Gull	37	i
Larus californicus	California Gull	3 4	a e
Larus canus	Common Gull	2 3 16 55	a b g
Larus cirrocephalus	Gray-headed Gull	2 6 8 10	b c d
Larus crassirostris	Black-tailed Gull	2 3 16	a b g
Larus delawarensis	Ring-billed Gull	3 4 5 6	a d e
Larus dominicanus	Kelp Gull	6 8 10 36 37	c d i
Larus eburnea	Ivory Gull	2 3	a b
Larus fulginosus	Lava Gull	46	
Larus fuscus	Lesser Black-backed Gull	2 3 8 15	a b c f
Larus genei	Slender-billed Gull	2 8 15	b c f
Larus glaucescens	Glaucous-winged Gull	2 3 4 16	a b e g
Larus glaucoides	Iceland Gull	2 3	a b
Larus heermanni	Heermann's Gull	3 4	a e
Larus hemprichii	Sooty Gull	2 8 15	b c f
Larus hyperboreus	Glaucous Gull	2 3 16	a b g
Larus ichthyaetus	Great Black-headed Gull	2 8 15 16 18	b c f g
Larus leucophthalmus	White-eyed Gull	2 8	b c
Larus maculipennis	Brown-hooded Gull	6	d
Larus marinus	Great Black-backed Gull	2 3	a b
Larus melanocephalus	Mediterranean Gull	2 16	b g
Larus minutus	Little Gull	2 3 15 16	a b f g
Larus modestus	Gray Gull	4 6	d e
Larus novaehollandiae	Silver Gull	35 36 38	i j k
Larus occidentalis	Western Gull	3 4	a e
Larus pacificus	Pacific Gull	36	i
Larus philadelphia	Bonaparte's Gull	3 4 5	a e
Larus pipixcan	Franklin's Gull	3 4 6	a d e
Larus relictus	Relict Gull	61	b
Larus ridibundus	Black-headed Gull	2 3 4 8 15 16 19 21 22	a b c e f g h
Larus rosea	Ross's Gull	2 3 26	a b g
Larus sabini	Sabine's Gull	2 3 4 6 8	a b c d e
Larus saundersi	Saunders's Gull	2 16	b g
Larus schistisagus	Slaty-backed Gull	2 3 16	a b g
Larus scoresbii	Dolphin Gull	6	d

Scientific Name	Common Name	Source Codes	Region Codes

LARIDAE · GULLS, TERNS *contd.*

Scientific Name	Common Name	Source Codes	Region Codes
Larus serranus	Andean Gull	6	d
Larus thayeri	Thayer's Gull	56	a b
Larus tridactylus	Black-legged Kittiwake	2 3 4 8 16	a b c e g
Creagrus furcatus	Swallow-tailed Gull	4 6	d e
Chlidonias hybrida	Whiskered Tern	2 8 15 16 18 19 21 22 35 36 55	b c f g h i j
Chlidonias leucoptera	White-winged Black Tern	2 3 8 10 15 16 18 19 21 22 35 36 37 55	a b c f g h i j
Chlidonias nigra	Black Tern	2 3 4 6 8	a b c d e
Phaetusa simplex	Large-billed Tern	6	d
Sterna acuticauda[2]	Black-bellied Tern	15 18 55	f g
Sterna albifrons	Least Tern	2 3 4 5 6 8 10 15 16 18 21 22 35 36 38 55	a b c d e f g h i j k
Sterna aleutica	Aleutian Tern	2 3	a b
Sterna anaethetus	Bridled Tern	2 3 4 5 6 8 10 15 16 18 19 21 35 36 38 55	a b c d e f g h i j k
Sterna aurantia	River Tern	15 18 55	f g
Sterna balaenarum	Damara Tern	8	c
Sterna bengalensis	Lesser Crested Tern	2 8 10 15 16 18 19 21 35 36 55	b c f g h i j
Sterna bergii	Greater Crested Tern	2 8 10 15 16 18 19 21 22 35 36 37 38 55	b c f g h i j k
Sterna caspia	Caspian Tern	2 3 4 5 6 8 10 15 16 18 22 36 37 55	a b c d e f g h i
Sterna dougallii	Roseate Tern	2 3 4 5 6 8 10 15 16 18 19 22 35 36 38 55	a b c d e f g h i j k
Sterna elegans	Elegant Tern	3 4 6	a d e
Sterna eurygnatha	Cayenne Tern	6	d
Sterna forsteri	Forster's Tern	3 4 5	a e
Sterna fuscata	Sooty Tern	3 4 5 6 8 15 16 18 19 21 22 35 36 37 38 55	a c d e f g h i j k
Sterna hirundinacea	South American Tern	6	d
Sterna hirundo	Common Tern	2 3 4 5 6 8 10 15 16 19 21 22 35 36 38 55	a b c d e f g h i j k
Sterna lorata	Peruvian Tern	6	d
Sterna lunata	Gray-backed Tern	38	k
Sterna maxima	Royal Tern	2 3 4 5 6 8	a b c d e
Sterna nereis	Fairy Tern	36 37 38	i k
Sterna nilotica	Gull-billed Tern	2 3 4 5 8 16 21 55	a b c d e f g h
Sterna paradisaea	Arctic Tern	2 3 6 8 36 37	a b c d i
Sterna repressa	White-cheeked Tern	2 8 15	b c f
Sterna sandvicensis	Sandwich Tern	2 3 4 5 6 8	a b c d e f
Sterna saundersi	Saunders's Little Tern	2 55	b g
Sterna striata	White-fronted Tern	36 37	i
Sterna sumatrana	Black-naped Tern	2 15 16 18 19 21 22 35 36 38 55	b f g h i j k
Sterna superciliaris	Yellow-billed Tern	6	d
Sterna trudeaui	Trudeau's Tern	6	d

Scientific Name	Common Name	Source Codes	Region Codes

LARIDAE · GULLS, TERNS contd.

Scientific Name	Common Name	Source Codes	Region Codes
Sterna virgata	Kerguelen Tern	50	l
Sterna vittata	Antarctic Tern	6 8 36 37	c d i
Sterna zimmermanni	Chinese Crested Tern	2 21 22 55	b g h
Larosterna inca	Inca Tern	6	d
Procelsterna caerulea	Blue-Gray Noddy	3 36 37 38	a i k
Anous stolidus	Brown Noddy	3 4 5 6 8 10 15 16 18 21 22 35 36 37 38 55	a c d e f g h i j k
Anous tenuirostris[3]	Black Noddy	3 4 6 8 10 15 19 22 35 36 37 38	a c d e f h i j k
Gygis alba	White Tern	4 10 15 16 19 35 36 37 38 55	c e f g h i j k

RYNCHOPIDAE · SKIMMERS   3 species recorded

Scientific Name	Common Name	Source Codes	Region Codes
Rhynchops albicollis	Indian Skimmer	15 16 18 55	f g
Rhynchops flavirostris	African Skimmer	2 8	b c
Rhynchops nigra	Black Skimmer	3 4 5 6	a d e

ALCIDAE · AUKS, AUKLETS, MURRES   21 species recorded

Scientific Name	Common Name	Source Codes	Region Codes
Alle alle	Dovekie	2 3	a b
Alca torda	Razorbill	2 3	a b
Uria aalge	Common Murre	2 3	a b
Uria lomvia	Thick-billed Murre	2 3	a b
Cepphus carbo	Spectacled Guillemot	2	b
Cepphus columba	Pigeon Guillemot	2 3	a b
Cepphus grylle	Black Guillemot	2 3	a b
Brachyramphus brevirostris	Kittlitz's Murrelet	2 3	a b
Brachyramphus hypoleuca[1,2]	Xantus's Murrelet	3 4	a e
Brachyramphus marmoratus	Marbled Murrelet	2 3 16	a b g
Synthliboramphus antiquus	Ancient Murrelet	2 3 4 16	a b e g
Synthliboramphus wumizusume	Japanese Murrelet	2	b
Ptychoramphus aleuticus	Cassin's Auklet	3 4	a e
Cyclorrhynchus psittacula	Parakeet Auklet	2 3	a b
Aethia cristatella	Crested Auklet	2 3	a b
Aethia pusilla	Least Auklet	2 3	a b
Aethia pygmaea	Whiskered Auklet	2 3	a b
Cerorhinca monocerata	Rhinoceros Auklet	2 3 4 16	a b e g
Fratercula arctica	Puffin	2 3	a b
Fratercula corniculata	Horned Puffin	2 3	a b
Lunda cirrhata	Tufted Puffin	2 3	a b

PTEROCLIDAE · SANDGROUSE   16 species recorded

Scientific Name	Common Name	Source Codes	Region Codes
Syrrhaptes paradoxus	Pallas's Sandgrouse	2 16	b g
Syrrhaptes tibetanus	Tibetan Sandgrouse	2 15 16	b f g
Pterocles alchata	Pin-tailed Sandgrouse	2 15	b f
Pterocles bicinctus	Double-banded Sandgrouse	8	c
Pterocles burchelli	Variegated Sandgrouse	8	c
Pterocles coronatus	Coroneted Sandgrouse	2 8 15	b c f

Scientific Name	Common Name	Source Codes	Region Codes
PTEROCLIDAE · SANDGROUSE contd.			
Pterocles decoratus	Black-faced Sandgrouse	8	c
Pterocles exustus	Chestnut-bellied Sandgrouse	2 8 15	b c f
Pterocles gutturalis	Yellow-throated Sandgrouse	8	c
Pterocles indicus	Painted Sandgrouse	15	f
Pterocles lichtensteinii	Lichtenstein's Sandgrouse	2 8	b c
Pterocles namaqua	Namaqua Sandgrouse	8	c
Pterocles orientalis	Black-bellied Sandgrouse	2 15 16	b f g
Pterocles personatus	Madagascar Sandgrouse	10	c
Pterocles quadricinctus	Four-banded Sandgrouse	8	c
Pterocles senegallus	Spotted Sandgrouse	2 8 15	b c f

COLUMBIDAE · PIGEONS, DOVES   280 species recorded

Scientific Name	Common Name	Source Codes	Region Codes
Columba albinucha	White-naped Pigeon	8	c
Columba albitorques	White-collared Dove	8	c
Columba araucana	Chilean Pigeon	6	d
Columba argentina	Gray Wood Pigeon	19 21	h
Columba arquatrix[1]	Olive Pigeon	8	c
Columba bollii[2]	Boll's Pigeon	51	c
Columba caribaea	Ring-tailed Pigeon	5	e
Columba cayennensis	Pale-vented Pigeon	4 6	d e
Columba chiriquensis	Chiriqui Pigeon	4	e
Columba corensis	Bare-eyed Pigeon	6	d
Columba delegorguei	Bronze-naped Pigeon	8	c
Columba elphinstonii	Nilgiri Wood Pigeon	15	f
Columba eversmanni	Eastern Stock Dove	2 15 16	b f g
Columba fasciata	Band-tailed Pigeon	3 4 6	a d e
Columba flavirostris	Red-billed Pigeon	3 4	a e
Columba goodsoni	Dusky Pigeon	6	d
Columba guinea	Speckled Pigeon	8	c
Columba hodgsonii	Speckled Wood Pigeon	2 15 16 18	b f g
Columba inornata	Plain Pigeon	5	e
Columba janthina	Japanese Wood Pigeon	2 16	b g
Columba jouyi	Jouyi's Wood Pigeon	2	b
Columba junoniae	Laurel Pigeon	2	b
Columba leucocephala	White-crowned Pigeon	3 4 5	a e
Columba leucomela[3]	White-headed Pigeon	36	i
Columba leuconota	Snow Pigeon	2 15 16 18	b f g
Columba livia	Rock Dove	2 3 4 8 15 16 18 36 37 55	a b c e f g h i
Columba maculosa	Spot-winged Pigeon	6	d
Columba malherbii[4]	Sao Thome Bronze-naped Pigeon	8	c
Columba mayeri[5]	Mauritius Pink Pigeon	14	c
Columba nigrirostris	Short-billed Pigeon	4 6	d e
Columba oenas	Stock Dove	2 16	b g
Columba oenops	Peruvian Pigeon	6	d
Columba olivae	Somali Rock Pigeon	8	c
Columba pallidiceps	Yellow-legged Pigeon	38	k
Columba palumboides	Andaman Wood Pigeon	15	f
Columba palumbus	Wood Pigeon	2 15 16	b f g
Columba picazuro	Picazuro Pigeon	6	d
Columba plumbea	Plumbeous Pigeon	6	d
Columba polleni	Comoro Olive Pigeon	14	c
Columba pulchricollis	Ashy Wood Pigeon	2 15 16 18 55	b f g

Scientific Name	Common Name	Source Codes	Region Codes

COLUMBIDAE · PIGEONS, DOVES *contd.*

Scientific Name	Common Name	Source Codes	Region Codes
Columba punicea	Purple Wood Pigeon	15 16 18 55	f g
Columba rupestris	Blue Hill Pigeon	2 15 16	b f g
Columba speciosa	Scaled Pigeon	4 6	d e
Columba squamosa	Scaly-naped Pigeon	3 5 6	a d
Columba subvinacea	Ruddy Pigeon	4 6	d e
Columba torringtoni	Ceylon Wood Pigeon	15	f
Columba trocaz	Long-toed Pigeon	2	b
Columba unicincta	Scaly Gray Pigeon	8	c
Columba versicolor	Kittlitz's Wood Pigeon	2	b
Columba vitiensis	Metallic Wood Pigeon	19 21 22 35 38	h j k
Streptopelia bitorquata	Javanese Turtle Dove	19 21 22 38	h k
Streptopelia capicola	Ring-necked Dove	8	c
Streptopelia chinensis	Spotted Dove	2 3 15 16 18 19 21 36 37 38 55	a b f g h i k
Streptopelia decaocto	Collared Turtle Dove	2 15 16 18	b f g
Streptopelia decipiens	African Mourning Dove	8	c
Streptopelia lugens[6]	Pink-breasted Dove	8	c
Streptopelia orientalis	Rufous Turtle Dove	2 15 16 18 55	b f g
Streptopelia picturata	Madagascar Turtle Dove	10 14	c
Streptopelia reichenowi	White-winged Collared Dove	8	c
Streptopelia risoria	Ringed Turtle Dove	3	a
Streptopelia roseogrisea	Pink-headed Turtle Dove	2 8	b c
Streptopelia semitorquata	Red-eyed Dove	8	c
Streptopelia senegalensis	Laughing Dove	2 8 15 16 36	b c f g i
Streptopelia tranquebarica	Red Turtle Dove	2 15 16 18 22 55	b f g h
Streptopelia turtur	Turtle Dove	2 8 15 16	b c f g
Streptopelia vinacea	Vinaceous Dove	8	c
Geopelia cuneata	Diamond Dove	36	i
Geopelia humeralis	Bar-shouldered Ground-Dove	35 36	i j
Geopelia striata	Barred Ground-Dove	18 19 21 22 35 36 55	g h i j k
Aplopelia larvata	Lemon Dove	8	c
Turacoena manandensis	White-faced Pigeon	29 31	h j
Turacoena modesta	Timor Black Pigeon	29	h
Macropygia amboinensis	Amboina Cuckoo-Dove	35 36	i j
Macropygia mackinlayi	Mackinlay's Cuckoo-Dove	35 38	j k
Macropygia magna	Large Cuckoo-Dove	27	h
Macropygia nigrirostris	Black-billed Cuckoo-Dove	35	j
Macropygia phasianella	Red Cuckoo-Dove	16 19 21 22 55	g h
Macropygia ruficeps	Lesser Red Cuckoo-Dove	18 19 21	h
Macropygia ruftpennis	Andaman Cuckoo-Dove	15	f
Macropygia unchall	Barred Cuckoo-Dove	15 16 18 19 55	f g h
Reinwardtoena browni	Brown's Long-tailed Pigeon	34	j
Reinwardtoena crassirostris	Crested Long-tailed Pigeon	38	k
Reinwardtoena reinwardtsi	Reinwardt's Long-tailed Pigeon	35	j
Oena capensis	Namaqua Dove	8 10	c
Turtur abyssinicus	Black-billed Blue-spotted Wood-Dove	8	c
Turtur afer	Blue-spotted Wood-Dove	8	c
Turtur brehmeri	Blue-headed Dove	8	c
Turtur chalcospilos	Emerald-spotted Wood-Dove	8	c
Turtur tympanistria	Tambourine Dove	8	c
Chalcophaps indica	Emerald Dove	15 16 18 19 21 22 35 38 55	f g h i j k
Chalcophaps stephani	Brown-backed Ground Pigeon	35 38	j k
Henicophaps albifrons	White-capped Ground Pigeon	35	j
Henicophaps foersteri	New Britain Ground Pigeon	34	j

Scientific Name	Common Name	Source Codes	Region Codes

COLUMBIDAE · PIGEONS, DOVES *contd.*

Scientific Name	Common Name	Source Codes	Region Codes
Petrophassa albipennis[7]	White-quilled Rock Pigeon	36	i
Petrophassa plumifera	Plumed Pigeon	36	i
Petrophassa rufipennis	Chestnut-quilled Rock Pigeon	63	i
Petrophassa scripta	Squatter Pigeon	36	i
Petrophassa smithii	Partridge Pigeon	36	i
Phaps chalcoptera	Common Bronzewing	36	i
Phaps elegans	Brush Bronzewing	36	i
Phaps histrionica[8]	Flock Pigeon	36	i
Ocyphaps lophotes	Crested Pigeon	36	i
Leucosarcia melanoleuca	Wonga Pigeon	36	i
Zenaida asiatica	White-winged Dove	3 4 5 6	a d e
Zenaida auriculata	Eared Dove	5 6	d e
Zenaida aurita	Zenaida Dove	3 4 5	a e
Zenaida galapagoensis	Galapagos Dove	51	
Zenaida macroura	Mourning Dove	3 4 5	a e
Columbina cruziana[9]	Croaking Ground-Dove	6	d
Columbina cyanopis	Blue-eyed Ground-Dove	6	d
Columbina minuta	Plain-breasted Ground-Dove	6	d e
Columbina passerina	Common Ground-Dove	3 4 5 6	a d e
Columbina picui	Picui Ground-Dove	6	d
Columbina squammata[10]	Scaled Dove	3 4 6	a d e
Columbina talpacoti[11]	Ruddy Ground-Dove	6	d e
Claravis godefrida	Purple-winged Ground-Dove	6	d
Claravis mondetoura	Maroon-chested Ground-Dove	4 6	d e
Claravis pretiosa	Blue Ground-Dove	4 6	d e
Metriopelia aymara	Golden-spotted Ground-Dove	6	d
Metriopelia ceciliae	Bare-faced Ground-Dove	6	d
Metriopelia melanoptera	Black-winged Ground-Dove	6	d
Metriopelia morenoi	Bare-eyed Ground-Dove	6	d
Uropelia campestris	Long-tailed Ground-Dove	6	d
Leptotila cassinii	Gray-chested Dove	4 6	d e
Leptotila conoveri	Tolima Dove	6	d
Leptotila jamaicensis	White-bellied Dove	4 5	e
Leptotila megalura	Large-tailed Dove	6	d
Leptotila ochraceiventris	Ochre-bellied Dove	6	d
Leptotila pallida	Pallid Dove	6	d
Leptotila plumbeiceps	Gray-headed Dove	4 6	d e
Leptotila rufaxilla	Gray-fronted Dove	6	d
Leptotila verreauxi	White-fronted Dove	3 4 6	a d e
Leptotila wellsi	Grenada Dove	5 53	e
Geotrygon caniceps	Gray-headed Quail-Dove	5	e
Geotrygon chrysia	Key West Quail-Dove	3 5	a e
Geotrygon costaricensis	Buff-fronted Quail-Dove	4	e
Geotrygon frenata	White-throated Quail-Dove	6	d
Geotrygon goldmani	Russet-crowned Quail-Dove	4 6	d e
Geotrygon lawrencii	Purplish-backed Quail-Dove	4	e
Geotrygon linearis	Lined Quail-Dove	4 6	d e
Geotrygon montana	Ruddy Quail-Dove	3 4 5 6	a d e
Geotrygon mystacea	Bridled Quail-Dove	5	e
Geotrygon saphirina	Sapphire Quail-Dove	6	d
Geotrygon veraguensis	Olive-backed Quail-Dove	4 6	d e
Geotrygon versicolor	Crested Quail-Dove	5	e
Geotrygon violacea	Violaceous Quail-Dove	4 6	d e
Gallicolumba beccarii	Gray-throated Ground Dove	35 38	j k
Gallicolumba canifrons	Palau Ground Dove	38	k
Gallicolumba erythroptera	Ground Dove	42	k
Gallicolumba hoedtii	Wetar Island Ground Dove	32	j

COLUMBIDAE · PIGEONS, DOVES *contd.*

Scientific Name	Common Name	Source Codes	Region Codes
Gallicolumba jobiensis	White-breasted Ground Dove	35 38	j k
Gallicolumba luzonica[12]	Luzon Bleeding-Heart Pigeon	22	h
Gallicolumba rubescens	Marquesas Ground Dove	51	k
Gallicolumba rufigula	Red-throated Ground Dove	35	j
Gallicolumba salamonis	Thick-billed Ground Dove	38	k
Gallicolumba sanctaecrucis	Santa Cruz Ground Pigeon	38	k
Gallicolumba stairii	Friendly Ground Dove	38	k
Gallicolumba tristigmata	Celebes Quail-Dove	27	h
Gallicolumba xanthonura[13]	White-throated Ground Dove	38	k
Starnoenas cyanocephala	Blue-headed Quail-Dove	5	g
Otidiphaps nobilis	Pheasant Pigeon	35	j
Caloenas nicobarica	Nicobar Pigeon	15 18 19 21 22 35 38 55	f g h j k
Trugon terrestris	Thick-billed Ground Pigeon	35	j
Goura cristata	Common Crowned Pigeon	35	j
Goura scheepmakeri	Sheepmaker's Crowned Pigeon	35	j
Goura victoria	Victoria Crowned Pigeon	35	j
Didunculus strigirostris	Tooth-billed Pigeon	38	k
Phapitreron amethystina	Greater Brown Fruit Dove	22	h
Phapitreron leucotis	Lesser Brown Fruit Dove	22	h
Microgoura meeki	Solomon Island Crowned Pigeon	52	j
Treron apicauda[14]	Pintailed Green Pigeon	15 18 55	f g
Treron australis[15]	African Green Pigeon	8 10	c
Treron bicincta	Orange-breasted Green Pigeon	15 16 18 19 55	f g h
Treron capellei	Large Green Pigeon	18 19 21 55	g h
Treron curvirostra	Thick-billed Green Pigeon	15 16 18 19 21 22 55	f g h
Treron floris	Flores Green Pigeon	32	j
Treron formosae	Whistling Green Pigeon	2 16 22	b g h
Treron fulvicollis	Cinnamon-headed Green Pigeon	18 19 21 55	g h
Treron griseicauda	Gray-cheeked Green Pigeon	19	h j
Treron olax	Little Green Pigeon	19 21 55	g h
Treron oxyura	Yellow-bellied Pintail Green Pigeon	19	h
Treron phoenicoptera	Yellow-footed Green Pigeon	15 18 55	f g h
Treron pompadora	Pompadour Green Pigeon	15 18 22 55	f g h
Treron psittacea	Timor Green Pigeon	32	j
Treron seimundi	White-bellied Pintail Green Pigeon	19 55	g h
Treron sieboldii	Green Pigeon	2 16 55	b g
Treron sphenurus	Wedge-tailed Green Pigeon	15 16 18 19 55	f g h
Treron teysmanni	Sumba Island Green Pigeon	32	j
Treron vernans	Pink-necked Green Pigeon	18 19 21 22 55	g h
Treron waalia	Bruce's Green Pigeon	8	c
Ptilinopus arcanus[16]	Ripley's Fruit Dove	63	h
Ptilinopus aurantiifrons	Orange-fronted Fruit Dove	35	j
Ptilinopus cinctus	Black-backed Fruit Dove	19 36	h i
Ptilinopus coronulatus	Little Coroneted Fruit Dove	35	j
Ptilinopus dohertyi	Red-naped Fruit Dove	32	j
Ptilinopus dupetithouarsii	White-capped Fruit Dove	51	h
Ptinilopus mercierii	Red-moustached Fruit Dove	63	i
Ptinilopus eugeniae	White-headed Fruit Dove	63	i
Ptilinopus fischeri	Fischer's Fruit Dove	27	h
Ptilinopus formosus	Scarlet-breasted Fruit Dove	31	j

Scientific Name	Common Name	Source Codes	Region Codes

Scientific Name	Common Name	Source Codes	Region Codes
Ptilinopus granulifrons	Carunculated Fruit Dove	31	j
Ptilinopus greyii	Red-bellied Fruit Dove	38	k
Ptilinopus huttoni	Rapa-Island Fruit Dove	51	h
Ptilinopus hyogastra	Gray-headed Fruit Dove	29	h
Ptilinopus insolitus	Knob-billed Fruit Dove	34	j
Ptilinopus iozonus	Orange-bellied Fruit Dove	35	j
Ptilinopus jambu	Jambu Fruit Dove	19 21 55	g h
Ptilinopus layardi	Velvet Dove	38	k
Ptilinopus leclancheri	Black-chinned Fruit Dove	16 22	g h
Ptilinopus luteovirens	Golden Dove	38	k
Ptilinopus magnificus	Magnificent Fruit Dove	35 36	i j
Ptilinopus marchei	Marche's Fruit Dove	22	h
Ptilinopus melanospila	Black-naped Fruit Dove	19 22	h
Ptilinopus mercierii	Red Moustached Fruit Dove	63	i
Ptilinopus merrilli	Merrill's Fruit Dove	22	h
Ptilinopus monachus	Blue-capped Fruit Dove	31	j
Ptilinopus naina	Small Green Fruit Dove	35	j
Ptilinopus occipitalis	Yellow-breasted Fruit Dove	22	h
Ptilinopus ornatus	Ornate Fruit Dove	35	j
Ptilinopus perlatus	Pink-spotted Fruit Dove	35	j
Ptilinopus perousii	Many-coloured Fruit Dove	38	k
Ptilinopus porphyraceus	Crimson-crowned Fruit Dove	38	k
Ptilinopus porphyreus	Pink-necked Fruit Dove	19	h
Ptilinopus pulchellus	Beautiful Fruit Dove	35	j
Ptilinopus purpuratus	Gray-Green Fruit Dove	43	k
Ptilinopus rarotongensis	Rarotongan Fruit Dove	43	k
Ptilinopus regina	Swainson's Fruit Dove	35 36	i j
Ptilinopus richardsii	Silver-capped Fruit Dove	38	k
Ptilinopus rivoli	White-breasted Fruit Dove	35	j
Ptilinopus roseicapillus	Marianas Fruit Dove	38	k
Ptilinopus solomonensis	Splendid Fruit Dove	35 38	j k
Ptilinopus subgularis	Dark-chinned Fruit Dove	29 31	h j
Ptilinopus superbus	Superb Fruit Dove	22 35 36 38	h i j k
Ptilinopus tannensis	Tanna Fruit Dove	38	k
Ptilinopus victor	Orange Dove	38	k
Ptilinopus viridis	Red-breasted Fruit Dove	35 38	j k
Ptilinopus wallacii	Wallace's Green Fruit Dove	35	j
Drepanoptila holosericea	Cloven-feathered Dove	38	k
Alectroenas madagascariensis	Madagascar Blue Pigeon	10	c
Alectroenas pulcherrima	Seychelles Blue Pigeon	14	c
Alectroenas sganzini	Comoro Blue Pigeon	14	c
Ducula aenea	Green Imperial Pigeon	15 16 18 19 21 22 55	f g h
Ducula aurorae	Society Island Pigeon	43	k
Ducula badia	Imperial Pigeon	15 16 18 19 21 55	f g h
Ducula bakeri	Baker's Pigeon	38	k
Ducula basilica	Moluccan Rufous-bellied Pigeon	63	i
Ducula bicolor	Pied Imperial Pigeon	15 18 19 21 22 35 55	f g h j
Ducula brenchleyi	Chestnut-bellied Pigeon	38	k
Ducula carola	Spotted Imperial Pigeon	22	h
Ducula chalconota	Red-breasted Imperial Pigeon	35	j
Ducula cineracea	Timor Imperial Pigeon	32	j
Ducula concinna	Elegant Imperial Pigeon	35	j
Ducula finschi	Finsch's Imperial Pigeon	34	j
Ducula forsteni	Green and White Zone-tailed Pigeon	27	h

Scientific Name	Common Name	Source Codes	Region Codes
COLUMBIDAE · PIGEONS, DOVES *contd.*			
Ducula galeata	Marquesas Pigeon	63	k
Ducula goliath	Giant Pigeon	38	k
Ducula lacernulata	Black-backed Imperial Pigeon	19	h
Ducula latrans	Peale's Pigeon	38	k
Ducula melanochroa	Black Imperial Pigeon	34	j
Ducula mindorensis	Mindoro Imperial Pigeon	22	h
Ducula mullerii	Muller's Imperial Pigeon	35	j
Ducula myristicivora	Island Imperial Pigeon	35	j
Ducula oceanica	Micronesian Pigeon	38	k
Ducula pacifica	Pacific Pigeon	35 38	j k
Ducula perspicillata	White-eyed Imperial Pigeon	29	h
Ducula pickeringi	Gray Imperial Pigeon	19 21 22	h
Ducula pinon	Pinon Imperial Pigeon	35	j
Ducula pistrinaria	Gray Imperial Pigeon	35 38	j k
Ducula poliocephala	Pink-bellied Imperial Pigeon	22	h
Ducula radiata	Gray-headed Zone-tailed Pigeon	29	h
Ducula rubricera	Red-knobbed Pigeon	38	k
Ducula rufigaster	Purple-tailed Imperial Pigeon	35	j
Ducula spilorrhoa	Torres Strait Imperial Pigeon	35 36	i j
Ducula whartoni	Christmas Island Imperial Pigeon	14	c
Ducula zoeae	Banded Imperial Pigeon	35	j
Hemiphaga novaeseelandiae	New Zealand Pigeon	37	i
Lopholaimus antarcticus	Topknot Pigeon	36	i
Cryptophaps poecilorrhoa	Celebes Dusky Pigeon	27	h
Gymnophaps albertisii	Bare-eyed Mountain Pigeon	35	j
Gymnophaps mada	Long-tailed Mountain Pigeon	31	j
Gymnophaps solomonensis	Pale Mountain Pigeon	38	k

PSITTACIDAE · LORY, LORIKEETS, PARROTS, PARROTLETS 328 species recorded

Scientific Name	Common Name	Source Codes	Region Codes
Chalcopsitta atra	Black Lory	35	j
Chalcopsitta cardinalis[1]	Cardinal Lory	38	k
Chalcopsitta duivenbodei	Brown Lory	35	j
Chalcopsitta scintillata	Yellow-streaked Lory	35	j
Eos bornea	Red Lory	31	j
Eos cyanogenia	Black-winged Lory	35	j
Eos historio	Red-and-blue Lory	31	j
Eos reticulara	Blue-streaked Lory	31	j
Eos semilarvata	Blue-eared Lory	31	j
Eos squamata	Violet-necked Lory	35	j
Pseudeos fuscata	Dusky Lory	35	j
Trichoglossus chlorolepidotus	Scaly-breasted Lorikeet	36	i
Trichoglossus euteles	Perfect Lorikeet	32	j
Trichoglossus flavoviridis	Yellow-and-green Lory	29	h
Trichoglossus goldiei[2]	Goldie's Lorikeet	35	j
Trichoglossus haematodus	Rainbow Lory	19 35 36 38	h i j k
Trichoglossus iris	Iris Lorikeet	32	j
Trichoglossus johnstoni	Johnstone's Lorikeet	22	h
Trichoglossus orantus	Ornate Lorikeet	28	h
Trichoglossus rubiginosus	Ponape Lory	38	k
Trichoglossus versicolor	Varied Lorikeet	36	i
Lorius albidinucha[3]	White-naped Lory	31	j
Lorius amabilis	Stresemann's Lory	34	j

Scientific Name	Common Name	Source Codes	Region Codes
PSITTACIDAE · LORY, LORIKEETS, PARROTS, PARROTLETS *contd.*			
Lorius chlorocercus	Yellow-bibbed Lory	31	j
Lorius domicellus[4]	Purple-naped Lory	31	j
Lorius garrulus	Chattering Lory	29	h j
Lorius hypoinochrous	Purple-bellied Lory	35	j
Lorius lory	Black-capped Lory	29	h j
Phigys solitarius	Collared Lory	38	k
Vini australis	Blue-crowned Lory	z8	k
Vini kuhlii	Kuhl's Lory	45	k
Vini peruviana	Tahitain Lory	43	k
Vini stepheni	Stephen's Lory	45	k
Vini ultramarina	Ultramarine Lory	64	k
Glossopsitta concinna	Musk Lorikeet	36	i
Glossopsitta porphyrocephala	Purple-crowned Lorikeet	36	i
Glossopsitta pusilla	Little Lorikeet	36	i
Charmosyna amabilis	Red-throated Lorikeet	38	k
Charmosyna diadema	New Caledonian Lorikeet	38	k
Charmosyna josefinae	Josephine's Lory	35	j
Charmosyna margarethae	Duchess Lorikeet	38	k
Charmosyna meeki	Meek's Lorikeet	38	k
Charmosyna multistriata	Striated Lorikeet	35	j
Charmosyna palmarum	Palm Lorikeet	38	k
Charmosyna papou	Papuan Lory	35	j
Charmosyna placentis	Red-flanked Lorikeet	35 38	j k
Charmosyna pulchella	Fairy Lorikeet	35	j
Charmosyna rubrigularis	Red-chinned Lorikeet	35	j
Charmosyna rubronotata	Red-spotted Lorikeet	35	j
Charmosyna toxopei	Blue-fronted Lorikeet	31	j
Charmosyna wilhelminae	Wilhelmina's Lorikeet	35	j
Oreopsittacus arfaki	Whiskered Lorikeet	35	j
Neopsittacus musschenbroekii	Musschenbroek's Lorikeet	35	j
Neopsittacus pullicauda	Emerald Lorikeet	35	j
Probosciger aterrimus	Palm Cockatoo	35 36	i j
Calyptorhynchus funereus	Black Cockatoo	36	i
Calyptorhynchus lathami	Glossy Cockatoo	36	i
Calyptorhynchus magnificus	Red-tailed Cockatoo	36	i
Callocephalon fimbriatum	Gang-gang Cockatoo	36	i
Eolophus roseicapillus	Galah	64	i
Cacatua alba	White Cockatoo	29 31	h j
Cacatua ducorpsi	Ducorp's Cockatoo	38	k
Cacatua galerita	Sulphur-crested Cockatoo	35 36 37	i j
Cacatua goffini[5]	Goffin's Cockatoo	64	j
Cacatua haematuropygia	Red-vented Cockatoo	22	h
Cacatua leadbeateri	Major Mitchell's Cockatoo	36	i
Cacatua moluccensis	Salmon-crested Cockatoo	31	j
Cacatua ophthalmica[6]	Blue-eyed Cockatoo	64	j
Cacatua sanguinea	Little Corella	35 36	i j
Cacatua sulphurea	Lesser Sulphur-crested Cockatoo	19	h
Cacatua tenuirostris	Long-billed Corella	36	i
Nymphicus hollandicus	Cockatiel	36	i
Nestor meridionalis	Kaka	37	i
Nestor notabilis	Kea	37	i
Micropsitta bruijnii	Red-breasted Pygmy Parrot	35 38	j k
Micropsitta finschii	Finsch's Pygmy Parrot	38	k
Micropsitta geelvinkiana	Geelvink Pygmy Parrot	35	j
Micropsitta keiensis	Yellow-capped Pygmy Parrot	35	j
Micropsitta meeki	Meek's Pygmy Parrot	64	j

44

Scientific Name	Common Name	Source Codes	Region Codes

PSITTACIDAE · LORY, LORIKEETS, PARROTS, PARROTLETS *contd.*

Scientific Name	Common Name	Source Codes	Region Codes
Micropsitta pusio	Buff-faced Pygmy Parrot	35	j
Opopsitta diophthalma	Double-eyed Fig Parrot	35 36	i j
Opopsitta gulielmiterti	Orange-breasted Fig Parrot	35	j
Psittaculirostris desmarestii	Desmarest's Fig Parrot	35	j
Psittaculirostris edwardsii	Edwards's Fig Parrot	35	j
Psittaculirostris salvadorii	Salvadori's Fig Parrot	35	j
Bolbopsittacus lunulatus	Guaiabero	22	h
Psittinus cyanurus	Blue-rumped Parrot	18 19 21 55	g h
Psittacella brehmii	Brehm's Parrot	35	j
Psittacella madaraszi	Madarasz's Parrot	35	j
Psittacella modesta	Modest Parrot	35	j
Psittacella picta	Painted Parrot	35	j
Geoffroyus geoffroyi	Red-cheeked Parrot	35 36	i j
Geoffroyus heteroclitus	Singing Parrot	35 36	i j
Geoffroyus simplex	Blue-collared Parrot	35	j
Prioniturus discurus	Blue-crowned Racket-tailed Parrot	22	h
Prioniturus flavicans	Red-spotted Racket-tailed Parrot	22	h
Prioniturus luconensis	Green Racket-tailed Parrot	22	h
Prioniturus mada	Buru Racket-tailed Parrot	22	h
Prioniturus montanus	Mountain Racket-tailed Parrot	24	h
Prioniturus platurus	Golden-mantled Racket-tailed Parrot	29	h
Tanygnathus gramineus	Black-lored Parrot	31	j
Tanygnathus lucionensis	Blue-naped Parrot	19 21 22	h
Tanygnathus megalorhynchus	Great-billed Parrot	22 35	h j
Tanygnathus sumatranus[7]	Muller's Parrot	30	h
Eclectus roratus	Eclectus Parrot	34 36 38	i j k
Psittrichas fulgidus	Pesquet's Parrot	36	j
Prosopeia personata	Masked Shining Parrot	38	h k
Prosopeia tabuensis	Red Shining Parrot	38	k
Alisterus amboinensis	Amboina King Parrot	35	j
Alisterus chloropterus	Green-winged King Parrot	35	j
Alisterus scapularis	Australian King Parrot	36	i
Aprosmictus erythropterus	Red-winged Parrot	32 35 36	i j
Aprosmictus jonquillaceus	Timor Red-winged Parrot	32	j
Polytelis anthopeplus	Regent Parrot	36	i
Polytelis alexandrae	Princess Parrot	36	i
Polytelis swainsonii	Superb Parrot	36	i
Purpureicephalus spurius	Red-capped Parrot	36	i
Barnardius barnardi	Mallee Ringneck Parrot	36	i
Barnardius zonarius	Port Lincoln Parrot	36	i
Platycercus adelaidae	Adelaide Rosella	64	i
Platycercus adscitus	Pale-headed Rosella	36	i
Platycercus caledonicus	Green Rosella	36	i
Platycercus elegans	Crimson Rosella	36 37	i
Platercercus eximius	Eastern Rosella	36	i
Platercercus flaveolus	Yellow Rosella	36	i
Platycercus icterotis	Western Rosella	36	i
Platycercus venustus	Northern Rosella	36	i
Psephotus chrysopterygius	Golden-shouldered Parrot	36	i
Psephotus haematogaster	Blue-Bonnet	36	i
Psephotus haematonotus	Red-rumped Parrot	36	i
Psephotus pulcherrimus	Paradise Parrot	36	i
Psephotus varius	Mulga Parrot	36	i

45

Scientific Name	Common Name	Source Codes	Region Codes
PSITTACIDAE · LORY, LORIKEETS, PARROTS, PARROTLETS contd.			
Cyanoramphus auriceps	Yellow-fronted Parakeet	37	i
Cyanoramphus malherbi	Orange-fronted Parakeet	37	i
Cyanoramphus novaezelandiae	Red-fronted Parakeet	36 37 38	i k
Cyanoramphus unicolor	Antipodes Green Parrot	37	i
Eunymphicus cornutus	Horned Parakeet	38	k
Neophema bourkii	Bourke's Parrot	36	i
Neophema chrysogaster	Orange-bellied Parrot	36	i
Neophema chrysostoma	Blue-winged Parrot	36	i
Neophema elegans	Elegant Parrot	36	i
Neophema petrophila	Rock Parrot	36	i
Neophema pulchella	Turquoise Parrot	36	i
Neophema splendida	Scarlet-chested Parrot	36	i
Lathamus discolor	Swift Parrot	36	i
Melopsittacus undulatus	Budgerigar	3 36 38	a i k
Pezoporus wallicus	Ground Parrot	36	i
Geopsittacus occidentalis	Night Parrot	64	i
Stringops habroptilus	Kakapo	37	i
Coracopsis nigra	Black Parrot	10 14	c
Coracopsis vasa	Vasa Parrot	14	c
Psittacus erithacus	Gray Parrot	8	c
Poicephalus crassus	Niam-Niam Parrot	8	c
Poicephalus cryptoxanthus	Brown-headed Parrot	8	c
Poicephalus flavifrons	Yellow-faced Parrot	8	c
Poicephalus gulielmi	Jardine's Parrot	8	c
Poicephalus meyeri	Meyer's Parrot	8	c
Poicephalus robustus	Cape Parrot	8	c
Poicephalus ruepellii	Rüpell's Parrot	8	c
Poicephalus rufiventris	Red-bellied Parrot	8	c
Poicephalus senegalus	Senegal Parrot	8	c
Agapornis cana	Gray-headed Lovebird	8 10	c
Agapornis fischeri	Fischer's Lovebird	8	c
Agapornis lilianae	Nyasa Lovebird	8	c
Agapornis nigrigensis	Black-cheeked Lovebird	64	c
Agapornis personata	Masked Lovebird	8	c
Agapornis pullaria	Red-faced Lovebird	8	c
Agapornis roseicollis	Peach-faced Lovebird	8	c
Agapornis swinderniana	Black-collared Lovebird	8	c
Agapornis taranta	Black-winged Lovebird	8	c
Loriculus amabilis	Moluccan Hanging Parrot	64	j
Loriculus aurantiifrons	Orange-fronted Hanging Parrot	35	j
Loriculus beryllinus	Ceylon Hanging Parrot	15	f
Loriculus exilis	Green Hanging Parrot	64	h
Loriculus flosculus	Wallace's Hanging Parrot	64	h
Loriculus galgulus	Blue-crowned Hanging Parrot	19 21 55	g h
Loriculus philippensis	Philippine Hanging Parrot	22	h
Loirculus pusillus	Yellow-throated Hanging Parrot	64	h
Loriculus stigmatus	Celebes Hanging Parrot	28 29	h
Loriculus vernalis	Vernal Hanging Parrot		
Psittacula alexandri	Moustached Parakeet	15 16 18 19 21 55	f g h
Psittacula calthorpae	Emerald-collared Parakeet	15	f
Psittacula caniceps	Blyth's Parakeet	15	f
Psittacula columboides	Malabar Parakeet	15	f
Psittacula cyanicephala	Plum-headed Parakeet	15 16 18 55	f g
Psittacula echo[6]	Mauritius Parakeet[2]	64	c
Psittacula eupatria	Alexandrine Parakeet	15 18 55	f g

46

Scientific Name	Common Name	Source Codes	Region Codes

PSITTACIDAE · LORY, LORIKEETS, PARROTS, PARROTLETS *contd.*

Scientific Name	Common Name	Source Codes	Region Codes
Psittacula derbiana	Lord Derby's Parakeet	2 15 16	b f g
Psittacula himalayana[9], [10]	Slaty-headed Parakeet	2 15 16 18 55	b f g
Psittacula krameri	Rose-ringed Parakeet	8 15 16 18	c f g
Psittacula longicauda	Long-tailed Parakeet	15 16 19 21 55	f g h
Psittacula roseata	Blossom-headed Parakeet	55	g
Anodorhynchus glaucus	Glaucous Macaw	6	d
Anodorhynchus hyacinthinus	Hyacinthine Macaw	6	d
Anodorhynchus leari	Indigo Macaw	6	d
Cyanopsitta spixii[11]	Little Blue Macaw	6	d
Ara ambigua	Great Green Macaw	4 6	d e
Ara ararauna[12]	Blue-and-Yellow Macaw	4 6	d e
Ara auricollis	Golden-collared Macaw	6	d
Ara chloroptera	Red-and-Green Macaw	4 6	d e
Ara couloni	Blue-headed Macaw	6	d
Ara macao	Scarlet Macaw	4 6	d e
Ara manilata	Red-bellied Macaw	6	d
Ara maracana	Blue-winged Macaw	6	d
Ara militaris	Military Macaw	4 6	d e
Ara nobilis	Red-shouldered Macaw	6	d
Ara rubrogenys	Red-fronted Macaw	6	d
Ara severa	Chestnut-fronted Macaw	4 6	d e
Aratinga acuticauda	Blue-crowned Parakeet	6	d
Aratinga aurea	Peach-fronted Parakeet	6	d
Aratinga auricapilla[13]	Golden-capped Parakeet	64	d
Aratinga cactorum	Cactus Parakeet	6	d
Aratinga canicularis	Orange-fronted Parakeet	4	e
Aratinga chloroptera	Hispaniolan Parakeet	5	a
Aratinga erythrogenys	Red-masked Parakeet	6	d
Aratinga euops	Cuban Parakeet	5	e
Aratinga finschi	Crimson-fronted Parakeet	4	e
Aratinga guarouba	Golden Parakeet	6	d
Aratinga holochlora	Green Parakeet	4	e
Aratinga jandaya[14]	Jandaya Parakeet	64	d
Aratinga leucophthalmus	White-eyed Parakeet	6	d
Aratinga mitrata	Mitred Parakeet	6	d
Aratinga nana[15]	Olive-throated Parakeet	64	d
Aratinga pertinax	Brown-throated Parakeet	4 5 6	d e
Aratinga solstitialis	Sun Parakeet	6	d
Aratinga wagleri	Scarlet-fronted Parakeet	6	d
Aratinga weddellii	Dusky-headed Parakeet	6	d
Nandayus nenday	Black-hooded Parakeet	6	d
Leptosittaca branickii	Golden-plumed Parrot	6	d
Rhynchopsitta pachyrhyncha	Thick-billed Parrot	3	a e
Cyanoliseus patagonus	Burrowing Parrot	6 4	d
Ognorhynchus icterotis	Yellow-eared Parakeet	6	d
Pyrrhura albipectus	White-breasted Parakeet	6	d
Pyrrhura calliptera	Flame-winged Parakeet	6	d
Pyrrhura cruentata	Ochre-marked Parakeet	6	d
Pyrrhura devillei	Blaze-winged Parakeet	6	d
Pyrrhura egregia	Fiery-shouldered Parakeet	6	d
Pyrrhura frontalis	Reddish-bellied Parakeet	6	d
Pyrrhura hoematotis	Blood-eared Parakeet	6	d
Pyrrhura hoffmanni	Sulphur-winged Parakeet	4	e
Pyrrhura hypoxantha	Yellow-sided Parakeet	6	d
Pyrrhura leucotis	Maroon-faced Parakeet	6	d
Pyrrhura melanura[16]	Maroon-tailed Parakeet	6	d
Pyrrhura molinae	Green-cheeked Parakeet	6	d

Scientific Name	Common Name	Source Codes	Region Codes
PSITTACIDAE · LORY, LORIKEETS, PARROTS, PARROTLETS contd.			
Pyrrhura perlata	Pearly Parakeet	6	d
Pyrrhura picta	Painted Parakeet	6	d
Pyrrhura rhodocephala	Rose-headed Parakeet	6	d
Pyrrhura rhodogaster	Crimson-bellied Parakeet	6	d
Pyrrhura rupicola	Rock Parakeet	6	d
Pyrrhura viridicata	Santa Marta Parakeet	6	d
Enicognathus ferrugineus	Austral Parakeet	6	d
Enicognathus leptorhynchus	Slender-billed Parakeet	6	d
Myiopsitta monachus	Monk Parakeet	6	d
Bolborhynchus aurifrons	Mountain Parakeet	6	d
Bolborhynchus aymara	Gray-hooded Parakeet	6	d
Bolborhynchus ferrugineifrons	Rufous-fronted Parakeet	6	d
Bolborhynchus lineola	Barred Parakeet	4 6	d e
Bolborhynchus orbygnesius	Andean Parakeet	6	d
Forpus coelestis	Pacific Parrotlet	6	d
Forpus conspicillatus	Spectacled Parrotlet	4 6	d e
Forpus cyanopygius	Blue-rumped Parrotlet	4	e
Forpus passerinus	Green-rumped Parrotlet	4 5 6	d e
Forpus sclateri	Dusky-billed Parrotlet	6	d
Forpus xanthops	Yellow-faced Parrotlet	6	d
Forpus xanthopterygius	Blue-winged Parrotlet	6	d
Brotogeris chrysopterus	Golden-winged Parakeet	6	d
Brotogeris cyanoptera	Cobalt-winged Parakeet	6	d
Brotogeris jugularis	Orange-chinned Parakeet	4 6	d e
Brotogeris pyrrhopterus	Gray-cheeked Parakeet	6	d
Brotogeris sanctithomae	Tui Parakeet	6	d
Brotogeris tirica	Plain Parakeet	6	d
Brotogeris versicolurus	Canary-winged Parakeet	6	d
Nannopsittaca panychlora	Tepui Parrotlet	6	d
Touit batavica	Lilac-tailed Parrotlet	6	d
Touit dilectissima	Red-winged Parrotlet	4 6	d e
Touit huetii	Scarlet-shouldered Parrotlet	6	d
Touit melanonota	Black-eared Parrotlet	6	d
Touit purpurata	Sapphire-rumped Parrotlet	6	d
Touit stictoptera	Spot-winged Parrotlet	6	d
Touit surda	Golden-tailed Parrotlet	6	d
Pionites leucogaster	White-bellied Parrot	6	d
Pionites melanocephala	Black-headed Parrot	6	d
Pionopsitta barrabandi	Orange-cheeked Parrot	6	d
Pionopsitta caica	Caica Parrot	6	d
Pionopsitta haematotis	Brown-hooded Parrot	4 6	d e
Pionopsitta pileata	Red-capped Parrot	6	d
Pionopsitta pulchra[17]	Beautiful Parrot	64	d
Pionopsitta pyrilia	Saffron-headed Parrot	4 6	d e
Gypopsitta vulturina	Vulturine Parrot	6	d
Hapalopsittaca amazonina	Rusty-faced Parrot	6	d
Hapalopsittaca melanotis	Black-eared Parrot	6	d
Graydidascalus brachyurus	Short-tailed Parrot	6	d
Pionus chalcopterus	Bronze-winged Parrot	6	d
Pionus fuscus	Dusky Parrot	6	d
Pionus maximiliani	Scaly-headed Parrot	6	d
Pionus menstruus	Blue-headed Parrot	4 6	d e
Pionus senilus	White-crowned Parrot	4	e
Pionus seniloides	White-capped Parrot	4 6	d e
Pionus sordidus	Red-billed Parrot	6	d
Pionus tumultuosus	Plum-crowned Parrot	6	d
Amazona aestiva	Turquoise-fronted Parrot	6	d

48

Scientific Name	Common Name	Source Codes	Region Codes
PSITTACIDAE · LORY, LORIKEETS, PARROTS, PARROTLETS contd.			
Amazona agilis	Black-billed Parrot	5	e
Amazona albifrons	White-fronted Parrot	4	e
Amazona amazonica	Orange-winged Parrot	6	d
Amazona arausiaca	Red-necked Parrot	5	e
Amazona autumnalis	Red-lored Parrot	4 6	d e
Amazona barbadensis	Yellow-shouldered Parrot	6	d
Amazona brasiliensis	Red-tailed Parrot	6	d
Amazona collaria	Yellow-billed Parrot	5	e
Amazona dufresniana[18]	Blue-cheeked Parrot	64	d
Amazona farinosa	Mealy Parrot	4 6	d e
Amazona festiva	Festive Parrot	6	d
Amazon finschia	Lilac-crowned Parrot	4	e
Amazona guildingii	St. Vincent Parrot	5	e
Amazona imperialis	Imperial Parrot	5	e
Amazona leucocephala	Cuban Parrot	5	e
Amazona mercenaria	Scaly-naped Parrot	6	d
Amazona ochrocephala	Yellow-headed Parrot	4 6	d e
Amazona pretrei	Red-spectacled Parrot	6	d
Amazona tucumana	Alder Parrot	6	d
Amazona ventralis	Hispaniolan Parrot	5	e
Amazona versicolor	St. Lucia Parrot	5	e
Amazona vinacea	Vinaceous-breasted Parrot	6	d
Amazona viridigenalis	Red-crowned Parrot	4	e
Amazona vittata	Puerto Rican Parrot	5	e
Amazona xantholora	Yellow-lored Parrot	4	e
Amazona xanthops	Yellow-faced Parrot	6	d
Deroptyus accipitrinus	Red-Fan Parrot	6	d
Triclaria malachitacea	Blue-bellied Parrot	6	d

MUSOPHAGIDAE · PLANTAIN-EATERS, TURACOS, GO-AWAY BIRDS

22 species recorded

Scientific Name	Common Name	Source Codes	Region Codes
Tauraco bannermani	Bannerman's Turaco	8	c
Tauraco corythaix	Knysna Turaco	8	c
Tauraco erythrolophus	Angola Red-crested Turaco	8	c
Tauraco fischeri	Fisher's Turaco	8	c
Tauraco hartlaubi	Hartlaub's Turaco	8	c
Tauraco johnstoni	Ruwenzori Turaco	8	c
Tauraco leucolophus	White-crested Turaco	8	c
Tauraco leucotis	White-cheeked Turaco	8	c
Tauraco livingstonii	Livingstone's Turaco	8	c
Tauraco macrorhynchus	Crested Turaco	8	c
Tauraco persa	Guinea Turaco	8	c
Tauraco porphyreolophus	Violet-crested Turaco	8	c
Tauraco ruspolii	Prince Ruspoli's Turaco	8 53	c
Tauraco schuttii	Black-billed Turaco	8	c
Musophaga rossae	Lady Ross's Turaco	8	c
Musophaga violacea	Violet Turaco	8	c
Corythaeola cristata	Great Blue Turaco	8	c
Crinifer piscator	Gray Plantain-Eater	8	c
Crinifer zonurus	Eastern Gray Plantain-Eater	8	c
Corythaixoides concolor	Go-Away Bird	8	c
Corythaixoides leucogaster	White-bellied Go-Away Bird	8	c
Corythaixoides personata	Bare-faced Go-Away Bird	8	c

Scientific Name	Common Name	Source Codes	Region Codes

CUCULIDAE · CUCKOOS, ROADRUNNERS, ANIS 127 species recorded

Scientific Name	Common Name	Source Codes	Region Codes
Clamator coromandus	Red-winged Crested Cuckoo	15 16 18 19 21 22 55	f g h
Clamator glandarius	Great Spotted Cuckoo	2 8	b c
Clamator jacobinus	Jacobin Cuckoo	2 8 15 16 18	b c f g
Clamator levaillantii	Levaillant's Cuckoo	8	c
Pachycoccyx audeberti	Thick-billed Cuckoo	8 10	c
Cuculus canorus	Cuckoo	2 8 15 16 18 19 22 35 55	b c f g h j
Cuculus clamosus	Black Cuckoo	8	c
Cuculus fugax	Fugitive Hawk-Cuckoo	2 15 16 18 19 21 22 55	b f g h
Cuculus merulinus	Plaintive Cuckoo	16	g
Cuculus micropterus	Short-winged Cuckoo	2 15 16 18 19 21 22 55	b f g h
Cuculus pallidus	Pallid Cuckoo	35 36 37	i j
Cuculus poliocephalus	Eurasian Little Cuckoo	2 8 10 15 16 18 19 21 55	b c f g h
Cuculus saturatus	Oriental Cuckoo	2 3 15 16 18 21 22 35 36 37 38 55	a b f g h i j k
Cuculus solitarius	Red-chested Cuckoo	8	c
Cuculus sparverioides	Large Hawk-Cuckoo	2 15 16 18 19 21 22 55	b f g h
Cuculus vagans	Lesser Hawk-Cuckoo	18 19 21 55	g h
Cuculus varius	Common Hawk-Cuckoo	15 18	f g
Cercococcyx mechowi	Dusky Long-tailed Cuckoo	8	c
Cercococcyx montanus	Barred Long-tailed Cuckoo	8	c
Cercococcyx olivinus	Olive Long-tailed Cuckoo	8	c
Cacomantis castaneiventris	Chestnut-breasted Brush Cuckoo	35 36	i j
Cacomantis heinrichi	Heinrich's Brush Cuckoo	31	j
Cacomantis merulinus	Gray-breasted Brush Cuckoo	15 18 19 21 22 55	f g h
Cacomantis pyrrhophanus	Fan-tailed Brush Cuckoo	35 36 37 38	i j k
Cacomantis sonneratii	Banded Bay Cuckoo	15 18 19 21 22 55	f g h
Cacomantis variolosus	Brush Cuckoo	19 21 22 35 36 38 55	g h i j k
Rhamphomantis megarhynchus	Little Long-billed Cuckoo	35	j
Chrysococcyx basalis	Horsfield's Bronze Cuckoo	36	h i j
Chrysococcyx caprius	Didric Cuckoo	8	c
Chrysococcyx crassirostris[1]	Moluccan Bronze Cuckoo	31	j
Chrysococcyx cupreus	African Emerald Cuckoo	8	c
Chrysococcyx flavigularis	Yellow-throated Green Cuckoo	8	c
Chrysococcyx klaas	Klaas's Cuckoo	8	c
Chrysococcyx lucidus	Golden Bronze Cuckoo	35 36 37 38	i j k
Chrysococcyx maculatus	Emerald Cuckoo	15 16 18 19 55	f g h
Chrysococcyx malayanus	Malaysian Bronze Cuckoo	19 21 22 35 55	g h j
Chrysococcyx meyerii	Myer's Bronze Cuckoo	35	j
Chrysococcyx minutillus	Rufous-breasted Bronze Cuckoo	36	i
Chrysococcyx osculans[2]	Black-eared Cuckoo	35 36	i j
Chrysococcyx ruficollis	Reddish-throated Bronze Cuckoo	35	j
Chrysococcyx xanthorhynchus	Violet Cuckoo	15 16 18 19 21 22 55	f g h
Caliechthrus leucolophus	White-crowned Koel	35	j
Surniculus lugubris	Drongo Cuckoo	15 16 18 19 21 22 55	f g h

50

Scientific Name	Common Name	Source Codes	Region Codes
CUCULIDAE · CUCKOOS, ROADRUNNERS, ANIS *contd.*			
Microdynamis parva	Black-capped Cuckoo	35	j
Eudynamis scolopacea	Koel	15 16 18 19 21 22 35 38 55	f g h j k
Eudynamis taitensis	Long-tailed Koel	35 36 37 38	i j k
Scythrops novaehollandiae	Channel-billed Cuckoo	35 36 37	i j
Coccyzus americanus	Yellow-billed Cuckoo	3 4 5 6	a d e
Coccyzus cinereus	Ash-colored Cuckoo	6	d
Coccyzus erythropthalmus	Black-billed Cuckoo	3 4 5 6	a d e
Coccyzus euleri[3]	Pearly-breasted Cuckoo	6	d
Coccyzus lansbergi	Gray-capped Cuckoo	4 6	d e
Coccyzus melacoryphus	Dark-billed Cuckoo	6	d
Coccyzus minor	Mangrove Cuckoo	3 4 5 6	a d e
Coccyzus pumilus	Dwarf Cuckoo	6	d
Piaya cayana	Squirrel Cuckoo	4 6	d e
Piaya melanogaster	Black-bellied Cuckoo	6	d
Piaya minuta	Little Cuckoo	4 6	d e
Piaya pluvialis[4]	Chestnut-bellied Cuckoo	5	e
Piaya rufigularis	Bay-breasted Cuckoo	5	e
Saurothera merlini[5]	Great Lizard Cuckoo	5	e
Saurothera vetula[6]	Jamaican Lizard Cuckoo	5	e
Ceuthmochares aereus	Yellow-Bill	8	c
Phaenicophaeus calorhynchus[7]	Celebes Malcoha	28 29	h
Phaenicophaeus chlorophaeus	Raffles's Malcoha	18 19 21 55	g h
Phaenicophaeus cummingi[8]	Scale-feathered Cuckoo	22	h
Phaenicophaeus curvirostris	Chestnut-breasted Malcoha	18 19 21 55	g h
Phaenicophaeus diardi	Lesser Green-billed Malcoha	18 19 21	h
Phaenicophaeus javanicus	Red-billed Malcoha	18 19 21	h
Phaenicophaeus leschenaultii[9]	Sirkeer Cuckoo	15	f
Phaenicophaeus pyrrhocephalus	Red-faced Malcoha	15 53	f
Phaenicophaeus sumatranus	Rufous-bellied Malcoha	18 19 21 55	g h
Phaenicophaeus superciliosus	Rough-crested Cuckoo	22	h
Phaenicophaeus tristis[10]	Greater Green-billed Malcoha	15 16 18 19 55	f g h
Phaenicophaeus viridirostris	Small Green-billed Malcoha	15	f
Crotophaga ani	Smooth-billed Ani	3 4 5 6	a d e
Crotophaga major	Greater Ani	4 6	d e
Crotophaga sulcirostris	Groove-billed Ani	3 4 6	a d e
Guira guira	Guira Cuckoo	6	d
Tapera naevia	Striped Cuckoo	4 6	d e
Morococcyx erythropygus	Lesser Ground-Cuckoo	4	e
Dromococcyx pavoninus	Pavonine Cuckoo	6	d
Dromococcyx phasianellus	Pheasant Cuckoo	4 6	d e
Geococcyx californianus	Roadrunner	3 4	a e
Geococcyx velox	Lesser Roadrunner	4	e
Neomorphus geoffroyi	Rufous-vented Ground-Cuckoo	4 6	d e
Neomorphus pucheranii	Red-billed Ground-Cuckoo	6	d
Neomorphus radiolosus	Banded Ground-Cuckoo	6	d
Neomorphus rufipennis	Rufous-winged Ground-Cuckoo	6	d
Neomorphus squamiger	Scaled Ground-Cuckoo	6	d
Carpococcyx radiceus	Ground-Cuckoo	19 21	h
Carpococcyx renauldi	Coral-billed Ground-Cuckoo	55	g
Coua caerulea	Blue Coua	10	c
Coua coquereli	Coquerel's Coua	10	c
Coua cristata	Crested Coua	10	c
Coua cursor	Running Coua	10	c
Coua delalandei[11]	Delalande's Coua	10	c
Coua gigas	Giant Coua	10	c

Scientific Name	Common Name	Source Codes	Region Codes

CUCULIDAE · CUCKOOS, ROADRUNNERS, ANIS *contd.*

Scientific Name	Common Name	Source Codes	Region Codes
Coua reynaudii	Red-fronted Coua	10	c
Coua ruficeps	Red-capped Coua	10	c
Coua serriana	Red-breasted Coua	10	c
Coua verreauxi	Verreaux's Coua	10	c
Centropus anselli	Gabon Coucal	8	c
Centropus ateralbus	New Britain Coucal	34	j
Centropus bengalensis	Lesser Coucal	16 18 19 21 22	g h
Centropus bernsteinii	Bernstein's Coucal	35	j
Centropus celebensis	Celebes Coucal	19	h
Centropus chalybeus	Biak Island Coucal	35	j
Centropus chlororhynchus	Ceylon Coucal	15	f
Centropus cupreicaudus	Copper-tailed Coucal	8	c
Centropus leucogaster	Black-throated Coucal	8	c
Centropus melanops	Black-faced Coucal	22	h
Centropus menbeki	Greater Coucal	35	j
Centropus milo	Buff-headed Coucal	38	k
Centropus monachus	Blue-headed Coucal	8	c
Centropus nigrorufus	Sunda Coucal	19	h
Centropus phasianinus	Pheasant-Coucal	35 36	i j
Centropus rectunguis	Short-toed Coucal	19 21	h
Centropus senegalensis	Senegal Coucal	2 8	b c
Centropus sinensis	Common Coucal	15 16 18 19 21 22 55	f g h
Centropus spilopterus	Moluccan Coucal	31	j
Centropus steerei	Steere's Coucal	22	h
Centropus superciliosus	White-browed Coucal	8	c
Centropus toulou	Black Coucal	8 10 15 55	c f g
Centropus unirufus	Rufous Coucal	22	h
Centropus violaceus	Violet Coucal	34	j
Centropus viridis	Philippine Coucal	22	h

TYTONIDAE · BARN OWLS 10 species recorded

Scientific Name	Common Name	Source Codes	Region Codes
Tyto alba	Barn Owl	2 4 6 8 15 18 35 36 38 55	a b c d e f g h i j k
Tyto aurantia	New Britain Barn Owl	34	j
Tyto capensis	Grass Owl	8 15 16 18 35 55	c f g j
Tyto inexpectata	Minahassa Barn Owl	50	h
Tyto novaehollandiae	Masked Owl	35 36	i j
Tyto rosenbergii	Celebes Barn Owl	31	j
Tyto soumagnei	Madagascar Grass Owl	10 22 36 38	h i k
Tyto tenebricosa	Sooty Owl	35 36	i j
Phodilus badius	Bay Owl	15 18 19 21 22 55	f g h
Phodilus prigoginei	Tanzanian Bay Owl	48	c

STRIGIDAE · TYPICAL OWLS 126 species recorded

Scientific Name	Common Name	Source Codes	Region Codes
Otus albogularis	White-throated Screech-Owl	6	d
Otus alfredi	Flores Scops-Owl	32	j
Otus asio[1]	Screech-Owl	3 4	a e
Otus atricapillus	Long-tufted Screech-Owl	6	d
Otus bakkamoena[2]	Collared Scops-Owl	2 15 16 18 19 21 22 55	b f g h

52

Scientific Name	Common Name	Source Codes	Region Codes
STRIGIDAE · TYPICAL OWLS *contd*.			
Otus balli	Andaman Scops-Owl	15	f
Otus barbarus	Bearded Screech-Owl	4	e
Otus brookei	Rajah's Scops-Owl	19 21	h
Otus brucei[3]	Striated Scops-Owl	2 15 16	b f g
Otus choliba	Tropical Screech-Owl	4 6	d e
Otus clarkii	Bare-shanked Screech-Owl	4 6	d e
Otus cooperi	Pacific Screech-Owl	4	e
Otus flammeolus	Flammulated Owl	3 4	a e
Otus guatemalae	Vermiculated Screech-Owl	4 6	d e
Otus gurneyi	Giant Scops-Owl	22	h
Otus icterorhynchus	Sandy Scops-Owl	8	c
Otus ingens	Rufescent Screech-Owl	6	d
Otus ireneae	Sokoke Scops-Owl	62	c
Otus lawrencii	Bare-legged Owl	5	e
Otus leucotis	White-faced Scops-Owl	2 8	b c
Otus manadensis[4]	Celebes Scops-Owl	29	h
Otus nudipes	Puerto Rican Screech-Owl	5	e
Otus podarginus	Palau Scops Owl	38	k
Otus roboratus	West Peruvian Screech-Owl	6	d
Otus rufescens	Reddish Scops-Owl	19 21 22 55	g h
Otus rutilus	Madagascan Scops-Owl	8 10	c
Otus sagittatus	White-fronted Scops-Owl	18 19 55	g h
Otus scops[5]	Scops-Owl	2 8 15 16 18 19 21 22 55	b c f g h
Otus spilocephalus	Spotted Scops-Owl	15 16 18 19 21 55	f g h
Otus sylvicolus	Lesser Sunda Scops-Owl	32	j
Otus trichopsis	Whiskered Owl	3 4	a e
Otus watsonii	Tawny-bellied Screech-Owl	6	d
Otus umbra	Mentaur Scops-Owl	62	c
Lophostrix cristata	Crested Owl	4 6	d e
Lophostrix letti	Akun Scops-Owl	8	c
Bubo africanus	Spotted Eagle-Owl	2 8	b c
Bubo bubo	Great Eagle-Owl	2 8 15 16 18	b c f g
Bubo capensis	Cape Eagle-Owl	8	c
Bubo coromandus	Dusky Eagle-Owl	15 16 18 19 55	f g h
Bubo lacteus	Verreaux's Eagle-Owl	8	c
Bubo leucostictus	Akun Eagle-Owl	8	c
Bubo nipalensis	Forest Eagle-Owl	15 18 55	f g h
Bubo philippensis	Philippine Horned Owl	22	h
Bubo poensis	Fraser's Eagle-Owl	8	c
Bubo shelleyi	Banded Eagle-Owl	8	c
Bubo sumatranus	Malay Eagle-Owl	18 19 21 55	g h
Bubo virginianus	Great Horned Owl	3 4 6	a d e
Ketupa blakistoni	Blakiston's Fish-Owl	2	b
Ketupa flavipes	Tawny Fish-Owl	2 15 16 18 55	b f g
Ketupa ketupu	Malay Fish-Owl	14 18 19 21 55	f g h
Ketupa zeylonensis	Brown Fish-Owl	2 15 16 18 55	b f g h
Scotopelia bouvieri	Vermiculated Fishing-Owl	8	c
Scotopelia peli	Pel's Fishing-Owl	8	c
Scotopelia ussheri	Rufous Fishing-Owl	8	c
Pulsatrix koeniswaldiana	Tawny-browed Owl	6	d
Pulsatrix melanota	Band-bellied Owl	6	d
Pulsatrix perspicillata	Spectacled Owl	4 6	d e
Sceloglaux albifacies[6]	Laughing Owl	37 53	i
Nyctea scandiaca	Snowy Owl	2 3 15	a b f g
Surnia ulula	Hawk Owl	2 3	a b
Glaucidium brasilianum[7]	Ferruginous Pygmy-Owl	3 4 6	a d e

Scientific Name	Common Name	Source Codes	Region Codes

STRIGIDAE · TYPICAL OWLS *contd.*

Scientific Name	Common Name	Source Codes	Region Codes
Glaucidium brodiei	Collared Pygmy-Owl	2 15 16 18 19 21 55	b f g h
Glaucidium capense[8]	Barred Owlet	8	c
Glaucidium cuculoides	Cuckoo Owl	15 16 18 19 55	f g h
Glaucidium gnoma	Northern Pygmy-Owl	3 4	a e
Glaucidium minutissimum	Least Pygmy-Owl	4 6	d e
Glaucidium passerinum	Eurasian Pygmy-Owl	2	b
Glaucidium perlatum	Pearl-spotted Owlet	8	c
Glaucidium radiatum	Jungle Owlet	15 18	f g
Glaucidium siju	Cuban Pygmy-Owl	5	e
Glaucidium sjostedti	Sjostedt's Barred Owlet	8	c
Glaucidium tephronotum	Red-chested Owlet	8	c
Micrathene whitneyi	Elf Owl	3 4	a e
Uroglaux dimorpha	Papuan Hawk-Owl	35	j
Ninox affinis	Andaman Brown Hawk-Owl	15	f
Ninox connivens	Barking Owl	35 36	i j
Ninox jacquinoti	Solomon Islands Hawk-Owl	38	k
Ninox meeki	Admiralty Island Hawk-Owl	50	j
Ninox novaeseelandiae	Boobook Owl	35 36 37	i j
Ninox odiosa	New Britain Hawk-Owl	34	j
Ninox perversa	Ochre-bellied Hawk-Owl	28	h
Ninox philippensis[9]	Philippine Boobook Owl	22	h
Ninox punctulata	Speckled Hawk-Owl	29	h
Ninox rufa	Rufous Owl	35 36	i j
Ninox scutulata	Brown Hawk-Owl	2 15 16 18 19 21 22 55	b f g h
Ninox solomonis	New Ireland Hawk-Owl	34	j
Ninox squamipila	Indonesian Hawk-Owl	14	f h j
Ninox strenua	Powerful Owl	36	i
Ninox superciliaris	White-browed Owl	10	c
Ninox theomacha	Brown Owl	35	j
Athene blewitti	Forest Spotted Owlet	15	f
Athene brama	Spotted Little Owl	2 15 16 18 55	b f g
Athene cunicularia[10]	Burrowing Owl	3 4 5 6	a d e
Athene noctua	Little Owl	2 8 15 16 37	b c f g i
Ciccaba albitarsus	Rufous-banded Owl	6	d
Ciccaba huhula	Black-banded Owl	6	d
Ciccaba nigrolineata	Black-and-White Owl	4 6	d e
Ciccaba virgata	Mottled Owl	4 6	d e
Ciccaba woodfordii	African Wood-Owl	8	c
Strix aluco	Tawny Owl	2 15 16 18 55	b f g
Strix butleri	Hume's Tawny Owl	2 15	b f
Strix hylophila	Rusty-barred Owl	6	d
Strix leptogrammica	Brown Wood Owl	2 15 16 18 19 21 55	b f g h
Strix nebulosa	Great Gray Owl	2 3 16	a b g
Strix occidentalis	Spotted Owl	3 4	a e
Strix ocellata	Mottled Wood Owl	15 18	f g
Strix rufipes	Rufous-legged Owl	6	d
Strix seloputo	Spotted Wood Owl	18 19 55	g h
Strix uralensis	Ural Owl	2 16	b g
Strix varia	Barred Owl	3 4	a e
Rhinoptynx clamator	Striped Owl	4 6	d e
Asio capensis	African Marsh Owl	2 8	b c
Asio flammeus	Short-eared Owl	2 3 4 5 6 8 15 16 18 19 21 22 38 55	a b c d e f g h k

Scientific Name	Common Name	Source Codes	Region Codes

STRIGIDAE · TYPICAL OWLS contd.

Scientific Name	Common Name	Source Codes	Region Codes
Asio madagascariensis	Madagascar Long-Eared Owl	10	c
Asio otus	Long-eared Owl	2 3 4 8 15 16 55	a b c e f g
Asio stygius	Stygian Owl	4 5 6	d e
Pseudoscops grammicus	Jamaican Owl	5	e
Nesasio solomonensis	Fearful Owl	38	k
Aegolius àcadicus	Saw-Whet Owl	3 4	a e
Aegolius funereus	Boreal Owl	2 3 15 16	a b f g
Aegolius harrisii	Buff-fronted Owl	6	d
Aegolius ridgwayi	Unspotted Saw-Whet Owl	4	e

STEATORNITHIDAE · OILBIRD   1 species recorded

Scientific Name	Common Name	Source Codes	Region Codes
Steatornis caripensis	Oilbird	6	d

PODARGIDAE · FROGMOUTHS   12 species recorded

Scientific Name	Common Name	Source Codes	Region Codes
Podargus ocellatus	Marbled Frogmouth	35 36 38	i j k
Podargus papuensis	Papuan Frogmouth	35 36	i j
Podargus strigoides	Tawny Frogmouth	36	i
Batrachostomus affinis	Blyth's Frogmouth	19 21 55	g h
Batrachostomus auritus	Large Frogmouth	19 21 55	g h
Batrachostomus harterti	Dulit Frogmouth	19 21	h
Batrachostomus hodgsoni	Hodgson's Frogmouth	15 18 55	f g
Batrachostomus javensis	Javan Frogmouth	18 19 21 55	g h
Batrachostomus moniliger	Ceylon Frogmouth	15	f
Batrachostomus poliolophus	Pale-headed Frogmouth	19 21	h
Batrachostomus septimus	Philippine Frogmouth	22	h
Batrachostomus stellatus	Gould's Frogmouth	19 21 55	g h

NYCTIBIIDAE · POTOOS   5 species recorded

Scientific Name	Common Name	Source Codes	Region Codes
Nyctibius aethereus	Long-tailed Potoo	6	d
Nyctibius bracteatus	Rufous Potoo	6	d
Nyctibius grandis	Great Potoo	4 6	d e
Nyctibius griseus	Common Potoo	4 5 6	d e
Nyctibius leucopterus	White-winged Potoo	6	d

AEGOTHELIDAE · OWLET-NIGHTJARS   7 species recorded

Scientific Name	Common Name	Source Codes	Region Codes
Aegotheles albertisi	Mountain Owlet-Nightjar	35	j
Aegotheles bennettii	Barred Owlet-Nightjar	35	j
Aegotheles crinifrons	Halmahera Owlet-Nightjar	31	j
Aegotheles cristatus	Owlet-Nightjar	35 36	i j
Aegotheles insignis	Large Owlet-Nightjar	35	j
Aegotheles savesi	New Caledonian Owlet-Nightjar	38	k
Aegotheles wallacii	Wallace's Owlet-Nightjar	35	j

Scientific Name	Common Name	Source Codes	Region Codes

CAPRIMULGIDAE · GOATSUCKERS, NIGHTJARS   72 species recorded

Scientific Name	Common Name	Source Codes	Region Codes
Lurocalis semitorquatus	Semicollared Nighthawk	4 6	d e
Chordeiles acutipennis	Lesser Nighthawk	3 4 6	a d e
Chordeiles minor	Common Nighthawk	3 4 5 6	a d e
Chordeiles pusillus	Least Nighthawk	6	d
Chordeiles rupestris	Sand-colored Nighthawk	6	d
Nyctiprogne leucopyga	Band-tailed Nighthawk	6	d
Podager nacunda	Nacunda Nighthawk	6	d
Eurostopodus archboldi	Archbold's Nightjar	35	j
Eurostopodus diabolicus	Devilish Nightjar	47	j
Eurostopodus guttatus	Spotted Nightjar	35 36	i j
Eurostopodus macrotis	Great Eared Nightjar	15 16 18 19 22 55	f g h
Eurostopodus mystacalis	White-throated Nightjar	36 38	i k
Eurostopodus papuensis	Papuan Nightjar	35	j
Eurostopodus temmincki	Malaysian Eared Nightjar	19 21	h
Nyctidromus albicollis	Pauraque	3 4 6	a d e
Phalaenoptilus nuttallii	Poorwill	3 4	a e
Siphonorhis americanus[1]	Least Pauraque	5	e
Otophanes mcleodii	Eared Poorwill	4	e
Otophanes yucatanicus	Yucatan Poorwill	4	e
Nyctiphrynus ocellatus	Ocellated Poorwill	4 6	d e
Caprimulgus aegyptius	Egyptian Nightjar	2 8 16	b c g
Caprimulgus affinis[2]	Franklin's Nightjar	15 16 18 19 21 22 55	f g h
Caprimulgus asiaticus	Indian Nightjar	2 15 18 55	b f g
Caprimulgus batesi	Bates's Nightjar	8	c
Caprimulgus binotatus	Brown Nightjar	8	c
Caprimulgus candicans	White-winged Nightjar	6	d
Caprimulgus carolinensis	Chuck-Will's-Widow	3 4 5 6	a d e
Caprimulgus cayennensis	White-tailed Nightjar	4 5 6	d e
Caprimulgus centralasicus	Vaurie's Nightjar	2	b
Caprimulgus climacurus	Long-tailed Nightjar	8	c
Caprimulgus concretus	Bonaparte's Nightjar	19 21	h
Caprimulgus cubanensis	Greater Antillean Nightjar	5	e
Caprimulgus enarratus	Collared Nightjar	10	c
Caprimulgus donaldsoni	Donaldson Smith's Nightjar	8	c
Caprimulgus europaeus	Eurasian Nightjar	2 8 15 16	b c f g
Caprimulgus eximius	Golden Nightjar	2 8	b c
Caprimulgus fossii	Gabon Nightjar	8	c
Caprimulgus fraenatus	Northern Dusky Nightjar	8	c
Caprimulgus hirundinaceus	Pygmy Nightjar	6	d
Caprimulgus indicus	Jungle Nightjar	2 15 16 18 19 21 22 35 38 55	b f g h j k
Caprimulgus inornatus	Plain Nightjar	2 8	b c
Caprimulgus longirostris	Band-winged Nightjar	6	d
Caprimulgus macrurus	Long-tailed Nightjar	15 16 18 19 21 22 35 36 55	f g h i j
Caprimulgus maculicaudus	Spot-tailed Nightjar	4 6	d e
Caprimulgus maculosus	Cayenne Nightjar	6	d
Caprimulgus madagascariensis	Madagascar Nightjar	10	c
Caprimulgus mahrattensis	Sykes's Nightjar	2 15	b f
Caprimulgus natalensis	White-tailed Nightjar	8	c
Caprimulgus nigrescens	Blackish Nightjar	6	d
Caprimulgus noctitherus[3]	Puerto Rico Whip-Poor-Will	53	e
Caprimulgus nubicus	Nubian Nightjar	2 8	b c
Caprimulgus parvulus	Little Nightjar	6	d
Caprimulgus pectoralis	Dusky Nightjar	8	c

Scientific Name	Common Name	Source Codes	Region Codes

CAPRIMULGIDAE · GOATSUCKERS, NIGHTJARS contd.

Scientific Name	Common Name	Source Codes	Region Codes
Caprimulgus poliocephalus	Abyssinian Nightjar	8	f
Caprimulgus pulchellus	Salvadori's Nightjar	19	h
Caprimulgus ridgwayi	Ridgway's Whip-Poor-Will	4	e
Caprimulgus ruficollis	Red-necked Nightjar	2 8	b c
Caprimulgus rufigena	Rufous-cheeked Nightjar	8	c
Caprimulgus rufus[4]	Rufous Nightjar	4 5 6	d e
Caprimulgus saturatus	Dusky Nightjar	4	e
Caprimulgus sericocaudatus	Silky-tailed Nightjar	6	d
Caprimulgus stellatus	Star-spotted Nightjar	8	c
Caprimulgus tristigma	Freckled Nightjar	8	c
Caprimulgus vociferus	Whip-Poor-Will	3 4 5	a e
Caprimulgus whiteleyi	Roraiman Nightjar	6	d
Macrodipteryx longipennis	Standard-winged Nightjar	8	c
Macrodipteryx vexillarius	Pennant-winged Nightjar	8	c
Hydropsalis brasiliana	Scissor-tailed Nightjar	6	d
Hydropsalis climacocerca	Ladder-tailed Nightjar	6	d
Uropsalis lyra	Lyre-tailed Nightjar	6	d
Uropsalis segmentata	Swallow-tailed Nightjar	6	d
Macropsalis creagra	Long-trained Nightjar	6	d
Eleothreptus anomalus	Sickle-winged Nightjar	6	d

HEMIPROCNIDAE · CRESTED SWIFTS 3 species recorded

Scientific Name	Common Name	Source Codes	Region Codes
Hemiprocne comata	Lesser Tree Swift	18 19 22 55	g h
Hemiprocne longipennis[1]	Crested Tree Swift	18 19 55	g h
Hemiprocne mystacea	Whiskered Tree Swift	35 38	j k

APODIDAE · SWIFTS 71 species recorded

Scientific Name	Common Name	Source Codes	Region Codes
Collocalia brevirostris	Himalayan Swiftlet	2 15 16 18 55	b f g h
Collocalia esculenta	White-bellied Swiftlet	15 18 19 21 22 35 36 38 55	f g h i j k
Collocalia francica	Gray-rumped Swiftlet	10 21	c h
Collocalia fuciphaga[1]	Thunberg's Swiftlet	15 19 21 55	f g h
Collocalia gigas	Giant Swiftlet	19	h
Collocalia hirundinacea	Mountain Swiftlet	35	i
Collocalia inexpectata	Edible-Nest Swiftlet	15 18 19 22 35 38	f h j k
Collocalia inquieta	Carolines Swiftlet	38	k
Collocalia leucophaea	Tahitian Swiftlet	41	k
Collocalia lowi	Low's Swiftlet	18 19 21 55	g h
Collocalia spodiopygia	White-rumped Swiftlet	36 38	i k
Collocalia troglodytes	Pygmy Swiftlet	22	h
Collocalia vanikorensis	Uniform Swiftlet	35 36 38	i j k
Collocalia vestita	Brown-rumped Swiftlet	19 21 22	h
Collocalia whiteheadi	Whitehead's Swiftlet	22 35 38	h j k
Hirundapus caudacutus[2]	White-throated Spinetail Swift	2 15 16 18 19 21 37 38 55	b f g h i j k
Hirundapus giganteus	Large Brown-throated Spinetail Swift	15 18 19 21 22 55	f g h
Hirundapus sylvatica	Indian White-rumped Spinetail Swift	15	f
Cypseloides biscutata[3]	Biscutate Swift	6	d
Cypseloides cherriei	Spot-fronted Swift	4 6	d e
Cypseloides cryptus	White-chinned Swift	4 6	d e

57

Scientific Name	Common Name	Source Codes	Region Codes
APODIDAE · SWIFTS contd.			
Cypseloides fumigatus	Sooty Swift	6	d
Cypseloides lemosi[4]	White-chested Swift	6	d
Cypseloides niger	Black Swift	3　4　5　6	a　d　e
Cypseloides phelpsi	Phelps's Swift	66	d
Cypseloides rutilus	Chestnut-collared Swift	4　6	d　e
Cypseloides semicollaris	White-naped Swift	4	e
Cypseloides senex	Great Dusky Swift	6	d
Cypseloides zonaris	White-collared Swift	4　5　6	d　e
Chaetura andrei[5]	Ashy-tailed Swift	4　6	d　e
Chaetura boehmi	Boehm's Spinetailed Swift	8	c
Chaetura brachyura	Short-tailed Swift	5　6	d　e
Chaetura cassini	Cassin's Spinetailed Swift	8	c
Chaetura chapmani	Chapman's Swift	4　6	d　e
Chaetura cinereiventris	Gray-rumped Swift	4　5　6	d　e
Chaetura egregia	Pale-rumped Swift	6	d
Chaetura grandidieri	Madagascar Spinetailed Swift	10	c
Chaetura leucopygialis	White-rumped Spinetailed Swift	18　19　21	h
Chaetura martinica	Lesser Antillean Swift	5	e
Chaetura melanopygia	Ituri Mottled-throated Spinetailed Swift	8	c
Chaetura novaeguineae	New Guinea Spinetailed Swift	35	j
Chaetura pelagica	Chimney Swift	3　4　5　6	a　d　e
Chaetura picina	Philippine Spinetailed Swift	22	h
Chaetura sabini	Sabine's Spinetailed Swift	8	c
Chaetura spinicauda	Band-rumped Swift	4　6	d　e
Chaetura thomensis	Sao Thome Spinetailed Swift	8	c
Chaetura ussheri	Mottled-throated Spinetailed Swift	8	c
Chaetura vauxi	Vaux's Swift	3　4　6	a　d　e
Apus acuticaudus	Dark-backed Swift	15	f
Apus aequatorialis	Mottled Swift	8	c
Apus affinis	House Swift	2　8　15　16　18　19 21　22　55	b　c　f　g　h
Apus apus	Common Swift	2　3　8　10　15　16	a　b　c　f　g
Apus barbatus	African Black Swift	8	c
Apus batesi	Bates's Swift	8	c
Apus caffer	White-rumped Swift	8	b　c
Apus horus	Horus Swift	8	c
Apus melba	Alpine Swift	2　8　10　15	b　c　f
Apus myioptilus	Scarce Swift	8	c
Apus niansae	Nyanza Swift	8	c
Apus pacificus	Northern White-rumped Swift	2　3　15　16　18　19 22　35　36　37　38　55	a　b　f　g　h　i　j　k
Apus pallidus	Pallid Swift	2　8	b　c
Apus toulsoni	Loanda Swift	8	c
Apus unicolor	Plain Swift	2	b
Aeronautes andecolus	Andean Swift	6	d
Aeronautes montivagus	White-tipped Swift	6	d
Aeronautes saxatalis	White-throated Swift	3　4	a　e
Panyptila cayennensis	Lesser Swallow-tailed Swift	4　6	d　e
Panyptila sanctihieronymi	Great Swallow-tailed Swift	4	c
Tachornis furcata[6]	Pygmy Swift	6	d
Tachornis phoenicobia	Antillean Palm Swift	5	e
Tachornis squamata[7]	Fork-tailed Palm Swift	6	d
Cypsiurus parvus[8]	Palm Swift	8　10　15　16　18　19 21　22　55	c　f　g　h

Scientific Name	Common Name	Source Codes	Region Codes

TROCHILIDAE · HUMMINGBIRDS 315 species recorded

Scientific Name	Common Name	Source Codes			Region Codes	
Tilmatura dupontii	Sparkling-tailed Hummingbird	4			e	
Androdon aequatorialis	Tooth-billed Hummingbird	4	6		d	e
Ramphodon dohrnii	Hook-billed Hermit	6			d	
Ramphodon naevius	Saw-billed Hermit	6			d	
Glaucis aenea	Bronzy Hermit	4	6		d	e
Glaucis hirsuta	Rufous-breasted Hermit	4	5	6	d	e
Threnetes leucurus	Pale-tailed Barbthroat	6			d	
Threnetes loehkeni	Bronze-tailed Barbthroat	6			d	
Threnetes niger	Sooty Barbthroat	6			d	
Threnetes ruckeri	Band-tailed Barbthroat	4	6		d	e
Phaethornis anthophilus	Pale-bellied Hermit	4	6		d	e
Phaethornis augusti	Sooty-capped Hermit	6			d	
Phaethornis bourcieri	Straight-billed Hermit	6			d	
Phaethornis eurynome	Scale-throated Hermit	6			d	
Phaethornis gounellei	Broad-tipped Hermit	6			d	
Phaethornis griseogularis	Gray-chinned Hermit	6			d	
Phaethornis guy	Green Hermit	4	6		d	e
Phaethornis hispidus	White-bearded Hermit	6			d	
Phaethornis idaliae	Minute Hermit	6			d	
Phaethornis longuemareus	Little Hermit	4	6		d	e
Phaethornis malaris	Great-billed Hermit	6			d	
Phaethornis maranhaoensis	Maranhao Hermit	6			d	
Phaethornis nattereri	Cinnamon-throated Hermit	6			d	
Phaethornis philippi	Needle-billed Hermit	6			d	
Phaethornis pretrei	Planalto Hermit	6			d	
Phaethornis ruber	Reddish Hermit	6			d	
Phaethornis squalidus	Dusky-throated Hermit	6			d	
Phaethornis stuarti	White-browed Hermit	6			d	
Phaethornis subochraceus	Buff-bellied Hermit	6			d	
Phaethornis superciliosus	Long-tailed Hermit	4	6		d	e
Phaethornis syrmatophorus	Tawny-bellied Hermit	6			d	
Phaethornis yaruqui	White-whiskered Hermit	6			d	
Eutoxeres aquila	White-tipped Sicklebill	4	6		d	e
Eutoxeres condamini	Buff-tailed Sicklebill	6			d	
Doryfera johannae	Blue-fronted Lancebill	6			d	
Doryfera ludoviciae	Green-fronted Lancebill	4	6		d	e
Phaeochroa cuvierii	Scaly-breasted Hummingbird	4	6		d	e
Campylopterus curvipennis	Wedge-tailed Sabrewing	4			e	
Campylopterus duidae	Buff-breasted Sabrewing	6			d	
Campylopterus ensipennis	White-tailed Sabrewing	6			d	
Campylopterus falcatus	Lazuline Sabrewing	6			d	
Campylopterus hemileucurus	Violet Sabrewing	4			e	
Campylopterus hyperythrus	Rufous-breasted Sabrewing	6			d	
Campylopterus largipennis	Gray-breasted Sabrewing	6			d	
Campylopterus phainopeplus	Santa Marta Sabrewing	6			d	
Campylopterus rufus	Rufous Sabrewing	4			e	
Campylopterus villaviscensio	Napo Sabrewing	6			d	
Eupetomena macroura	Swallow-tailed Hummingbird	6			d	
Florisuga mellivora	White-necked Jacobin	4	6		d	e
Melanotrochilus fuscus	Black Jacobin	6			d	
Colibri coruscans	Sparkling Violetear	6			d	
Colibri delphinae	Brown Violetear	4	6		d	e
Colibri serrirostris	White-vented Violetear	6			d	
Colibri thalassinus	Green Violetear	4	6		d	e
Anthracothorax dominicus	Antillean Mango	5			e	
Anthracothorax mango	Jamaican Mango	5			e	

59

Scientific Name	Common Name	Source Codes	Region Codes

TROCHILIDAE · HUMMINGBIRDS *contd.*

Scientific Name	Common Name	Source Codes	Region Codes
Anthracothorax nigricollis	Black-throated Mango	4 6	d e
Anthracothorax prevostii	Green-breasted Mango	4 5 6	d e
Anthracothorax veraguensis	Veraguan Mango	4	e
Anthracothorax viridigula	Green-throated Mango	6	d
Anthracothorax viridis	Green Mango	5	e
Avocettula recurvirostris	Fiery-throated Awlbill	6	d
Eulampis jugularis	Purple-throated Carib	5	e
Sericotes holosericeus	Green-throated Carib	5	e
Chrysolampis mosquitus	Ruby-Topaz Hummingbird	6	d
Orthorhyncus cristatus	Antillean Crested Hummingbird	5	e
Klais guimeti	Violet-headed Hummingbird	4 6	d e
Abeillia abeillei	Emerald-chinned Hummingbird	4	e
Stephanoxis lalandi	Black-breasted Plovercrest	6	d
Lophornis chalybea	Festive Coquette	6	d
Lophornis delattrei	Rufous-crested Coquette	4 6	d e
Lophornis gouldii	Dot-eared Coquette	6	d
Lophornis magnifica	Frilled Coquette	6	d
Lophornis ornata	Tufted Coquette	6	d
Lophornis pavonina	Peacock Coquette	6	d
Lophornis stictolopha	Spangled Coquette	6	d
Paphosia adorabilis	White-crested Coquette	4	e
Paphosia helenae	Black-crested Coquette	4	e
Popelairia conversii	Green Thorntail	4 6	d e
Popelairia langsdorffi	Black-bellied Thorntail	6	d
Popelairia letitiae	Coppery Thorntail	6	d
Popelairia popelairii	Wire-crested Thorntail	6	d
Discosura longicauda	Racket-tailed Coquette	6	d
Chlorestes notatus	Blue-chinned Sapphire	6	d
Chlorostilbon alice	Green-tailed Emerald	6	d
Chlorostilbon aureoventris	Glittering-bellied Emerald	6	d
Chlorostilbon canivetii	Fork-tailed Emerald	4	e
Chlorostilbon gibsoni	Red-billed Emerald	6	d
Chlorostilbon maugaeus	Puerto Rican Emerald	5	e
Chlorostilbon mellisugus	Blue-tailed Emerald	6	d
Chlorostilbon poortmanni	Short-tailed Emerald	6	d
Chlorostilbon ricordii	Cuban Emerald	5	e
Chlorostilbon russatus	Coppery Emerald	6	d
Chlorostilbon stenura	Narrow-tailed Emerald	6	d
Chlorostilbon swainsonii	Hispaniolan Emerald	5	e
Cynanthus latirostris	Broad-billed Hummingbird	3 4	a e
Cynanthus sordidus	Dusky Hummingbird	4	e
Cyanophaia bicolor	Blue-headed Hummingbird	5	e
Thalurania colombica	Blue-crowned Woodnymph	4	e
Thalurania fannyi	Green-crowned Woodnymph	4	e
Thalurania furcata	Fork-tailed Woodnymph	6	d
Thalurania glaucopis	Violet-capped Woodnymph	6	d
Thalurania watertonii	Long-tailed Woodnymph	6	d
Panterpe insignis	Fiery-throated Hummingbird	4	e
Damophila julie	Violet-bellied Hummingbird	4 6	d e
Lepidopyga coeruleogularis	Sapphire-throated Hummingbird	4 6	d e
Lepidopyga goudoti	Shining Green Hummingbird	6	d
Lepidopyga lillae	Sapphire-bellied Hummingbird	6	d
Hylocharis chrysura	Gilded Hummingbird	6	d
Hylocharis cyanus	White-chinned Sapphire	6	d

60

Scientific Name	Common Name	Source Codes	Region Codes

TROCHILIDAE · HUMMINGBIRDS *contd.*

Scientific Name	Common Name	Source Codes	Region Codes
Hylocharis eliciae	Blue-throated Goldentail	4	e
Hylocharis grayi	Blue-headed Sapphire	4 6	d c
Hylocharis leucotis	White-eared Hummingbird	3 4	a e
Hylocharis sapphirina	Rufous-throated Sapphire	6	d
Hylocharis xantusii	Black-fronted Hummingbird	4	e
Chrysuronia oenone	Golden-tailed Sapphire	6	d
Goldmania violiceps	Violet-capped Hummingbird	4 6	d e
Goethalsia bella	Pirre Hummingbird	4 6	d e
Trochilus polytmus	Streamertail	5	e
Leucochloris albicollis	White-throated Hummingbird	6	d
Polytmus guainumbi	White-tailed Goldenthroat	6	d
Polytmus milleri	Tepui Goldenthroat	6	d
Polytmus theresiae	Green-tailed Goldenthroat	6	d
Leucippus baeri	Tumbes Hummingbird	6	d
Leucippus chlorocercus	Olive-spotted Hummingbird	6	d
Leucippus fallax	Buffy Hummingbird	6	d
Leucippus taczanowskii	Spot-throated Hummingbird	6	d
Taphrospilus hypostictus	Many-spotted Hummingbird	6	d
Amazilia amabilis	Blue-chested Hummingbird	4 6	d e
Amazilia amazilia	Amazilia Hummingbird	6	d
Amazilia beryllina	Berylline Hummingbird	4	e
Amazilia boucardi	Mangrove Hummingbird	4	e
Amazilia candida	White-bellied Emerald	4	e
Amazilia castaneiventris	Chestnut-bellied Hummingbird	6	d
Amazilia chionogaster	White-bellied Hummingbird	6	d
Amazilia chionopectus	White-chested Emerald	6	d
Amazilia cyanifrons	Indigo-capped Hummingbird	4 6	d e
Amazilia cyanocephala	Red-billed Azurecrown	4	e
Amazilia cyanura	Blue-tailed Hummingbird	4	e
Amazilia distans	Tachira Emerald	6	d
Amazilia edward	Snowy-breasted Hummingbird	4	e
Amazilia fimbriata	Glittering-throated Emerald	6	d
Amazilia franciae	Andean Emerald	6	d
Amazilia lactea	Sapphire-spangled Emerald	6	d
Amazilia leucogaster	Plain-bellied Emerald	6	d
Amazilia luciae	Honduras Emerald	4	e
Amazilia microrhyncha	Small-billed Azurecrown	4	e
Amazilia rosenbergi	Purple-chested Hummingbird	6	d
Amazilia rutila	Cinnamon Hummingbird	4	e
Amazilia saucerottei	Steely-vented Hummingbird	4 6	d e
Amazilia tobaci	Copper-rumped Hummingbird	6	d
Amazilia tzacatl	Rufous-tailed Hummingbird	3 4 6	a d e
Amazilia versicolor	Versicolored Emerald	6	d
Amazilia violiceps	Violet-crowned Hummingbird	3 4	a e
Amazilia viridicauda	Green-and-White Hummingbird	6	d
Amazilia viridifrons	Green-fronted Hummingbird	4	e
Amazilia viridigaster	Green-bellied Hummingbird	6	d
Amazilia yucatanensis	Buff-bellied Hummingbird	3 4	a e
Eupherusa eximia	Stripe-tailed Hummingbird	4	e
Eupherusa nigriventris	Black-bellied Hummingbird	4	e
Elvira chionura	White-tailed Emerald	4	e
Elvira cupreiceps	Coppery-headed Emerald	4	e
Microchera albocoronata	Snowcap	4	e
Chalybura buffonii	White-veined Plumeleteer	4 6	d e
Chalybura melanorrhoa	Dusky Plumeleteer	4	e
Chalybura urochrysia	Bronze-tailed Plumeleteer	4 6	d e

Scientific Name	Common Name	Source Codes	Region Codes
TROCHILIDAE · HUMMINGBIRDS *contd.*			
Aphantochroa cirrhochloris	Sombre Hummingbird	6	d
Adelomyia melanogenys	Speckled Hummingbird	6	d
Anthocephala floriceps	Blossomcrown	6	d
Urosticte benjamini	Whitetip	6	d
Phlogophilus harterti	Peruvian Piedtail	6	d
Phlogophilus hemileucurus	Ecuadorean Piedtail	6	d
Clytolaema rubricauda	Brazilian Ruby	6	d
Polyplancta aurescens	Gould's Jewelfront	6	d
Lampornis amethystinus	Amethyst-throated Hummingbird	4	e
Lampornis calolaema	Purple-throated Mountain-Gem	4	e
Lampornis castaneoventris	White-throated Mountain-Gem	4	e
Lampornis cinereicauda	Gray-tailed Mountain-Gem	4	e
Lampornis clemenciae	Blue-throated Hummingbird	3 4	a e
Lampornis hemileucus	White-bellied Mountain-Gem	4	e
Lampornis viridipallens	Green-throated Mountain-Gem	4	e
Lamprolaima rhami	Garnet-throated Hummingbird	4	e
Heliodoxa branickii	Rufous-webbed Brilliant	6	d
Heliodoxa gularis	Pink-throated Brilliant	6	d
Heliodoxa imperatrix	Empress Brilliant	6	d
Heliodoxa jacula	Green-crowned Brilliant	4 6	d e
Heliodoxa leadbeateri	Violet-fronted Brilliant	6	d
Heliodoxa rubinoides	Fawn-breasted Brilliant	6	d
Heliodoxa schreibersii	Black-throated Brilliant	6	d
Heliodoxa xanthogonys	Velvet-browed Brilliant	6	d
Eugenes fulgens	Rivoli's Hummingbird	3 4	a e
Hylonympha macrocerca	Scissor-tailed Hummingbird	6	d
Sternoclyta cyanopectus	Violet-chested Hummingbird	6	d
Topaza pella	Crimson Topaz	6	d
Topaza pyra	Fiery Topaz	6	d
Oreotrochilus adela	Wedge-tailed Hillstar	6	d
Oreotrochilus estella	Andean Hillstar	6	d
Oreotrochilus leucopleurus	White-sided Hillstar	6	d
Oreotrochilus melanogaster	Black-breasted Hillstar	6	d
Urochroa bougueri	White-tailed Hillstar	6	d
Patagona gigas	Giant Hummingbird	6	d
Aglaeactis aliciae	Purple-backed Sunbeam	6	d
Aglaeactis castelnaudii	White-tufted Sunbeam	6	d
Aglaeactis cupripennis	Shining Sunbeam	6	d
Aglaeactis pamela	Black-hooded Sunbeam	6	d
Lafresnaya lafresnayi	Mountain Velvetbreast	6	d
Pterophanes cyanopterus	Great Sapphirewing	6	d
Coeligena bonapartei	Golden-bellied Starfrontlet	6	d
Coeligena coeligena	Bronzy Inca	6	d
Coeligena helianthea	Blue-throated Starfrontlet	6	d
Coeligena iris	Rainbow Starfrontlet	6	d
Coeligena lutetiae	Buff-winged Starfrontlet	6	d
Coeligena orina	Dusky Starfrontlet	6	d
Coeligena phalerata	White-tailed Starfrontlet	6	d
Coeligena prunellei	Black Inca	6	d
Coeligena torquata	Collared Inca	6	d
Coeligena violifer	Violet-throated Starfrontlet	6	d
Coeligena wilsoni	Brown Inca	6	d
Ensifera ensifera	Sword-billed Hummingbird	6	d

Scientific Name	Common Name	Source Codes	Region Codes

TROCHILIDAE · HUMMINGBIRDS *contd.*

Scientific Name	Common Name	Source Codes	Region Codes
Sephanoides fernandensis	Fernandez Firecrown	47	d
Sephanoides sephanoides	Green-backed Firecrown	6	d
Boissonneaua flavescens	Buff-tailed Coronet	6	d
Boissonneaua jardini	Velvet-Purple Coronet	6	d
Boissonneaua matthewsii	Chestnut-breasted Coronet	6	d
Heliangelus amethysticollis	Amethyst-throated Sunangel	6	d
Heliangelus exortis	Tourmaline Sunangel	6	d
Heliangelus mavors	Orange-throated Sunangel	6	d
Heliangelus spencei	Merida Sunangel	6	d
Heliangelus strophianus	Gorgeted Sunangel	6	d
Heliangelus viola	Purple-throated Sunangel	6	d
Eriocnemis alinae	Emerald-bellied Puffleg	6	d
Eriocnemis cupreoventris	Coppery-bellied Puffleg	6	d
Eriocnemis derbyi	Black-thighed Puffleg	6	d
Eriocnemis glaucopoides	Blue-capped Puffleg	6	d
Eriocnemis godini	Turquoise-throated Puffleg	6	d
Eriocnemis luciani	Sapphire-vented Puffleg	6	d
Eriocnemis mirabilis	Colorful Puffleg	6	d
Eriocnemis mosquera	Golden-breasted Puffleg	6	d
Eriocnemis nigrivestis	Black-breasted Puffleg	6	d
Eriocnemis vestitus	Glowing Puffleg	6	d
Haplophaedia aureliae	Greenish Puffleg	4 6	d e
Haplophaedia lugens	Hoary Puffleg	6	d
Ocreatus underwoodii	Booted Racket-Tail	6	d
Lesbia nuna	Green-tailed Trainbearer	6	d
Lesbia victoriae	Black-tailed Trainbearer	6	d
Sappho sparganura	Red-tailed Comet	6	d
Polyonymus caroli	Bronze-tailed Comet	6	d
Ramphomicron dorsale	Black-backed Thornbill	6	d
Ramphomicron microrhynchum	Purple-backed Thornbill	6	d
Metallura aneocauda	Scaled Metaltail	6	d
Metallura baroni	Violet-throated Metaltail	6	d
Metallura eupogon	Fire-throated Metaltail	6	d
Metallura iracunda	Perija Metaltail	6	d
Metallura phoebe	Black Metaltail	6	d
Metallura theresiae	Coppery Metaltail	6	d
Metallura tyrianthina	Tyrian Metaltail	6	d
Metallura williami	Viridian Metaltail	6	d
Chalcostigma herrani	Rainbow-bearded Thornbill	6	d
Chalcostigma heteropogon	Bronze-tailed Thornbill	6	d
Chalcostigma olivaceum	Olivaceous Thornbill	6	d
Chalcostigma ruficeps	Rufous-capped Thornbill	6	d
Chalcostigma stanleyi	Blue-mantled Thornbill	6	d
Oxypogon guerinii	Bearded Helmetcrest	6	d
Opisthoprora euryptera	Mountain Avocetbill	6	d
Tephrolesbia griseiventris	Gray-bellied Comet	6	d
Aglaiocercus coelestis	Violet-tailed Sylph	6	d
Aglaiocercus kingi	Long-tailed Sylph	6	d
Oreonympha nobilis	Bearded Mountaineer	6	d
Augastes lumachellus	Hooded Visorbearer	6	d
Augastes scutatus	Hyacinth Visorbearer	6	d
Schistes geoffroyi	Wedge-billed Hummingbird	6	d
Heliothryx aurita	Black-eared Fairy	6	d
Heliothryx barroti	Purple-crowned Fairy	4 6	d e
Heliactin cornuta	Horned Sungem	6	d
Loddigesia mirabilis	Marvellous Spatuletail	6	d
Heliomaster constanti	Plain-capped Starthroat	4	e

63

Scientific Name	Common Name	Source Codes	Region Codes

TROCHILIDAE · HUMMINGBIRDS contd.

Scientific Name	Common Name	Source Codes			Region Codes	
Heliomaster furcifer	Blue-tufted Starthroat	6			d	
Heliomaster longirostris	Long-billed Starthroat	4	6		d	e
Heliomaster squamosus	Stripe-breasted Starthroat	6			d	
Rhodopis vesper	Oasis Hummingbird	6			d	
Thaumastura cora	Peruvian Sheartail	6			d	
Philodice bryantae	Magenta-throated Woodstar	4			e	
Philodice mitchellii	Purple-throated Woodstar	6			d	
Doricha eliza	Mexican Sheartail	4			e	
Doricha enicura	Slender Sheartail	4			e	
Microstilbon burmeisteri	Slender-tailed Woodstar	6			d	
Calothorax lucifer	Lucifer Hummingbird	3	4		a	e
Calothorax pulcher	Beautiful Hummingbird	4			e	
Archilochus alexandri	Black-chinned Hummingbird	3	4		a	e
Archilochus colubris	Ruby-throated Hummingbird	3	4	5	a	e
Calliphlox amethystina	Amethyst Woodstar	6			d	
Calliphlox evelynae	Bahama Woodstar	5			e	
Mellisuga helenae	Bee Hummingbird	5			e	
Mellisuga minima	Vervain Hummingbird	5			e	
Calypte anna	Anna's Hummingbird	3	4		a	e
Calypte costae	Costa's Hummingbird	3	4		a	e
Stellula calliope	Calliope Hummingbird	3	4		a	e
Atthis ellioti	Wine-throated Hummingbird	4			e	
Atthis heloisa	Bumblebee Hummingbird	3	4		a	e
Myrtis fanny	Purple-collared Woodstar	6			d	
Eulidia yarrellii	Chilean Woodstar	6			d	
Myrmia micrura	Short-tailed Woodstar	6			d	
Acestrura berlepschi	Esmeraldas Woodstar	6			d	
Acestrura bombus	Little Woodstar	6			d	
Acestrura heliodor	Gorgeted Woodstar	4	6		d	e
Acestrura mulsant	White-bellied Woodstar	6			d	
Chaetocercus jourdanii	Rufous-shafted Woodstar	6			d	
Selasphorus ardens	Glow-throated Hummingbird	4			e	
Selasphorus flammula	Rose-throated Hummingbird	4			e	
Selasphorus platycercus	Broad-tailed Hummingbird	3	4		a	e
Selasphorus rufus	Rufous Hummingbird	3	4		a	e
Selasphorus sasin	Allen's Hummingbird	3	4		a	e
Selasphorus scintilla	Scintillant Hummingbird	4			e	
Selasphorus simoni	Cerise-throated Hummingbird	4			e	
Selasphorus torridus	Heliotrope-throated Hummingbird	4			e	

COLIIDAE · MOUSEBIRDS, COLIES 6 species recorded

Scientific Name	Common Name	Source Codes	Region Codes
Colius castanotus	Red-backed Mousebird	8	c
Colius colius	White-backed Mousebird	8	c
Colius indicus	Red-faced Mousebird	8	c
Colius leucocephalus	White-headed Mousebird	8	c
Colius macrourus	Blue-naped Mousebird	8	c
Colius striatus	Speckled Mousebird	8	c

TROGONIDAE · TROGONS 36 species recorded

Scientific Name	Common Name	Source Codes	Region Codes
Pharomachrus antisianus	Crested Quetzal	6	d
Pharomachrus fulgidus	White-tipped Quetzal	6	d

Scientific Name	Common Name	Source Codes	Region Codes

TROGONIDAE · TROGONS *contd.*

Scientific Name	Common Name	Source Codes	Region Codes
Pharomachrus mocinno	Resplendent Quetzal	1	e
Pharomachrus pavoninus[1]	Golden-headed Quetzal	4 6	d e
Euptilotis neoxenus	Eared Trogon	4	e
Trogon aurantiiventris	Orange-bellied Trogon	4	e
Trogon citreolus	Citreoline Trogon	4	e
Trogon clathratus	Lattice-tailed Trogon	4	e
Trogon collaris	Collared Trogon	4 6	d e
Trogon comptus	Blue-tailed Trogon	6	d
Trogon curucui	Blue-crowned Trogon	6	d
Trogon elegans	Coppery-tailed Trogon	3 4	a e
Trogon massena	Slaty-tailed Trogon	4 6	d e
Trogon melanurus	Black-tailed Trogon	4 6	d e
Trogon mexicanus	Mountain Trogon	4	e
Trogon personatus	Masked Trogon	6	d
Trogon rufus	Black-throated Trogon	4 6	d e
Trogon surrucura	Surucua Trogon	6	d
Trogon violaceus	Violaceous Trogon	4 6	d e
Trogon viridis	White-tailed Trogon	4 6	d e
Priotelus temnurus	Cuban Trogon	5	e
Temnotrogon roseigaster	Hispaniolan Trogon	5	e
Apaloderma aequatoriale	Bare-cheeked Trogon	8	c
Apaloderma narina	Narina's Trogon	8	c
Apaloderma vittatum[2]	Bar-tailed Trogon	8	c
Harpactes ardens	Philippine Trogon	22	h
Harpactes diardi	Diard's Trogon	19 21 55	g h
Harpactes duvauceli	Scarlet-rumped Trogon	18 19 21 55	g h
Harpactes erythrocephalus	Red-headed Trogon	15 16 18 19 55	f g h
Harpactes fasciatus	Malabar Trogon	15	f
Harpactes kasumba	Red-naped Trogon	19 21 55	g h
Harpactes oreskios	Orange-breasted Trogon	16 18 19 21 55	g h
Harpactes orrophaeus	Cinnamon-rumped Trogon	19 21 55	g h
Harpactes reinwardti	Reinwardt's Blue-tailed Trogon	19	h
Harpactes wardi	Ward's Trogon	18 55	g
Harpactes whiteheadi	Whitehead's Trogon	19 21	h

ALCEDINIDAE · KINGFISHERS   90 species recorded

Scientific Name	Common Name	Source Codes	Region Codes
Ceryle alcyon	Belted Kingfisher	3 4 5 6	a d e
Ceryle lugubris	Greater Pied Kingfisher	2 15 16 18 55	b f g
Ceryle maxima	Giant Kingfisher	8	c
Ceryle rudis	Lesser Pied Kingfisher	2 8 15 16 18 55	b c f g
Ceryle torquata	Ringed Kingfisher	3 4 5 6	a d c
Chloroceryle aenea	Pygmy Kingfisher	4 6	d e
Chloroceryle amazona	Amazon Kingfisher	4 6	d e
Chloroceryle americana	Green Kingfisher	3 4 6	a d e
Chloroceryle inda	Green-and-Rufous Kingfisher	4 6	d e
Alcedo atthis	Common Kingfisher	2 8 15 16 18 19 21 22 35 38 55	b c f g h j k
Alcedo coerulescens	Small Blue Kingfisher	19	h
Alcedo cristata	Malachite Kingfisher	8 10	c
Alcedo euryzona	Broad-zoned Kingfisher	18 19 21 55	g h
Alcedo hercules	Blyth's Kingfisher	15 16 18 55	f g
Alcedo leucogaster	White-bellied Kingfisher	8	c
Alcedo meninting	Blue-eared Kingfisher	15 18 19 21 22 55	f g h
Alcedo quadribrachys	Shining-Blue Kingfisher	8	c

Scientific Name	Common Name	Source Codes	Region Codes
ALCEDINIDAE · KINGFISHERS contd.			
Alcedo semitorquata	Half-collared Kingfisher	8	c
Ceyx argentatus	Silvery Kingfisher	22	h
Ceyx azurea	Azure Kingfisher	35 36	i j
Ceyx cyanopectus	Dwarf River Kingfisher	22	h
Ceyx erithacus	Three-toed Kingfisher	15 16 18 19 21 22 55	f g h
Ceyx fallax	Celebes Pygmy Kingfisher	28 29	h
Ceyx lecontei	African Dwarf Kingfisher	8	c
Ceyx lepidus	Dwarf Kingfisher	22 35 38	h j k
Ceyx madagascariensis	Madagascar Pygmy Kingfisher	10	c
Ceyx melanurus	Philippine Forest Kingfisher	22	h
Ceyx picta	African Pygmy Kingfisher	8	c
Ceyx pusillus	African Mangrove Kingfisher	38	k
Ceyx rufidorsus	Malay Forest Kingfisher	19 22 55	g h
Ceyx websteri	Bismarck Pygmy Kingfisher	34	j
Pelargopsis amauroptera	Brown-winged Kingfisher	15 18 55	f g h
Pelargopsis capensis	Stork-billed Kingfisher	15 18 19 21 22 55	f g h
Pelargopsis melanorhynca	Black-bellied Kingfisher	31	h
Lacedo pulchella	Banded Kingfisher	18 19 21 55	g h
Dacelo gaudichaud	Rufous-bellied Giant Kingfisher	35	j
Dacelo leachii	Blue-winged Kookaburra	35 36	i j
Dacelo novaeguineae[1]	Laughing Kookaburra	36 37	i
Dacelo tyro	Aru Giant Kingfisher	35	j
Clytoceyx rex	Shovel-billed Kingfisher	35	j
Melidora macrorhina	Hook-billed Kingfisher	35	j
Cittura cyanotis	Celebes Blue-eared Kingfisher	29	h
Halcyon albiventris	Brown-hooded Kingfisher	8	c
Halcyon albonotata	White-backed Kingfisher	34	j
Halcyon australasia	Timor Kingfisher	32	j
Halcyon badia	Chocolate-backed Kingfisher	8	c
Halcyon bougainvillei	Moustached Kingfisher	38	k
Halcyon chelicuti	Striped Kingfisher	8	c
Halcyon chloris	White-collared Kingfisher	8 16 18 19 21 22 35 36 38 55	c f g h i j k
Halcyon cinnamomina	Micronesian Kingfisher	38	k
Halcyon concreta	Chestnut-collared Kingfisher	18 19 21 55	g h
Halcyon coromanda	Ruddy Kingfisher	2 15 16 18 19 21 22 55	b f g h
Halcyon cyanoleuca	Angolan Woodland Kingfisher	8	c
Halcyon cyanoventris	Java Kingfisher	19	h
Halcyon diops	Moluccan Kingfisher	29	h
Halcyon farquhari	Chestnut-bellied Kingfisher	38	k
Halcyon fulgidus	Glittering Kingfisher	32	j
Halcyon funebris	Sombre Kingfisher	29	h
Halcyon gambieri	Tuamotu Kingfisher	47	i
Halcyon godeffroyi	Marquenan Kingfisher	47	i
Halcyon hombroni	Blue-capped Wood Kingfisher	22	h
Halcyon leucocephala	Gray-headed Kingfisher	8	c
Halcyon leucopygia	Ultramarine Kingfisher	38	k
Halcyon lindsayi	Spotted Wood Kingfisher	22	h
Halcyon macleayii	Forest Kingfisher	35 36	i j
Halcyon malimbica	Blue-breasted Kingfisher	8	c
Halcyon megarhynchus	Mountain Yellow-billed Kingfisher	35	j
Halcyon monachus	Lonely Kingfisher	28	h
Halcyon nigrocyanea	Blue-Black Kingfisher	35	j

66

ALCEDINIDAE · KINGFISHERS *contd.*

Scientific Name	Common Name	Source Codes	Region Codes
Halcyon pileata	Black-capped Kingfisher	2 15 16 10 19 21 22	b f g h
Halcyon princeps	Princely Kingfisher	47	i
Halcyon pyrrhopygia	Red-backed Kingfisher	36	i
Halcyon recurvirostris	Flat-billed Kingfisher	38	k
Halcyon sancta	Sacred Kingfisher	19 21 35 36 37 38	h i j k
Halcyon saurophaga[2]	White-headed Kingfisher	35 38	j k
Halcyon senegalensis	Woodland Kingfisher	8	c
Halcyon senegaloides	Mangrove Kingfisher	8	c
Halcyon smyrnensis	White-breasted Kingfisher	2 15 16 18 19 22 55	b f g h
Halcyon torotoro	Lesser Yellow-billed Kingfisher	35 36	i j
Halcyon tuta	Borabora Kingfisher	43	k
Halcyon venerata	Tahitian Kingfisher	43	k
Halcyon winchelli	Winchell's Kingfisher	22	h
Tanysiptera carolinae	Numfor Paradise Kingfisher	35	j
Tanysiptera danae	Brown-backed Paradise Kingfisher	35	j
Tanysiptera ellioti	Kofiau Paradise Kingfisher	35	j
Tanysiptera galatea	Common Paradise Kingfisher	35	j
Tanysiptera hydrocharis	Aru Paradise Kingfisher	35	j
Tanysiptera nympha	Pink-breasted Paradise Kingfisher	35	j
Tanysiptera riedelii	Biak Paradise Kingfisher	35	j
Tanysiptera sylvia	White-tailed Kingfisher	35 36	i j

TODIDAE · TODIES 5 species recorded

Scientific Name	Common Name	Source Codes	Region Codes
Todus angustirostris	Narrow-billed Tody	5	e
Todus mexicanus	Puerto Rican Tody	5	e
Todus multicolor	Cuban Tody	5	e
Todus subulatus	Broad-billed Tody	5	e
Todus todus	Jamaican Tody	5	e

MOTMOTIDAE · MOTMOTS 8 species recorded

Scientific Name	Common Name	Source Codes	Region Codes
Hylomanes momotula	Tody Motmot	4 6	d e
Aspatha gularis	Blue-throated Motmot	4	e
Electron carinatum	Keel-billed Motmot	4	e
Electron platyrhynchum	Broad-billed Motmot	4 6	d e
Eumomota superciliosa	Turquoise-browed Motmot	4	e
Baryphthengus ruficapillus	Rufous Motmot	4 6	d e
Momotus mexicanus	Russet-crowned Motmot	4	e
Momotus momota	Blue-crowned Motmot	4 6	d e

MEROPIDAE · BEE-EATERS 23 species recorded

Scientific Name	Common Name	Source Codes	Region Codes
Nyctyornis amicta	Red-bearded Bee-Eater	18 19 21 55	g h
Nyctyornis athertoni	Blue-bearded Bee-Eater	15 16 18 55	f g
Meropogon forsteni	Celebes Bearded Bee-Eater	29	h
Merops albicollis	White-throated Bee-Eater	2 8	b c

Scientific Name	Common Name	Source Codes	Region Codes
MEROPIDAE · BEE-EATERS contd.			
Merops apiaster	Common Bee-Eater	2 8 15 16	b c f g
Merops boehmi	Boehm's Bee-Eater	8	c
Merops breweri[1]	Black-headed Bee-Eater	8	c
Merops bulocki[2]	Red-throated Bee-Eater	8	c
Merops gularis	Black Bee-Eater	8	c
Merops hirundineus	Swallow-tailed Bee-Eater	8	c
Merops lafresnayii	Cinnamon-chested Bee-Eater	8	c
Merops leschenaulti	Chestnut-headed Bee-Eater	15 16 18 19 55	f g h
Merops malimbicus	Rosy Bee-Eater	8	c
Merops muelleri	Blue-headed Bee-Eater	8	c
Merops nubicus[1]	Carmine Bee-Eater	8	c
Merops orientalis	Little Green Bee-Eater	2 8 15 16 18 55	b c f g h
Merops ornatus	Rainbow Bee-Eater	35 36 38	i j k
Merops philippinus	Blue-tailed Bee-Eater	15 18 35 38 55	f g h j k
Merops pusillus	Little Bee-Eater	8	c
Merops revoilii	Somali Bee-Eater	8	c
Merops superciliosus	Blue-cheeked Bee-Eater	2 8 10 15 16 19 21 22	b c f g h
Merops variegatus	Blue-breasted Bee-Eater	8	c
Merops viridis	Blue-throated Bee-Eater	16 19 21 22 55	g h

LEPTOSOMATIDAE · COUROL   1 species recorded

Leptosomus discolor	Kirombo Courol	10	c

CORACIIDAE · ROLLERS   16 species recorded

Atelornis crossleyi	Crossley's Ground Roller	10	c
Atelornis pittoides	Pitta-like Ground Roller	10	c
Brachypteracias leptosomus	Short-legged Ground Roller	10	c
Brachypteracias squamigera	Scaled Ground Roller	10	c
Coracias abyssinicus	Abyssinian Roller	2	b
Coracias benghalensis	Indian Roller	2 15 16 18 55	b f g
Coracias caudata	Lilac-breasted Roller	8	c
Coracias cyanogaster	Blue-bellied Roller	8	c
Coracias garrulus	Blue Roller	2 8 15 16	b c f g
Coracias naevia	Rufous-crowned Roller	8	c
Coracias spatulata	Racquet-tailed Roller	8	c
Coracias temminckii	Temminck's Roller	29	h
Uratelornis chimaera	Long-tailed Ground Roller	10	c
Eurystomus glaucurus	African Broad-billed Roller	8 10	c
Eurystomus gularis	Blue-throated Roller	8	c
Eurystomus orientalis[1]	Broad-billed Roller	2 15 16 18 19 21 22 35 36 37 38 55	b f g h i j k

UPUPIDAE · HOOPOE   1 species recorded

Upupa epops	Hoopoe	2 8 10 15 16 18 19 21 55	b c f g h

68

Scientific Name	Common Name	Source Codes	Region Codes

PHOENICULIDAE · WOOD-HOOPOES   8 species recorded

Scientific Name	Common Name	Source Codes	Region Codes
Phoeniculus aterrimus[1]	Black Wood-Hoopoe	8	c
Phoeniculus bollei	White-headed Wood-Hoopoe	8	c
Phoeniculus castaneiceps	Forest Wood-Hoopoe	8	c
Phoeniculus cyanomelas	Scimitar-Bill	8	c
Phoeniculus damarensis	Violet Wood-Hoopoe	8	c
Phoeniculus granti[2]	Grant's Wood-Hoopoe	8	c
Phoeniculus minor	Abyssinian Scimitar-Bill	8	c
Phoeniculus purpureus	Green Wood-Hoopoe	8	c

BUCEROTIDAE · HORNBILLS   44 species recorded

Scientific Name	Common Name	Source Codes	Region Codes
Tockus alboterminatus	Crowned Hornbill	8	c
Tockus birostris	Common Gray Hornbill	15	f
Tockus bradfieldi	Bradfield's Hornbill	8	c
Tockus camurus	Red-billed Dwarf-Hornbill	8	c
Tockus deckeni	Von der Decken's Hornbill	8	c
Tockus erythrorhynchus	Red-billed Hornbill	8	c
Tockus fasciatus	Pied Hornbill	8	c
Tockus flavirostris	Yellow-billed Hornbill	8	c
Tockus griseus	Malabar Gray Hornbill	15	f
Tockus hartlaubi	Black Dwarf-Hornbill	8	c
Tockus hemprichii	Hemprich's Hornbill	8	c
Tockus monteiri	Monteiro's Hornbill	8	c
Tockus nasutus	African Gray Hornbill	8	c
Tockus pallidirostris	Pale-billed Hornbill	8	c
Berenicornis albocristatus[1]	African White-crested Hornbill	8	c
Berenicornis comatus	Asiatic White-crested Hornbill	18 19 21 55	g h
Ptilolaemus tickelli	White-throated Brown Hornbill	15 18 55	f g
Anorrhinus galeritus	Bushy-crested Hornbill	18 19 21 55	g h
Penelopides exarhatus	Temminck's Hornbill	29	h
Penelopides panini	Rufous-tailed Hornbill	22	h
Aceros cassidix[2]	Celebes Hornbill	28 29	h
Aceros everetti	Everett's Hornbill	32	j
Aceros leucocephalus[3]	Wrinkled Hornbill	19 21 22 55	g h
Aceros nipalensis	Rufous-necked Hornbill	15 18 55	f g
Aceros plicatus	Blyth's Hornbill	18 19 35 38 55	g h j k
Aceros undulatus[4]	Wreathed Hornbill	15 18 19 21 55	f g h
Anthracoceros coronatus	Malabar Pied Hornbill	15 18 21 55	f g h
Anthracoceros malabaricus	Indian Pied Hornbill	15 16 19	f h
Anthracoceros malayanus	Black Hornbill	19 21 55	g h
Anthracoceros marchei[5]	Palawan Hornbill	22	h
Anthracoceros montani	Sulu Hornbill	22	h
Bycanistes brevis	Silvery-cheeked Hornbill	8	c
Bycanistes bucinator	Trumpeter Hornbill	8	c
Bycanistes cylindricus	Brown-cheeked Hornbill	8	c
Bycanistes fistulator	Piping Hornbill	8	c
Bycanistes subcylindricus	Black-and-White Casqued Hornbill	8	c
Ceratogymna atrata	Black-casqued Hornbill	8	c
Ceratogymna elata	Yellow-casqued Hornbill	8	c
Buceros bicornis	Great Pied Hornbill	15 16 18 19	f g h
Buceros hydrocorax	Rufous Hornbill	22	h

Scientific Name	Common Name	Source Codes	Region Codes
BUCEROTIDAE · HORNBILLS *contd.*			
Buceros rhinoceros	Rhinoceros Hornbill	19 21 55	g h
Rhinoplax vigil	Helmeted Hornbill	18 19 21 55	g h
Bucorvus abyssinicus	Abyssinian Ground Hornbill	8	c
Bucorvus cafer	Southern Ground Hornbill	8	c

GALBULIDAE · JACAMARS 15 species recorded

Scientific Name	Common Name	Source Codes	Region Codes
Galbalcyrhynchus leucotis	Chestnut Jacamar	6	d
Brachygalba albogularis	White-throated Jacamar	6	d
Brachygalba goeringi	Pale-headed Jacamar	6	d
Brachygalba lugubris	Brown Jacamar	6	d
Brachygalba salmoni	Dusky-backed Jacamar	4 6	d e
Jacamaralcyon tridactyla	Three-toed Jacamar	6	d
Galbula albirostris	Yellow-billed Jacamar	6	d
Galbula cyanescens	Bluish-fronted Jacamar	6	d
Galbula dea	Paradise Jacamar	6	d
Galbula galbula	Green-tailed Jacamar	6	d
Galbula leucogastra	Bronzy Jacamar	6	d
Galbula pastazae	Coppery-chested Jacamar	6	d
Galbula ruficauda	Rufous-tailed Jacamar	4 6	d e
Galbula tombacea	White-chinned Jacamar	6	d
Jacamerops aurea	Great Jacamar	4 6	d e

BUCCONIDAE · PUFFBIRDS 32 species recorded

Scientific Name	Common Name	Source Codes	Region Codes
Notharchus macrorhynchus	White-necked Puffbird	4 6	d e
Notharchus ordii	Brown-banded Puffbird	6	d
Notharchus pectoralis	Black-breasted Puffbird	4 6	d e
Notharchus tectus	Pied Puffbird	4 6	d e
Bucco capensis	Collared Puffbird	6	d
Bucco macrodactylus	Chestnut-capped Puffbird	6	d
Bucco noanamae	Sooty-capped Puffbird	6	d
Bucco tamatia	Spotted Puffbird	6	d
Nystalus chacuru	White-eared Puffbird	6	d
Nystalus maculatus	Spot-backed Puffbird	6	d
Nystalus radiatus	Barred Puffbird	4 6	d e
Nystalus striolatus	Striolated Puffbird	6	d
Hypnelus ruficollis	Russet-throated Puffbird	6	d
Malacoptila fulvogularis	Black-streaked Puffbird	6	d
Malacoptila fusca	White-chested Puffbird	6	d
Malacoptila mystacalis	Moustached Puffbird	6	d
Malacoptila panamensis	White-whiskered Puffbird	4 6	d e
Malacoptila rufa	Rufous-necked Puffbird	6	d
Malacoptila semicincta	Semicollared Puffbird	6	d
Malacoptila striata	Crescent-chested Puffbird	6	d
Micromonacha lanceolata	Lanceolated Monklet	4 6	d e
Nonnula amaurocephala	Chestnut-headed Nunlet	6	d
Nonnula brunnea	Brown Nunlet	6	d
Nonnula rubecula	Rusty-breasted Nunlet	6	d
Nonnula ruficapilla[1]	Gray-cheeked Nunlet	4 6	d e
Nonnula sclateri	Fulvous-chinned Nunlet	6	d
Hapaloptila castanea	White-faced Nunbird	6	d
Monasa atra	Black Nunbird	6	d

Scientific Name	Common Name	Source Codes	Region Codes

BUCCONIDAE · PUFFBIRDS contd.

Scientific Name	Common Name	Source Codes	Region Codes
Monasa flavirostris	Yellow-billed Nunbird	6	d
Monasa morphoeus	White-fronted Nunbird	4 6	d e
Monasa nigrifrons	Black-fronted Nunbird	6	d
Chelidoptera tenebrosa	Swallow-Wing	6	d

CAPITONIDAE · BARBETS   78 species recorded

Scientific Name	Common Name	Source Codes	Region Codes
Capito aurovirens	Scarlet-crowned Barbet	6	d
Capito dayi	Black-girdled Barbet	6	d
Capito hypoleucus	White-mantled Barbet	6	d
Capito maculicoronatus	Spot-crowned Barbet	4 6	d e
Capito niger	Black-spotted Barbet	6	d
Capito quinticolor	Five-colored Barbet	6	d
Capito squamatus	Orange-fronted Barbet	6	d
Eubucco bourcierii	Red-headed Barbet	4 6	d e
Eubucco richardsoni	Lemon-throated Barbet	6	d
Eubucco tucinkae	Scarlet-hooded Barbet	6	d
Eubucco versicolor	Versicolored Barbet	6	d
Semnornis frantzii	Prong-billed Barbet	4	e
Semnornis ramphastinus	Toucan Barbet	6	d
Psilopogon pyrolophus	Fire-tufted Barbet	19	h
Megalaima armillaris	Blue-crowned Barbet	19	h
Megalaima asiatica	Blue-throated Barbet	15 16 18 55	f g h
Megalaima australis	Blue-eared Barbet	15 18 19 21 55	f g h
Megalaima chrysopogon	Gold-whiskered Barbet	19 21 55	g h
Megalaima corvina	Brown-throated Barbet	19	h
Megalaima exima	Black-throated Barbet	21	h
Megalaima faiostricta	Green-eared Barbet	16 55	g
Megalaima flavifrons	Yellow-fronted Barbet	15	f
Megalaima franklinii	Golden-throated Barbet	15 16 18 19 55	f g h
Megalaima haemacephala	Crimson-breasted Barbet	15 16 18 19 22 55	f g h
Megalaima henrici	Yellow-crowned Barbet	19 21 55	g h
Megalaima incognita	Hume's Blue-throated Barbet	18 55	g
Megalaima juvensis	Black-banded Barbet	19	h
Megalaima lagrandieri	Red-vented Barbet	55	g
Megalaima lineata	Lineated Barbet	15 55	f g
Megalaima monticola	Mountain Barbet	19 21	h
Megalaima mystacophanes	Gaudy Barbet	18 19 21 55	g h
Megalaima oorti	Muller's Barbet	16 19 55	g h
Megalaima pulcherrima	Golden-naped Barbet	19 21	h
Megalaima rafflesi	Many-colored Barbet	18 19 21 55	g h
Megalaima rubricapilla	Crimson-throated Barbet	15	f
Megalaima virens	Great Barbet	15 16 18 55	f g
Megalaima viridis	Small Green Barbet	15	f
Megalaima zeylanica	Oriental Green Barbet	15 18 19 55	f g h
Calorhamphus fuliginosus	Brown Barbet	18 19 21 55	g h
Gymnobucco bonapartei	Gray-throated Barbet	8	c
Gymnobucco calvus	Naked-faced Barbet	8	c
Gymnobucco peli	Bristle-nosed Barbet	8	c
Buccanodon anchietae	Yellow-headed Barbet	8	c
Buccanodon duchaillui	Yellow-spotted Barbet	8	c
Buccanodon leucotis	White-eared Barbet	8	c
Buccanodon olivaceum	Green Barbet	8	c
Buccanodon whytii	Whyte's Barbet	8	c
Pogoniulus atroflavus	Red-rumped Tinkerbird	8	c

Scientific Name	Common Name	Source Codes	Region Codes

CAPITONIDAE · BARBETS contd.

Scientific Name	Common Name	Source Codes	Region Codes
Pogoniulus bilineatus	Golden-rumped Tinkerbird	8	c
Pogoniulus chrysoconus	Yellow-fronted Tinkerbird	8	c
Pogoniulus coryphaeus	Western Green Tinkerbird	8	c
Pogoniulus leucomystax	Moustached Green Tinkerbird	8	c
Pogoniulus makawai	Black-chinned Tinkerbird	49	c
Pogoniulus pusillus	Red-fronted Tinkerbird	8	c
Pogoniulus scolopaceus	Speckled Tinkerbird	8	c
Pogoniulus simplex	Green Tinkerbird	8	c
Pogoniulus subsulphureus	Yellow-throated Tinkerbird	8	c
Lybius bidentatus[1]	Double-toothed Barbet	8	c
Lybius diadematum	Red-fronted Barbet	47	e
Lybius dubius	Bearded Barbet	8	c
Lybius guifsobalito	Black-billed Barbet	8	c
Lybius hirsutus	Hairy-breasted Barbet	8	c
Lybius lacrymosus	Spotted-flanked Barbet	8	c
Lybius leucocephalus[2]	White-headed Barbet	8	c
Lybius leucomelas	Pied Barbet	8	c
Lybius melanocephalus	African Black-throated Barbet	8	c
Lybius melanopterus	Brown-breasted Barbet	8	c
Lybius minor	Black-backed Barbet	8	c
Lybius rolleti	Black-breasted Barbet	8	c
Lybius rubrifacies	Red-faced Barbet	8	c
Lybius torquatus	Black-collared Barbet	8	c
Lybius undatus	Banded Barbet	8	c
Lybius vieilloti	Vieillot's Barbet	8	c
Trachyphonus darnaudii	D'Arnaud's Barbet	8	c
Trachyphonus erythrocephalus	Red-and-Yellow Barbet	8	c
Trachyphonus margaritatus	Yellow-breasted Barbet	8	c
Trachyphonus purpuratus	Yellow-billed Barbet	8	c
Trachyphonus vaillantii	Levaillant's Barbet	8	c

INDICATORIDAE · HONEYGUIDES 14 species recorded

Scientific Name	Common Name	Source Codes	Region Codes
Prodotiscus insignis	Cassin's Honeybird	8	c
Prodotiscus regulus	Wahlberg's Honeybird	8	c
Melignomon zenkeri	Zenker's Honeyguide	8	c
Indicator archipelagicus	Malay Honeyguide	19 21 55	g h
Indicator exilis	Least Honeyguide	8	c
Indicator indicator	Black-throated Honeyguide	8	c
Indicator maculatus	Spotted Honeyguide	8	c
Indicator meliphilus	Eastern Least Honeyguide	8	c
Indicator minor[1]	Lesser Honeyguide	8	c
Indicator pumilio	Pygmy Honeyguide	8	c
Indicator variegatus	Scaly-throated Honeyguide	8	c
Indicator willcocksi	Willcocks's Honeyguide	8	c
Indicator xanthonotus	Indian Honeyguide	15 18	f g
Melichneutes robustus	Lyre-tailed Honeyguide	8	c

RAMPHASTIDAE · TOUCANS 38 species recorded

Scientific Name	Common Name	Source Codes	Region Codes
Aulacorhynchus calorhynchus	Yellow-billed Toucanet	6	d
Aulacorhynchus coeruleicinctis	Blue-banded Toucanet	6	d
Aulacorhynchus derbianus	Chestnut-tipped Toucanet	6	d
Aulacorhynchus haematopygus	Crimson-rumped Toucanet	6	d

Scientific Name	Common Name	Source Codes	Region Codes

RAMPHASTIDAE · TOUCANS contd.

Scientific Name	Common Name	Source Codes	Region Codes
Aulacorhynchus huallagae	Yellow-browed Toucanet	6	d
Aulacorhynchus prasinus[1]	Emerald Toucanet	4 6	d e
Aulacorhynchus sulcatus	Groove-billed Toucanet	6	d
Pteroglossus aracari	Black-necked Aracari	6	d
Pteroglossus beauharnaesii	Curl-crested Aracari	6	d
Pteroglossus bitorquatus	Red-necked Aracari	6	d
Pteroglossus castanotis	Chestnut-eared Aracari	6	d
Pteroglossus erythropygius	Pale-mandibled Aracari	6	d
Pteroglossus flavirostris	Ivory-billed Aracari	6	d
Pteroglossus mariae	Brown-mandibled Aracari	6	d
Pteroglossus pluricinctus	Many-banded Aracari	6	d
Pteroglossus sanguineus	Stripe-billed Aracari	6	d
Pteroglossus torquatus[2]	Collared Aracari	4 6	d e
Pteroglossus viridis[3]	Green Aracari	6	d
Selenidera culik	Guianan Toucanet	6	d
Selenidera maculirostris	Spot-billed Toucanet	6	d
Selenidera nattereri	Tawny-tufted Toucanet	6	d
Selenidera reinwardtii	Golden-collared Toucanet	6	d
Selenidera spectabilis	Yellow-eared Toucanet	4 6	d e
Andigena bailloni[4]	Saffron Toucanet	6	d
Andigena cucullata	Hooded Mountain-Toucan	6	d
Andigena hypoglauca	Gray-breasted Mountain-Toucan	6	d
Andigena laminirostris	Plate-billed Mountain-Toucan	6	d
Andigena nigrirostris	Black-billed Mountain-Toucan	6	d
Ramphastos ambiguus[5]	Black-mandibled Toucan	4 6	d e
Ramphastos aurantiirostris	Orange-billed Toucan	6	d
Ramphastos citreolaemus	Citron-throated Toucan	6	d
Ramphastos culminatus[6]	Yellow-ridged Toucan	6	d
Ramphastos cuvieri	Cuvier's Toucan	6	d
Ramphastos dicolorus	Red-breasted Toucan	6	d
Ramphastos sulfuratus	Keel-billed Toucan	4 6	d e
Ramphastos swainsonii	Chestnut-mandibled Toucan	4 6	d e
Ramphastos toco	Toco Toucan	6	d
Ramphastos vitellinus	Channel-billed Toucan	6	d

PICIDAE · WOODPECKERS, PICULETS 206 species recorded

Scientific Name	Common Name	Source Codes	Region Codes
Jynx ruficollis	Red-breasted Wryneck	8	c
Jynx torquilla	Wryneck	2 3 8 15 16 18 55	a b c f g
Picumnus aurifrons	Gold-fronted Piculet	6	d
Picumnus borbae	Bar-breasted Piculet	6	d
Picumnus castelnau	Plain-breasted Piculet	6	d
Picumnus cinnamomeus	Chestnut Piculet	6	d
Picumnus cirratus	White-barred Piculet	6	d
Picumnus dorbygnianus	Ocellated Piculet	6	d
Picumnus exilis	Golden-spangled Piculet	6	d
Picumnus granadensis	Grayish Piculet	6	d
Picumnus innominatus	Speckled Piculet	2 15 16 18 19 21 55	b f g h
Picumnus limae	Ochraceous Piculet	6	d
Picumnus minutissimus[1]	Arrowhead Piculet	6	d
Picumnus nebulosus	Mottled Piculet	6	d
Picumnus nigropunctatus	Black-dotted Piculet	6	d

Scientific Name	Common Name	Source Codes	Region Codes
PICIDAE · WOODPECKERS, PICULETS contd.			
Picumnus olivaceus	Olivaceous Piculet	4 6	d e
Picumnus pumilus	Orinoco Piculet	6	d
Picumnus pygmaeus	Spotted Piculet	6	d
Picumnus rufiventris	Rufous-breasted Piculet	6	d
Picumnus sclateri	Ecuadorean Piculet	6	d
Picumnus spilogaster[2]	White-bellied Piculet	6	d
Picumnus squamulatus	Scaled Piculet	6	d
Picumnus steindachneri	Speckle-chested Piculet	6	d
Picumnus temminckii	Ochre-collared Piculet	6	d
Picumnus varzeae	Varzea Piculet	6	d
Nesoctites micromegas	Antillean Piculet	5	e
Verreauxia africana	African Piculet	8	c
Sasia abnormis	Rufous Piculet	18 19 21 55	g h
Sasia ochracea	White-browed Rufous Piculet	15 16 18 55	f g
Geocolaptes olivaceus	Ground Woodpecker	8	c
Colaptes auratus[3]	Common Flicker	3 5	a e
Colaptes campestris	Campo Flicker	6	d
Colaptes campestroides	Field Flicker	6	d
Colaptes fernandinae[4]	Fernandina's Flicker	5	e
Colaptes pitius	Chilean Flicker	6	d
Colaptes rupicola	Andean Flicker	6	d
Chrysoptilus atricollis	Black-necked Woodpecker	6	d
Chrysoptilus melanochloros	Green-barred Woodpecker	6	d
Chrysoptilus melanolaimus	Golden-breasted Woodpecker	6	d
Chrysoptilus punctigula	Spot-breasted Woodpecker	4 6	d e
Piculus aeruginosus	Bronze-winged Woodpecker	4	e
Piculus auricularis	Gray-crowned Woodpecker	4	e
Piculus aurulentus	White-browed Woodpecker	6	d
Piculus chrysochloros	Golden-green Woodpecker	4 6	d e
Piculus flavigula	Yellow-throated Woodpecker	6	d
Piculus leucolaemus	White-throated Woodpecker	6	d
Piculus rivolii	Crimson-mantled Woodpecker	6	d
Piculus rubiginosus	Golden-Olive Woodpecker	4 6	d e
Piculus simplex[5]	Rufous-winged Woodpecker	4	e
Campethera abingoni	Golden-tailed Woodpecker	8	c
Campethera bennettii	Bennett's Woodpecker	8	c
Campethera cailliautii	Little Spotted Woodpecker	8	c
Campethera caroli	Brown-eared Woodpecker	8	c
Campethera maculosa	Western Golden-backed Woodpecker	8	c
Campethera nivosa	Buff-spotted Woodpecker	8	c
Campethera notata	Knysna Woodpecker	8	c
Campethera nubica	Nubian Woodpecker	8	c
Campethera punctuligera	Fine-spotted Woodpecker	8	c
Campethera tullbergi	Tullberg's Woodpecker	8	c
Celeus castaneus	Chestnut-colored Woodpecker	4	e
Celeus elegans	Chestnut Woodpecker	6	d
Celeus flavescens	Blond-crested Woodpecker	6	d
Celeus flavus	Cream-colored Woodpecker	6	d
Celeus grammicus	Scale-breasted Woodpecker	6	d
Celeus loricatus	Cinnamon Woodpecker	4 6	d e
Celeus lugubris	Pale-crested Woodpecker	6	d
Celeus spectabilis	Rufous-headed Woodpecker	6	d
Celeus torquatus	Ringed Woodpecker	6	d
Celeus undatus	Waved Woodpecker	6	d
Micropternus brachyurus	Rufous Woodpecker	15 16 18 19 21 55	f g h
Picus awokera	Japanese Green Woodpecker	2	b

Scientific Name	Common Name	Source Codes	Region Codes
PICIDAE WOODPECKERS, PICULETS contd.			
Picus canus	Gray-headed Woodpecker	2 15 16 18 19 55	b f g h
Picus chlorolophus	Lesser Yellow-naped Woodpecker	15 16 18 19 55	f g h
Picus erythropygius	Red-rumped Green Woodpecker	18 55	g
Picus flavinucha	Greater Yellow-naped Woodpecker	15 16 18 19 55	f g h
Picus mentalis	Checker-throated Woodpecker	18 19 55	g h
Picus miniaceus	Banded Red Woodpecker	18 19 21 55	g h
Picus myrmecophoneus	Little Scaly-bellied Woodpecker	55	g
Picus puniceus	Crimson-winged Woodpecker	18 19 21 55	g h
Picus rabieri	Red-collared Woodpecker	55	g
Picus squamatus	Scaly-bellied Green Woodpecker	2 15	b f
Picus viridanus	Burmese Scaly-bellied Woodpecker	18 55	g h
Picus viridis	Green Woodpecker	2 15 18 55	b f g
Picus vittatus[6]	Laced Green Woodpecker	15 16 18 19 55	f g h
Dinopium benghalense	Lesser Golden-backed Woodpecker	15 18	f g
Dinopium javanense	Golden-backed Three-toed Woodpecker	15 16 18 19 21 55	f g h
Dinopium rafflesi	Olive-backed Three-toed Woodpecker	18 19 21 55	g h
Dinopium shorii	Himalayan Three-toed Woodpecker	15 18	f g
Geniculus viridis	Bamboo Woodpecker	55	h
Geniculus grantia	Pale-headed Woodpecker	15 16 18 19 55	f g h
Meiglyptes jugularis	Black-and-Buff Woodpecker	18 55	g
Meiglyptes tristis	Fulvous-rumped Barred Woodpecker	18 19 21 55	g h
Meiglyptes tukki	Buff-necked Barred Woodpecker	18 19 21 55	g h
Mulleripicus funebris	Sooty Woodpecker	22	h
Mulleripicus pulverulentus	Great Slaty Woodpecker	15 18 19 21 55	f g h
Mulleripicus fulvus[7]	Fulvous Woodpecker	29	h
Dryocopus galeatus	Helmeted Woodpecker	6	d
Dryocopus javensis	White-bellied Black Woodpecker	2 15 16 18 19 21 22 55	b f g h
Dryocopus lineatus	Lineated Woodpecker	4 6	d e
Dryocopus martius	Black Woodpecker	2 16	b g
Dryocopus pileatus	Pileated Woodpecker	3	a
Dryocopus schulzi	Black-bodied Woodpecker	6	d
Phloeoceastes gayaquilensis	Guayaquil Woodpecker	6	d
Phloeoceastes guatemalensis	Pale-bellied Woodpecker	4	e
Phloeoceastes haematogaster	Crimson-bellied Woodpecker	4 6	d e
Phloeoceastes leucopogon	Cream-backed Woodpecker	6	d
Phloeoceastes melanoleucos	Crimson-crested Woodpecker	4 6	d e
Phloeoceastes pollens	Powerful Woodpecker	6	d
Phloeoceastes robustus	Robust Woodpecker	6	d
Phloeoceastes rubricollis	Red-necked Woodpecker	6	d
Leuconerpes candidus	White Woodpecker	6	d
Melanerpes aurifrons[8, 9]	Golden-fronted Woodpecker	3 4	a e
Melanerpes carolinus	Red-bellied Woodpecker	3	a
Melanerpes chrusauchen	Golden-naped Woodpecker	4 6	d e
Melanerpes chrysogenys	Golden-cheeked Woodpecker	4	e

Scientific Name	Common Name	Source Codes	Region Codes
PICIDAE · WOODPECKERS, PICULETS *contd.*			
Melanerpes cruentatus	Yellow-Tufted Woodpecker	6	d
Melanerpes erythrocephalus	Red-headed Woodpecker	3	a
Melanerpes flavifrons	Yellow-fronted Woodpecker	6	d
Melanerpes formicivorus	Acorn Woodpecker	3 4 6	a d e
Melanerpes herminieri	Guadeloupe Woodpecker	5	e
Melanerpes hypopolius	Gray-breasted Woodpecker	4	e
Melanerpes lewis[10]	Lewis's Woodpecker	3 4	a e
Melanerpes portoricensis	Puerto Rican Woodpecker	5	e
Melanerpes pucherani	Black-cheeked Woodpecker	4 6	d e
Melanerpes radiolatus	Jamaican Woodpecker	5	e
Melanerpes rubricapillus[11]	Red-crowned Woodpecker	4 6	d e
Melanerpes rubricomus	Red-vented Woodpecker	4	e
Melanerpes rubrifrons	Red-fronted Woodpecker	6	d
Melanerpes striatus	Hispaniolan Woodpecker	5	e
Melanerpes superciliaris	West Indian Red-bellied Woodpecker	5	e
Sphyrapicus nuchalis[12]	Red-naped Sapsucker	56	a
Sphyrapicus ruber[12]	Red-breasted Sapsucker	56	a
Sphyrapicus thyroideus	Williamson's Sapsucker	3 4	a e
Sphyrapicus varius	Yellow-bellied Sapsucker	3 4 5 6	a d e
Trichopicus cactorum	White-fronted Woodpecker	6	d
Veniliornis affinis	Red-stained Woodpecker	6	d
Veniliornis callonotus	Scarlet-backed Woodpecker	6	d
Veniliornis cassini	Golden-collared Woodpecker	6	d
Veniliornis dignus	Yellow-fronted Woodpecker	6	d
Veniliornis frontalis	Dot-fronted Woodpecker	6	d
Veniliornis fumigatus	Smoky-brown Woodpecker	4 6	d e
Veniliornis kirkii	Red-rumped Woodpecker	4 6	d e
Veniliornis maculifrons	Yellow-eared Woodpecker	6	d
Veniliornis nigriceps	Bar-bellied Woodpecker	6	d
Veniliornis passerinus	Little Woodpecker	6	d
Veniliornis sanguineus	Blood-colored Woodpecker	6	d
Veniliornis spilogaster	White-spotted Woodpecker	6	d
Dendropicos abyssinicus	Golden-backed Woodpecker	8	c
Dendropicos elachus	Little Gray Woodpecker	8	c
Dendropicos fuscescens	Cardinal Woodpecker	8	c
Dendropicos gabonensis	Gabon Woodpecker	8	c
Dendropicos poecilolaemus	Uganda Spotted Woodpecker	8	c
Dendropicos stierlingi	Stierling's Woodpecker	8	c
Picoides albolarvatus[13]	White-headed Woodpecker	3	a
Picoides arcticus	Black-backed Three-toed Woodpecker	3	a
Picoides assimilis	Sind Pied Woodpecker	2 15	b f
Picoides atratus	Stripe-breasted Pied Woodpecker	15 16 18 55	f g
Picoides auriceps	Brown-fronted Pied Woodpecker	2 15	b f
Picoides borealis	Red-cockaded Woodpecker	3	a
Picoides canicapillus	Gray-headed Pygmy Woodpecker	2 15 16 19 21 55	b f g h
Picoides cathpharius	Lesser Pied Woodpecker	2 15 16 18 55	b f g
Picoides darjeelensis	Darjeeling Pied Woodpecker	2 15 16 18 55	b f g
Picoides dorae	Arabian Woodpecker	2 8	b c
Picoides hardwickei	Pygmy Pied Woodpecker	18	h
Picoides himalayensis	Himalayan Pied Woodpecker	2 15	b f
Picoides hyperythrus[14]	Rufous-bellied Pied Woodpecker	2 15 16 18 55	b f g

Scientific Name	Common Name	Source Codes	Region Codes

PICIDAE · WOODPECKERS, PICULETS *contd.*

Scientific Name	Common Name	Source Codes	Region Codes
Picoides kizuki	Japanese Pygmy Woodpecker	2 16	b g
Picoides leucopterus	White-winged Spotted Woodpecker	2 16	b g
Picoides leucotos	White-backed Woodpecker	2 16	b g
Picoides lignarius	Striped Woodpecker	6	d
Picoides macei	Fulvous-breasted Pied Woodpecker	15 18 19 55	f g h
Picoides maculatus	Philippine Pygmy Woodpecker	22	h
Picoides mahrattensis	Yellow-fronted Pied Woodpecker	15 18 55	f g
Picoides major	Great Spotted Woodpecker	2 15 16 18 55	b f g
Picoides medius	Middle Spotted Woodpecker	2	b
Picoides minor	Lesser Spotted Woodpecker	2 16	b g
Picoides mixtus	Checkered Woodpecker	6	d
Picoides moluccensis	Brown-capped Pied Woodpecker	19 21 55	g h
Picoides nanus	Pygmy Woodpecker	15	f
Picoides nuttallii	Nuttall's Woodpecker	3 4	a e
Picoides obsoletus	Brown-backed Woodpecker	8	c
Picoides pubescens	Downy Woodpecker	3	a
Picoides scalaris	Ladder-backed Woodpecker	3 4	a e
Picoides stricklandi[15]	Brown-backed Woodpecker	3 4	a e
Picoides syriacus	Syrian Woodpecker	2	b
Picoides tridactylus	Three-toed Woodpecker	2 3 15 16	a b f g
Picoides villosus	Hairy Woodpecker	3 4 5	a e
Sapheopico noguchii	Pryer's Woodpecker	2 53	b
Xiphidiopicus percussus	Cuban Green Woodpecker	5	e
Mesopicos elliotii	Elliot's Woodpecker	8	c
Mesopicos goertae	Gray Woodpecker	8	c
Mesopicos griseocephalus	African Gray-headed Woodpecker	8	c
Mesopicos pyrrhogaster	Fire-bellied Woodpecker	8	c
Mesopicos xantholophus	Yellow-crested Woodpecker	8	c
Thripias namaquus	Bearded Woodpecker	8	c
Hemicircus canente	Heart-spotted Woodpecker	15 18 55	f g
Hemicircus concretus	Malaysian Gray-breasted Woodpecker	18 19 21 55	g h
Blythipicus pyrrhotis	Bay Woodpecker	15 16 18 19 55	f g h
Blythipicus rubiginosus	Lesser Bay Woodpecker	18 19 21 55	g h
Chrysocolaptes festivus	Black-backed Woodpecker	15	f
Chrysocolaptes lucidus	Crimson-backed Woodpecker	15 16 18 19 21 22 55	f g h
Chrysocolaptes validus	Orange-backed Woodpecker	19 21 55	g h
Campephilus imperialis	Imperial Woodpecker	4 53	e
Campephilus magellanicus	Magellanic Woodpecker	6	d
Campephilus principalis	Ivory-billed Woodpecker	3 5 53	a e

EURYLAIMIDAE · BROADBILLS 14 species recorded

Scientific Name	Common Name	Source Codes	Region Codes
Smithornis capensis	Delacour's Broadbill	8	c
Smithornis rufolateralis	Rufous-sided Broadbill	8	c
Smithornis sharpei	Gray-headed Broadbill	8	c
Pseudocalyptomena graueri	Green Broadbill	8	c

Scientific Name	Common Name	Source Codes	Region Codes

EURYLAIMIDAE · BROADBILLS contd.

Scientific Name	Common Name	Source Codes	Region Codes
Corydon sumatranus	Dusky Broadbill	18 19 21 55	g h
Cymbirhynchus macrorhynchus	Black-and-Red Broadbill	18 19 21 55	g h
Eurylaimus javanicus	Banded Broadbill	18 19 21 55	g h
Eurylaimus ochromalus	Black-and-Yellow Broadbill	18 19 21 55	g h
Eurylaimus steerii	Wattled Broadbill	22	h
Serilophus lunatus[1]	Silver-breasted Broadbill	15 17 18 19 55	f g h
Psarisomus dalhousiae	Long-tailed Broadbill	15 17 18 19 21 55	f g h
Calyptomena hosei	Magnificent Green Broadbill	19 21	h
Calyptomena viridis	Lesser Green Broadbill	18 19 21 55	g h
Calyptomena whiteheadi	Black-throated Green Broadbill	19 21	h

DENDROCOLAPTIDAE · WOODCREEPERS 50 species recorded

Scientific Name	Common Name	Source Codes	Region Codes
Dendrocincla anabatina	Tawny-winged Woodcreeper	4	e
Dendrocincla fuliginosa	Plain-Brown Woodcreeper	4 6	d e
Dendrocincla homochroa	Ruddy Woodcreeper	4 6	d e
Dendrocincla merula	White-chinned Woodcreeper	6	d
Dendrocincla tyrannina	Tyrannine Woodcreeper	6	d
Deconychura longicauda	Long-tailed Woodcreeper	4 6	d e
Deconychura stictolaema	Spot-throated Woodcreeper	6	d
Sittasomus griseicapillus	Olivaceous Woodcreeper	4 6	d e
Glyphorynchus spirurus	Wedge-billed Woodcreeper	4 6	d e
Drymornis bridgesii	Scimitar-billed Woodcreeper	6	d
Nasica longirostris	Long-billed Woodcreeper	6	d
Dendrexetastes rufigula	Cinnamon-throated Woodcreeper	6	d
Hylexetastes perrotii	Red-billed Woodcreeper	6	d
Hylexetastes stresemanni	Bar-bellied Woodcreeper	6	d
Xiphocolaptes albicollis	White-throated Woodcreeper	6	d
Xiphocolaptes falcirostris	Moustached Woodcreeper	6	d
Xiphocolaptes franciscanus	Snethlage's Woodcreeper	6	d
Xiphocolaptes major	Great Rufous Woodcreeper	6	d
Xiphocolaptes promeropirhynchus	Strong-billed Woodcreeper	4 6	d e
Dendrocolaptes certhia	Barred Woodcreeper	4 6	d e
Dendrocolaptes concolor	Concolor Woodcreeper	6	d
Dendrocolaptes hoffmannsi	Hoffmann's Woodcreeper	6	d
Dendrocolaptes picumnus	Black-banded Woodcreeper	4 6	d e
Dendrocolaptes platyrostris	Planalto Woodcreeper	6	d
Xiphorhynchus elegans	Elegant Woodcreeper	6	d
Xiphorhynchus erythropygius	Spotted Woodcreeper	4 6	d e
Xiphorhynchus eytoni	Dusky-billed Woodcreeper	6	d
Xiphorhynchus flavigaster	Ivory-billed Woodcreeper	4	e
Xiphorhynchus guttatus	Buff-throated Woodcreeper	4 6	d e
Xiphorhynchus lachrymosus	Black-striped Woodcreeper	4 6	d e
Xiphorhynchus necopinus	Zimmer's Woodcreeper	6	d
Xiphorhynchus obsoletus	Striped Woodcreeper	6	d
Xiphorhynchus ocellatus	Ocellated Woodcreeper	6	d
Xiphorhynchus pardalotus	Chestnut-rumped Woodcreeper	6	d
Xiphorhynchus picus	Straight-billed Woodcreeper	4 6	d e
Xiphorhynchus spixii	Spix's Woodcreeper	6	d
Xiphorhynchus striatigularis	Stripe-throated Woodcreeper	4	e
Xiphorhynchus triangularis	Olive-backed Woodcreeper	6	d

Scientific Name	Common Name	Source Codes	Region Codes

DENDROCOLAPTIDAE · WOODCREEPERS *contd.*

Scientific Name	Common Name	Source Codes	Region Codes
Lepidocolaptes affinis	Spot-crowned Woodcreeper	4 6	d e
Lepidocolaptes albolineatus	Lineated Woodcreeper	6	d
Lepidocolaptes angustirostris	Narrow-billed Woodcreeper	6	d
Lepidocolaptes fuscus	Lesser Woodcreeper	6	d
Lepidocolaptes leucogaster	White-striped Woodcreeper	4	e
Lepidocolaptes souleyetii	Streak-headed Woodcreeper	4 6	d e
Lepidocolaptes squamatus	Scaled Woodcreeper	6	d
Campylorhamphus falcularius	Black-billed Scythebill	6	d
Campylorhamphus procurvoides	Curve-billed Scythebill	6	d
Campylorhamphus pucheranii	Greater Scythebill	6	d
Campylorhamphus pusillus	Brown-billed Scythebill	4 6	d e
Campylorhamphus trochilirostris	Red-billed Scythebill	4 6	d e

FURNARIIDAE · OVENBIRDS 217 species recorded

Scientific Name	Common Name	Source Codes	Region Codes
Geobates poecilopterus	Campo Miner	6	d
Geositta antarctica	Short-billed Miner	6	d
Geositta crassirostris	Thick-billed Miner	6	d
Geositta cunicularia	Common Miner	6	d
Geositta isabellina	Creamy-rumped Miner	6	d
Geositta maritima	Grayish Miner	6	d
Geositta peruviana	Coastal Miner	6	d
Geositta punensis	Puna Miner	6	d
Geositta rufipennis	Rufous-banded Miner	6	d
Geositta saxicolina	Dark-winged Miner	6	d
Geositta tenuirostris	Slender-billed Miner	6	d
Upucerthia andaecola	Rock Earthcreeper	6	d
Upucerthia certhioides	Chaco Earthcreeper	6	d
Upucerthia dumetaria	Scale-throated Earthcreeper	6	d
Upucerthia harterti	Bolivian Earthcreeper	6	d
Upucerthia jelskii	Plain-breasted Earthcreeper	6	d
Upucerthia ruficauda	Straight-billed Earthcreeper	6	d
Upucerthia serrana	Striated Earthcreeper	6	d
Upucerthia validirostris	Buff-breasted Earthcreeper	6	d
Upucerthia albigula	White-throated Earthcreeper	6	d
Eremobius phoenicurus	Band-tailed Earthcreeper	6	d
Chilia melanura	Crag Chilia	6	d
Cinclodes antarcticus	Blackish Cinclodes	6	d
Cinclodes atacamensis	White-winged Cinclodes	6	d
Cinclodes excelsior	Stout-billed Cinclodes	6	d
Cinclodes fuscus	Bar-winged Cinclodes	6	d
Cinclodes nigrofumosus	Seaside Cinclodes	6	d
Cinclodes oustaleti	Gray-flanked Cinclodes	6	d
Cinclodes pabsti	Long-tailed Cinclodes	6	d
Cinclodes palliatus	White-bellied Cinclodes	6	d
Cinclodes patagonicus	Dark-bellied Cinclodes	6	d
Clibanornis dendrocolaptoides	Canebrake Groundcreeper	6	d
Furnarius cristatus	Crested Hornero	6	d
Furnarius figulus	Wing-banded Hornero	6	d
Furnarius leucopus	Pale-legged Hornero	6	d
Furnarius minor	Lesser Hornero	6	d
Furnarius rufus	Rufous Hornero	6	d
Furnarius torridus	Pale-billed Hornero	6	d

Scientific Name	Common Name	Source Codes	Region Codes

Scientific Name	Common Name	Source Codes	Region Codes
Limnornis curvirostris	Curve-billed Reedhaunter	6	d
Sylviorthorhynchus desmursii	Des Murs's Wiretail	6	d
Aphrastura masafuerae[1]	Masafuera Island Rayadito	6	d
Aphrastura spinicauda	Thorn-tailed Rayadito	6	d
Leptasthenura aegithaloides	Plain-mantled Tit-Spinetail	6	d
Leptasthenura andicola	Andean Tit-Spinetail	6	d
Leptasthenura fuliginiceps	Brown-capped Tit-Spinetail	6	d
Leptasthenura pileata	Rusty-crowned Tit-Spinetail	6	d
Leptasthenura platensis	Tufted Tit-Spinetail	6	d
Leptasthenura setaria	Araucaria Tit-Spinetail	6	d
Leptasthenura striata	Streaked Tit-Spinetail	6	d
Leptasthenura striolata	Striolated Tit-Spinetail	6	d
Leptasthenura xenothorax	White-browed Tit-Spinetail	6	d
Leptasthenura yanacensis	Tawny Tit-Spinetail	6	d
Phleocryptes melanops	Wren-like Rushbird	6	d
Spartanoica maluroides	Bay-capped Wren-Spinetail	6	d
Schizoeaca coryi	Ochre-browed Thistletail	6	d
Schizoeaca fuliginosa	White-chinned Thistletail	6	d
Schizoeaca griseomurina	Mouse-colored Thistletail	6	d
Schizoeaca harterti	Black-throated Thistletail	6	d
Schizoeaca helleri	Puna Thistletail	6	d
Schizoeaca palpebralis	Eye-ringed Thistletail	6	d
Schoeniophylax phryganophila	Chotoy Spinetail	6	d
Oreophylax moreirae	Itatiaia Spinetail	6	d
Synallaxis albescens	Pale-breasted Spinetail	4 6	d e
Synallaxis albigularis	Dark-breasted Spinetail	6	d
Synallaxis azarae	Azara's Spinetail	6	d
Synallaxis brachyura	Slaty Spinetail	4 6	d e
Synallaxis cabanisi	Cabanis's Spinetail	6	d
Synallaxis cherriei	Chestnut-throated Spinetail	6	d
Synallaxis cinerascens	Gray-bellied Spinetail	6	d
Synallaxis cinnamomea	Stripe-breasted Spinetail	6	d
Synallaxis erythrothorax	Rufous-breasted Spinetail	4	e
Synallaxis frontalis	Sooty-fronted Spinetail	6	d
Synallaxis fuscorufa	Rusty-headed Spinetail	6	d
Synallaxis gujanensis	Plain-crowned Spinetail	6	d
Synallaxis gularis	White-browed Spinetail	6	d
Synallaxis hypospodia	Cinereous-breasted Spinetail	6	d
Synallaxis moesta	Dusky Spinetail	6	d
Synallaxis poliophrys	Gray-browed Spinetail	6	d
Synallaxis propinqua	White-bellied Spinetail	6	d
Synallaxis ruficap[?]	Rufous-capped Spinetail	6	d
Synallaxis rutilans	Ruddy Spinetail	6	d
Synallaxis spixi	Chicli Spinetail	6	d
Synallaxis stictothorax	Necklaced Spinetail	6	d
Synallaxis subpudica	Silvery-throated Spinetail	6	d
Synallaxis superciliosa	Buff-browed Spinetail	6	d
Synallaxis tithys	Blackish-headed Spinetail	6	d
Synallaxis unirufa	Rufous Spinetail	6	d
Synallaxis zimmeri	Russet-bellied Spinetail	6 49	d
Gyalophylax hellmayri	Red-shouldered Spinetail	6	d
Certhiaxis cinnamomea	Yellow-throated Spinetail	6	d
Certhiaxis mustelina	Red-and-White Spinetail	6	d
Limnoctites rectirostris	Straight-billed Reedhaunter	6	d
Poecilurus candei	White-whiskered Spinetail	6	d
Poecilurus kollari	Hoary-throated Spinetail	6	d
Poecilurus scutatus	Ochre-cheeked Spinetail	6	d

Scientific Name	Common Name	Source Codes	Region Codes
FURNARIIDAE · OVENBIRDS *contd.*			
Cranioleuca albicapilla	Creamy-crested Spinetail	6	d
Cranioleuca albiceps	Light-crowned Spinetail	6	d
Cranioleuca antisiensis	Line-cheeked Spinetail	6	d
Cranioleuca curtata	Ash-browed Spinetail	6	d
Cranioleuca demissa	Tepui Spinetail	6	d
Cranioleuca erythrops	Red-faced Spinetail	4 6	d e
Cranioleuca gutturata	Speckled Spinetail	6	d
Cranioleuca hellmayri	Streak-capped Spinetail	6	d
Cranioleuca marcapatae	Marcapata Spinetail	6	d
Cranioleuca muelleri	Scaled Spinetail	6	d
Cranioleuca obsoleta	Olive Spinetail	6	d
Cranioleuca pallida	Pallid Spinetail	6	d
Cranioleuca pyrrhophia	Stripe-crowned Spinetail	6	d
Cranioleuca semicinerea	Gray-headed Spinetail	6	d
Cranioleuca subscristata	Crested Spinetail	6	d
Cranioleuca sulphurifera	Sulphur-bearded Spinetail	6	d
Cranioleuca vulpina	Rusty-backed Spinetail	6	d
Siptornopsis hypochondriacus	Great Spinetail	6	d
Asthenes anthoides	Austral Canastero	6	d
Asthenes baeri	Short-billed Canastero	6	d
Asthenes berlepschi	Berlepsch's Canastero	6	d
Asthenes cactorum	Cactus Canastero	6	d
Asthenes dorbignyi	Creamy-breasted Canastero	6	d
Asthenes flammulata	Many-striped Canastero	6	d
Asthenes hudsoni	Hudson's Canastero	6	d
Asthenes humicola	Dusky-tailed Canastero	6	d
Asthenes humilis	Streak-throated Canastero	6	d
Asthenes maculicauda	Scribble-tailed Canastero	6	d
Asthenes modesta	Cordilleran Canastero	6	d
Asthenes ottonis	Rusty-fronted Canastero	6	d
Asthenes patagonica	Patagonian Canastero	6	d
Asthenes pudibunda	Canyon Canastero	6	d
Asthenes pyrrholeuca	Lesser Canastero	6	d
Asthenes sclateri	Cordoba Canastero	6	d
Asthenes steinbachi	Chestnut Canastero	6	d
Asthenes urubambensis	Line-fronted Canastero	6	d
Asthenes virgata	Junin Canastero	6	d
Asthenes wyatti	Streak-backed Canastero	6	d
Thripophaga berlepschi	Russet-mantled Softtail	6	d
Thripophaga cherriei	Orinoco Softtail	6	d
Thripophaga fusciceps	Plain Softtail	6	d
Thripophaga macroura	Striated Softtail	6	d
Phacellodomus dorsalis	Chestnut-backed Thornbird	6	d
Phacellodomus erythrophthalmus	Red-eyed Thornbird	6	d
Phacellodomus ruber	Greater Thornbird	6	d
Phacellodomus rufifrons	Rufous-fronted Thornbird	6	d
Phacellodomus sibilatrix	Little Thornbird	6	d
Phacellodomus striaticeps	Streak-fronted Thornbird	6	d
Phacellodomus striaticollis	Freckle-breasted Thornbird	6	d
Coryphistera alaudina	Lark-like Brushrunner	6	d
Siptornis striaticollis	Spectacled Prickletail	6	d
Xenerpestes minlosi	Double-banded Graytail	4 6	d e
Xenerpestes singularis	Equatorial Graytail	6	d
Metopothrix aurantiacus	Orange-fronted Plushcrown	6	d
Roraimia adusta	Roraiman Barbtail	6	d
Margarornis bellulus	Beautiful Treerunner	4	e
Margarornis rubiginosus	Ruddy Treerunner	4	e

81

Scientific Name	Common Name	Source Codes	Region Codes
FURNARIIDAE · OVENBIRDS *contd.*			
Margarornis squamiger	Pearled Treerunner	6	d
Margarornis stellatus	Fulvous-dotted Treerunner	6	d
Anumbius annumbi	Firewood-Gatherer	6	d
Premnornis guttuligera	Rusty-winged Barbtail	6	d
Premnoplex brunnescens	Spotted Barbtail	4 6	d e
Premnoplex tatei	White-throated Barbtail	6	d
Pseudocolaptes boissonneautii	Streaked Tuftedcheek	6	d
Pseudocolaptes lawrencii	Buffy Tuftedcheek	4 6	d e
Berlepschia rikeri	Point-tailed Palmcreeper	6	d
Pseudoseisura cristata	Rufous Cacholote	6	d
Pseudoseisura gutturalis	White-throated Cacholote	6	d
Pseudoseisura lophotes	Brown Cacholote	6	d
Hyloctistes subulatus	Striped Woodhaunter	4 6	d e
Ancistrops strigilatus	Chestnut-winged Hookbill	6	d
Anabazenops fuscus	White-collared Foliage-Gleaner	6	d
Syndactyla guttulata	Guttulated Foliage-Gleaner	6	d
Syndactyla rufosuperciliata	Buff-browed Foliage-Gleaner	6	d
Syndactyla subalaris	Lineated Foliage-Gleaner	4 6	d e
Simoxenops striatus	Bolivian Recurvebill	6	d
Simoxenops ucayalae	Peruvian Recurvebill	6	d
Anabacerthia amaurotis	White-browed Foliage-Gleaner	6	d
Anabacerthia striaticollis	Montane Foliage-Gleaner	6	d
Anabacerthia variegaticeps	Scaly-throated Foliage-Gleaner	4 6	d e
Philydor atricapillus	Black-capped Foliage-Gleaner	6	d
Philydor dimidiatus	Russet-mantled Foliage-Gleaner	6	d
Philydor erythrocercus	Rufous-rumped Foliage-Gleaner	4 6	d e
Philydor erythropterus	Chestnut-winged Foliage-Gleaner	6	d
Philydor hylobius	Neblina Foliage-Gleaner	6	d
Philydor lichtensteini	Ochre-breasted Foliage-Gleaner	6	d
Philydor phyrrhodes	Cinnamon-rumped Foliage-Gleaner	6	d
Philydor ruficaudatus	Rufous-tailed Foliage-Gleaner	6	d
Philydor rufus	Buff-fronted Foliage-Gleaner	4 6	d e
Automolus dorsalis	Crested Foliage-Gleaner	6	d
Automolus infuscatus	Olive-backed Foliage-Gleaner	6	d
Automolus leucophthalmus	White-eyed Foliage-Gleaner	6	d
Automolus melanopezus	Brown-rumped Foliage-Gleaner	6	d
Automolus ochrolaemus	Buff-throated Foliage-Gleaner	4 6	d e
Automolus roraimae	White-throated Foliage-Gleaner	6	d
Automolus rubiginosus	Ruddy Foliage-Gleaner	4 6	d e
Automolus ruficollis	Rufous-necked Foliage-Gleaner	6	d
Automolus rufipileatus	Chestnut-crowned Foliage-Gleaner	6	d
Hylocryptus erythrocephalus	Henna-hooded Foliage-Gleaner	6	d
Hylocryptus rectirostris	Chestnut-capped Foliage-Gleaner	6	d

82

Scientific Name	Common Name	Source Codes	Region Codes

FURNARIIDAE · OVENBIRDS contd.

Scientific Name	Common Name	Source Codes	Region Codes
Cichlocolaptes leucophrys	Pale-browed Treehunter	6	d
Heliobletus contaminatus	Sharp-billed Treehunter	6	d
Thripadectes flammulatus	Flammulated Treehunter	6	d
Thripadectes holostictus	Striped Treehunter	6	d
Thripadectes ignobilis	Uniform Treehunter	6	d
Thripadectes melanorhynchus	Black-billed Treehunter	6	d
Thripadectes rufobrunneus	Streak-breasted Treehunter	4	e
Thripadectes scrutator	Buff-throated Treehunter	6	d
Thripadectes virgaticeps	Streak-capped Treehunter	6	d
Xenops milleri	Rufous-tailed Xenops	6	d
Xenops minutus	Plain Xenops	4 6	d e
Xenops rutilans	Streaked Xenops	4 6	d e
Xenops tenuirostris	Slender-billed Xenops	6	d
Megaxenops parnaguae	Great Xenops	6	d
Pygarrhichas albogularis	White-throated Treerunner	6	d
Sclerurus albigularis	Gray-throated Leafscraper	4 6	d e
Sclerurus caudacutus	Black-tailed Leafscraper	6	d
Sclerurus guatemalensis	Scaly-throated Leafscraper	4 6	d e
Sclerurus mexicanus	Tawny-throated Leafscraper	4 6	d e
Sclerurus rufigularis	Short-billed Leafscraper	6	d
Sclerurus scansor	Rufous-breasted Leafscraper	6	d
Lochmias nematura	Sharp-tailed Streamcreeper	4 6	d e

FORMICARIIDAE · ANTBIRDS   230 species recorded

Scientific Name	Common Name	Source Codes	Region Codes
Cymbilaimus lineatus	Fasciated Antshrike	4 6	d e
Hypoedaleus guttatus	Spot-backed Antshrike	6	d
Batara cinerea	Giant Antshrike	6	d
Mackenziaena leachii	Large-tailed Antshrike	6	d
Mackenziaena severa	Tufted Antshrike	6	d
Frederickena unduligera	Undulated Antshrike	6	d
Frederickena viridis	Black-throated Antshrike	6	d
Taraba major	Great Antshrike	4 6	d e
Sakesphorus bernardi	Collared Antshrike	6	d
Sakesphorus canadensis	Black-crested Antshrike	6	d
Sakesphorus cristatus	Silvery-cheeked Antshrike	6	d
Sakesphorus luctuosus	Glossy Antshrike	6	d
Sakesphorus melanonotus	Black-backed Antshrike	6	d
Sakesphorus melanothorax	Band-tailed Antshrike	6	d
Biatas nigropectus	White-bearded Antshrike	6	d
Thamnophilus aethiops	White-shouldered Antshrike	6	d
Thamnophilus amazonicus	Amazonian Antshrike	6	d
Thamnophilus aroyae	Upland Antshrike	6	d
Thamnophilus bridgesi	Black-hooded Antshrike	4	e
Thamnophilus caerulescens	Variable Antshrike	6	d
Thamnophilus cryptoleucus	Castelnau's Antshrike	6	d
Thamnophilus doliatus	Barred Antshrike	4 6	d e
Thamnophilus insignis	Streak-backed Antshrike	6	d
Thamnophilus multistriatus	Bar-crested Antshrike	6	d
Thamnophilus murinus	Mouse-colored Antshrike	6	d
Thamnophilus nigriceps	Black Antshrike	4 6	d e
Thamnophilus nigrocinereus	Blackish-gray Antshrike	6	d
Thamnophilus palliatus	Lined Antshrike	6	d
Thamnophilus praecox	Cocha Antshrike	6	d
Thamnophilus punctatus	Slaty Antshrike	4 6	d e
Thamnophilus ruficapillus	Rufous-capped Antshrike	6	d

FORMICARIIDAE · ANTBIRDS *contd.*

Scientific Name	Common Name	Source Codes	Region Codes
Thamnophilus schistaceus	Black-capped Antshrike	6	d
Thamnophilus torquatus	Rufous-winged Antshrike	6	d
Thamnophilus unicolor	Uniform Antshrike	6	d
Pygiptila stellaris	Spot-winged Antshrike	6	d
Megastictus margaritatus	Pearly Antshrike	6	d
Neoctantes niger	Black Bushbird	6	d
Clytoctantes alixi	Recurve-billed Bushbird	6	d
Xenornis setifrons	Speckle-breasted Antshrike	4 6	d e
Thamnistes anabatinus	Russet Antshrike	4 6	d e
Dysithamnus mentalis	Plain Antvireo	4 6	d e
Dysithamnus puncticeps	Spot-crowned Antvireo	4 6	d e
Dysithamnus stictothorax	Spot-breasted Antvireo	6	d
Dysithamnus striaticeps	Streak-crowned Antvireo	4	e
Dysithamnus xanthopterus	Rufous-backed Antvireo	6	d
Thamnomanes ardesiacus	Dusky-throated Antshrike	6	d
Thamnomanes caesius	Cinereous Antshrike	6	d
Thamnomanes occidentalis	Western Antshrike	6	d
Thamnomanes plumbeus	Plumbeous Antshrike	6	d
Thamnomanes saturninus	Saturnine Antshrike	6	d
Thamnomanes schistogynus	Bluish-slate Antshrike	6	d
Myrmotherula ambigua	Yellow-throated Antwren	6	d
Myrmotherula assimilis	Leaden Antwren	6	d
Myrmotherula axillaris	White-flanked Antwren	4 6	d e
Myrmotherula behni	Plain-winged Antwren	6	d
Myrmotherula brachyura	Pygmy Antwren	4 6	d e
Myrmotherula cherriei	Cherrie's Antwren	6	d
Myrmotherula erythronotos	Black-hooded Antwren	6	d
Myrmotherula erythrura	Rufous-tailed Antwren	6	d
Myrmotherula fulviventris	Checker-throated Antwren	4 6	d e
Myrmotherula grisea	Ashy Antwren	6	d
Myrmotherula gularis	Star-throated Antwren	6	d
Myrmotherula guttata	Rufous-bellied Antwren	6	d
Myrmotherula gutturalis	Brown-bellied Antwren	6	d
Myrmotherula haematonota	Stipple-throated Antwren	6	d
Myrmotherula hauxwelli	Plain-throated Antwren	6	d
Myrmotherula iheringi	Ihering's Antwren	6	d
Myrmotherula klagesi	Klages's Antwren	6	d
Myrmotherula leucophthalma	White-eyed Antwren	6	d
Myrmotherula longicauda	Stripe-chested Antwren	6	d
Myrmotherula longipennis	Long-winged Antwren	6	d
Myrmotherula menetriesii	Gray Antwren	6	d
Myrmotherula minor	Salvadori's Antwren	6	d
Myrmotherula obscura	Short-billed Antwren	6	d
Myrmotherula ornata	Ornate Antwren	6	d
Myrmotherula schisticolor	Slaty Antwren	4 6	d e
Myrmotherula sclateri	Sclater's Antwren	6	d
Myrmotherula sunensis	Rio Suno Antwren	6	d
Myrmotherula surinamensis	Streaked Antwren	4 6	d e
Myrmotherula unicolor	Unicolored Antwren	6	d
Myrmotherula urosticta	Band-tailed Antwren	6	d
Dichrozona cincta	Banded Antbird	6	d
Myrmochilus strigilatus	Stripe-backed Antbird	6	d
Herpsilochmus axillaris	Yellow-breasted Antwren	6	d
Herpsilochmus dorsimaculatus	Spot-backed Antwren	6	d
Herpsilochmus longirostris	Large-billed Antwren	6	d
Herpsilochmus pectoralis	Pectoral Antwren	6	d
Herpsilochmus pileatus	Black-capped Antwren	6	d

Scientific Name	Common Name	Source Codes	Region Codes
FORMICARIIDAE · ANTBIRDS contd.			
Herpsilochmus roraimae	Roraiman Antwren	6	d
Herpsilochmus rufimarginatus	Rufous-winged Antwren	4 6	d e
Herpsilochmus stictocephalus	Todd's Antwren	6	d
Herpsilochmus sticturus	Spot-tailed Antwren	6	d
Microrhopias quixensis	Dot-winged Antwren	4 6	d e
Formicivora grisea	White-fringed Antwren	4 6	d e
Formicivora iheringi	Narrow-billed Antwren	6	d
Formicivora melanogaster	Black-bellied Antwren	6	d
Formicivora rufa	Rusty-backed Antwren	6	d
Formicivora serrana	Serra Antbird	6	d
Drymophila caudata	Long-tailed Antbird	6	d
Drymophila devillei	Striated Antbird	6	d
Drymophila ferruginea	Ferruginous Antbird	6	d
Drymophila genei	Rufous-tailed Antbird	6	d
Drymophila malura	Dusky-tailed Antbird	6	d
Drymophila ochropyga	Ochre-rumped Antbird	6	d
Drymophila squamata	Scaled Antbird	6	d
Terenura callinota	Rufous-rumped Antwren	4 6	d e
Terenura humeralis	Chestnut-shouldered Antwren	6	d
Terenura maculata	Streak-capped Antwren	6	d
Terenura sharpei	Yellow-rumped Antwren	6	d
Terenura spodioptila	Ash-winged Antwren	6	d
Cercomacra brasiliana	Rio de Janeiro Antbird	6	d
Cercomacra carbonaria	Rio Branco Antbird	6	d
Cercomacra cinerascens	Gray Antbird	6	d
Cercomacra ferdinandi	Bananal Antbird	6	d
Cercomacra melanaria	Mato Grosso Antbird	6	d
Cercomacra nigrescens	Blackish Antbird	6	d
Cercomacra nigricans	Jet Antbird	4 6	d e
Cercomacra serva	Black Antbird	6	d
Cercomacra tyrannina	Dusky Antbird	4 6	d e
Sipia berlepschi	Stub-tailed Antbird	6	d
Sipia rosenbergi	Esmeraldas Antbird	6	d
Pyriglena atra	Fringe-backed Fire-Eye	6	d
Pyriglena leuconota	White-backed Fire-Eye	6	d
Pyriglena leucoptera	White-shouldered Fire-Eye	6	d
Rhopornis ardesiaca	Slender Antbird	6	d
Myrmoborus leucophrys	White-browed Antbird	6	d
Myrmoborus lugubris	Ash-breasted Antbird	6	d
Myrmoborus melanurus	Black-tailed Antbird	6	d
Myrmoborus myotherinus	Black-faced Antbird	6	d
Hypocnemis cantator	Warbling Antbird	6	d
Hypocnemis hypoxantha	Yellow-browed Antbird	6	d
Hypocnemoides maculicauda	Band-tailed Antbird	6	d
Hypocnemoides melanopogon	Black-chinned Antbird	6	d
Myrmochanes hemileucus	Black-and-White Antbird	6	d
Gymnocichla nudiceps	Bare-crowned Antbird	4 6	d e
Sclateria naevia	Silvered Antbird	6	d
Percnostola caurensis	Caura Antbird	6	d
Percnostola leucostigma	Spot-winged Antbird	6	d
Percnostola lophotes	Rufous-crested Antbird	6	d
Percnostola macrolopha	White-lined Antbird	6	d
Percnostola rufifrons	Black-headed Antbird	6	d
Percnostola schistacea	Slate-colored Antbird	6	d
Myrmeciza atrothorax	Black-throated Antbird	6	d
Myrmeciza disjuncta	Yapacana Antbird	6	d
Myrmeciza exsul	Chestnut-backed Antbird	4 6	d e

Scientific Name	Common Name	Source Codes	Region Codes

Scientific Name	Common Name	Source Codes	Region Codes
Myrmeciza ferruginea	Ferruginous-backed Antbird	6	d
Myrmeciza fortis	Sooty Antbird	6	d
Myrmeciza goeldii	Goeldi's Antbird	6	d
Myrmeciza griseiceps	Gray-headed Antbird	6	d
Myrmeciza hemimelaena	Chestnut-tailed Antbird	6	d
Myrmeciza hyperythra	Plumbeous Antbird	6	d
Myrmeciza immaculata	Immaculate Antbird	4 6	d e
Myrmeciza laemosticta	Dull-mantled Antbird	4 6	d e
Myrmeciza longipes	White-bellied Antbird	4 6	d e
Myrmeciza loricata	White-bibbed Antbird	6	d
Myrmeciza melanoceps	White-shouldered Antbird	6	d
Myrmeciza pelzelni	Gray-bellied Antbird	6	d
Myrmeciza ruficauda	Scalloped Antbird	6	d
Myrmeciza squamosa	Squamate Antbird	6	d
Myrmeciza stictothorax	Spot-breasted Antbird	6	d
Formicarius analis	Black-faced Antthrush	4 6	d e
Formicarius colma	Rufous-capped Antthrush	6	d
Formicarius nigricapillus	Black-headed Antthrush	4 6	d e
Formicarius rufifrons	Rufous-fronted Antthrush	6	d
Formicarius rufipectus	Rufous-breasted Antthrush	4 6	d e
Chamaeza campanisona	Short-tailed Antthrush	6	d
Chamaeza mollissima	Barred Antthrush	6	d
Chamaeza nobilis	Striated Antthrush	6	d
Chamaeza ruficauda	Rufous-tailed Antthrush	6	d
Pithys albifrons	White-plumed Antbird	6	d
Pithys castanea	White-masked Antbird	6	d
Gymnopithys leucaspis	Bicolored Antbird	4 6	d e
Gymnopithys lunulata	Lunulated Antbird	6	d
Gymnopithys rufigula	Rufous-throated Antbird	6	d
Gymnopithys salvini	White-throated Antbird	6	d
Rhegmatorhina berlepschi	Harlequin Antbird	6	d
Rhegmatorhina cristata	Chestnut-crested Antbird	6	d
Rhegmatorhina gymnops	Bare-eyed Antbird	6	d
Rhegmatorhina hoffmannsi	White-breasted Antbird	6	d
Rhegmatorhina melanosticta	Hairy-crested Antbird	6	d
Hylopezus berlepschi	Amazonian Antpitta	6	d
Hylopezus fulviventris	Fulvous-bellied Antpitta	6	d
Hylopezus macularius	Spotted Antpitta	6	d
Hylopezus ochroleucus	Speckle-breasted Antpitta	6	d
Hylopezus perspicillatus	Streak-chested Antpitta	6	d
Hylophylax naevia	Spot-backed Antbird	6	d
Hylophylax naevioides	Spotted Antbird	4 6	d e
Hylophylax poecilonota	Scale-backed Antbird	6	d
Hylophylax punctulata	Dot-backed Antbird	6	d
Skutchia borbae	Pale-faced Bare-Eye	6	d
Phlegopsis barringeri	Argus Bare-Eye	6	d
Phlegopsis erythroptera	Reddish-winged Bare-Eye	6	d
Phlegopsis nigromaculata	Black-spotted Bare-Eye	6	d
Phaenostictus mcleannani	Ocellated Antbird	4 6	d e
Myrmornis torquata	Wing-banded Antbird	4 6	d e
Pittasoma michleri	Black-crowned Antpitta	4 6	d e
Pittasoma rufopileatum	Rufous-crowned Antpitta	6	d
Grallaricula cucullata	Hooded Antpitta	6	d
Grallaricula ferrugineipectus	Rusty-breasted Antpitta	6	d
Grallaricula flavirostris	Ochre-breasted Antpitta	4 6	d e
Grallaricula lineifrons	Crescent-faced Antpitta	6	d
Grallaricula loricata	Scallop-breasted Antpitta	6	d

Scientific Name	Common Name	Source Codes	Region Codes

FORMICARIIDAE · ANTBIRDS *contd.*

Scientific Name	Common Name	Source Codes	Region Codes
Grallaricula nana	Slate-crowned Antpitta	6	d
Grallaricula peruviana	Peruvian Antpitta	6	d
Myrmothera campanisona	Thrush-like Antpitta	6	d
Myrmothera simplex	Brown-breasted Antpitta	6	d
Grallaria albigula	White-throated Antpitta	6	d
Grallaria alleni	Moustached Antpitta	6	d
Grallaria andicola	Stripe-headed Antpitta	6	d
Grallaria bangsi	Santa Marta Antpitta	6	d
Grallaria chthonia	Tachira Antpitta	6	d
Grallaria dignissima	Ochre-striped Antpitta	6	d
Grallaria eludens	Elusive Antpitta	6	d
Grallaria erythrotis	Rufous-faced Antpitta	6	d
Grallaria excelsa	Great Antpitta	6	d
Grallaria fulviventris	Fulvous-bellied Antpitta	4	e
Grallaria gigantea	Giant Antpitta	6	d
Grallaria griseonucha	Gray-naped Antpitta	6	d
Grallaria guatimalensis	Scaled Antpitta	4 6	d e
Grallaria haplonota	Plain-backed Antpitta	6	d
Grallaria hypoleuca	Bay-backed Antpitta	6	d
Grallaria milleri	Brown-banded Antpitta	6	d
Grallaria nuchalis	Chestnut-naped Antpitta	6	d
Grallaria perspicillata	Streak-chested Antpitta	4	e
Grallaria quitensis	Tawny Antpitta	6	d
Grallaria ruficapilla	Chestnut-crowned Antpitta	6	d
Grallaria rufocinerea	Bicolored Antpitta	6	d
Grallaria rufula	Rufous Antpitta	6	d
Grallaria squamigera	Undulated Antpitta	6	d
Grallaria varia	Variegated Antpitta	6	d

CONOPOPHAGIDAE · GNATEATERS 8 species recorded

Scientific Name	Common Name	Source Codes	Region Codes
Conopophaga ardesiaca	Slaty Gnateater	6	d
Conopophaga aurita	Chestnut-belted Gnateater	6	d
Conopophaga castaneiceps	Chestnut-crowned Gnateater	6	d
Conopophaga lineata	Rufous Gnateater	6	d
Conopophaga melanogaster	Black-bellied Gnateater	6	d
Conopophaga melanops	Black-cheeked Gnateater	6	d
Conopophaga peruviana	Ash-throated Gnateater	6	d
Conopophaga roberti	Hooded Gnateater	6	d

RHINOCRYPTIDAE · TAPACULOS 29 species recorded

Scientific Name	Common Name	Source Codes	Region Codes
Pteroptochos castaneus	Chestnut-throated Huet-Huet	6	d
Pteroptochos megapodius	Moustached Turca	6	d
Pteroptochos tarnii	Black-throated Huet-Huet	6	d
Scelorchilus albicollis	White-throated Tapaculo	6	d
Scelorchilus rubecula	Chucao Tapaculo	6	d
Rhinocrypta lanceolata	Crested Gallito	6	d
Teledromas fuscus	Sandy Gallito	6	d
Liosceles thoracicus	Rusty-belted Tapaculo	6	d
Merulaxis ater	Slaty Bristle-front	6	d
Merulaxis stresemanni	Stresemann's Bristle-front	6	d
Melanopareia elegans	Elegant Crescent-Chest	6	d
Melanopareia maranonica	Maranon Crescent-Chest	6	d
Melanopareia maximiliani	Olive-crowned Crescent-Chest	6	d

Scientific Name	Common Name	Source Codes	Region Codes
Melanopareia torquata	Collared Crescent-Chest	6	d
Scytalopus argentifrons	Silvery-fronted Tapaculo	4	e
Scytalopus femoralis	Rufous-vented Tapaculo	6	d
Scytalopus indigoticus	White-breasted Tapaculo	6	d
Scytalopus latebricola	Brown-rumped Tapaculo	6	d
Scytalopus macropus	Large-footed Tapaculo	6	d
Scytalopus magellanicus	Andean Tapaculo	6	d
Scytalopus novacapitalis	Brasilia Tapaculo	6	d
Scytalopus panamensis	Pale-throated Tapaculo	4 6	d e
Scytalopus speluncae	Mouse-colored Tapaculo	6	d
Scytalopus superciliaris	White-browed Tapaculo	6	d
Scytalopus unicolor	Unicolored Tapaculo	6	d
Myornis senilis	Ash-colored Tapaculo	6	d
Psilorhamphus guttatus	Spotted Bamboowren	6	d
Eugralla paradoxa	Ochre-flanked Tapaculo	6	d
Acropternis orthonyx	Ocellated Tapaculo	6	d

PITTIDAE · PITTAS 26 species recorded

Scientific Name	Common Name	Source Codes	Region Codes
Pitta anerythra	Black-faced Pitta	38	k
Pitta angolensis	African Pitta	8	c
Pitta arcuata	Blue-banded Pitta	19 21	h
Pitta baudi	Blue-headed Pitta	19 21	h
Pitta brachyura[1]	Blue-winged Pitta	1 15 17 18 19 21 22	h f g h
Pitta caerulea	Great Blue Pitta	18 19 21 55	g h
Pitta cyanea	Lesser Blue Pitta	15 18 55	f g
Pitta elioti	Bar-bellied Pitta	55	g
Pitta erythrogaster[2]	Red-breasted Pitta	22 35	h j
Pitta granatina	Garnet Pitta	18 19 21 55	f h
Pitta guajana	Blue-tailed Pitta	19 21 55	g h
Pitta gurneyi	Gurney's Pitta	18 55	g
Pitta kochi	Koch's Pitta	22	h
Pitta iris	Rainbow Pitta	36	i
Pitta maxima	Halmahera Pitta	47	j
Pitta mollucensis	Moluccan Pitta	47	g
Pitta nipalensis	Blue-naped Pitta	15 17 18 55	f g
Pitta oatesi	Fulvous Pitta	18 55	g
Pitta phayrei	Phayre's Pitta	17 18 55	g
Pitta reichenowi	Green-breasted Pitta	8	c
Pitta schneideri	Schneider's Pitta	19	h
Pitta sordida	Black-headed Pitta	15 17 18 19 21 22 35 55	f g h j
Pitta soror	Blue-backed Pitta	17 55	g
Pitta steerei	Steere's Pitta	22	h
Pitta venusta	Mueller's Pitta	47	h
Pitta versicolor	Noisy Pitta	35 36	i j

PHILEPITTIDAE · ASITIES, FALSE-SUNBIRDS 4 species recorded

Scientific Name	Common Name	Source Codes	Region Codes
Philepitta castanea	Velvet Asity	10	c
Philepitta schlegeli	Schlegel's Asity	10	c
Neodrepanis coruscans	Wattled False-Sunbird	10	c
Neodrepanis hypoxantha	Small-billed False-Sunbird	10 53	c

88

Scientific Name	Common Name	Source Codes	Region Codes

ACANTHISITTIDAE · NEW ZEALAND WRENS 3 species recorded

Xenicus gilviventris	Rock Wren	37	i
Xenicus longipes	Bush Wren	37 53	i
Acanthisitta chloris	Rifleman	37	i

TYRANNIDAE · TYRANT FLYCATCHERS 362 species recorded

Agriornis albicauda	White-tailed Shrike-Tyrant	6	d
Agriornis livida	Great Shrike-Tyrant	6	d
Agriornis microptera	Gray-bellied Shrike-Tyrant	6	d
Agriornis montana	Black-bellied Shrike-Tyrant	6	d
Neoxolmis rufiventris	Chocolate-vented Tyrant	6	d
Xolmis cinerea	Gray Monjita	6	d
Xolmis coronata	Black-crowned Monjita	6	d
Xolmis dominicana	Black-and-White Monjita	6	d
Xolmis irupero	White Monjita	6	d
Xolmis murina	Mouse-Brown Monjita	6	d
Xolmis rubetra	Rusty-backed Monjita	6	d
Xolmis rufipennis	Rufous-webbed Tyrant	6	d
Xolmis velata	White-rumped Monjita	6	d
Pyrope pyrope	Fire-eyed Diucon	6	d
Muscisaxicola albifrons	White-fronted Ground-Tyrant	6	d
Muscisaxicola albilora	White-browed Ground-Tyrant	6	d
Muscisaxicola alpina	Plain-capped Ground-Tyrant	6	d
Muscisaxicola capistrata	Cinnamon-bellied Ground-Tyrant	6	d
Muscisaxicola flavinucha	Ochre-naped Ground-Tyrant	6	d
Muscisaxicola fluviatilis	Little Ground-Tyrant	6	d
Muscisaxicola frontalis	Black-fronted Ground-Tyrant	6	d
Muscisaxicola juninensis	Puna Ground-Tyrant	6	d
Muscisaxicola macloviana	Dark-faced Ground-Tyrant	6	d
Muscisaxicola maculirostris	Spot-billed Ground-Tyrant	6	d
Muscisaxicola rufivertex	Rufous-naped Ground-Tyrant	6	d
Muscigralla brevicauda	Short-tailed Field-Tyrant	6	d
Lessonia rufa	Rufous-backed Negrito	6	d
Myiotheretes erythropygius	Red-rumped Bush-Tyrant	6	d
Myiotheretes fumigatus	Smoky Bush-Tyrant	6	d
Myiotheretes fuscorufus	Rufous-bellied Bush-Tyrant	6	d
Myiotheretes pernix	Santa Marta Bush-Tyrant	6	d
Myiotheretes signatus	Jelski's Bush-Tyrant	6	d
Myiotheretes striaticollis	Streak-throated Bush-Tyrant	6	d
Ochthoeca cinnamomeiventris	Slaty-backed Chat-Tyrant	6	d
Ochthoeca diadema	Yellow-bellied Chat-Tyrant	6	d
Ochthoeca frontalis	Crowned Chat-Tyrant	6	d
Ochthoeca fumicolor	Brown-backed Chat-Tyrant	6	d
Ochthoeca leucophrys	White-browed Chat-Tyrant	6	d
Ochthoeca oenanthoides	D'Orbigny's Chat-Tyrant	6	d
Ochthoeca piurae	Piura Chat-Tyrant	6	d
Ochthoeca pulchella	Golden-browed Chat-Tyrant	6	d
Ochthoeca rufipectoralis	Rufous-breasted Chat-Tyrant	6	d
Sayornis nigricans	Black Phoebe	3 4 6	a d e
Sayornis phoebe	Eastern Phoebe	3 4	a e
Sayornis saya	Say's Phoebe	3 4	a e
Colonia colonus	Long-tailed Tyrant	4 6	d e
Gubernetes yetapa	Streamer-tailed Tyrant	6	d
Alectrurus tricolor	Cock-tailed Tyrant	6	d

89

Scientific Name	Common Name	Source Codes	Region Codes

TYRANNIDAE · TYRANT FLYCATCHERS *contd.*

Scientific Name	Common Name	Source Codes	Region Codes
Yetapa risora	Strange-tailed Tyrant	6	d
Knipolegus aterrimus	White-winged Black-Tyrant	6	d
Knipolegus cabanisi	Plumbeous Tyrant	6	d
Knipolegus cyanirostris	Blue-billed Black-Tyrant	6	d
Knipolegus lophotes	Crested Black-Tyrant	6	d
Knipolegus nigerrimus	Velvety Black-Tyrant	6	d
Knipolegus orenocensis	Riverside Tyrant	6	d
Knipolegus poecilurus	Rufous-tailed Tyrant	6	d
Phaeotriccus hudsoni	Hudson's Black-Tyrant	6	d
Phaeotriccus poecilocercus	Amazonian Black-Tyrant	6	d
Entotriccus striaticeps	Cinereous Tyrant	6	d
Hymenops perspicillata	Spectacled Tyrant	6	d
Muscipipra vetula	Shear-tailed Gray-Tyrant	6	d
Fluvicola nengeta	Masked Water-Tyrant	6	d
Fluvicola pica	Pied Water-Tyrant	4 6	d e
Arundinicola leucocephala	White-headed Marsh-Tyrant	6	d
Pyrocephalus rubinus[1]	Vermilion Flycatcher	3 4 6	a d e
Ochthornis littoralis	Drab Water-Tyrant	6	d
Tumbezia salvini	Tumbes Tyrant	6	d
Satrapa icterophrys	Yellow-browed Tyrant	6	d
Machetornis rixosus	Cattle Tyrant	6	d
Sirystes sibilator	Sirystes	4 6	d e
Muscivora tyrannus	Fork-tailed Flycatcher	3 4 5 6	a d e
Tyrannus albogularis	White-throated Kingbird	6	d
Tyrannus caudifasciatus	Loggerhead Kingbird	5	e
Tyrannus couchii[2]	Couch's Kingbird		a e
Tyrannus crassirostris	Thick-billed Kingbird	3 4	a e
Tyrannus cubensis	Giant Kingbird	4 5	e
Tyrannus dominicensis	Gray Kingbird	3 4 5 6	a d e
Tyrannus forficatus	Scissor-tailed Flycatcher	3 4	a e
Tyrannus melancholicus	Tropical Kingbird	3 4 5 6	a d e
Tyrannus niveigularis	Snowy-throated Kingbird	6	d
Tyrannus tyrannus	Eastern Kingbird	3 4 5 6	a d e
Tyrannus verticalis	Western Kingbird	3 4	a e
Tyrannus vociferans	Cassin's Kingbird	3 4	a e
Tyrannopsis luteiventris	Dusky-chested Flycatcher	6	d
Tyrannopsis sulphurea	Sulphury Flycatcher	6	d
Empidonomus aurantioatrocristatus	Crowned Slaty-Flycatcher	6	d
Empidonomus varius	Variegated Flycatcher	6	d
Legatus leucophaius	Piratic Flycatcher	4 6	d e
Conopias cinchoneti	Lemon-browed Flycatcher	6	d
Conopias parva	White-ringed Flycatcher	6	d
Conopias trivirgata	Three-striped Flycatcher	6	d
Megarhynchus pitangua	Boat-billed Flycatcher	4 6	d e
Myiodynastes bairdi[3]	Baird's Flycatcher	6	d
Myiodynastes chrysocephalus	Golden-crowned Flycatcher	6	d
Myiodynastes hemichrysus	Golden-bellied Flycatcher	4	e
Myiodynastes luteiventris	Sulphur-bellied Flycatcher	3 4 6	a d e
Myiodynastes maculatus	Streaked Flycatcher	4 6	d e
Coryphotriccus albovittatus	White-ringed Flycatcher	4	e
Myiozetetes cayanensis	Rusty-margined Flycatcher	4 6	d e
Myiozetetes granadensis	Gray-capped Flycatcher	4 6	d e
Myiozetetes inornatus	White-bearded Flycatcher	6	d
Xenopsaris albinucha	White-naped Xenopsaris	6	d
Myiozetetes similis	Social Flycatcher	4 6	d e
Attila bolivianus	Dull-capped Attila	6	d

90

Scientific Name	Common Name	Source Codes	Region Codes
TYRANNIDAE · TYRANT FLYCATCHERS contd.			
Attila cinnamomeus	Cinnamon Attila	6	d
Attila citriniventris	Citron-bellied Attila	6	d
Attila rufus	Gray-hooded Attila	6	d
Attila spadiceus[4]	Bright-rumped Attila	4 6	d e
Attila torridus	Ochraceous Attila	6	d
Casiornis fusca	Ash-throated Casiornis	6	d
Casiornis rufa	Rufous Casiornis	6	d
Laniocera hypopyrrha	Cinereous Mourner	6	d
Laniocera rufescens[4]	Speckled Mourner	4 6	d e
Pitangus lictor	Lesser Kiskadee	4 6	d e
Pitangus sulphuratus	Great Kiskadee	3 4 6	a d e
Pseudattila phoenicurus	Rufous-tailed Attila	6	d
Rhytipterna holerythra[4]	Rufous Mourner	4 6	d e
Rhytipterna immunda	Pale-bellied Mourner	6	d
Rhytipterna simplex	Grayish Mourner	6	d
Myiarchus apicalis	Apical Flycatcher	6	d
Myiarchus barbirostris	Jamaican Flycatcher	5	e
Myiarchus cephalotes	Pale-edged Flycatcher	6	d
Myiarchus cinerascens	Ash-throated Flycatcher	3 4	a e
Myiarchus crinitus	Great-crested Flycatcher	3 4 5 6	a d e
Myiarchus ferox	Short-crested Flycatcher	4 6	d e
Myiarchus magnirostris	Galapagos Flycatcher	46	d
Myiarchus nuttingi	Pale-throated Flycatcher	4	e
Myiarchus phaeocephalus	Sooty-crowned Flycatcher	6	d
Myiarchus semirufus	Rufous Flycatcher	6	d
Myiarchus stolidus	Stolid Flycatcher	5	e
Myiarchus swainsoni	Swainson's Flycatcher	6	d
Myiarchus tuberculifer	Dusky-capped Flycatcher	3 4 6	a d e
Myiarchus tyrannulus	Wied's Crested Flycatcher	3 4 5 6	a d e
Myiarchus validus	Rufous-tailed Flycatcher	5	e
Myiarchus yucatanensis	Yucatan Flycatcher	4	e
Nesotriccus ridgwayi	Cocos Island Flycatcher	4	e
Deltarhynchus flammulatus	Flammulated Flycatcher	4	e
Contopus albogularis	White-throated Pewee	6	d
Contopus borealis	Olive-sided Flycatcher	3 4 6	a d e
Contopus caribaeus	Greater Antillean Pewee	5	e
Contopus cinereus	Tropical Pewee	4 6	d e
Contopus fumigatus[5]	Greater Pewee	6	d
Contopus latirostris	Lesser Antillean Pewee	5	e
Contopus nigrescens	Blackish Pewee	6	d
Contopus ochraceus	Ochraceous Pewee	4	e
Contopus pertinax	Coues's Flycatcher	3 4	a e
Contopus sordidulus	Western Wood Pewee	3	a
Contopus virens[6]	Eastern Wood Pewee	3 4 5 6	a d e
Empidonax affinis	Pine Flycatcher	4	e
Empidonax albigularis	White-throated Flycatcher	4	e
Empidonax alnorum	Alder Flycatcher	56	a d e
Empidonax atriceps	Black-capped Flycatcher	4	e
Empidonax difficilis	Western Flycatcher	3 4	a e
Empidonax euleri	Euler's Flycatcher	5 6	d e
Empidonax flavescens	Yellowish Flycatcher	4	e
Empidonax flaviventris	Yellow-bellied Flycatcher	3 4	a e
Empidonax fulvifrons	Buff-breasted Flycatcher	3 4	a e
Empidonax griseipectus	Gray-breasted Flycatcher	6	d
Empidonax hammondii	Hammond's Flycatcher	3 4	a e
Empidonax minimus	Least Flycatcher	3 4	a e
Empidonax oberholseri	Dusky Flycatcher	3 4	a e

Scientific Name	Common Name	Source Codes	Region Codes

TYRANNIDAE · TYRANT FLYCATCHERS *contd.*

Scientific Name	Common Name	Source Codes	Region Codes
Empidonax traillii	Willow Flycatcher	3 4 6	a d e
Empidonax virescens	Acadian Flycatcher	3 4 5 6	a d e
Empidonax wrightii	Gray Flycatcher	3 4	a e
Aechmolophus mexicanus	Pileated Flycatcher	4	e
Xenotriccus callizonus	Belted Flycatcher	4	e
Cnemotriccus fuscatus	Fuscous Flycatcher	6	d
Mitrephanes phaeocercus	Tufted Flycatcher	4 6	d e
Terenotriccus erythrurus	Ruddy-tailed Flycatcher	4 6	d e
Aphanotriccus audax	Black-billed Flycatcher	4 6	d e
Aphanotriccus capitalis	Tawny-chested Flycatcher	4	e
Myiobius atricaudus	Black-tailed Flycatcher	4 6	d e
Myiobius barbatus[7]	Sulphur-rumped Flycatcher	6	d
Myiobius villosus	Tawny-breasted Flycatcher	6	d
Myiotriccus ornatus	Ornate Flycatcher	6	d
Pyrrhomyias cinnamomea	Cinnamon Flycatcher	6	d
Myiophobus cryptoxanthus	Olive-chested Flycatcher	6	d
Myiophobus fasciatus	Bran-colored Flycatcher	4 6	d e
Myiophobus flavicans	Flavescent Flycatcher	6	d
Myiophobus inornatus	Unadorned Flycatcher	6	d
Myiophobus lintoni	Orange-banded Flycatcher	6	d
Myiophobus ochraceiventris	Ochraceous-breasted Flycatcher	6	d
Myiophobus phoenicomitra	Orange-crested Flycatcher	6	d
Myiophobus pulcher	Handsome Flycatcher	6	d
Myiophobus roraimae	Roraiman Flycatcher	6	d
Hirundinea ferruginea	Cliff Flycatcher	6	d
Onychorhynchus coronatus[8]	Royal Flycatcher	6	d
Platyrinchus coronatus	Golden-crowned Spadebill	4 6	d e
Platyrinchus flavigularis	Yellow-throated Spadebill	6	d
Platyrinchus leucoryphus	Russet-winged Spadebill	6	d
Platyrinchus mystaceus	White-throated Spadebill	4 6	d e
Platyrinchus platyrhynchos	White-crested Spadebill	6	d
Platyrinchus saturatus	Cinnamon-crested Spadebill	6	d
Cnipodectes subbrunneus	Brownish Flycatcher	4 6	d e
Tolmomyias assimilis	Yellow-margined Flycatcher	4 6	d e
Tolmomyias flaviventris	Yellow-breasted Flycatcher	6	d
Tolmomyias poliocephalus	Gray-crowned Flycatcher	6	d
Tolmomyias sulphurescens	Yellow-Olive Flycatcher	4 6	d e
Rhynchocyclus brevirostris	Eye-ringed Flatbill	4 6	d e
Rhynchocyclus fulvipectus	Fulvous-breasted Flatbill	6	d
Rhynchocyclus olivaceus	Olivaceous Flatbill	4 6	d e
Ramphotrigon fuscicauda	Dusky-tailed Flatbill	6	d
Ramphotrigon megacephala	Large-headed Flatbill	6	d
Ramphotrigon ruficauda	Rufous-tailed Flatbill	6	d
Todirostrum albifacies	White-cheeked Tody-Flycatcher	6	d
Todirostrum calopterum	Golden-winged Tody-Flycatcher	6	d
Todirostrum capitale	Black-and-White Tody-Flycatcher	6	d
Todirostrum chrysocrotaphum	Painted Tody-Flycatcher	6	d
Todirostrum cinereum	Common Tody-Flycatcher	4 6	d e
Todirostrum fumifrons	Smoky-fronted Tody-Flycatcher	6	d
Todirostrum latirostre	Rusty-fronted Tody-Flycatcher	6	d
Todirostrum maculatum	Spotted Tody-Flycatcher	6	d
Todirostrum nigriceps	Black-headed Tody-Flycatcher	4 6	d e

Scientific Name	Common Name	Source Codes	Region Codes

Scientific Name	Common Name	Source Codes		Region Codes	
Todirostrum plumbeiceps	Ochre-faced Tody-Flycatcher	6		d	
Todirostrum poliocephalum	Gray-headed Tody-Flycatcher	6		d	
Todirostrum russatum	Ruddy Tody-Flycatcher	6		d	
Todirostrum sylvia	Slate-headed Tody-Flycatcher	4	6	d	e
Ceratotriccus furcatus	Fork-tailed Pygmy-Tyrant	6		d	
Oncostoma cinereigulare[9]	Bentbill	4	6	d	e
Idioptilon aenigma	Zimmer's Tody-Tyrant	6		d	
Idioptilon granadense	Black-throated Tody-Tyrant	6		d	
Idioptilon margaritaceiventer	Pearly-vented Tody-Tyrant	6		d	
Idioptilon mirandae	Buff-breasted Tody-Tyrant	6		d	
Idioptilon nidipendulum	Hangnest Tody-Tyrant	6		d	
Idioptilon orbitatum	Eye-ringed Tody-Tyrant	6		d	
Idioptilon rufigulare	Buff-throated Tody-Tyrant	6		d	
Idioptilon spodiops	Yungas Tody-Tyrant	6		d	
Idioptilon striaticolle	Stripe-necked Tody-Tyrant	6		d	
Idioptilon zosterops	White-eyed Tody-Tyrant	6		d	
Microcochlearius josephinae	Boat-billed Tody-Tyrant	6		d	
Snethlagea minor	Snethlage's Tody-Tyrant	6		d	
Poecilotriccus ruficeps	Rufous-crowned Tody-Tyrant	6		d	
Taeniotriccus andrei	Black-chested Tyrant	6		d	
Lophotriccus eulophotes	Long-crested Pygmy-Tyrant	6		d	
Lophotriccus pileatus	Scale-crested Pygmy-Tyrant	4	6	d	e
Lophotriccus vitiosus	Double-banded Pygmy-Tyrant	6		d	
Colopteryx galeatus	Helmeted Pygmy-Tyrant	6		d	
Atalotriccus pilaris	Pale-eyed Pygmy-Tyrant	4	6	d	e
Myiornis auricularis	Eared Pygmy-Tyrant	6		d	
Myiornis ecaudatus[10]	Short-tailed Pygmy-Tyrant	4	6	d	e
Pseudotriccus pelzelni	Streak-crowned Pygmy-Tyrant	4	6	d	e
Pseudotriccus ruficeps	Rufous-headed Pygmy-Tyrant	6		d	
Pseudotriccus simplex	Hazel-fronted Pygmy-Tyrant	6		d	
Hemitriccus diops	Drab-breasted Pygmy-Tyrant	6		d	
Hemitriccus flammulatus	Flammulated Pygmy-Tyrant	6		d	
Hemitriccus obsoletus	Brown-breasted Pygmy-Tyrant	6		d	
Pogonotriccus eximius	Southern Bristle-Tyrant	6		d	
Pogonotriccus flaviventris	Yellow-bellied Bristle-Tyrant	6		d	
Pogonotriccus gualaquizae	Ecuadorean Bristle-Tyrant	6		d	
Pogonotriccus ophthalmicus	Marbled-faced Bristle-Tyrant	6		d	
Pogonotriccus orbitalis	Spectacled Bristle-Tyrant	6		d	
Pogonotriccus poecilotis	Variegated Bristle-Tyrant	6		d	
Pogonotriccus venezuelanus	Venezuelan Bristle-Tyrant	6		d	
Leptotriccus sylviolus	Bay-ringed Tyrannulet	6		d	
Phylloscartes chapmani	Chapman's Tyrannulet	6		d	
Phylloscartes difficilis	Serra Do Mar Tyrannulet	6		d	
Phylloscartes flavovirens	Yellow-Green Tyrannulet	4		e	
Phylloscartes nigrifrons	Black-fronted Tyrannulet	6		d	
Phylloscartes oustaleti	Oustalet's Tyrannulet	6		d	
Phylloscartes paulistus	Sao Paulo Tyrannulet	6		d	
Phylloscartes roquettei	Minas Gerais Tyrannulet	6		d	
Phylloscartes superciliaris	Rufous-browed Tyrannulet	4	6	d	e
Phylloscartes ventralis	Mottle-cheeked Tyrannulet	6		d	
Phylloscartes virescens	Olive-Green Tyrannulet	6		d	
Capsiempis flaveola	Yellow Tyrannulet	4	6	d	e
Euscarthmus meloryphus	Tawny-crowned Pygmy-Tyrant	6		d	
Euscarthmus rufomarginatus	Rufous-sided Pygmy-Tyrant	6		d	
Pseudocolopteryx acutipennis	Subtropical Doradito	6		d	
Pseudocolopteryx dinellianus	Dinelli's Doradito	6		d	
Pseudocolopteryx flaviventris	Warbling Doradito	6		d	

93

Scientific Name	Common Name	Source Codes	Region Codes

TYRANNIDAE · TYRANT FLYCATCHERS *contd.*

Scientific Name	Common Name	Source Codes	Region Codes
Pseudocolopteryx scalteri	Crested Doradito	6	d
Polystictus pectoralis	Bearded Tachuri	6	d
Polystictus superciliaris	Gray-backed Tachuri	6	d
Culicivora caudacuta	Sharp-tailed Tyrant	6	d
Tachuris rubrigastra	Many-colored Rush-Tyrant	6	d
Anairetes alpinus	Ash-breasted Tit-Tyrant	6	d
Anairetes flavirostris	Yellow-billed Tit-Tyrant	6	d
Anairetes parulus	Tufted Tit-Tyrant	6	d
Anairetes reguloides	Pied-crested Tit-Tyrant	6	d
Uromyias agilis	Agile Tit-Tyrant	6	d
Uromyias agraphia	Unstreaked Tit-Tyrant	6	d
Stigmatura budytoides	Greater Wagtail-Tyrant	6	d
Stigmatura napensis	Lesser Wagtail-Tyrant	6	d
Serpophaga araguayae	Bananal Tyrannulet	6	d
Serpophaga cinerea	Torrent Tyrannulet	4 6	d e
Serpophaga griseiceps	Gray-crowned Tyrannulet	6	d
Serpophaga hypoleuca	River Tyrannulet	6	d
Serpophaga munda	White-bellied Tyrannulet	6	d
Serpophaga nigricans	Sooty Tyrannulet	6	d
Serpophaga subcristata	White-crested Tyrannulet	6	d
Inezia inornata	Plain Tyrannulet	6	d
Inezia subflava	Pale-tipped Tyrannulet	6	d
Inezia tenuirostris	Slender-billed Tyrannulet	6	d
Mecocerculus calopterus	Rufous-winged Tyrannulet	6	d
Mecocerculus hellmayri	Buff-banded Tyrannulet	6	d
Mecocerculus leucophrys	White-throated Tyrannulet	6	d
Mecocerculus minor	Sulphur-bellied Tyrannulet	6	d
Mecocerculus poecilocercus	White-tailed Tyrannulet	6	d
Mecocerculus stictopterus	White-banded Tyrannulet	6	d
Colorhamphus parvirostris	Patagonian Tyrant	6	d
Elaenia albiceps	White-crested Elaenia	6	d
Elaenia chiriquensis	Lesser Elaenia	4 6	d e
Elaenia cristata	Plain-crested Elaenia	6	d
Elaenia dayi	Great Elaenia	6	d
Elaenia fallax	Greater Antillean Elaenia	5	e
Elaenia flavogaster	Yellow-bellied Elaenia	4 5 6	d e
Elaenia frantzii[11]	Mountain Elaenia	4 6	d e
Elaenia gigas	Mottle-backed Elaenia	6	d
Elaenia martinica	Caribbean Elaenia	4 5 6	d e
Elaenia mesoleuca	Olivaceous Elaenia	6	d
Elaenia obscura	Highland Elaenia	6	d
Elaenia pallatangae	Sierran Elaenia	6	d
Elaenia parvirostris	Small-billed Elaenia	6	d
Elaenia pelzelni	Brownish Elaenia	6	d
Elaenia ruficeps	Rufous-crowned Elaenia	6	d
Elaenia spectabilis	Large Elaenia	6	d
Elaenia strepera	Slaty Elaenia	6	d
Myiopagis caniceps	Gray Elaenia	6	d
Myiopagis cotta	Jamaican Elaenia	5	e
Myiopagis flavivertex	Yellow-crowned Elaenia	6	d
Myiopagis gaimardii	Forest Elaenia	4 6	d e
Myiopagis subplacens	Pacific Elaenia	6	d
Myiopagis viridicata	Greenish Elaenia	4 6	d e
Suiriri suiriri	Suiriri Flycatcher	6	d
Sublegatus modestus	Scrub Flycatcher	4 6	d e
Phaeomyias leucospodia	Gray-and-White Tyrannulet	6	d
Phaeomyias murina	Mouse-colored Tyrannulet	4 6	d e

94

Scientific Name	Common Name	Source Codes	Region Codes

TYRANNIDAE · TYRANT FLYCATCHERS *contd*

Scientific Name	Common Name	Source Codes	Region Codes
Camptostoma imberbe	Beardless Flycatcher	3 4	a e
Camptostoma obsoletum	Southern Beardless Tyrannulet	4 6	d e
Xanthomyias reiseri	Reiser's Tyrannulet	6	d
Xanthomyias sclateri	Sclater's Tyrannulet	6	d
Xanthomyias virescens	Greenish Tyrannulet	6	d
Phyllomyias fasciatus	Planalto Tyrannulet	6	d
Phyllomyias griseiceps	Sooty-headed Tyrannulet	4 6	d e
Tyranniscus australis	Olrog's Tyrannulet	6	d
Tyranniscus bolivianus	Bolivian Tyrannulet	6	d
Tyranniscus cinereicapillus	Red-billed Tyrannulet	6	d
Tyranniscus cinereiceps	Ashy-headed Tyrannulet	6	d
Tyranniscus gracilipes	Slender-footed Tyrannulet	6	d
Tyranniscus nigrocapillus	Black-capped Tyrannulet	6	d
Tyranniscus uropygialis	Tawny-rumped Tyrannulet	6	d
Tyranniscus vilissimus	Paltry Tyrannulet	4 6	d e
Tyranniscus viridiflavus	Golden-faced Tyrannulet	6	d
Oreotriccus griseocapillus	Gray-capped Tyrannulet	6	d
Oreotriccus plumbeiceps	Plumbeous-crowned Tyrannulet	6	d
Tyrannulus elatus	Yellow-crowned Tyrannulet	4 6	d e
Acrochordopus burmeisteri	Rough-legged Tyrannulet	6	d
Acrochordopus zeledoni	White-fronted Tyrannulet	4	e
Ornithion brunneicapillum	Brown-capped Tyrannulet	4	e
Ornithion inerme	White-lored Tyrannulet	6	d
Ornithion semiflavum	Yellow-bellied Tyrannulet	4 6	d e
Leptopogon amaurocephalus	Sepia-capped Flycatcher	4 6	d e
Leptopogon rufipectus	Rufous-breasted Flycatcher	6	d
Leptopogon superciliaris	Slaty-capped Flycatcher	4 6	d e
Leptopogon taczanowskii	Inca Flycatcher	6	d
Mionectes olivaceus	Olive-striped Flycatcher	4 6	d e
Mionectes striaticollis	Streak-necked Flycatcher	6	d
Pipromorpha macconnelli	McConnell's Flycatcher	6	d
Pipromorpha oleaginea	Ochre-bellied Flycatcher	4 6	d e
Pipromorpha rufiventris	Gray-hooded Flycatcher	6	d
Corythopis delalandi	Southern Antpipit	6	d
Corythopis torquata	Ringed Antpipit	6	d

OXYRUNCIDAE · SHARPBILL 1 species recorded

Scientific Name	Common Name	Source Codes	Region Codes
Oxyruncus cristatus	Sharpbill	4 6	d e

PIPRIDAE · MANAKINS 53 species recorded

Scientific Name	Common Name	Source Codes	Region Codes
Pipra aureola	Crimson-hooded Manakin	6	d
Pipra caeruleocapilla	Cerulean-capped Manakin	6	d
Pipra chloromeros	Round-tailed Manakin	6	d
Pipra cornuta	Scarlet-horned Manakin	6	d
Pipra coronata	Blue-crowned Manakin	4 6	d e
Pipra erythrocephala	Golden-headed Manakin	4 6	d e
Pipra fasciicauda	Band-tailed Manakin	6	d
Pipra iris	Opal-crowned Manakin	6	d
Pipra isidorei	Blue-rumped Manakin	6	d
Pipra mentalis	Red-capped Manakin	4 6	d e

Scientific Name	Common Name	Source Codes	Region Codes

Scientific Name	Common Name	Source Codes	Region Codes
Pipra nattereri	Snow-capped Manakin	6	d
Pipra pipra	White-crowned Manakin	4 6	d e
Pipra rubrocapilla	Red-headed Manakin	6	d
Pipra serena	White-fronted Manakin	6	d
Pipra vilasboasi	Golden-crowned Manakin	6	d
Teleonema filicauda	Wire-tailed Manakin	6	d
Antilophia galeata	Helmeted Manakin	6	d
Chiroxiphia caudata	Swallow-tailed Manakin	6	d
Chiroxiphia lanceolata	Sharp-tailed Manakin	4 6	d e
Chiroxiphia linearis	Long-tailed Manakin	4	e
Chiroxiphia pareola	Blue-backed Manakin	6	d
Masius chrysopterus	Golden-winged Manakin	6	d
Ilicura militaris	Pin-tailed Manakin	6	d
Corapipo gutturalis	White-throated Manakin	6	d
Corapipo leucorrhoa	White-ruffed Manakin	4 6	d e
Manacus cerritus	Almirante Manakin	4	e
Manacus manacus	White-bearded Manakin	6	d
Manacus vitellinus[1]	Golden-collared Manakin	4 6	d e
Allocotopterus deliciosus	Club-winged Manakin	6	d
Machaeropterus pyrocephalus	Fiery-capped Manakin	6	d
Machaeropterus regulus	Striped Manakin	6	d
Xenopipo atronitens	Black Manakin	6	d
Chloropipo flavicapilla	Yellow-headed Manakin	6	d
Chloropipo holochlora	Green Manakin	4 6	d e
Chloropipo unicolor	Jet Manakin	6	d
Chloropipo uniformis	Olive Manakin	6	d
Neopipo cinnamomea	Cinnamon Manakin	6	d
Heterocercus aurantiivertex	Orange-crowned Manakin	6	d
Heterocercus flavivertex	Yellow-crowned Manakin	6	d
Heterocercus linteatus	Flame-crowned Manakin	6	d
Neopelma aurifrons	Wied's Tyrant-Manakin	6	d
Neopelma chrysocephalum	Saffron-crested Tyrant-Manakin	6	d
Neopelma pallescens	Pale-bellied Tyrant-Manakin	6	d
Neopelma sulphureiventer	Sulphur-bellied Tyrant-Manakin	6	d
Tyranneutes stolzmanni	Dwarf Tyrant-Manakin	6	d
Tyranneutes virescens	Tiny Tyrant-Manakin	6	d
Piprites chloris	Wing-barred Manakin	6	d
Piprites griseiceps	Gray-headed Manakin	4	e
Piprites pileatus	Black-capped Manakin	6	d
Sapayoa aenigma	Broad-billed Manakin	4 6	d e
Schiffornis major	Greater Manakin	6	d
Schiffornis turdinus	Thrush-like Manakin	4 6	d e
Schiffornis virescens	Greenish Manakin	6	d

COTINGIDAE · COTINGAS, COCKS-OF-THE-ROCK, BECARDS 79 species recorded

Scientific Name	Common Name	Source Codes	Region Codes
Laniisoma elegans	Shrike-like Cotinga	6	d
Rupicola peruviana	Andean Cock-of-the-Rock	6	d
Rupicola rupicola	Guianan Cock-of-the-Rock	6	d
Phibalura flavirostris	Swallow-tailed Cotinga	6	d
Tijuca atra	Black-and-Gold Cotinga	6	d
Carpornis cucullatus	Hooded Berryeater	6	d

Scientific Name	Common Name	Source Codes	Region Codes
COTINGIDAE COTINGAS, COCKS-OF-THE-ROCK, BECARDS contd.			
Carpornis melanocephalus	Black-headed Berryeater	6	d
Porphyrolaema porphyrolaema	Purple-throated Cotinga	6	d
Cotinga amabilis[1]	Lovely Cotinga	4	e
Cotinga cayana	Spangled Cotinga	6	d
Cotinga cotinga	Purple-breasted Cotinga	6	d
Cotinga maculata	Banded Cotinga	6	d
Cotinga maynana	Plum-throated Cotinga	6	d
Cotinga nattererii	Blue Cotinga	4 6	d e
Cotinga ridgwayi[1]	Turquoise Cotinga	4	e
Xipholena atropurpurea	White-winged Cotinga	6	d
Xipholena lamellipennis	White-tailed Cotinga	6	d
Xipholena punicea	Pompadour Cotinga	6	d
Carpodectes antoniae	Yellow-billed Cotinga	4	e
Carpodectes hopkei	White Cotinga	4 6	d e
Carpodectes nitidus	Snowy Cotinga	4	e
Conioptilon mcilhennyi	Black-faced Cotinga	6	d
Ampelion rubrocristatus[2]	Red-crested Cotinga	6	d
Ampelion rufaxilla	Chestnut-crested Cotinga	6	d
Ampelion sclateri	Bay-vented Cotinga	6	d
Ampelion stresemanni	White-cheeked Cotinga	6	d
Pipreola arcuata	Barred Fruiteater	6	d
Pipreola aureopectus[3]	Golden-breasted Fruiteater	6	d
Pipreola chlorolepidota	Fiery-throated Fruiteater	6	d
Pipreola formosa	Handsome Fruiteater	6	d
Pipreola frontalis	Scarlet-breasted Fruiteater	6	d
Pipreola intermedia	Band-tailed Fruiteater	6	d
Pipreola riefferii	Green-and-Black Fruiteater	6	d
Pipreola whitelyi	Red-banded Fruiteater	6	d
Ampelioides tschudii	Scaled Fruiteater	6	d
Iodopleura fusca	Dusky Purpletuft	6	d
Iodopleura isabellae	White-browed Purpletuft	6	d
Iodopleura pipra	Buff-throated Purpletuft	6	d
Calyptura cristata	Kinglet Calyptura	6	d
Lipaugus cryptolophus	Olivaceous Piha	6	d
Lipaugus fuscocinereus	Dusky Piha	6	d
Lipaugus lanioides	Cinnamon-vented Piha	6	d
Lipaugus streptophorus	Rose-collared Piha	6	d
Lipaugus subalaris	Gray-tailed Piha	6	d
Lipaugus unirufus	Rufous Piha	4 6	d e
Lipaugus vociferans	Screaming Piha	6	d
Chirocylla uropygialis	Scimitar-winged Piha	6	d
Pachyramphus aglaiae[4]	Rose-throated Becard	3 4	a c
Pachyramphus albogriseus	Black-and-White Becard	4 6	d e
Pachyramphus castaneus	Chestnut-crowned Becard	6	d
Pachyramphus cinnamomeus	Cinnamon Becard	4 6	d e
Pachyramphus major	Gray-collared Becard	4	e
Pachyramphus marginatus	Black-capped Becard	6	d
Pachyramphus minor	Pink-throated Becard	6	d
Pachyramphus niger	Jamaican Becard	5	c
Pachyramphus polychopterus	White-winged Becard	4 6	d e
Pachyramphus rufus	Cinereous Becard	4 6	d e
Pachyramphus spodiurus	Slaty Becard	6	d
Pachyramphus surinamus	Glossy-backed Becard	6	d
Pachyramphus validus	Plain Becard	6	d
Pachyramphus versicolor	Barred Becard	4 6	d e
Pachyramphus viridis	Green-backed Becard	6	d
Tityra cayana	Black-tailed Tityra	6	d

97

Scientific Name	Common Name	Source Codes	Region Codes

COTINGIDAE · COTINGAS, COCKS-OF-THE-ROCK, BECARDS *contd.*

Scientific Name	Common Name	Source Codes	Region Codes
Tityra inquisitor	Black-crowned Tityra	4 6	d e
Tityra semifasciata	Masked Tityra	4 6	d e
Haematoderus militaris	Crimson Fruitcrow	6	d
Querula purpurata	Purple-throated Fruitcrow	4 6	d e
Pyroderus scutatus	Red-ruffed Fruitcrow	6	d
Cephalopterus glabricollis	Bare-necked Umbrellabird	4	e
Cephalopterus ornatus	Amazonian Umbrellabird	6	d
Cephalopterus penduliger	Long-wattled Umbrellabird	6	d
Perissocephalus tricolor	Capuchinbird	6	d
Gymnoderus foetidus	Bare-necked Fruitcrow	6	d
Procnias alba	White Bellbird	6	d
Procnias averano	Bearded Bellbird	6	d
Procnias nudicollis	Bare-throated Bellbird	6	d
Procnias tricarunculata	Three-wattled Bellbird	4	e
Phoenicircus carnifex	Guianan Red-Cotinga	6	d
Phoenicircus nigricollis	Black-necked Red-Cotinga	6	d

PHYTOTOMIDAE · PLANTCUTTERS   3 species recorded

Scientific Name	Common Name	Source Codes	Region Codes
Phytotoma raimondii	Peruvian Plantcutter	6	d
Phytotoma rara	Rufous-tailed Plantcutter	6	d
Phytotoma rutila	White-tipped Plantcutter	6	d

MENURIDAE · LYREBIRDS   2 species recorded

Scientific Name	Common Name	Source Codes	Region Codes
Menura alberti	Albert's Lyrebird	36	i
Menura novaehollandiae	Superb Lyrebird	36	i

ATRICHORNITHIDAE · SCRUB-BIRDS   2 species recorded

Scientific Name	Common Name	Source Codes	Region Codes
Atrichornis clamosus	Noisy Scrub-Bird	36	i
Atrichornis rufescens	Rufous Scrub-Bird	36	i

ALAUDIDAE · LARKS   76 species recorded

Scientific Name	Common Name	Source Codes	Region Codes
Mirafra africana	Rufous-naped Lark	8	c
Mirafra africanoides	Fawn-colored Lark	8	c
Mirafra albescens[1]	Karoo Lark	8	c
Mirafra albicauda	Northern White-tailed Bush-Lark	8	c
Mirafra angolensis	Angolan Lark	8	c
Mirafra apiata	Clapper Lark	8	c
Mirafra assamica	Rufous-winged Bush-Lark	15 18 55	f g
Mirafra burra	Ferruginous Lark	8	c
Mirafra cantillans	Northern Singing Bush-Lark	9	c
Mirafra cheniana	Southern Singing Bush-Lark	8	c
Mirafra chuana	Short-clawed Lark	8	c
Mirafra collaris	Collared Lark	8	c
Mirafra cordofanica	Kordofan Bush-Lark	8	c

98

Scientific Name	Common Name	Source Codes	Region Codes
ALAUDIDAE · LARKS contd.			
Mirafra curvirostris[1]	Long-billed Lark	8	c
Mirafra erythroptera	Indian Red-winged Bush-Lark	15	f
Mirafra gilletti	Gillett's Lark	8	c
Mirafra hova	Madagascar Bush-Lark	10	c
Mirafra hypermetra	Red-winged Bush-Lark	9	c
Mirafra javanica	Singing Bush-Lark	8 15 17 18 19 21 22 35 36 55	c f g h i j
Mirafra nigricans	Dusky Lark	8	c
Mirafra passerina	Monotonous Lark	9	c
Mirafra poecilosterna	Pink-breasted Lark	8	c
Mirafra pulpa	Friedmann's Bush-Lark	8	c
Mirafra ruddi[2]	Rudd's Lark	8	c
Mirafra rufa	Rusty Bush-Lark	8	c
Mirafra rufocinnamomea	Flappet Lark	8	c
Mirafra sabota	Sabota Lark	8	c
Mirafra somalica	Somali Long-billed Lark	8	c
Mirafra williamsi	Marsabit Lark	9	c
Chersomanes albofasciata	Spike-heeled Lark	8	c
Eremopterix australis	Black-eared Finch-Lark	8	c
Eremopterix grisea	Ashy-crowned Finch-Lark	15	f
Eremopterix leucopareia	Fischer's Finch-Lark	8	c
Eremopterix leucotis	Chestnut-backed Finch-Lark	8	c
Eremopterix nigriceps	Black-crowned Finch-Lark	1 8 15	b c f
Eremopterix signata	Chestnut-headed Finch-Lark	8	c
Eremopterix verticalis	Gray-backed Finch-Lark	8	c
Ammomanes cincturus	Bar-tailed Desert Lark	1 8	b c
Ammomanes deserti	Desert Lark	1 8 15	b c f
Ammomanes grayi	Gray's Lark	8	c
Ammomanes phoenicurus	Rufous-tailed Finch-Lark	15	f
Alaemon alaudipes	Bifasciated Lark	1 8 15	b c f
Alaemon hamertoni	Lesser Hoopoe-Lark	8	c
Rhamphocoris clot-bey	Thick-billed Lark	1	b
Melanocorypha bimaculata	Eastern Calandra Lark	1 8 15 17	b c f g
Melanocorypha calandra	Calandra Lark	1	b
Melanocorypha leucoptera	White-winged Lark	1	b
Melanocorypha maxima	Long-billed Calandra Lark	1 15 17	b f g
Melanocorypha mongolica	Mongolian Lark	1 3 17	b g k
Melanocorypha yeltoniensis	Black Lark	1	b
Calandrella acutirostris	Hume's Short-toed Lark	1 15 17	b f g
Calandrella cinerea[3]	Short-toed Lark	1 8 15 17 18	b c f g
Calandrella conirostris	Pink-billed Lark	8	c
Calandrella dunni[4]	Dunn's Lark	1 8 9	b c
Calandrella fringillaris	Botha's Lark	8	c
Calandrella obbiensis	Obbia Lark	8	c
Calandrella personata	Masked Lark	8	c
Calandrella raytal	Sandlark	15 18	f g
Calandrella razae	Raza Short-toed Lark	1 53	b
Calandrella rufescens[5]	Lesser Short-toed Lark	1 8 17 18	b c g
Calandrella sclateri	Sclater's Short-toed Lark	8	c
Calandrella somalica	Rufous Short-toed Lark	9	c
Calandrella starki	Stark's Short-toed Lark	8	c
Chersophilus duponti	Dupont's Lark	1	b
Galerida cristata	Crested Lark	1 8 15 17	b c f g
Galerida deva	Sykes's Crested Lark	15	f
Galerida fremantlii[6]	Short-tailed Lark	9	c
Galerida magnirostris	Thick-billed Lark	8	c
Galerida malabarica	Malabar Crested Lark	15	f

Scientific Name	Common Name	Source Codes	Region Codes

ALAUDIDAE · LARKS contd.

Scientific Name	Common Name	Source Codes	Region Codes
Galerida modesta	Sun Lark	8	c
Galerida thecklae	Thekla Lark	1 8	b c
Lullula arborea	Wood Lark	1	b
Alauda arvensis	Skylark	1 3 8 15 17 18 21 22 37	a b c f g h i k
Alauda gulgula	Small Skylark	1 15 17	b f g h
Eremophila alpestris	Horned Lark	1 3 4 6 15 17	a b d e f g
Eremophila bilopha	Temminck's Horned Lark	1	b

HIRUNDINIDAE · SWALLOWS, MARTINS 74 species recorded

Scientific Name	Common Name	Source Codes	Region Codes
Pseudochelidon eurystomina	African River-Martin	8	c
Pseudochelidon sirintarae	White-eyed River-Martin	55	g
Tachycineta albilinea[1]	Mangrove Swallow	4 6	d e
Tachycineta albiventer	White-winged Swallow	6	d
Tachycineta bicolor	Tree Swallow	3 4 5 6	a d e
Tachycineta leucopyga	Chilean Swallow	6	d
Tachycineta leucorrhoa	White-rumped Swallow	6	d
Tachycineta thalassina	Violet-Green Swallow	3 4	a e
Callichelidon cyaneoviridis	Bahama Swallow	3 5	a e
Kalochelidon euchrysea	Golden Swallow	5	e
Progne chalybea	Gray-breasted Martin	3 4 6	a d e
Progne dominicensis	Caribbean Martin	6	d
Progne modesta	Southern Martin	6	d
Progne subis	Purple Martin	3 4 5 6	a d e
Progne tapera	Brown-chested Martin	4 6	d e
Notiochelidon cyanoleuca	Blue-and-White Swallow	4 6	d e
Notiochelidon flavipes	Pale-footed Swallow	6	d
Notiochelidon murina	Brown-bellied Swallow	6	d
Notiochelidon pileata	Black-capped Swallow	4	e
Atticora fasciata	White-banded Swallow	6	d
Atticora melanoleuca	Black-collared Swallow	6	d
Neochelidon tibialis	White-thighed Swallow	4 6	d e
Alopochelidon fucata	Tawny-headed Swallow	6	d
Stelgidopteryx ruficollis	Rough-winged Swallow	3 4 5 6	a d e
Cheramoeca leucosterna	White-backed Swallow	36	i
Riparia cincta	Banded Martin	8	c
Riparia congica	Congo Sand Martin	8	c
Riparia paludicola	Brown-throated Sand Martin	1 8 10 15 17 18 22 55	b c f g h
Riparia riparia	Bank Swallow	1 3 4 5 6 8 10 15 17 18 19 21 22 55	a b c d e f g h
Phedina borbonica	Mascarene Martin	8	c
Phedina brazzae	Congo Martin	8	c
Hirundo abyssinica[2]	Lesser Striped Swallow	8	c
Hirundo aethiopica	Ethiopian Swallow	8	c
Hirundo albigularis	White-throated Swallow	8	c
Hirundo angolensis	Angola Swallow	8	c
Hirundo atrocaerulea	Blue Swallow	8	c
Hirundo concolor	Dusky Crag Martin	15 18 55	f g
Hirundo cucullata	Greater Striped Swallow	8	c
Hirundo daurica	Red-rumped Swallow	1 8 15 17 18	b c f g h
Hirundo dimidiata	Pearl-breasted Swallow	8	c
Hirundo fluvicola	Indian Cliff Swallow	1 15	b f

100

Scientific Name	Common Name	Source Codes	Region Codes

HIRUNDINIDAE · SWALLOWS, MARTINS contd.

Scientific Name	Common Name	Source Codes	Region Codes
Hirundo fuliginosa	Cameroon Cliff Swallow	8	c
Hirundo fuligula	African Rock Martin	8	c
Hirundo griseopyga	Gray-rumped Swallow	8	c
Hirundo leucosoma	Pied-winged Swallow	8	c
Hirundo lucida	Red-chested Swallow	9	c
Hirundo megaensis	White-tailed Swallow	8	c
Hirundo neoxena	Welcome Swallow	36 37	i
Hirundo nigricans	Tree Martin	35 36 37 38	i j k
Hirundo nigrita	Little Blue Swallow	8	c
Hirundo nigrorufa	Congo Swallow	8	c
Hirundo obsoleta	Pale Crag Martin	1 15	b f
Hirundo preussi	Preuss's Cliff Swallow	9	c
Hirundo rupestris	Crag Martin	1 8 15 17	b c f g
Hirundo rustica	Barn Swallow	1 3 4 5 6 8 10 15 17 18 19 21 22 35 36 55	a b c d e f g h i j
Hirundo semirufa	Rufous-chested Swallow	8	c
Hirundo senegalensis	Mosque Swallow	8	c
Hirundo smithii	Wire-tailed Swallow	1 8 15 18 55	b c f g
Hirundo spilodera	African Cliff Swallow	8	c
Hirundo striolata	Striated Swallow	15 18 19 21 22 55	f g h
Hirundo tahitica[3]	Pacific Swallow	15 17 18 19 21 22 35 36 38 55	f g h i j k
Petrochelidon andecola	Andean Swallow	6	d
Petrochelidon ariel	Fairy Martin	36	i
Petrochelidon fulva	Cave Swallow	3 4 5 6	a d e
Petrochelidon nigricans	Australian Tree-Martin	36	i
Petrochelidon pyrrhonota	Cliff Swallow	3 4 5 6	a d e
Delichon dasypus	Asiatic House Martin	18 19 21 22 55	g h
Delichon nipalensis	Nepal House Martin	1 15 18 55	b f g
Delichon urbica	House Martin	1 8 15 17 18 55	b c f g
Psalidoprocne albiceps	White-headed Rough-winged Swallow	8	c
Psalidoprocne fuliginosa	Cameroon Mountain Rough-winged Swallow	8	c
Psalidoprocne nitens	Square-tailed Rough-winged Swallow	8	c
Psalidoprocne obscura	Fanti Rough-winged Swallow	8	c
Psalidoprocne pristoptera	Blue Rough-winged Swallow	8	c

MOTACILLIDAE · WAGTAILS, PIPITS 54 species recorded

Scientific Name	Common Name	Source Codes	Region Codes
Dendronanthus indicus[1]	Forest Wagtail	1 15 17 18 19 21 22 55	b f g h
Motacilla aguimp	African Pied Wagtail	9	c
Motacilla alba	White Wagtail	1 3 4 8 15 17 18 19 21 22 55	a b c e f g h
Motacilla capensis	Cape Wagtail	8	c
Motacilla cinerea	Gray Wagtail	1 8 17 18 19 22 35 55	b c g h j
Motacilla citreola	Yellow-headed Wagtail	1 15 17 18	b f g
Motacilla clara	Mountain Wagtail	8	c
Motacilla flava	Yellow Wagtail	1 3 8 15 17 18 19 21 22 35 36 55	a b c f g h i j
Motacilla flaviventris	Madagascar Wagtail	10	c

Scientific Name	Common Name	Source Codes	Region Codes

MOTACILLIDAE · WAGTAILS, PIPITS *contd.*

Scientific Name	Common Name	Source Codes	Region Codes
Motacilla grandis	Japanese Wagtail	1	b
Motacilla maderaspatensis	Large Pied Wagtail	1 15	b f
Tmetothylacus tenellus	Golden Pipit	8	c
Macronyx amerliae	Rosy-breasted Longclaw	8	c
Macronyx aurantigula	Pangani Longclaw	8	c
Macronyx capensis	Orange-throated Longclaw	8	c
Macronyx croceus	Yellow-throated Longclaw	8	c
Macronyx flavicollis	Ethiopian Longclaw	8	c
Macronyx fullebornii	Fulleborn's Longclaw	8	c
Macronyx grimwoodi	Grimwood's Longclaw	8	c
Macronyx sharpei	Sharpe's Longclaw	8	c
Anthus antarctica	Sub-antarctic Pipit	57	d
Anthus berthelotii	Berthelot's Pipit	1	b
Anthus bogotensis	Paramo Pipit	6	d
Anthus brachyurus	Short-tailed Pipit	9	c
Anthus caffer	Bushveld Tree-Pipit	9	c
Anthus campestris	Tawny Pipit	1 8 15 17	b c f g
Anthus cervinus	Red-throated Pipit	1 3 4 8 15 17 18 19 21 22 55	a b c e f g h
Anthus chacoensis	Chaco Pipit	6	d
Anthus chloris	Yellow-breasted Pipit	8	c
Anthus correndera	Correndera Pipit	6	d
Anthus crenatus	Rock Pipit	8	c
Anthus furcatus	Short-billed Pipit	6	d
Anthus godlewskii	Blyth's Pipit	1 8 15 55	b c f g
Anthus gustavi	Pechora Pipit	1 3 17 19 21 22	a b g h
Anthus gutturalis	New Guinea Pipit	35	j
Anthus hellmayri	Hellmayr's Pipit	6	d
Anthus hodgsoni	Oriental Tree-Pipit	1 15 17 18 19 21 22 55	b f g h
Anthus leucophrys	Plain-backed Pipit	8	c
Anthus lineiventris	Striped Pipit	8	c
Anthus lutescens	Yellowish Pipit	4 6	d e
Anthus melindae	Malindi Pipit	8	c
Anthus nattereri	Ochre-breasted Pipit	6	d
Anthus nilghiriensis	Nilgiri Pipit	15	f
Anthus novaeseelandiae[2]	Richard's Pipit	1 8 15 17 18 19 21 22 35 37 55	b c f g h i j
Anthus pallidiventris	Long-legged Pipit	8	c
Anthus pratensis	Meadow Pipit	1 15	b f
Anthus roseatus[3]	Hodgson's Pipit	1 15 17 18 55	b f g
Anthus similis	Long-billed Pipit	1 8 15 18	b c f
Anthus sokokensis	Sokoke Pipit	8	c
Anthus spinoletta[4]	Water Pipit	1 3 4 15 17 18 55	a b e f g h
Anthus spragueii	Sprague's Pipit	3 4	a e
Anthus sylvanus	Upland Pipit	1 15 17	b f g
Anthus trivialis	Tree Pipit	1 8 15 17	b c f g
Anthus vaalensis	Sandy Plain-backed Pipit	8	c

CAMPEPHAGIDAE · CUCKOO-SHRIKES 72 species recorded

Scientific Name	Common Name	Source Codes	Region Codes
Pteropodocys maxima	Ground Cuckoo-Shrike	36	i
Coracina abbotti[1]	Abbott's Cuckoo-Shrike	27	h
Coracina analis	Mountain Graybird	38	k
Coracina atriceps	Moluccan Cuckoo-Shrike	31	j

Scientific Name	Common Name	Source Codes	Region Codes

CAMPEPHAGIDAE · CUCKOO-SHRIKES *contd.*

Scientific Name	Common Name	Source Codes	Region Codes
Coracina azurea	Blue Cuckoo-Shrike	8	c
Coracina bicolor	Celebes Cuckoo-Shrike	29	h
Coracina boyeri	Rufous-underwing Graybird	35	j
Coracina caeruleogrisea	Stout-billed Graybird	35	j
Coracina caerulescens	Black Graybird	22	h
Coracina caesia	African Gray Cuckoo-Shrike	8	c
Coracina caledonica	Melanesian Graybird	38	k
Coracina cinerea	Madagascar Cuckoo-Shrike	10	c
Coracina dohertyi	Doherty's Graybird	32	j
Coracina fimbriata	Lesser Graybird	19 21 55	g h
Coracina fortis	Cheeky Cuckoo-Shrike	31	j
Coracina graueri	Grauer's Cuckoo-Shrike	8	c
Coracina holopolium	Black-bellied Graybird	38	k
Coracina larvata	Black-faced Graybird	19 21	h
Coracina leucopygia	White-rumped Cuckoo-Shrike	29	h
Coracina lineata	Lineated Cuckoo-Shrike	35 36 38	i j k
Coracina longicauda	Black-hooded Graybird	35	j
Coracina macregori	Sharp-tailed Graybird	22 23	h
Coracina melanoptera	Black-headed Cuckoo-Shrike	15 18	f h
Coracina melaschistos	Lesser Cuckoo-Shrike	1 15 17 55	b f g
Coracina montana	Black-bellied Graybird	35	j
Coracina morio	Muller's Graybird	22 35	h j
Coracina newtoni	Reunion Cuckoo-Shrike	14	c
Coracina novaehollandiae	Large Cuckoo-Shrike	15 17 18 19 35 36 37 38 55	f g h i j k
Coracina panayensis	White-winged Graybird	22	h
Coracina papuensis [2]	Papuan Cuckoo-Shrike	35 36 38	i j k
Coracina parvula	Halmahera Graybird	31	j
Coracina pectoralis	White-breasted Cuckoo-Shrike	8	c
Coracina polioptera	Gray Cuckoo-Shrike	18 55	g
Coracina pollens	Able Cuckoo-Shrike	31	j
Coracina robusta	Little Cuckoo-Shrike	36	i
Coracina schistacea	Slaty Cuckoo-Shrike	31	j
Coracina schisticeps	Gray's Graybird	35	j
Coracina striata	Barred Cuckoo-Shrike	15 19 21 22 55	f g h
Coracina temminckii	Temminck's Cuckoo-Shrike	29	h
Coracina tenuirostris	Long-billed Graybird	35 36 38	i j k
Coracina typica	Mauritius Cuckoo-Shrike	14	c
Campochaera sloetii	Orange Cuckoo-Shrike	35	j
Chlamydochaera jefferyi	Black-breasted Triller	19 21	h
Lalage atrovirens	Black-browed Triller	35	j
Lalage aurea	Moluccan Triller	29	h
Lalage leucomela	White-browed Triller	35 36	i j
Lalage leucopyga	Long-tailed Triller	38	k
Lalage maculosa	Polynesian Triller	38	k
Lalage melanoleuca	Black-and-White Triller	22	h
Lalage nigra	Pied Triller	21 22 55	g h
Lalage sharpei	Samoan Triller	38	k
Lalage suerii	White-winged Triller	19 35 36	h i j
Campephaga flava [3]	Black Cuckoo-Shrike	9	c
Campephaga lobata	Wattled Cuckoo-Shrike	8	c
Campephaga oriolina [4]	Oriole Cuckoo-Shrike	9	c
Campephaga petiti	Petit's Cuckoo-Shrike	9	c
Campephaga phoenicea	Red-shouldered Cuckoo-Shrike	8	c
Campephaga quiscalina	Purple-throated Cuckoo-Shrike	8	c

Scientific Name	Common Name	Source Codes	Region Codes

CAMPEPHAGIDAE · CUCKOO-SHRIKES *contd.*

Scientific Name	Common Name	Source Codes	Region Codes
Pericrocotus brevirostris	Short-billed Minivet	15 17 18 55	f g
Pericrocotus cinnamomeus[5]	Small Minivet	15 18 19 21 55	f g h
Pericrocotus divaricatus	Ashy Minivet	1 55	b g
Pericrocotus erythropygius	White-bellied Minivet	15 18	f g
Pericrocotus ethologus	Flame-colored Minivet	1 15 17 18 55	b f g
Pericrocotus flammeus	Scarlet Minivet	15 17 18 19 21 22 55	f g h
Pericrocotus miniatus	Sunda Minivet	19	h
Pericrocotus roseus	Rosy Minivet	15 17 18 19 21 22 55	f g h
Pericrocotus solaris	Mountain Minivet	15 17 18 19 21 55	f g h
Pericrocotus lansbergi	Flores Minivet	32	j
Hemipus hirundinaceus	Black-winged Flycatcher-Shrike	18 19 21 55	g h
Hemipus picatus	Pied Flycatcher-Shrike	15 17 18 19 21 55	f g h
Tephrodornis gularis	Brown-tailed Wood Shrike	17 18 19 21 55	g h
Tephrodornis pondicerianus	Common Wood Shrike	15 18 55	f g

PYCNONOTIDAE · BULBULS   118 species recorded

Scientific Name	Common Name	Source Codes	Region Codes
Spizixos canifrons	Finch-billed Bulbul	1 15 17 18 55	b f g
Spizixos semitorques	Collared Finch-billed Bulbul	1 17 55	b g
Andropadus ansorgei[1]	Ansorge's Gray Greenbul	9	c
Andropadus curvirostris	Sombre Bulbul	8	c
Andropadus gracilirostris	Slender-billed Greenbul	8	c
Andropadus gracilis	Little Gray Bulbul	8	c
Andropadus hallae	Hall's Greenbul	67	c
Andropadus importunus	Sombre Greenbul	8	c
Andropadus latirostris	Yellow-whiskered Greenbul	8	c
Andropadus masukuensis	Shelley's Greenbul	9	c
Andropadus milanjensis	Stripe-cheeked Greenbul	8	c
Andropadus montanus	Mountain Bulbul	8	c
Andropadus tephrolaemus	Gray-throated Bulbul	8	c
Andropadus virens	Little Greenbul	8	c
Pycnonotus atriceps	Black-headed Bulbul	15 18 19 21 55	f g h
Pycnonotus aurigaster	White-eared Bulbul	18 55	g
Pycnonotus barbatus[2]	Common Bulbul	1 8	b c
Pycnonotus bimaculatus	Orange-spotted Bulbul	19	h
Pycnonotus blanfordi	Blanford's Olive Bulbul	18 55	g
Pycnonotus brunneus	Red-eyed Brown Bulbul	18 19 21 55	g h
Pycnonotus cafer	Red-vented Bulbul	15 17 18 19 37 38 55	f g h i k
Pycnonotus capensis	Cape Bulbul	8	c
Pycnonotus cyaniventris	Gray-bellied Bulbul	18 19 21 55	g h
Pycnonotus erythrophthalmos	Lesser Brown Bulbul	18 19 21 55	g h
Pycnonotus eutilotus	Puff-backed Brown Bulbul	18 19 21 55	g h
Pycnonotus finlaysoni	Stripe-throated Bulbul	17 18 19 55	g h
Pycnonotus flavescens	Pale-faced Bulbul	15 17 18 19 21 55	f g h
Pycnonotus goiavier	Yellow-vented Bulbul	18 19 21 22 55	g h
Pycnonotus jocosus	Red-whiskered Bulbul	3 15 17 18 19 55	a f g h
Pycnonotus leucogenys	White-cheeked Bulbul	1 15	b f
Pycnonotus leucogrammicus	Striated Bulbul	19	h
Pycnonotus luteolus	White-browed Bulbul	15	f
Pycnonotus melanicterus	Black-headed Yellow Bulbul	15 17 18 19 21 55	f g h
Pycnonotus melanoleucos	Black-and-White Bulbul	19 21 55	g h

104

Scientific Name	Common Name	Source Codes	Region Codes

Scientific Name	Common Name	Source Codes	Region Codes
Pycnonotus nieuwenhuisi	Malaysian Wattled Bulbul	19 21	h
Pycnonotus nigricans	Black-fronted Bulbul	8	c
Pycnonotus penicillatus	Yellow-eared Bulbul	15	f
Pycnonotus plumosus	Olive-Brown Bulbul	18 19 21 55	g h
Pycnonotus priocephalus	Grey-headed Bulbul	15	f
Pycnonotus simplex	White-eyed Brown Bulbul	19 21 55	g h
Pycnonotus sinensis	Chinese Bulbul	17 55	g
Pycnonotus squamatus	Scaly-breasted Bulbul	18 19 21 55	g h
Pycnonotus striatus	Striated Green Bulbul	15 17 18 55	f g
Pycnonotus taivanus	Formosan Bulbul	17	g
Pycnonotus tympanistrigus	Olive-crowned Bulbul	19	h
Pycnonotus urostictus	Wattled Bulbul	22	h
Pycnonotus xantholaemus	Yellow-throated Bulbul	15	f
Pycnonotus xanthorrhous	Anderson's Bulbul	1 17 18 55	b g
Pycnonotus zeylanicus	Yellow-crowned Bulbul	18 19 21 55	g h
Calyptocichla serina	Golden Bulbul	8	c
Baeopogon clamans	Sjostedt's White-tailed Bulbul	8	c
Baeopogon indicator	White-tailed Bulbul	8	c
Ixonotus guttatus	Spotted Bulbul	8	c
Chlorocichla falkensteini	Yellow-throated Bulbul	8	c
Chlorocichla flavicollis	Yellow-throated Leaf-Love	8	c
Chlorocichla flaviventris	Yellow-bellied Greenbul	8	c
Chlorocichla laetissima	Joyful Greenbul	8	c
Chlorocichla simplex	Simple Bulbul	8	c
Thescelocichla leucopleura	Swamp Bulbul	8	c
Phyllastrephus albigularis	African White-throated Bulbul	8	c
Phyllastrephus baumanni[3]	Baumann's Bulbul	8	c
Phyllastrephus cerviniventris	Gray-Olive Greenbul	9	c
Phyllastrephus cinereiceps	Gray-crowned Foditany	10	c
Phyllastrephus debilis	Slender Greenbul	8	c
Phyllastrephus fischeri	Fischer's Greenbul	8	c
Phyllastrephus flavostriatus	Yellow-streaked Greenbul	8	c
Phyllastrephus fulviventris	Pale-Olive Greenbul	8	c
Phyllastrephus icterinus	Lesser Icterine Bulbul	8	c
Phyllastrephus lorenzi	Lorenz's Bulbul	8	c
Phyllastrephus madagascariensis	Tetraka	10	c
Phyllastrephus orostruthus	Dappled Mountain-Greenbul	8 53	c
Phyllastrephus poensis	Olive Bulbul	8	c
Phyllastrephus poliocephalus	Yellow-bellied Greenbul	9	c
Phyllastrephus scandens	Leaf-Love	8	c
Phyllastrephus strepitans	Northern Brownbul	8	c
Phyllastrephus tenebrosus[4]	Dusky Tetraka	10	c
Phyllastrephus terrestris	Brownbul	8	c
Phyllastrephus xanthophrys	Yellow-browed Foditany	10	c
Phyllastrephus xavieri	Greater Icterine Bulbul	8	c
Phyllastrephus zosterops	Short-billed Tetraka	10	c
Bleda canicapilla	Gray-headed Bristle-Bill	8	c
Bleda eximia	Green-tailed Bristle-Bill	8	c
Bleda syndactyla	Common Bristle-Bill	8	c
Nicator chloris[5]	African Nicator	8	c
Nicator vireo	Yellow-throated Nicator	8	c
Criniger barbatus	Bearded Bulbul	8	c
Criniger bres	Olive White-throated Bulbul	18 19 21 55	g h
Criniger calurus	White-bearded Greenbul	8	c
Criniger finschi	Dwarf Bearded Bulbul	19 21 55	g h
Criniger flaveolus	Ashy-fronted Bearded Bulbul	15 55	f g
Criniger ndussumensis	White-bearded Bulbul	9	c

Scientific Name	Common Name	Source Codes	Region Codes

PYCNONOTIDAE · BULBULS *contd.*

Scientific Name	Common Name	Source Codes	Region Codes
Criniger ochraceus	Brown White-throated Bulbul	18 19 21 55	g h
Criniger olivaceus	Yellow-throated Olive Bulbul	8	c
Criniger pallidus	Olivaceous Bearded Bulbul	17 55	g
Criniger phaeocephalus	Crestless White-throated Bulbul	18 19 21	h
Setornis criniger	Hook-billed Bulbul	19 21	h
Hypsipetes affinis	Moluccan Bulbul	29 31	h j
Hypsipetes amaurotis	Brown-eared Bulbul	1 17 22	b g h
Hypsipetes borbonicus	Reunion Bulbul	47 53	c
Hypsipetes charlottae	Crested Olive Bulbul	17 18 19 21 55	g h
Hypsipetes crassirostris	Seychelles Bulbul	14	c
Hypsipetes criniger	Hairy-backed Bulbul	18 19 21 55	g h
Hypsipetes everetti	Yellow-washed Bulbul	23	h
Hypsipetes flavala[6]	Oriental Brown-eared Bulbul	15 16 17 18 19 55	f g h
Hypsipetes indicus	Yellow-browed Bulbul	15	f
Hypsipetes madagascariensis	Black Bulbul	1 10 15 17 18 55	b c f g
Hypsipetes malaccensis	Green-backed Bulbul	55	g h
Hypsipetes mcclellandii	McClelland's Bulbul	18 55	g
Hypsipetes nicobariensis	Nicobar Bulbul	15	f
Hypsipetes palawanensis	Golden-eyed Bulbul	47	h
Hypsipetes philippinus	Rufous-breasted Bulbul	22 23	h
Hypsipetes propinquus	Gray-eyed Bulbul	18 55	g
Hypsipetes siquijorensis	Mottled-breasted Bulbul	22	h
Hypsipetes thompsoni	Bingham's Bulbul	18 55	g
Hypsipetes virescens	Green-winged Bulbul	15 17 18 19 21	f g h
Hypsipetes viridescens	Blyth's Olive Bulbul	15 18	f h
Neolestes torquatus	Black-collared Bulbul	8	c
Tylas eduardi	Kinkimavo	10	c

IRENIDAE · LEAFBIRDS 14 species recorded

Scientific Name	Common Name	Source Codes	Region Codes
Aegithina lafresnayei	Great Iora	17 18 19 55	g h
Aegithina nigrolutea	Marshall's Iora	15	f
Aegithina tiphia	Common Iora	15 17 18 19 21 55	f g h
Aegithina viridissima	Green Iora	18 19 21	g h
Chloropsis aurifrons	Golden-fronted Leafbird	15 17 18 19	f g h
Chloropsis cochinchinensis	Blue-winged Leafbird	15 17 18 19 21 55	f g h
Chloropsis cyanopogon	Lesser Green Leafbird	18 19 21 55	g h
Chloropsis flavipennis	Yellow-quilled Leafbird	22	h
Chloropsis hardwickii	Orange-bellied Leafbird	15 17 18 19 55	f g h
Chloropsis palawanensis	Palawan Leafbird	19	h
Chloropsis sonnerati	Greater Green Leafbird	18 19 21 55	g h
Chloropsis venusta	Blue-masked Leafbird	19	h
Irena cyanogaster	Philippine Fairy Bluebird	22	h
Irena puella	Fairy Bluebird	15 17 18 19 21 55	f g h

PRIONOPIDAE · HELMET SHRIKES 9 species recorded

Scientific Name	Common Name	Source Codes	Region Codes
Eurocephalus anguitimens	White-crowned Shrike	8	c
Eurocephalus rueppelli	Rueppell's White-crowned Shrike	9	c
Prionops alberti	Yellow-crested Helmet Shrike	8	c
Prionops caniceps	Red-billed Shrike	8	c

Scientific Name	Common Name	Source Codes	Region Codes

Prionops gabela	Angola Red-billed Shrike	8 49	c
Prionops plumata	Long-crested Helmet Shrike	8	c
Prionops poliolopha	Gray-crested Helmet Shrike	8	c
Prionops retzii	Retz's Red-billed Shrike	8	c
Prionops scopifrons	Chestnut-fronted Shrike	8	c

LANIIDAE · SHRIKES 70 species recorded

Lanioturdus torquatus	Chat Shrike	8	c
Nilaus afer	Brubru Shrike	8	c
Dryoscopus angolensis	Pink-footed Puff-Back	8	c
Dryoscopus cubla	Black-backed Puff-Back	8	c
Dryoscopus gambensis	Puff-Back	8	c
Dryoscopus pringlii	Pringle's Puff-Back	8	c
Dryoscopus sabini	Sabine's Puff-Back	8	c
Dryoscopus senegalensis	Red-eyed Puff-Back	8	c
Tchagra australis	Black-crowned Bush Shrike	8	c
Tchagra cruenta	Rosy-patched Bush Shrike	8	c
Tchagra jamesi	Three-streaked Bush Shrike	8	c
Tchagra minuta	Lesser Bush Shrike	8	c
Tchagra senegala	Black-headed Bush Shrike	1 8	b c
Tchagra tchagra	Levaillant's Bush Shrike	8	c
Laniarius aethiopicus[1]	Tropical Boubou	9	c
Laniarius atrococcineus	Crimson-breasted Shrike	9	c
Laniarius atroflavus	Yellow-breasted Shrike	8	c
Laniarius barbarus	Gonolek	8	c
Laniarius bicolor[1]	Ngami Boubou Shrike	9	c
Laniarius erythrogaster[2]	Black-headed Gonolek	9	c
Laniarius ferrugineus	Southern Boubou	8	c
Laniarius fulleborni	Fulleborn's Black Boubou	8	c
Laniarius funebris	Slate-colored Boubou	8	c
Laniarius leucorhynchus	Sooty Boubou	8	c
Laniarius luhderi	Luhder's Bush Shrike	8	c
Laniarius mufumbiri	Mufumbiri Shrike	8	c
Laniarius poensis[3]	Mountain Sooty Boubou	9	c
Laniarius ruficeps	Red-naped Bush Shrike	8	c
Malaconotus alius[4]	Black-cap Bush Shrike	8	c
Malaconotus blanchoti	Gray-headed Bush Shrike	8	c
Malaconotus bocagei	Bocage's Bush Shrike	8	c
Malaconotus cruentus	Fiery-breasted Bush Shrike	8	c
Malaconotus dohertyi	Doherty's Bush Shrike	8	c
Malaconotus gladiator	Pugnacious Bush Shrike	8	c
Malaconotus kupeensis	Mt. Kupe Bush Shrike	8	c
Malaconotus lagdeni	Lagden's Bush Shrike	8	c
Malaconotus monteiri[5]	Monteiro's Bush Shrike	9	c
Malaconotus multicolor	Many-colored Bush Shrike	8	c
Malaconotus nigrifrons	Black-fronted Bush Shrike	9	c
Malaconotus olivaceus	Olive Bush Shrike	8	c
Malaconotus quadricolor	Gorgeous Bush Shrike	9	c
Malaconotus sulfureopectus	Orange-breasted Bush Shrike	8	c
Malaconotus viridis	Perrin's Bush Shrike	8	c
Malaconotus zeylonus	Bokmakierie	8	c
Corvinella corvina	Western Long-tailed Shrike	8	c
Corvinella melanoleuca	Eastern Long-tailed Shrike	8	c
Lanius bucephalus	Bull-headed Shrike	1 17	b g
Lanius cabanisi	Long-tailed Fiscal Shrike	8	c

Scientific Name	Common Name	Source Codes	Region Codes
LANIIDAE · SHRIKES contd.			
Lanius collaris[6]	Fiscal Shrike	8	c
Lanius collurio	Red-backed Shrike	1 8 15	b c f
Lanius collurioides	Chestnut-backed Shrike	15 17 18 55	f g
Lanius cristatus	Brown Shrike	1 15 17 18 19 21 22 55	b f g h
Lanius dorsalis	Taita Fiscal Shrike	8	c
Lanius excubitor	Northern Shrike	1 3 8 15 17	a b c f g
Lanius excubitoroides[7]	Gray-backed Fiscal Shrike	8	c
Lanius gubernator	Emin's Red-backed Shrike	8	c
Lanius ludovicianus	Loggerhead Shrike	3 4	a e
Lanius mackinnoni	MacKinnon's Gray Shrike	8	c
Lanius minor	Lesser Gray Shrike	1 8 15 17	b c f g
Lanius nubicus	Masked Shrike	1 8	b c
Lanius schach	Black-headed Shrike	1 15 17 18 19 21 22 35 55	b f g h j
Lanius senator	Woodchat-Shrike	1 8 15	b c f
Lanius somalicus	Somali Fiscal Shrike	8	c
Lanius souzae	Souza's Shrike	8	c
Lanius sphenocercus	Long-tailed Gray Shrike	1 17	b g
Lanius tephronotus	Tibetan Shrike	1 17 55	b g
Lanius tigrinus	Thick-billed Shrike	1 17 18 19 21 22 55	b g h
Lanius validirostris	Strong-billed Shrike	22	h
Lanius vittatus	Bay-backed Shrike	1 15	b f
Pityriasis gymnocephala	Bornean Bristle-head	21	h

VANGIDAE · VANGA SHRIKES   13 species recorded

Scientific Name	Common Name	Source Codes	Region Codes
Calicalicus madagascariensis	Red-tailed Vanga	10	c
Schetba rufa	Rufous Vanga	10	c
Vanga curvirostris	Hook-billed Vanga	10	c
Xenopirostris damii	Van Dam's Vanga	10	c
Xenopirostris polleni	Pollen's Vanga	10	c
Xenopirostris xenopirostris	Lafresnaye's Vanga	10	c
Falculea palliata	Sicklebill Falculea	10	c
Leptopterus chabert	Chabert Vanga	10	c
Leptopterus madagascarinus	Blue Vanga	10	c
Leptopterus viridis	White-headed Vanga	10	c
Oriolia bernieri	Bernier's Vanga	10	c
Euryceros prevostii	Helmet Bird	10	c
Hypositta corallirostris	Madagascar Nuthatch	10	c

PTILOGONATIDAE · SILKY FLYCATCHERS, WAXWINGS, HYPOCOLIUS
8 species recorded

Scientific Name	Common Name	Source Codes	Region Codes
Bombycilla cedrorum	Cedar Waxwing	3 4 5 6	a d e
Bombycilla garrulus	Bohemian Waxwing	1 3 17	a b g
Bombycilla japonica	Japanese Waxwing	1 17	b g
Ptilogonys caudatus	Long-tailed Silky Flycatcher	4	e
Ptilogonys cinereus	Gray Silky Flycatcher	4	e
Phainopepla nitens	Phainopepla	3 4	a e
Phainoptila melanoxantha	Black-and-Yellow Silky Flycatcher	4	e
Hypocolius ampelinus	Hypocolius	1 8 15	b c f

Scientific Name	Common Name	Source Codes	Region Codes

DULIDAE · PALMCHAT 1 species recorded

Scientific Name	Common Name	Source Codes	Region Codes
Dulus dominicus	Palmchat	5	e

CINCLIDAE · DIPPERS 4 species recorded

Scientific Name	Common Name	Source Codes	Region Codes
Cinclus cinclus	Dipper	1 15 17 18	b f g
Cinclus leucocephalus[1]	White-capped Dipper	6	d
Cinclus mexicanus	American Dipper	3 4	a e
Cinclus pallasii	Brown Dipper	1 15 17 18 55	b f g

TROGLODYTIDAE · WRENS 59 species recorded

Scientific Name	Common Name	Source Codes	Region Codes
Campylorhynchus brunneicapillus	Cactus Wren	3 4	a e
Campylorhynchus fasciatus	Fasciated Wren	6	d
Campylorhynchus griseus[1]	Bicolored Wren	6	d
Campylorhynchus gularis	Mexican Wren	4 6	d e
Campylorhynchus jocosus	Spotted Wren	4	e
Campylorhynchus megalopterus	Gray-barred Wren	4	e
Campylorhynchus nuchalis	Stripe-backed Wren	6	d
Campylorhynchus rufinucha	Rufous-naped Wren	4	e
Campylorhynchus turdinus[2]	Thrush-like Wren	6	d
Campylorhynchus yucatanicus	Giant Wren	4	d
Campylorhynchus zonatus	Band-backed Wren	4 6	d e
Odontorchilus branickii	Gray-mantled Wren	6	d
Odontorchilus cinereus	Tooth-billed Wren	6	d
Salpinctes mexicanus	Canyon Wren	3 4	a e
Salpinctes obsoletus	Rock Wren	3 4	a e
Hylorchilus sumichrasti	Slender-billed Wren	4	e
Cinnycerthia peruana	Sepia-Brown Wren	6	d
Cinnycerthia unirufa	Rufous Wren	6	d
Cistothorus apolinari	Apolinar's Marsh Wren	6	d
Cistothorus meridae	Paramo Wren	6	d
Cistothorus palustris[3]	Long-billed Marsh Wren	3 4	a e
Cistothorus platensis	Short-billed Marsh Wren	3 4 6	a d e
Thryomanes bewickii	Bewick's Wren	3 4	a e
Thryomanes sissonii	Socorro Wren	4	e
Ferminia cerverai	Zapata Wren	5	e
Thryothorus atrogularis[4]	Black-throated Wren	4 6	e
Thryothorus coraya	Coraya Wren	6	d
Thryothorus euophrys	Plain-tailed Wren	6	d
Thryothorus fasciatoventris	Black-bellied Wren	4 6	e
Thryothorus felix	Happy Wren	4	e
Thryothorus genibarbis	Moustached Wren	6	d
Thryothorus griseus	Gray Wren	6	d
Thryothorus guarayanus	Fawn-breasted Wren	6	d
Thryothorus leucotis	Buff-breasted Wren	4 6	d e
Thryothorus longirostris	Long-billed Wren	6	d
Thryothorus ludovicianus	Carolina Wren	3 4	a e
Thryothorus maculipectus	Spot-breasted Wren	4 6	d e
Thryothorus modestus[5]	Plain Wren	4	e
Thryothorus nicefori[6]	Nicefero's Wren	6	d
Thryothorus nigricapillus[7]	Bay Wren	4 6	d e

109

Scientific Name	Common Name	Source Codes	Region Codes
TROGLODYTIDAE · WRENS contd.			
Thryothorus pleurostictus	Banded Wren	4	e
Thryothorus rufalbus	Rufous-and-White Wren	4 6	d e
Thryothorus rutilus	Rufous-breasted Wren	4 6	d e
Thryothorus sinaloa	Bar-vented Wren	4	e
Thryothorus superciliaris	Superciliated Wren	6	d
Thryothorus thoracicus[8]	Stripe-throated Wren	4 6	d e
Troglodytes aedon[9]	House Wren	3 4 5 6	a d e
Troglodytes browni[10]	Timberline Wren	4	e
Troglodytes rufulus	Tepui Wren	6	d
Troglodytes solstitialis[11]	Mountain Wren	4 6	d
Troglodytes troglodytes	Common Wren	1 3 15 17 18	a b f g
Uropsila leucogastra	White-bellied Wren	4	e
Henicorhina leucophrys	Gray-breasted Wood-Wren	4 6	d e
Henicorhina leucosticta	White-breasted Wood-Wren	4 6	d e
Microcerculus bambla	Wing-banded Wren	6	d
Microcerculus marginatus	Nightingale Wren	4 6	d
Microcerculus ustulatus	Flutist Wren	6	d
Cyphorhinus aradus	Song Wren	4 6	d
Cyphorhinus thoracicus[12]	Chestnut-breasted Wren	6	d

MIMIDAE · THRASHERS, MOCKINGBIRDS   30 species recorded

Scientific Name	Common Name	Source Codes	Region Codes
Dumetella carolinensis	Gray Catbird	3 4 5	a e
Dumetella glabrirostris[1]	Black Catbird	4	e
Melanotis caerulescens	Blue Mockingbird	4	e
Melanotis hypoleucus	Blue-and-White Mockingbird	4	e
Mimus dorsalis	Brown-backed Mockingbird	6	d
Mimus gundlachii	Bahama Mockingbird	5	e
Mimus longicaudatus	Long-tailed Mockingbird	6	d
Mimus patagonicus	Patagonian Mockingbird	6	d
Mimus polyglottos[2]	Mockingbird	3 4 5 6	a d e
Mimus saturninus	Chalk-browed Mockingbird	6	d
Mimus thenca	Chilean Mockingbird	6	d
Mimus triurus	White-banded Mockingbird	6	d
Nesomimus trifasciatus	Galapagos Mockingbird	47	d
Mimodes graysoni	Socorro Thrasher	4	e
Toxostoma bendirei	Bendire's Thrasher	3 4	a e
Toxostoma cinereum	Gray Thrasher	4	e
Toxostoma curvirostre	Curve-billed Thrasher	3 4	a e
Toxostoma dorsale	Crissal Thrasher	3 4	a e
Toxostoma guttatum	Cozumel Thrasher	4	e
Toxostoma lecontei	Le Conte's Thrasher	3 4	a e
Toxostoma longirostre	Long-billed Thrasher	3 4	a e
Toxostoma montanus[3]	Sage Thrasher	3 4	a e
Toxostoma ocellatum	Ocellated Thrasher	4	e
Toxostoma redivivum	California Thrasher	3 4	a e
Toxostoma rufum	Brown Thrasher	3	a
Cinclocerthia brachyurus	White-breasted Thrasher	5	e
Cinclocerthia ruficauda	Brown Trembler	5	e
Donacobius atricapillus	Black-capped Mockingthrush	4 6	d e
Margarops fuscatus[4]	Pearly-eyed Thrasher	5 6	d e
Margarops fuscus	Scaly-breasted Thrasher	5	e

Scientific Name	Common Name	Source Codes	Region Codes

PRUNELLIDAE · ACCENTORS 13 species recorded

Scientific Name	Common Name	Source Codes	Region Codes
Prunella atrogularis	Black-throated Accentor	1 15 17	b f g
Prunella collaris	Alpine Accentor	1 15 17 18	b f g
Prunella fagani[1]	Yemeni Accentor	8	c
Prunella fulvescens	Brown Accentor	1 15 17	b f g
Prunella himalayana	Himalayan Accentor	1 15 17	b f g
Prunella immaculata	Maroon-backed Accentor	1 15 17 18	b f g
Prunella koslowi	Kozlov's Accentor	1 17	b g
Prunella modularis	Dunnock	1 37	b i
Prunella montanella	Siberian Accentor	1 3 17	a b g
Prunella ocularis	Radde's Accentor	1	b
Prunella rubeculoides	Robin Accentor	1 15 17	b f g
Prunella rubida	Japanese Accentor	1	b
Prunella strophiata	Rufous-breasted Accentor	1 15 17 18	b f g

MUSCICAPIDAE · TURDINAE · THRUSHES, WREN-THRUSHES 304 species recorded

Scientific Name	Common Name	Source Codes	Region Codes
Stiphornis erythrothorax	Forest Robin	8	c
Brachypterex calligyna	Celebes Shortwing	27	h
Brachypteryx hyperythra	Rusty-bellied Shortwing	15	f
Brachypteryx leucophrys	Lesser Shortwing	15 17 18 19 55	f g h
Brachypteryx major	Rufous-bellied Shortwing	15	f
Brachypteryx montana	Blue Shortwing	1 15 17 18 19 21 22 55	b f g h
Brachypteryx stellata	Gould's Shortwing	1 15 17 18 55	b f g
Zeledonia coronata	Wren-Thrush	4	e
Namibornis herero	Herero Thrush-Flycatcher	8	c
Cercotrichas barbata[1]	Bearded Scrub Robin	8	c
Cercotrichas coryphaeus	Karroo Scrub Robin	8	c
Cercotrichas galactotes	Rufous Bush Robin	1 8 15	b c f
Cercotrichas hartlaubi	Brown backed Scrub Robin	8	c
Cercotrichas leucophrys	White-winged Scrub Robin	8	c
Cercotrichas leucosticta	Western Bearded Scrub Robin	8	c
Cercotrichas paena	Kalahari Sandy Scrub Robin	8	c
Cercotrichas podobe	Black Bush Robin	1 8	b c
Cercotrichas quadrivirgata	Eastern Bearded Scrub Robin	8	c
Cercotrichas signata	Brown Robin-Chat	8	c
Pinarornis plumosus	Sooty Rock Chat	8	c
Chaetops frenatus	Rufous Rock Jumper	8	c
Drymodes brunneopygia	Southern Scrub Robin	36	i
Drymodes superciliaris	Northern Scrub Robin	35 36	i j
Pogonocichla stellata	White-starred Bush Robin	8	c
Pogonocichla swynnertoni	Swynnerton's Bush Robin	8	c
Erithacus rubecula	Eurasian Robin	1	b
Sheppardia aequatorialis[2]	Equatorial Akalat	8	c
Sheppardia cyornithopsis	Whiskered Akalat	8	c
Sheppardia gabela	Gabela Akalat	8	c
Sheppardia gunningi	East Coast Akalat	8	c
Sheppardia roberti	White-bellied Akalat	9	c
Sheppardia sharpei	Sharpe's Akalat	8	c
Luscinia akahige[3]	Japanese Robin	1 3 17 55	b g k
Luscinia brunnea	Indian Blue Robin	1 15 17 18	b f g
Luscinia calliope	Siberian Rubythroat	1 3 15 17 18 22 55	a b f g h

Scientific Name	Common Name	Source Codes	Region Codes

MUSCICAPIDAE · TURDINAE · THRUSHES, WREN-THRUSHES *contd.*

Scientific Name	Common Name	Source Codes	Region Codes
Luscinia chrysaeus	Golden Bush Robin	1 15 17 18 55	b f g
Luscinia cyane	Siberian Blue Robin	1 15 17 18 19 21 55	b f g h
Luscinia cyanurus	Orange-flanked Bush Robin	1 15 17 18 55	b f g
Luscinia hyperythrus	Rufous-bellied Bush Robin	1 15 18	b f
Luscinia indicus	White-browed Bush Robin	1 15 17 18 55	b f g
Luscinia johnstoniae	Formosan Bush Robin	17	g
Luscinia komadori	Ryu Kyu Robin	1 3	b k
Luscinia luscinia	Thrush-Nightingale	1 8	b c
Luscinia megarhynchos	Nightingale	1 8 15 17	b c f g
Luscinia obscura	Black-throated Blue Robin	18 55	g
Luscinia pectardens	Père David's Orangethroat	1 15 17 55	b g
Luscinia pectoralis	Himalayan Rubythroat	1 15 17 18 55	b f g
Luscinia ruficeps	Rufous-headed Robin	1 17 53 55	b g
Luscinia sibilans	Swinhoe's Red-tailed Robin	17 55	g
Luscinia svecica	Bluethroat	1 3 8 15 17 18 55	a b c f g
Cossypha albicapilla	White-crowned Robin-Chat	8	c
Cossypha ansorgei	Angola Cave Chat	8	c
Cossypha archeri	Archer's Robin-Chat	8	c
Cossypha bocagei	Rufous-cheeked Robin-Chat	8	c
Cossypha caffra	Robin-Chat	8	c
Cossypha cyanocampter	Blue-shouldered Robin-Chat	8	c
Cossypha dichroa	Chorister Robin-Chat	8	c
Cossypha heinrichi	Heinrich's Robin-Chat	8	c
Cossypha heuglini	White-browed Robin-Chat	8	c
Cossypha humeralis	White-throated Robin-Chat	8	c
Cossypha isabellae	Mountain Robin-Chat	8	c
Cossypha natalensis	Red-capped Robin-Chat	8	c
Cossypha niveicapilla	Snowy-headed Robin-Chat	8	c
Cossypha polioptera	Gray-winged Robin-Chat	8	c
Cossypha roberti	White-bellied Robin-Chat	8	c
Cossypha semirufa	Ruppell's Robin-Chat	8	c
Modulatrix stictigula	Spot-throat	8	c
Cichladusa arquata	Morning Warbler	8	c
Cichladusa guttata	Spotted Morning Warbler	8	c
Cichladusa ruficauda	Red-tailed Morning Warbler	8	c
Alethe anomala[4, 5]	Olive-flanked Alethe	8	c
Alethe choloensis	Mt. Cholo Alethe	8	c
Alethe diademata	Fire-crested Alethe	8	c
Alethe fuelleborni	White-crested Alethe	8	c
Alethe lowei	Iringa Alethe	8	c
Alethe montana	Usambara Alethe	8	c
Alethe poliocephala	Brown-chested Alethe	8	c
Alethe poliophrys	Red-throated Alethe	8	c
Copsychus albospecularis	Madagascar Magpie-Robin	10	c
Copsychus luzoniensis	White-eyebrowed Shama	22	h
Copsychus malabaricus	White-rumped Shama	3 15 17 18 19 21 55	f g h k
Copsychus niger	Palawan Black Shama	22 23 53	h
Copsychus pyrrhopygus	Orange-tailed Shama	19 21	h
Copsychus saularis	Dyal	3 15 17 18 19 21 22 55	f g h k
Copsychus sechellarum	Seychelles Magpie-Robin	14 53	c
Copsychus stricklandii	Black Shama	22	h
Irania gutturalis	White-throated Robin	1 8	b c
Phoenicurus alaschanicus	Alashan Redstart	17	g

Scientific Name	Common Name	Source Codes	Region Codes

Scientific Name	Common Name	Source Codes	Region Codes
Phoenicurus auroreus	Daurian Redstart	1 15 17 18 55	b f g
Phoenicurus caeruleocephalus	Blue-headed Redstart	1 15 17	b f g
Phoenicurus erythrogaster	Guldenstadt's Redstart	1 15 17	b f g
Phoenicurus erythronotus	Eversmann's Redstart	1 15 17	b f g
Phoenicurus frontalis	Blue-fronted Redstart	1 15 17 18 55	b f g
Phoenicurus hodgsoni	Hodgson's Redstart	1 15 17 18	b f g
Phoenicurus moussieri	Moussier's Redstart	1	b
Phoenicurus ochruros	Black Redstart	1 8 15 17 18 55	b c f g
Phoenicurus phoenicurus	Redstart	1 8 15	b c f
Phoenicurus schisticeps	White-throated Redstart	1 15 17 18	b f g
Rhyacornis bicolor	Philippine Water Redstart	22	h
Rhyacornis fuliginosus	Plumbeous Water Redstart	1 15 55	b f g
Hodgsonius phoenicuroides	Hodgson's Shortwing	1 15 17 18 55	b f g
Cinclidium diana	Sunda Blue Robin	19	h
Cinclidium frontale	Blue-fronted Long-tailed Robin	15 55	f g
Cinclidium leucurum	White-tailed Blue Robin	15 55	f g
Grandala coelicolor	Grandala	1 15 17 18	b f g
Sialia currucoides	Mountain Bluebird	3 4	a e
Sialia mexicana	Western Bluebird	3 4	a e
Sialia sialis	Eastern Bluebird	3 4 5	a e
Enicurus immaculatus	Black-backed Forktail	15 18 55	f g
Enicurus leschenaulti	White-crowned Forktail	1 15 17 18 19 21 55	b f g h
Enicurus maculatus	Spotted Forktail	1 15 17 18 55	b f g
Enicurus ruficapillus	Chestnut-naped Forktail	18 19 21 55	g h
Enicurus schistaceus	Slaty-backed Forktail	15 17 18 19 55	f g h
Enicurus scouleri	Little Forktail	1 15 17 18 55	b f g
Enicurus velatus	Lesser Forktail	19	h
Cochoa azurea	Malaysian Cochoa	19	h
Cochoa purpurea	Purple Cochoa	15 17 18 55	f g
Cochoa viridis	Green Cochoa	15 17 18 55	f g
Myadestes elisabeth	Cuban Solitaire	5	e
Myadestes genibarbis	Rufous-throated Solitaire	5	e
Myadestes leucogenys	Rufous-brown Solitaire	6	d
Myadestes obscurus	Brown-backed Solitaire	4	e
Myadestes ralloides[6]	Andean Solitaire	4 6	d
Myadestes townsendi	Townsend's Solitaire	3 4	a e
Myadestes unicolor	Slate-colored Solitaire	4	e
Entomodestes coracinus	Black Solitaire	6	d
Entomodestes leucotis	White-eared Solitaire	6	d
Neocossyphus finschi[7]	Finsch's Rusty Flycatcher	9	c
Neocossyphus fraseri	Fraser's Rusty Flycatcher	8 9	c
Neocossyphus poensis	White-tailed Ant-Thrush	8	c
Neocossyphus rufus	Red-tailed Ant-Thrush	8	c
Cercomela dubia	Sombre Rock-Chat	8	c
Cercomela familiaris	Red-tailed Chat	8	c
Cercomela fusca	Brown Rock-Chat	15	f
Cercomela melanura	Blackstart	1 8	b c
Cercomela schlegelii	Schlegel's Chat	8	c
Cercomela scotocerca	Brown-tailed Rock-Chat	8	c
Cercomela sinuata	Sickle-wing Chat	8	c
Cercomela sordida	Hill Chat	8	c
Cercomela tractrac	Tractrac Chat	8	c
Saxicola caprata	Pied Stonechat	1 15 17 18 19 21 22 35 55	b f g h i
Saxicola dacotiae	Canary Islands Stonechat	1	b

113

Scientific Name	Common Name	Source Codes	Region Codes

MUSCICAPIDAE · TURDINAE · THRUSHES, WREN-THRUSHES *contd.*

Scientific Name	Common Name	Source Codes	Region Codes
Saxicola ferrea	Gray Bush Chat	1 15 17 18 55	b f g
Saxicola gutturalis	Timor Stonechat	47	j
Saxicola insignis	Hodgson's Stonechat	1 15 17	b f g
Saxicola jerdoni	Jerdon's Bush Chat	15 17 18 55	f g
Saxicola leucura	White-tailed Stonechat	15 18	f
Saxicola macrorhyncha	Stoliczka's Whinchat	1 15	b f
Saxicola rubetra	Whinchat	1 8	b c
Saxicola torquata	Stonechat	1 8 10 15 17 18 19 21 55	b c f g h
Myrmecocichla aethiops[8, 9]	Anteater Chat	8	c
Myrmecocichla albifrons	White-fronted Blackchat	8	c
Myrmecocichla arnotti	Arnot's Chat	8	c
Myrmecocichla cinnamomeiventris	Cliffchat	8	c
Myrmecocichla formicivora	Southern Anteater Chat	8	c
Myrmecocichla melaena	Ruppell's Chat	8	c
Myrmecocichla nigra	Sooty Chat	8	c
Myrmecocichla semirufa	White-winged Cliffchat	9	c
Myrmecocichla tholloni	Congo Moor Chat	8	c
Oenanthe alboniger	Hume's Wheatear	1 15	b f
Oenanthe bifasciata	Buff-streaked Chat	8	c
Oenanthe bottae	Red-breasted Wheatear	8	c
Oenanthe deserti	Desert Wheatear	1 8 15 17	b c f g
Oenanthe finschii	Finsch's Wheatear	1 15	b f
Oenanthe hispanica	Black-eared Wheatear	1 8 17	b c g
Oenanthe isabellina	Isabelline Wheatear	1 8 15 17	b c f g
Oenanthe leucopyga	White-rumped Black Wheatear	1 8	b c
Oenanthe leucura	Black Wheatear	1	b
Oenanthe lugens	Mourning Wheatear	1 8	b c
Oenanthe moesta	Red-rumped Wheatear	1	b
Oenanthe monacha	Hooded Wheatear	1 8 15	b c f
Oenanthe monticola	Mountain Wheatear	8	c
Oenanthe oenanthe	Wheatear	1 3 8 15 17 21 22	a b c f g h
Oenanthe phillipsi[10]	Somali Wheatear	9	c
Oenanthe picata	Eastern Pied Wheatear	1 15	b f
Oenanthe pileata	Capped Wheatear	8	c
Oenanthe pleschanka	Pied Wheatear	1 8 15	b c f
Oenanthe xanthoprymna	Red-tailed Wheatear	1 8 15	b c f
Chaimarrornis leucocephalus[11]	White-capped Water Redstart	1 15 17 55	b f g
Saxicoloides fulicata	Indian Robin	15	f
Pseudocossyphus imerinus	Madagascar Robin-Chat	10	c
Monticola angolensis	Mottled Rock Thrush	8	c
Monticola bensoni	Benson's Rock Thrush	68	c
Monticola brevipes	Short-toed Rock Thrush	8	c
Monticola cinclorhynchus[12]	Blue-headed Rock Thrush	1 15 17 18 19 55	b f g h
Monticola explorator	Sentinel Rock Thrush	8	c
Monticola rufiventris	Chestnut-bellied Rock Thrush	1 15 17 18 55	b f g
Monticola rufocinerea	Little Rock Thrush	8	c
Monticola rupestris	Cape Rock Thrush	8	c
Monticola saxatilis	Rock Thrush	1 8 15 17	b c f g
Monticola solitaria	Blue Rock Thrush	1 8 15 17 18 19 21 22 55	b c f g h
Myiophoneus blighi	Blyth's Whistling Thrush	15	f
Myiophoneus caeruleus	Blue Whistling Thrush	1 15 17 18 19 55	b f g h
Myiophoneus glaucinus	Sunda Whistling Thrush	19 21	h
Myiophoneus horsfieldii	Malabar Whistling Thrush	15 17	f g

Scientific Name	Common Name	Source Codes	Region Codes

Scientific Name	Common Name	Source Codes	Region Codes
Mylophoneus insularis	Formosan Whistling Thrush	17	g
Mylophoneus melanurus	Shiny Whistling Thrush	19	h
Myiophoneus robinsoni	Malayan Whistling Thrush	19	h
Geomalia heinrichi	Celebes Mountain Thrush	27	h
Zoothera andromedae[13]	Sunda Ground Thrush	19 22	h j
Zoothera cinerea	Ashy Ground Thrush	22	h
Zoothera citrina	Orange-headed Ground Thrush	15 17 18 19 21 55	f g h
Zoothera dauma	White's Thrush	1 15 17 18 19 22 35 36 38 55	b f g h i j k
Zoothera dixoni	Long-tailed Mountain Thrush	1 15 17 18 55	b f g
Zoothera dumasi	Moluccan Ground Thrush	31	j
Zoothera erythronota	Celebes Ground Thrush	47	h
Zoothera everetti	Everett's Ground Thrush	19 21	h
Zoothera interpres	Kuhl's Ground Thrush	19 21 22 55	g h
Zoothera margaretae	San Cristobal Ground Thrush	38	k
Zoothera marginata	Lesser Long-billed Thrush	15 17 18 55	f g
Zoothera mollissima	Plain-backed Mountain Thrush	1 15 17 18 55	b f g
Zoothera monticola	Greater Long-billed Thrush	15 18 55	f g
Zoothera naevia	Varied Thrush	3 4	a e
Zoothera peronii	Peroni's Ground Thrush	32	h j
Zoothera pinicola	Aztec Thrush	4	e
Zoothera schistacea	Tanimbar Ground Thrush	47	h
Zoothera sibirica	Siberian Ground Thrush	1 15 21 55	b f g h
Zoothera spiloptera	Spotted-winged Ground Thrush	15	f
Zoothera talaseae	New Britain Ground Thrush	47	j
Zoothera terrestris	Kittlitz's Thrush	1	b
Zoothera wardii	Pied Ground Thrush	15	f
Amalocichla incerta	Lesser New Guinea Thrush	35	j
Amalocichla sclateriana	Greater New Guinea Thrush	35	j
Cataponera turnoides	Cataponera Thrush	27	h
Nesocichla eremita	Starchy	11 53	c
Cichlherminia lherminieri	Forest Thrush	5	e
Phaeornis obscurus	Hawaiian Thrush	3	h
Phaeornis palmeri	Small Kauai Thrush	3	h
Catharus aurantiirostris	Orange-billed Nightingale-Thrush	4 6	d e
Catharus dryas	Spotted Nightingale-Thrush	4 6	d e
Catharus fuscater	Slaty-backed Nightingale-Thrush	4 6	d e
Catharus fuscescens	Veery	3 4 5 6	a d e
Catharus gracilirostris	Black-billed Nightingale-Thrush	4	e
Catharus guttatus	Hermit Thrush	3 4	a e
Catharus mexicanus	Black-headed Nightingale-Thrush	4	e
Catharus minimus	Gray-cheeked Thrush	1 3 4 5 6	a b d e
Catharus occidentalis	Russet Nightingale-Thrush	4	e
Catharus ustulatus	Swainson's Thrush	3 4 5 6	a d e
Hylocichla mustelina	Wood Thrush	3 4 5	a e
Platycichla flavipes	Yellow-legged Thrush	6	d
Platycichla leucops	Pale-eyed Thrush	6	d
Turdus abyssinicus[14]	Rufous Thrush	8	c
Turdus albicollis[15]	White-necked Thrush	4 6	d e
Turdus albocinctus	White-collared Blackbird	1 15 17 18	b f g
Turdus amaurochalinus	Creamy-bellied Thrush	6	d
Turdus aurantius	White-chinned Thrush	5	e

Scientific Name	Common Name	Source Codes	Region Codes

MUSCICAPIDAE · TURDINAE · THRUSHES, WREN-THRUSHES *contd.*

Scientific Name	Common Name	Source Codes	Region Codes
Turdus bewsheri	Comoro Thrush	14	c
Turdus boulboul	Gray-winged Blackbird	15 17 18 55	f g
Turdus camaronensis	Black-eared Ground Thrush	8	c
Turdus cardis	Gray Thrush	1 17 55	b g
Turdus celaenops	Seven Islands Thrush	1	b
Turdus chiguanco	Chiguanco Thrush	6	d
Turdus chrysolaus	Red-bellied Thrush	1 22	b h
Turdus dissimilis[16]	Black-breasted Thrush	1 15 17 18 55	b f g
Turdus falcklandii	Austral Thrush	6	d
Turdus feae	Fea's Thrush	1 15 17 18 55	b f g
Turdus fischeri[17]	Fischer's Thrush	8	c
Turdus fulviventris	Chestnut-bellied Thrush	6	d
Turdus fumigatus[18]	Pale-vented Robin	4 5 6	d e
Turdus fuscater	Great Thrush	6	d
Turdus grayi	Clay-colored Thrush	4 6	d e
Turdus gurneyi[19]	Orange Ground Thrush	8	c
Turdus haplochrous	Unicolored Thrush	6	d
Turdus ignobilis[20]	Black-billed Thrush	6	d
Turdus iliacus[21]	Redwing	1 15	b f
Turdus jamaicensis	White-eyed Thrush	5	e
Turdus kessleri	Kessler's Thrush	1 15 17	b f g
Turdus lawrencii	Lawrence's Thrush	6	d
Turdus leucomelas	Pale-breasted Thrush	6	d
Turdus libonyanus	Kurrichane Thrush	8	c
Turdus litsitsirupa	Ground-Scraper Thrush	8	c
Turdus maranonicus	Maranon Thrush	6	d
Turdus merula	Blackbird	1 15 17 18 37 55	b f g h i
Turdus migratorius	American Robin	3 4 5	a e
Turdus mupinensis	Verreaux's Song Thrush	1 17	b g
Turdus naumanni	Dusky Thrush	15 17 18 55	f g
Turdus nigrescens	Sooty Robin	4	e
Turdus nigriceps	Slaty Thrush	6	d
Turdus nudigenis	Bare-eyed Thrush	5 6	d e
Turdus oberlaenderi	Congo Thrush	8	c
Turdus obscurus	Eye-browed Thrush	1 15 18 19 22 55	b f g h
Turdus olivaceofuscus	Olivaceous Thrush	8	c
Turdus olivaceus	Olive Thrush	8	c
Turdus olivater	Black-hooded Thrush	6	d
Turdus pallidus	Pale Thrush	1 17 21 22	b g h
Turdus pelios[22]	African Thrush	8	c
Turdus philomelos	Song Thrush	1 8 37	b c i
Turdus piaggiae	Abyssinian Ground Thrush	8	c
Turdus pilaris	Fieldfare	1 3 15 17	a b f g
Turdus plumbeus	Red-legged Thrush	5	a
Turdus poliocephalus	Mountain Blackbird	19 21 22 35 38	h j k
Turdus princei	Gray Ground Thrush	8	c
Turdus ravidus	Grand Cayman Thrush	5 53	e
Turdus reevei	Plumbeous-backed Thrush	6	d
Turdus rubrocanus	Gray-headed Thrush	1 15 17 18	b f g
Turdus ruficollis	Red-throated Thrush	15 17 18	f g
Turdus rufitorques	Rufous-collared Robin	4	e
Turdus rufiventris	Rufous-bellied Thrush	6	d
Turdus rufopalliatus	Rufous-backed Robin	4	e
Turdus serranus[23]	Glossy-black Thrush	4 6	d e
Turdus swalesi	La Selle Thrush	5	e
Turdus tephronotus	African Bare-eyed Thrush	8	c
Turdus torquatus	Ring Ouzel	1 8	b c

116

Scientific Name	Common Name	Source Codes	Region Codes

MUSCICAPIDAE   TURDINAE   THRUSHES, WREN-THRUSHES contd.

Turdus unicolor	Tickell's Thrush	1 15	b f
Turdus viscivorus	Mistle Thrush	1 15 17	b f g

MUSCICAPIDAE · ORTHONYCHINAE · LOGRUNNERS 20 species recorded

Orthonyx spaldingi	Northern Logrunner	36	i	
Orthonyx temmincki	Southern Logrunner	35 36	i	j
Androphobus viridis	Green-backed Babbler	35	j	
Psophodes nigrogularis	Western Whip-Bird	36	i	
Psophodes olivaceus	Eastern Whip-Bird	36	i	
Sphenostoma cristatum	Wedgebill	36	i	
Cinclosoma ajax	Ajax Quail-Thrush	35 36	i	j
Cinclosoma castanotum	Chestnut Quail-Thrush	36	i	
Cinclosoma cinnamomeum	Cinnamon Quail-Thrush	36	i	
Cinclosoma punctatum	Spotted Quail-Thrush	36	i	
Eupetes caerulescens[1]	Lowland Eupetes	35	j	
Eupetes castanonotus	Mid-Mountain Eupetes	35	j	
Eupetes leucostictus	High Mountain Eupetes	35	j	
Eupetes macrocercus	Rail-Babbler	19 21 55	g	h
Melampitta gigantea	Greater Melampitta	35	j	
Melampitta lugubris	Lesser Melampitta	35	j	
Crateroscelis murina	Lowland Mouse-Babbler	35	j	
Crateroscelis nigrorufa	Mid-Mountain Mouse-Babbler	35	j	
Crateroscelis robusta	Mountain Mouse-Babbler	35	j	
Ifrita kowaldi	Blue-capped Babbler	35	j	

MUSCICAPIDAE · TIMALIINAE · BABBLERS, WREN-TITS 252 species recorded

Pellorneum albiventre	Brown Babbler	15 18 55	f	g	h
Pellorneum capistratum	Black-capped Babbler	18 19 21 55		g	h
Pellorneum fuscocapillum	Brown-capped Babbler	15	f		
Pellorneum palustre	Marsh Spotted Babbler	15	f		
Pellorneum ruficeps	Spotted Babbler	15 17 18 19 55	f	g	h
Trichastoma abbotti	Abbott's Babbler	15 18 19 21 55	f	g	h
Trichastoma albipectus	White-breasted Illadopsis	8	c		
Trichastoma bicolor	Ferruginous Babbler	18 19 21 55		g	h
Trichastoma celebensis	Celebes Jungle Babbler	27 29			h
Trichastoma cinereiceps	Ashy-headed Babbler	22			h
Trichastoma cleaveri	Blackcap Illadopsis	8	c		
Trichastoma fulvescens	Brown Illadopsis	8	c		
Trichastoma malaccensis	Short-tailed Jungle Babbler	19 21 55		g	h
Trichastoma perspicillatum	Black-browed Babbler	21			h
Trichastoma poliothorax	Gray-chested Illadopsis	8	c		
Trichastoma puveli	Puvel's Illadopsis	8	c		
Trichastoma pyrrhoptera	Mountain Illadopsis	8	c		
Trichastoma pyrrogenys	Temminck's Babbler	19 21			h
Trichastoma rostrata	Blyth's Babbler	18 19 21 55		g	h
Trichastoma rufescens	Rufous-winged Illadopsis	8	c		
Trichastoma rufipenne	Pale-breasted Illadopsis	8	c		
Trichastoma sepiaria	Horsfield's Babbler	19 21 55		g	h
Trichastoma tickelli	Tickell's Babbler	15 17 18 19 55	f	g	h
Leonardina woodi	Bagobo Babbler	22			h
Ptyrticus turdinus	White-bellied Thrush-Babbler	8	c		

Scientific Name	Common Name	Source Codes	Region Codes
MUSCICAPIDAE · TIMALIINAE · BABBLERS, WREN-TITS *contd.*			
Malacopteron affine	Plain Babbler	19 21 55	g h
Malacopteron albogulare	White-throated Babbler	19 21	h
Malacopteron cinereum	Lesser Red-headed Babbler	19 21 55	g h
Malacopteron magnirostre	Brown-headed Babbler	18 19 21 55	g h
Malacopteron magnum	Greater Red-headed Babbler	18 19 21 55	g h
Malacopteron palawanense	Palawan Babbler	47	h
Pomatorhinus erythrocnemis[1]	Chinese Rusty-cheeked Scimitar Babbler	1 55	b g
Pomatorhinus erythrogenys	Rusty-cheeked Scimitar Babbler	1 15 17 18 55	b f g
Pomatorhinus ferruginosus	Coral-billed Scimitar Babbler	15 18 55	f g
Pomatorhinus horsfieldii	Horsfield's Scimitar Babbler	47	f
Pomatorhinus hypoleucos	Large Scimitar Babbler	15 17 18 19 55	f g h
Pomatorhinus montanus	Chestnut-backed Scimitar Babbler	18 19 21	h
Pomatorhinus ochraceiceps	Red-billed Scimitar Babbler	15 18 55	f g
Pomatorhinus ruficollis	Rufous-necked Scimitar Babbler	1 15 17 18 55	b f g
Pomatorhinus schisticeps	Slaty-headed Scimitar Babbler	15 55	f g
Garritornis isidorei	Isadore's Rufous Babbler	35	j
Pomatostomus halli	Hall's White-throated Babbler	36 49	i
Pomatostomus ruficeps	Chestnut-crowned Babbler	36	i
Pomatostomus superciliosus	White-browed Babbler	36	i
Pomatostomus temporalis	Gray-crowned Babbler	35 36	i j
Xiphirhynchus superciliaris	Slender-billed Scimitar Babbler	15 17 18 55	f g
Jabouilleia danjoui	Danjou's Babbler	55	g
Rimator malacoptilus	Long-billed Wren-Babbler	15 18 19 55	f g h
Ptilocichla falcata	Falcated Ground Babbler	22	h
Ptilocichla leucogrammica	Bornean Wren-Babbler	19 21	h
Ptilocichla mindanensis[2]	Streaked Ground Babbler	24	h
Kenopia striata	Striped Wren-Babbler	19 21 55	g h
Napothera atrigularis	Black-throated Wren-Babbler	21	h
Napothera brevicaudata	Short-tailed Wren-Babbler	15 17 18 19 55	f g h
Napothera crassa	Mountain Wren-Babbler	21	h
Napothera crispifrons	Limestone Wren-Babbler	18 55	g
Napothera epilepidota	Small Wren-Babbler	15 17 18 19 21 55	f g h
Napothera macrodactyla[3]	Large-footed Wren-Babbler	19 55	g h
Napothera marmoratus	Muller's Wren-Babbler	19	h
Napothera rabori	Rabor's Wren-Babbler	24 47	h
Pnoepyga albiventer	Greater Scaly Wren-Babbler	15 17 18 55	f g
Pnoepyga pusilla	Lesser Scaly Wren-Babbler	1 15 17 18 19 55	b f g h
Spelaeornis cqudatus	Tailed Wren-Babbler	15	f
Spelaeornis chocolatinus	Streaked Long-tailed Wren-Babbler	15 17 18 55	f g
Spelaeornis formosus	Spotted Wren-Babbler	15 17 18	f g
Spelaeornis longicaudatus	Long-tailed Wren-Babbler	15	f
Spelaeornis troglodytoides	Barred-wing Wren-Babbler	1 15 17 18	b f g
Sphenocichla humei	Wedge-billed Wren-Babbler	15 18	f g
Neomixis flavoviridis	Wedge-tailed Jery	10	c
Neomixis striatigula	Stripe-throated Jery	10	c
Neomixis tenella	Northern Jery	10	c
Neomixis viridis	Green Jery	10	c
Stachyris ambigua	Equivocal Babbler	55	g
Stachyris capitalis	Rufous-crowned Tree Babbler	22	h
Stachyris chrysaea	Golden-headed Babbler	15 17 18 19 55	f g h
Stachyris erythroptera	Red-winged Babbler	18 19 21 55	g h
Stachyris grammiceps	White-breasted Tree Babbler	19	h

118

Scientific Name	Common Name	Source Codes	Region Codes

MUSCICAPIDAE · TIMALIINAE · BABBLERS, WREN-TITS *contd.*

Scientific Name	Common Name	Source Codes	Region Codes
Stachyris herberti	Laos Dusky Tree Babbler	55	g
Stachyris hypogrammica	Palawan Tree Babbler	25	h
Stachyris leucotis	White-eared Tree Babbler	19 21 55	g h
Stachyris maculata	Red-rumped Tree Babbler	19 21 55	g h
Stachyris melanothorax	Pearl-cheeked Tree Babbler	19	h
Stachyris nigriceps	Black-throated Babbler	15 17 18 19 21 55	f g h
Stachyris nigricollis	Black-necked Tree Babbler	19 21 55	g h
Stachyris nigrorum	Black-crowned Tree Babbler	22	h
Stachyris oglei	Austen's Spotted Babbler	15	f
Stachyris plateni	Pygmy Tree Babbler	22	h
Stachyris poliocephala	Gray-headed Tree Babbler	19 21 55	g h
Stachyris pyrrhops	Red-billed Babbler	15	f
Stachyris rodolphei	Deignan's Babbler	55	g
Stachyris ruficeps	Red-headed Tree Babbler	15 17 18 55	f g
Stachyris rufifrons	Red-fronted Babbler	15 18 19 21 55	f g h
Stachyris speciosa	Rough-templed Tree Babbler	22	h
Stachyris striata	Striped Tree Babbler	22	h
Stachyris striolata	Spotted Tree Babbler	17 18 19 55	g h
Stachyris thoracica	White-collared Tree Babbler	19	h
Stachyris whiteheadi	Whitehead's Tree Babbler	22	h
Dumetia hyperythra	Rufous-bellied Babbler	15	f
Rhopocichla atriceps	Black-headed Babbler	15	f
Macronous flavicollis	Yellow-collared Tit-Babbler	47	h
Macronous gularis	Striped Tit-Babbler	15 21 55	f g h
Macronous kellyi	Gray-faced Tit-Babbler	55	g
Macronous ptilosus	Fluffy-backed Tit-Babbler	17 18 19 21 55	g h
Macronous striaticeps	Brown Tit-Babbler	22	h
Micromacronus leytensis	Leyte Tit-Babbler	47	h
Timalia pileata	Red-capped Babbler	15 17 18 19 55	f g h
Chrysomma sinensis	Yellow-eyed Babbler	15 17 18 55	f g
Moupinia altirostre	Jerdon's Babbler	15 18	f g
Moupinia poecilotis	Chestnut-tailed Moupinia	1 17	b g
Chamaea fasciata	Wren-Tit	3 4	a e
Turdoides affinis	Indian White-headed Babbler	15	f
Turdoides altirostris	Iraq Babbler	1	b
Turdoides aylmeri	Scaly Chatterer	8	c
Turdoides bicolor	Pied Babbler	8	c
Turdoides caudatus	Common Babbler	1 15	b f
Turdoides earlei	Striated Babbler	15 18	f g
Turdoides fulvus	Fulvous Babbler	1 8	b c
Turdoides gularis	Burmese White-throated Babbler	18	g
Turdoides gymnogenys	Bare-cheeked Babbler	8	c
Turdoides hindei	Hinde's Pied Babbler	8	c
Turdoides hypoleucus	Northern Pied Babbler	8	c
Turdoides jardinei	Arrow-marked Babbler	8	c
Turdoides leucocephalus[4]	White-headed Babbler	9	c
Turdoides leucopygius	White-rumped Babbler	8	c
Turdoides longirostris	Slender-billed Babbler	15 18	f g
Turdoides malcolmi	Large Gray Babbler	15	f
Turdoides melanops	Black-lored Babbler	8	c
Turdoides nipalensis	Spiny Babbler	15	f
Turdoides plebejus	African Brown Babbler	8	c
Turdoides reinwardtii	Western Dusky Babbler	8	c
Turdoides rubiginosus	Rufous Chatterer	8	c
Turdoides sharpei[5]	Black-lored Babbler	9	c
Turdoides squamiceps	Arabian Brown Babbler	1 8	b c

Scientific Name	Common Name	Source Codes	Region Codes
MUSCICAPIDAE · TIMALIINAE · BABBLERS, WREN-TITS *contd.*			
Turdoides squamulatus	Scaly Babbler	8	c
Turdoides striatus	Jungle Babbler	15	f
Turdoides subrufus	Rufous Babbler	15	f
Turdoides tenebrosus	Dusky Babbler	8	c
Babax koslowi	Kozlov's Babax	1	b
Babax lanceolatus	Chinese Babax	1 15 17 18	b f g
Babax waddelli	Giant Babax	1 15 17	b f g
Garrulax affinis[6]	Black-faced Laughingthrush	1 15 17 18	b f g h
Garrulax albogularis	White-throated Laughing-thrush	1 3 15 17 55	b f g h
Garrulax austeni	Brown-capped Laughing-thrush	15 18 55	f g
Garrulax cachinnans[7]	Nilgiri Laughingthrush	15	f
Garrulax caerulatus[8]	Gray-sided Laughingthrush	1 15 17 18	b f g
Garrulax canorus	Hwa-Mei	1 3 17 55	b g k
Garrulax chinensis[9]	Black-throated Laughingthrush	3 15 17 18 55	f g k
Garrulax cineraceus	Ashy Laughingthrush	1 15 17 18	b f g h
Garrulax cinereifrons	Ashy-headed Laughingthrush	15	f
Garrulax davidi	Père David's Laughingthrush	1 17	b g
Garrulax delesserti[10]	Wynaad Laughingthrush	15 55	f g
Garrulax elliotii	Elliot's Laughingthrush	1 17	b g
Garrulax erythrocephalus	Red-headed Laughingthrush	1 15 17 18 19 55	b f g h
Garrulax formosus	Red-winged Laughingthrush	1 17 55	b g
Garrulax galbanus[11]	Austen's Laughingthrush	15 17 18	f g
Garrulax henrici	Prince d'Orlean's Laughing-thrush	1 15 17	b f g
Garrulax leucolophus	White-crested Laughingthrush	15 17 18 19 55	f g h
Garrulax lineatus	Streaked Laughingthrush	1 17	b g
Garrulax lugubris	Black Laughingthrush	19 21	h
Garrulax lunulatus[12]	Barred Laughingthrush	1 17	b g
Garrulax maesi	Maes's Laughingthrush	1 17 55	b g
Garrulax maximus	Giant Laughingthrush	1 15 17	b f g
Garrulax merulinus	Spotted-breasted Laughing-thrush	15 17 18 55	f g
Garrulax milleti	Millet's Laughingthrush	55	g
Garrulax milnei	Red-tailed Laughingthrush	17 18 55	g
Garrulax mitratus	Chestnut-capped Laughing-thrush	19 21	h
Garrulax moniliger	Lesser Necklaced Laughing-thrush	15 18 55	f g
Garrulax ocellatus	Spotted Laughingthrush	1 15 17 18	b f g
Garrulax palliatus	Gray-and-Brown Laughing-thrush	19 21	h
Garrulax pectoralis	Greater Necklaced Laughing-thrush	15 17 18 55	f g
Garrulax perspicillatus	Spectacled Laughingthrush	1 17 55	b g
Garrulax ruficollis	Rufous-necked Laughing-thrush	15 18	f g
Garrulax rufifrons	Red-fronted Laughingthrush	19	h
Garrulax rufogularis	Rufous-chinned Laughing-thrush	15 18	f g
Garrulax sannio	White-browed Laughingthrush	1 15 17 18 55	b f g
Garrulax squamatus	Blue-winged Laughingthrush	15 17 18 55	f g
Garrulax strepitans	Tickell's Laughingthrush	18 55	g
Garrulax striatus	Striated Laughingthrush	1 18	b g
Garrulax subunicolor	Plain-colored Laughingthrush	15 17 18 55	f g
Garrulax sukatschewi	Sukatschev's Laughingthrush	1 17	b g

120

Scientific Name	Common Name	Source Codes	Region Codes
MUSCICAPIDAE · TIMALIINAE · BABBLERS, WREN-TITS *contd.*			
Garrulax variegatus	Variegated Laughingthrush	1 15	b f
Garrulax vassali	White-cheeked Laughing-thrush	55	g
Garrulax virgatus	Streaked Laughingthrush	15 18	f g
Garrulax yersini	Collared Laughingthrush	55	g
Liocichla phoenicea	Crimson-winged Liocichla	15 17 18 55	f g
Liocichla steerii	Steere's Liocichla	17	g
Leiothrix argentauris	Silver-eared Mesia	15 17 18 19 55	f g h
Leiothrix lutea	Peking Robin	1 3 15 17 18	b g h k
Cutia nipalensis	Nepal Cutia	15 17 18 19 55	f g h
Pteruthius aenobarbus	Chestnut-fronted Shrike-Babbler	15 17 18 19 55	f g h
Pteruthius flaviscapis	Red-winged Shrike-Babbler	1 15 17 18 19 21 55	b f g h
Pteruthius melanotis	Chestnut-throated Shrike-Babbler	15 17 18 19 55	f g h
Pteruthius rufiventer	Rufous-bellied Shrike-Babbler	15 17 18 55	f g
Pteruthius xanthochlorus	Green Shrike-Babbler	1 15 17 18	b f g
Gampsorhynchus rufulus	White-headed Shrike-Babbler	15 18 19 55	f g h
Actinodura egertoni	Spectacled Barwing	15 17 18	f g
Actinodura morrisoniana	Formosan Barwing	17	g
Actinodura nipalensis	Hoary Barwing	15 17 18 55	f g
Actinodura ramsayi	Ramsay's Barwing	55	g
Actinodura souliei	Soule's Barwing	17 55	g
Actinodura waldeni	Austen's Barwing	15 18	f g
Minla cyanouroptera	Blue-winged Siva	15 17 18 19 55	f g h
Minla ignotincta	Fire-tailed Minla	15 17 18 55	f g
Minla strigula	Bar-throated Minla	15 17 18 19 55	f g h
Alcippe abyssinica	African Hill Babbler	8	c
Alcippe brunnea	Gould's Tit-Babbler	15 17 18 55	f g
Alcippe bruneicauda	Brown Quaker Babbler	21 55	g h
Alcippe castaneceps	Chestnut-headed Tit-Babbler	15 17 18 19 55	f g h
Alcippe chrysotis	Golden-breasted Tit-Babbler	1 15 17 18 55	b f g
Alcippe cinerea	Yellow-throated Tit-Babbler	15 18 55	f g
Alcippe cinereiceps	Gray-headed Tit-Babbler	1 15 17 18 55	b f g
Alcippe morrisonia	Gray-headed Quaker Babbler	17 18 55	g g
Alcippe nipalensis	White-eyed Quaker Babbler	15 18 19	f h
Alcippe peracensis	Mountain Nun Babbler	20 55	g h
Alcippe poioicephala	Quaker Babbler	15 17 18 19 55	f g h
Alcippe pyrrhoptera	Javan Nun Babbler	20	h
Alcippe ruficapilla	Verreaux's Rufous-headed Tit-Babbler	1 17 55	b g
Alcippe rufogularis	Red-throated Tit-Babbler	15 18 55	f g
Alcippe striaticollis	Mountain Tit-Babbler	1 17	b g
Alcippe variegaticeps	Yellow-fronted Tit-Babbler	17	g
Alcippe vinipectus	White-browed Tit-Babbler	1 15 17 18 55	b f g
Lioptilus chapini	Chapin's Flycatcher-Babbler	9	c
Lioptilus gilberti	White-throated Mountain Babbler	8	c
Lioptilus nigricapillus	Blackcap Babbler	8	c
Lioptilus rufocinctus	Rufous-collared Mountain Babbler	8	c
Parophasma galinieri	Abyssinian Catbird	8	c
Phyllanthus atripennis	Capuchin Babbler	8	c
Crocias albonotatus	Spotted Sibia	19	h
Crocias langbianis	Gray-crowned Sibia	55	g
Heterophasia annectens	Chestnut-backed Sibia	15 17 18 55	f g

Scientific Name	Common Name	Source Codes	Region Codes

Scientific Name	Common Name	Source Codes	Region Codes
Heterophasia auricularis	Formosan Sibia	17	g
Heterophasia capistrata	Black-headed Sibia	15 17	f g
Heterophasia gracilis	Gray Sibia	15 18	f g
Heterophasia melanoleuca[13]	Tickell's Sibia	17 18 55	g
Heterophasia picaoides	Long-tailed Sibia	15 18 19 55	f g h
Heterophasia pulchella	Beautiful Sibia	15 17 18	f g
Picathartes gymnocephalus	Guinea Bare-headed Rockfowl	8	c
Picathartes oreas	Cameroon Bare-headed Rockfowl	9	c
Yuhina bakeri	Baker's Chestnut-headed Yuhina	15 18	f g
Yuhina brunneiceps	Formosan Yuhina	17	g
Yuhina castaniceps[14]	Chestnut-headed Yuhina	15 55	f g
Yuhina diademata	White-collared Yuhina	1 17 18 55	b g
Yuhina flavicollis[15]	Yellow-naped Yuhina	15 17 18 55	f g
Yuhina gularis	Stripe-throated Yuhina	1 15 17 18 55	b f g
Yuhina nigrimenta	Black-chinned Yuhina	15 17 18 55	f g
Yuhina occipitalis	Rufous-vented Yuhina	15 17 18	f g
Yuhina zantholeuca	White-bellied Yuhina	15 17 18 19 21 55	f g h
Malia grata	Celebes Malia	27	h
Myzornis pyrrhoura	Fire-tailed Myzornis	15 17 18	f g
Horizorhinus dohrni	Dohrns Thrush-Babbler	8	c
Oxylabes madagascariensis	Foditany	10	c
Mystacornis crossleyi	Crossley's Babbler	10	c

MUSCICAPIDAE · PARADOXORNITHINAE · PARROTBILLS, SUTHORAS
19 species recorded

Scientific Name	Common Name	Source Codes	Region Codes
Panurus biarmicus	Bearded Reedling	1	b
Conostoma oemodium	Great Parrotbill	1 15 17 18	b f g
Paradoxornis alphonsianus	Ashy-throated Parrotbill		
Paradoxornis atrosuperciliaris	Black-browed Parrotbill	15 17 18 55	f g
Paradoxornis conspicillatus	Spectacled Parrotbill	1 17	b g
Paradoxornis davidianus	Short-tailed Parrotbill	17 18 55	g
Paradoxornis flavirostris	Gould's Parrotbill	15 17 18	f g
Paradoxornis fulvifrons	Fulvous-fronted Parrotbill	1 15 17 18	b f g
Paradoxornis gularis	Gray-headed Parrotbill	15 17 18 55	f g
Paradoxornis guttaticollis	Spot-breasted Parrotbill	55	g
Paradoxornis heudei	Yangtze Crowtit	17	g
Paradoxornis nipalensis[1]	Ashy-eared Parrotbill	1 15 17 18 55	b f g
Paradoxornis paradoxus	Three-toed Parrotbill	1 17	b g
Paradoxornis przewalskii	Przevalski's Parrotbill	1 17	b g
Paradoxornis ricketti	Yunnan Parrotbill	47	g
Paradoxornis ruficeps	Greater Red-headed Parrotbill	15 18 55	f g
Paradoxornis unicolor	Brown Parrotbill	1 15 17 18	b f g
Paradoxornis webbianus	Vinous-throated Parrotbill	1 17 18 55	b g
Paradoxornis zappeyi	Zappey's Parrotbill	1 17	b g

MUSCICAPIDAE · SYLVIINAE · OLD WORLD WARBLERS   339 species recorded

Scientific Name	Common Name	Source Codes	Region Codes
Microbates cinereiventris	Half-collared Gnatwren	4 6	d e
Microbates collaris	Collared Gnatwren	6	d
Ramphocaenus melanurus[1]	Long-billed Gnatwren	4 6	d e

Scientific Name	Common Name	Source Codes	Region Codes
MUSCICAPIDAE ' SYLVIINAE ' OLD WORLD WARBLERS *contd.*			
Polioptila albiloris	White-lored Gnatcatcher	4	e
Polioptila caerulea	Blue-Gray Gnatcatcher	3 4 5	a e
Polioptila dumicola	Masked Gnatcatcher	6	d
Polioptila guianensis[2]	Guianan Gnatcatcher	6	d
Polioptila lactea[3]	Cream-bellied Gnatcatcher	6	d
Polioptila lembeyei	Cuban Gnatcatcher	5	e
Polioptila melanura	Black-tailed Gnatcatcher	3 4	a e
Polioptila nigriceps	Black-capped Gnatcatcher	4	e
Polioptila plumbea	Tropical Gnatcatcher	4 6	d e
Polioptila schistaceigula	Slate-throated Gnatcatcher	4 6	d e
Tesia castaneocoronata	Chestnut-headed Ground Warbler	1 15 17 18 55	b f g
Tesia cyaniventer	Dull Slaty-bellied Ground Warbler	15 17 18 55	f g h
Tesia olivea	Bright Slaty-bellied Ground Warbler	15 17 18 55	f g
Tesia superciliaris	Javan Ground Warbler	19	h
Cettia acanthizoides	Verreaux's Bush Warbler	1 15 17 18	b f g
Cettia brunnifrons	Rufous-capped Bush Warbler	1 15 17 18	b f g
Cettia cetti	Cetti's Warbler	1 15 17	b f g
Cettia diphone[4]	Bush Warbler	1 3 15 17 22	b f g h k
Cettia flavolivaceus	Aberrant Bush Warbler	1 15 17 18 55	b f g
Cettia fortipes	Strong-footed Bush Warbler	15 17 18 19 21 55	f g h
Cettia major	Large Bush Warbler	1 15 17 55	b f g
Cettia montanus	Mountain Bush Warbler	1	b
Cettia pallidipes	Pale-footed Bush Warbler	15 17 18 55	f g
Cettia squamciceps	Short-tailed Bush Warbler	1 17 18 55	b g
Cettia subulata	Timor Bush Warbler	32	j
Cettia whiteheadi	Short-tailed Bush Warbler	19 21	h
Bradypterus accentor	Kinabalu Scrub Warbler	19 21	h
Bradypterus alfredi	Bamboo Warbler	8	c
Bradypterus baboecala	African Sedge Warbler	8	c
Bradypterus barratti	Scrub Warbler	8	c
Bradypterus carpalis	White-winged Warbler	8	c
Bradypterus castaneus	East Indies Bush Warbler	31	h j
Bradypterus caudatus	Long-tailed Ground Warbler	22	h
Bradypterus cinnamomeus	Cinnamon Bracken Warbler	8	c
Bradypterus grandis	Giant Swamp Warbler	9	c
Bradypterus graueri	Grauer's Warbler	8	c
Bradypterus luteoventris	Brown Bush Warbler	1 15 17 18 22 55	b f g h
Bradypterus major	Large-billed Bush Warbler	1 15 17	b f g
Bradypterus palliseri	Palliser's Warbler	15	f
Bradypterus seebohmi	Mountain Scrub Warbler	17 55	g
Bradypterus sylvaticus	Knysna Scrub Warbler	8	c
Bradypterus tacsanowskius	Chinese Bush Warbler	1 15 17 18 55	b f g
Bradypterus thoracicus	Spotted Bush Warbler	1 15 17 18 55	b f g
Bradypterus victorini	Victorin's Bush Warbler	8	c
Psamathia annae	Palau Warbler	38	k
Schoenicola platyura	Broadtailed Grass Warbler	8 15	c f
Megalurus albolimbatus	Fly River Grass Warbler	35	j
Megalurus gramineus	Little Grass Warbler	35 36	i j
Megalurus palustris	Striated Marsh Warbler	15 17 18 19 22 55	f g h
Megalurus pryeri	Japanese Marsh Warbler	1 17	b g
Megalurus timoriensis	Rufous-capped Grass Warbler	22 35 36	h i j
Chaetornis striatus	Bristled Grass Warbler	15	f
Locustella certhiola	Pallas's Grasshopper Warbler	1 15 17 18 19 21 22 55	b f g h

Scientific Name	Common Name	Source Codes	Region Codes
MUSCICAPIDAE · SYLVIINAE · OLD WORLD WARBLERS *contd.*			
Locustella fasciolata	Gray's Grasshopper Warbler	1 17 22 35	b g h j
Locustella fluviatilis	River Warbler	1 8	b c
Locustella lanceolata	Lanceolated Warbler	1 15 17 18 19 21 22 55	b f g h
Locustella luscinioides	Savi's Warbler	1 8	b c
Locustella naevia	Grasshopper Warbler	1 8 15 17	b c f g
Locustella ochotensis	Middendorff's Grasshopper Warbler	3 17 21 55	a g h
Acrocephalus aedon[5]	Thick-billed Reed Warbler	1 18 55	b g
Acrocephalus aequinoctalis	Polynesian Warbler	48	k
Acrocephalus agricola	Paddy-Field Warbler	1 15 17 18 55	b f g
Acrocephalus arundinaceus	Great Reed Warbler	1 8 15 17 18 19 21 22 35 38 55	b c f g h j k
Acrocephalus atypha	Atoll Warbler	44	k
Acrocephalus bistrigiceps	Black-browed Reed Warbler	1 15 17 18 55	b f g
Acrocephalus boeticatus	Tropical African Reed Warbler	8	c
Acrocephalus brevipennis	Cape Verde Island Cane Warbler	9	c
Acrocephalus caffra	Long-billed Warbler	41	k
Acrocephalus concinens	Blunt-winged Paddy-Field Warbler	1 15 55	b f g
Acrocephalus dumetorum	Blyth's Reed Warbler	1 15 18	b f
Acrocephalus familiaris	Millerbird	3	k
Acrocephalus gracilirostris	Cape Reed Warbler	8	c
Acrocephalus luscinia	Nightingale Reed Warbler	38	k
Acrocephalus melanopogon[6]	Moustached Warbler	1 8 15	b c f
Acrocephalus newtoni	Madagascar Swamp Warbler	10	c
Acrocephalus orinus	Large-billed Reed Warbler	1 15	b f
Acrocephalus paludicola	Aquatic Warbler	1	b
Acrocephalus palustris	Marsh Warbler	1 8	b c
Acrocephalus rufescens	Greater Swamp Warbler	8	c
Acrocephalus schoenobaenus	Sedge Warbler	1 8 17	b c g
Acrocephalus scirpaceus	Reed Warbler	1 8	b c
Acrocephalus sorghophilus	Speckled Reed Warbler	1 17 22	b g h
Acrocephalus stentoreus	Southern Great Reed Warbler	1 8 15 17 55	b c f g
Acrocephalus vaughani	Pitcairn Warbler	45	k
Chloropeta gracilirostris	Thin-billed Flycatcher	8	c
Chloropeta natalensis	Yellow Flycatcher	8	c
Chloropeta similis	Mountain Yellow Flycatcher	8	c
Sphenoeacus afer	Grassbird	8	c
Sphenoeacus mentalis	Moustache Warbler	8	c
Sphenoeacus pycnopygius	Damara Rock-Jumper	8	c
Hippolais caligata	Booted Warbler	1 15 17	b f g
Hippolais icterina	Icterine Warbler	1 8	b c
Hippolais languida	Upcher's Warbler	1 8 15	b c f
Hippolais olivetorum	Olive-Tree Warbler	1 8	b c
Hippolais pallida	Olivaceous Warbler	1 8	b c
Hippolais polyglotta	Melodious Warbler	1 8	b c
Sylvia althaea	Hume's Lesser Whitethroat	1 15	b f
Sylvia atricapilla	Blackcap	1 8	b c
Sylvia borin	Garden Warbler	1 8	b c
Sylvia cantillans	Subalpine Warbler	1 8	b c
Sylvia communis	Whitethroat	1 8 15 17	b c f g
Sylvia conspicillata	Spectacled Warbler	1	b
Sylvia curruca	Lesser Whitethroat	1 8 15 17	b c f g
Sylvia deserticola	Tristram's Warbler	1	b
Sylvia hortensis	Orphean Warbler	1 8 15	b c f

Scientific Name	Common Name	Source Codes	Region Codes
MUSCICAPIDAE · SYLVIINAE · OLD WORLD WARBLERS contd.			
Sylvia leucomelana	Red-Sea Warbler	8	c
Sylvia melanocephala	Sardinian Warbler	1 8	b e
Sylvia minula	Desert Lesser Whitethroat	1 15 17	b f g
Sylvia mystacea	Menetries's Warbler	1 8	b c
Sylvia nana	Desert Warbler	1 8 15 17	b c f g
Sylvia nisoria	Barred Warbler	1 8 17	b c g
Sylvia ruppelli	Ruppell's Warbler	1 8	b c
Sylvia sarda	Marmora's Warbler	1	b
Sylvia undata	Dartford Warbler	1	b
Phylloscopus affinis	Tickell's Willow Warbler	1 15 17 18	b f g
Phylloscopus amoenus	Kulambangra Warbler	38	k
Phylloscopus armandii	Milne-Edwards's Warbler	1 17 18 55	b g
Phylloscopus bonelli	Bonelli's Warbler	1 8	b c
Phylloscopus borealis	Arctic Warbler	1 3 15 17 18 19 21 22 55	a b f g h
Phylloscopus budongoensis	Uganda Woodland Warbler	8	c
Phylloscopus cantator[7]	Black-browed Willow Warbler	15 17 18 55	f g
Phylloscopus collybita	Chiffchaff	1 8 15 17	b c f g
Phylloscopus coronatus	Crowned Willow Warbler	17 18 55	g
Phylloscopus davisoni	White-tailed Willow Warbler	1 17 18 55	b g
Phylloscopus fuligiventer	Smoky Willow Warbler	15	f
Phylloscopus fuscatus	Dusky Warbler	1 15 17 18 55	b f g
Phylloscopus griseolus	Olivaceous Willow Warbler	1 15 17	b f g
Phylloscopus herberti	Black-capped Woodland Warbler	8	c
Phylloscopus ijimae	Ijima's Willow Warbler	1	b
Phylloscopus inornatus	Yellow-browed Warbler	1 15 17 18 19 55	b f g h
Phylloscopus laetus	Red-faced Woodland Warbler	8	c
Phylloscopus laurae	Mrs. Boulton's Woodland Warbler	9	c
Phylloscopus maculipennis	Gray-faced Willow Warbler	1 15 17 18 55	b f g
Phylloscopus magnirostris	Large-billed Willow Warbler	1 15 17 18	b f g
Phylloscopus neglectus	Plain Willow Warbler	1 15	b f
Phylloscopus nitidus	Green Warbler	1 15	b f
Phylloscopus occipitalis	Crowned Willow Warbler	1 15 19	b f h
Phylloscopus olivaceus	Philippine Leaf Warbler	22	h
Phylloscopus proregulus	Pallas's Leaf Warbler	1 15 17 18 55	b f g
Phylloscopus pulcher	Orange-barred Willow Warbler	1 15 17 18 55	b f g
Phylloscopus reguloides	Blyth's Crowned Willow Warbler	1 15 17 18 55	b f g
Phylloscopus ruficapilla	Yellow-throated Woodland Warbler	8	c
Phylloscopus schwarzi	Radde's Willow Warbler	1 17 18 55	b g
Phylloscopus sibilatrix	Wood Warbler	1 8	b c
Phylloscopus subaffinis	Buff-throated Willow Warbler	1 15 17 18 55	b f g
Phylloscopus subviridis	Brooks's Willow Warbler	1 15	b f
Phylloscopus tenellipes	Pale-legged Willow Warbler	1 17 18 55	b g
Phylloscopus trivirgatus	Mountain Leaf Warbler	1 19 21 22 35 38	b h j k
Phylloscopus trochiloides	Greenish Warbler	1 15 17 18 55	b f g
Phylloscopus trochilus	Willow Warbler	1 8 15	b c f
Phylloscopus tytleri	Tytler's Willow Warbler	1 15	b f
Phylloscopus umbrovirens	Brown Woodland Warbler	8	c
Seicercus affinis[8]	Allied Flycatcher-Warbler	15 17 18 55	f g
Seicercus burkii	Yellow-eyed Flycatcher-Warbler	1 15 17 18 55	b f g

Scientific Name	Common Name	Source Codes	Region Codes

MUSCICAPIDAE · SYLVIINAE · OLD WORLD WARBLERS *contd.*

Scientific Name	Common Name	Source Codes	Region Codes
Seicercus castaniceps	Chestnut-headed Flycatcher-Warbler	15 17 18 19 55	f g h
Seicercus grammiceps	Sunda Flycatcher-Warbler	19	h
Seicercus montis	Yellow-breasted Flycatcher-Warbler	19 21	h
Seicercus poliogenys	Gray-cheeked Flycatcher-Warbler	15 17 18 55	f g
Seicercus xanthoschistus	Gray-headed Flycatcher-Warbler	15 17 18	f g
Abrocsopus albogularis[9]	Fulvous-faced Flycacther-Warbler	15 17 18 55	f g
Abroscopus hodgsoni	Broad-billed Flycatcher-Warbler	15 18 55	f g
Abroscopus schisticeps	Black-faced Flycatcher-Warbler	15 17 18 55	f g
Abroscopus superciliaris	Yellow-bellied Flycatcher-Warbler	15 17 18 19 21 55	f g h
Regulus calendula[10]	Ruby-crowned Kinglet	3 4	a e
Regulus ignicapillus	Firecrest	1	b
Regulus regulus	Goldcrest	1 15 17	b f g
Regulus satrapa	Golden-crowned Kinglet	3	a
Leptopoecile elegans	Crested Tit-Warbler	1 15 17	b f g
Leptopoecile sophiae	Severtzov's Tit-Warbler	1 15 17	b f g
Bebrornis aldabranus	Aldabra Warbler	48	c
Bebrornis mariae	Comoro Brush Warbler	48	c
Bebrornis roderica	Rodriguez Brush Warbler	14	c
Bebrornis sechellensis	Seychelles Brush Warbler	14	c
Bebrornis typica	Tsikirity Brush Warbler	48	
Dromaeocercus brunneus	Brown Emu-Tail	10	c
Dromaeocercus seebohmi	Gray Emu-Tail	10	c
Prinia atrogularis	Black-throated Prinia	1 15 17 18 19 55	b f g h
Prinia bairdii	Banded Prinia	8	c
Prinia buchanani	Rufous-fronted Longtail Warbler	15	f
Prinia burnesii	Long-tailed Grass Warbler	15	f
Prinia cinereocapilla	Hodgson's Longtailed Warbler	15	f
Prinia clamans[11]	Cricket Warbler	1 8	b c
Prinia criniger	Hill Warbler	15 17 55	f g
Prinia epichlora	Green Longtail	8	c
Prinia erythroptera	Red-winged Warbler	8	c
Prinia familiaris	Bar-winged Wren-Warbler	19	h
Prinia flavicans	Black-chested Prinia	8	c
Prinia flaviventris	Yellow-bellied Wren-Warbler	15 17 18 19 21 55	f g h
Prinia gracilis	Graceful Prinia	1 8 15	b c f
Prinia hodgsoni	Franklin's Wren-Warbler	15 17 18 55	f g
Prinia inornata	Greater Brown Wren-Warbler	17 18 19 55	g h
Prinia leontica	Sierra Leone Prinia	8	c
Prinia leucopogon	White-chinned Prinia	8	c
Prinia maculosa	Karroo Prinia	8	c
Prinia molleri	Sao Tome Long-tailed Prinia	8	c
Prinia pectoralis	Rufous-eared Warbler	8	c
Prinia polychroa	Brown Prinia	1 17 18 19 55	b g h
Prinia pulchella	Buff-bellied Warbler	8	c
Prinia robertsi	Forest Prinia	8	c
Prinia rufescens	Dark-crowned Wren-Warbler	15 17 18 19 55	f g h
Prinia rufifrons[12]	Red-faced Apalis	9	c
Prinia socialis	Ashy Long-tailed Warbler	15	f

Scientific Name	Common Name	Source Codes	Region Codes
MUSCICAPIDAE · SYLVIINAE · OLD WORLD WARBLERS *contd.*			
Prinia somalica	Pale Prinia	8	c
Prinia subflava	Tawny Prinia	1 8 15	b c f
Prinia substriata	Namaqua Prinia	8	c
Prinia sylvatica	Jungle Long-tailed Warbler	15	f
Scotocerca inquieta	Streaked Scrub Warbler	1 15	b f
Thamnornis chloropetoides	Kiritika	10	c
Incana incana	Sokotra Grass Warbler	8	c
Randia pseudozosterops	Rand's Warbler	10	c
Cisticola aberrans	Rock-loving Cisticola	8	c
Cisticola anonyma	Chattering Cisticola	8	c
Cisticola aridula	Desert Cisticola	8	c
Cisticola ayresii	Ayres's Cloud Cisticola	8	c
Cisticola brachyptera	Short-winged Cisticola	8	c
Cisticola brunnescens	Pale-crowned Cloud Cisticola	8	c
Cisticola bulliens	Bubbling Cisticola	8	c
Cisticola cantans	Singing Cisticola	8	c
Cisticola carruthersi	Carruther's Cisticola	8	c
Cisticola cherina	Madagascar Cisticola	10	c
Cisticola chiniana	Rattling Cisticola	8	c
Cisticola chubbi	Chubb's Cisticola	9	c
Cisticola cinereola	Ashy Cisticola	8	c
Cisticola dambo	Cloud-Scraper Cisticola	8	c
Cisticola erythrops	Red-faced Cisticola	8	c
Cisticola exilis	Golden-headed Cisticola	15 17 18 19 22 35 36 55	f g h i j
Cisticola eximia	Black-backed Cisticola	8	c
Cisticola fulvicapilla	Piping Cisticola	8	c
Cisticola galactotes	Winding Cisticola	8	c
Cisticola haesitata	Socotra Cisticola	9	c
Cisticola hunteri	Hunter's Cisticola	8	c
Cisticola juncidis	Zitting Cisticola	1 8 15 17 18 19 22 36 55	b c f g h i
Cisticola lais	Wailing Cisticola	8	c
Cisticola lateralis	Whistling Cisticola	8	c
Cisticola melanura	Angola Slender-tailed Cisticola	8	c
Cisticola nana	Tiny Cisticola	8	c
Cisticola natalensis	Croaking Cisticola	8	c
Cisticola njombe	Churring Cisticola	8	c
Cisticola pipiens	Chirping Cisticola	8	c
Cisticola robusta	Stout Cisticola	8	c
Cisticola rufa	Rufous Grass Warbler	8	c
Cisticola ruficeps	Red-Pate Cisticola	8	c
Cisticola rufilata	Tinkling Cisticola	8	c
Cisticola subruficapilla	Gray-backed Cisticola	8	c
Cisticola textrix	Cloud Cisticola	8	c
Cisticola tinniens	Le Vaillant's Cisticola	8	c
Cisticola troglodytes	Foxy Cisticola	8	c
Cisticola woosnami	Trilling Cisticola	8	c
Rhopophilus pekinensis	White-browed Chinese Warbler	1	b
Graminocola bengalensis	Large Grass Warbler	15 17 18 55	f g
Orthotomus atrogularis	Black-necked Tailorbird	15 18 19 21 22 55	f g h
Orthotomus cinereiceps	White-eared Tailorbird	24	h
Orthotomus cucullatus	Mountain Tailorbird	15 17 18 19 21 22 55	f g h
Orthotomus derbianus	Luzon Tailorbird	24	h
Orthotomus nigriceps	Black-headed Tailorbird	22	h
Orthotomus samarensis	Samar Tailorbird	24	h

Scientific Name	Common Name	Source Codes	Region Codes
MUSCICAPIDAE · SYLVIINAE · OLD WORLD WARBLERS *contd.*			
Orthotomus sepium	Ashy Tailorbird	18 19 21 55	g h
Orthotomus sericeus	Red-headed Tailorbird	18 19 21 22 55	g h
Orthotomus sutorius	Common Tailorbird	15 17 18 19 55	f g h
Apalis alticola	Brown-headed Apalis	9	c
Apalis argentea	Kungewe Apalis	9	c
Apalis binotata	Masked Apalis	8	c
Apalis chariessa	White-winged Apalis	8	c
Apalis chirindensis	Melsetter Apalis	9	c
Apalis cinerea	Gray Apalis	8	c
Apalis flavida	Yellow-breasted Apalis	8	c
Apalis jacksoni	Black-throated Apalis	8	c
Apalis karamojae	Karamoja Apalis	8	c
Apalis melanocephala	Black-headed Apalis	8	c
Apalis moreaui	Long-billed Apalis	8	c
Apalis nigriceps	Black-capped Apalis	8	c
Apalis porphyrolaema	Chestnut-throated Apalis	8	c
Apalis pulchra	Black-collared Apalis	8	c
Apalis ruddi	Rudd's Apalis	8	c
Apalis rufogularis	Buff-throated Apalis	8	c
Apalis ruwenzori	Collared Apalis	9	c
Apalis sharpii	Bamenda Apalis	8	c
Apalis thoracica	Bar-throated Apalis	8	c
Artisornis metopias	Red-capped Forest Warbler	8	c
Scepomycter winifredae	Mrs. Moreau's Warbler	8	c
Drymocichla incana	Red-winged Gray Warbler	8	c
Eminia lepida	Gray-capped Warbler	8	c
Hypergerus atriceps	Oriole Babbler	8	c
Bathmocercus cerviniventris	Black-headed Stream-Warbler	8	c
Bathmocercus rufus	Black-faced Rufous Warbler	9	c
Camaroptera brachyura	Broad-tailed Camaroptera	8	c
Camaroptera brevicaudata	Gray-backed Camaroptera	9	c
Camaroptera chloronota	Green-backed Camaroptera	8	c
Camaroptera fasciolata	Barred Wren-Warbler	8	c
Camaroptera lopezi	White-tailed Warbler	8	c
Camaroptera simplex	Gray Wren-Warbler	8	c
Camaroptera stierlingi	Stierling's Barred Wren-Warbler	8	c
Camaroptera superciliaris	Yellow-browed Camaroptera	8	c
Euryptila subcinnamomea	Cinnamon-breasted Warbler	8	c
Eremomela atricollis	Black-necked Eremomela	8	c
Eremomela badiceps	Brown-crowned Eremomela	8	c
Eremomela canescens	Yellow-breasted Eremomela	9	c
Eremomela flavocrissalis	Yellow-vented Eremomela	8	c
Eremomela gregalis	Karroo Green Warbler	8	c
Eremomela icteropygialis	Yellow-backed Eremomela	8	c
Eremomela pusilla	Green-backed Eremomela	8	c
Eremomela salvadorii	Salvadori's Eremomela	9	c
Eremomela scotops	Green-capped Eremomela	8	c
Eremomela turneri	Turner's Eremomela	8	c
Eremomela usticollis	Brown-throated Eremomela	8	c
Sylvietta brachyura	Crombec	9	c
Sylvietta denti	Lemon-bellied Crombec	8	c
Sylvietta isabellina	Somali Long-billed Crombec	8	c
Sylvietta leucophrys	White-browed Crombec	8	c
Sylvietta philippae	Somali Short-billed Crombec	9	c
Sylvietta rufescens	Long-billed Crombec	8	c
Sylvietta ruficapilla	Red-capped Crombec	9	c

128

Scientific Name	Common Name	Source Codes	Region Codes

MUSCICAPIDAE · SYLVIINAE · OLD WORLD WARBLERS *contd.*

Scientific Name	Common Name	Source Codes	Region Codes
Sylvietta virens	Green Crombec	8	c
Sylvietta whytii	Red-faced Crombec	8	c
Hemitesia neumanni	Neumann's Bush Warbler	8	c
Macrosphenus concolor	Olive Bush-Creeper	8	c
Macrosphenus flavicans	Long-billed Bush-Creeper	8	c
Macrosphenus kempi	Kemp's Bush-Creeper	9	c
Macrosphenus kretschmeri	Kretschmer's Greenbul	8	c
Macrosphenus pulitzeri	Pulitzer's Greenbul	8	c
Graueri vittata	Grauer's Bush Warbler	8	c
Parisoma bohmi	Banded Tit-Flycatcher	8	c
Parisoma buryi	Yemen Tit-Babbler	8	c
Parisoma layardi	Layard's Tit-Babbler	8	c
Parisoma lugens	Brown Tit-Flycatcher	8	c
Parisoma subcaeruleum	Tit-Babbler	8	c
Hylia prasina	Green Hylia	8	c
Pholidornis rushiae	Tit-Weaver	8	c
Eremiornis carteri	Spinifex-Bird	36	i
Bowdleria punctata	Fernbird	37	i
Buettikoferella bivittata	Buettikoffer's Warbler	32	j
Ortygocichla rubiginosa	Rufous-faced Thicket Warbler	34	j
Megalurulus mariei	New Caledonian Grass Warbler	38	k
Cichlornis grosvenori	Whiteman Mountains Warbler	34	j
Cichlornis whitneyi	Thicket Warbler	38	k
Lamprolia victoriae	Silktail	38	k

MUSCICAPIDAE · MALURINAE · WREN-WARBLERS 29 species recorded

Scientific Name	Common Name	Source Codes	Region Codes
Malurus alboscapulatus	Black-and-White Wren-Warbler	35	j
Malurus amabilis	Lovely Wren-Warbler	36	i
Malurus assimilis	Purple-backed Wren-Warbler	47	i
Malurus callainus	Turquoise Wren-Warbler	36	i
Malurus coronatus	Purple-crowned Wren-Warbler	36	i
Malurus cyaneus	Superb Wren-Warbler	36	i
Malurus elegans	Red-winged Wren-Warbler	36	i
Malurus dulcis	Lavendar-flanked Wren-Warbler	36	i
Malurus lamberti	Variegated Wren-Warbler	36	i
Malurus leucopterus[1]	Blue-and-White Wren-Warbler	36	i
Malurus melanocephalus	Red-backed Wren-Warbler	36	i
Malurus melanotus	Black-backed Blue Wren	36	i
Malurus pulcherrimus	Blue-breasted Wren-Warbler	36	i
Malurus splendens	Splendid Blue Wren-Warbler	36	i
Clytomyias insignis	Rufous Wren-Warbler	35	j
Chenorhamphus grayi	Broad-billed Wren-Warbler	35	j
Todopsis cyanocephala	Blue Wren-Warbler	35	j
Todopsis wallacii	Wallace's Wren-Warbler	35	j
Stipiturus malachurus	Southern Emu-Wren	36	i
Stipiturus mallee	Mallee Emu-Wren	36	i
Stipiturus ruficeps	Rufous-crowned Emu-Wren	36	i
Amytornis barbatus	Gray Grass-Wren	71	i
Amytornis dorotheae	Dorothy's Grass-Wren	36	i
Amytornis goyderi	Eyrean Grass-Wren	36 53	i

129

Scientific Name	Common Name	Source Codes	Region Codes

MUSCICAPIDAE · MALURINAE · WREN-WARBLERS *contd.*

Scientific Name	Common Name	Source Codes	Region Codes
Amytornis housei	Black Grass-Wren	36	i
Amytornis purnelli	Dusky Grass-Wren	47	i
Amytornis striatus	Striated Grass-Wren	36	i
Amytornis textilis[2]	Western Grass-Wren	36	i
Amytornis woodwardi	White-throated Grass-Wren	36	i

MUSCICAPIDAE · ACANTHIZINAE · AUSTRALASIAN WARBLERS
59 species recorded

Scientific Name	Common Name	Source Codes	Region Codes
Dasyornis brachypterus[1]	Bristle-Bird	36	i
Dasyornis broadbenti	Rufous Bristle-Bird	36	i
Aphelocephala leucopsis[2]	Common Whiteface	36	i
Aphelocephala nigricincta	Banded Whiteface	36	i
Aphelocephala pectoralis	Chestnut-breasted Whiteface	36	i
Smicrornis brevirostris	Brown Weebill	36	i
Acanthiza chrysorrhoa	Yellow-tailed Thornbill	36	i
Acanthiza ewingi	Tasmanian Thornbill	36	i
Acanthiza inornata	Western Thornbill	36	i
Acanthiza iredalei	Slender Thornbill	36	i
Acanthiza lineata	Striated Thornbill	36	i
Acanthiza murina	De Vis Tree Warbler	35	j
Acanthiza nana	Little Thornbill	36	i
Acanthiza pusilla	Brown Thornbill	36	i
Acanthiza reguloides	Buff-tailed Thornbill	36	i
Acanthiza robustirostris	Robust Thornbill	36	i
Acanthiza uropygialis	Chestnut-tailed Thornbill	36	i
Pyrrholaemus brunneus	Redthroat	36	i
Finschia novaeseelandiae	Brown Creeper	37	i
Mohoua ochrocephala[3]	Whitehead	37	i
Pycnoptilus floccosus	Pilot-Bird	36	i
Calamanthus fulignosus[4]	Field-Wren	36	i
Hylacola cauta	Shy Ground-Wren	36	i
Hylacola pyrrhopygia	Chestnut-tailed Ground-Wren	36	i
Chthonicola sagittata	Speckled Warbler	36	i
Gerygone albofrontata[5]	Chatham Island Gerygone Warbler	37	i
Gerygone chloronota	Gray-headed Gerygone Warbler	35 36	i j
Gerygone chrysogaster	Yellow-bellied Gerygone Warbler	35	j
Gerygone cinerea	New Guinea Gerygone Warbler	35	j
Gerygone flavolateralis	New Caledonian Gerygone Warbler	38	k
Gerygone fusca	Western Gerygone Warbler	21 35 36	h i j
Gerygone igata	Gray Gerygone Warbler	37	i
Gerygone levigaster	Buff-breasted Gerygone Warbler	36	i
Gerygone magnirostris	Swamp Gerygone Warbler	35 36	i j
Gerygone olivacea	White-throated Gerygone Warbler	35 36	i j
Gerygone palpebrosa	Black-headed Gerygone Warbler	35 36	i j
Gerygone ruficollis	Treefern Gerygone Warbler	35	j

Scientific Name	Common Name	Source Codes	Region Codes

MUSCICAPIDAE · ACANTHIZINAE · AUSTRALASIAN WARBLERS *contd.*

Scientific Name	Common Name	Source Codes	Region Codes
Gerygone sulphurea	Yellow-breasted Gerygone Warbler	19 22 55	g h
Gerygone tenebrosa	Dusky Gerygone Warbler	36	i
Eugerygone rubra	Red-backed Warbler	35	j
Acanthornis magnus	Scrub-Tit	36	i
Oreoscopus gutturalis	Fern-Wren	36	i
Sericornis arfakianus	Gray-Green Sericornis	35	j
Sericornis beccarii[6]	Beccari's Sericornis	35	j
Sericornis citreogularis	Yellow-throated Scrub-Wren	36	i
Sericornis frontalis	White-browed Scrub-Wren	36	i
Sericornis humilis	Brown Scrub-Wren	36	i
Sericornis maculatus	Spotted Scrub-Wren	36	i
Sericornis magnirostris	Large-billed Scrub-Wren	36	i
Sericornis nigroviridis	Black-and-Green Sericornis	35	j
Sericornis nouhuysi	Large Mountain Sericornis	35	j
Sericornis papuensis	Papuan Sericornis	35	j
Sericornis perspicillatus	Buff-faced Sericornis	35	j
Sericornis spilodera	Pale-billed Sericornis	35	j
Vitia parens	Shade Warbler	38	k
Vitia ruficapilla[7, 8]	Fiji Warbler	38	k
Origma rubricata	Rock-Warbler	36	i
Cinclorhamphus cruralis	Brown Songlark	36	i
Cinclorhamphus mathewsi	Rufous Songlark	36	i

MUSCICAPIDAE · MUSCICAPINAE · OLD WORLD FLYCATCHERS

134 species recorded

Scientific Name	Common Name	Source Codes	Region Codes
Bradornis infuscus	African Brown Flycatcher	8	c
Bradornis mariquensis	Mariqua Flycatcher	8	c
Bradornis microrhynchus	Gray Flycatcher	8	c
Bradornis pallidus	Pale Flycatcher	8	c
Empidornis semipartitus	Silver-Bird	8	c
Melaenornis annamarulae	Liberian Flycatcher	69	c
Melaenornis ardesiaca	Western Mountain Flycatcher	8	c
Melaenornis chocolatina	Slaty Flycatcher	8	c
Melaenornis edolioides	Black Flycatcher	8	c
Melaenornis pannelaina	South African Black Flycatcher	8	c
Melaenornis silens	Fiscal-Flycatcher	8	c
Fraseria cinerascens	White-browed Forest Flycatcher	8	c
Fraseria ocreata	Forest Flycatcher	8	c
Rhinomyias addita	Buru Jungle Flycatcher	31	j
Rhinomyias brunneata	White-gorgetted Jungle Flycatcher	17 17	f g h
Rhinomyias colonus	Gleaning Jungle Flycatcher	63	j
Rhinomyias gularis	White-browed Jungle Flycatcher	19 21	h
Rhinomyias insignis[1]	Luzon Jungle Flycatcher	22	h
Rhinomyias olivacea	Olive-backed Jungle Flycatcher	17 18 19 21	g h
Rhinomyias oscillans	Flores Jungle Flycatcher	63	j
Rhinomyias ruficauda	Rufous-tailed Jungle Flycatcher	21 22	h
Rhinomyias umbratilis	White-throated Jungle Flycatcher		

Scientific Name	Common Name	Source Codes	Region Codes
MUSCICAPIDAE · MUSCICAPINAE · OLD WORLD FLYCATCHERS contd.			
Machaerirhynchus flaviventer	Boat-billed Flycatcher	35 36	i j
Machaerirhynchus nigripectus	Black-breast Boat-billed Flycatcher	35	j
Ficedula albicollis	Collared Flycatcher	1 8	b c
Ficedula basilanica	Little Slaty Flycatcher	22	h
Ficedula bonthaina	Lisping Flycatcher	27	h
Ficedula buruensis	Buru Flycatcher	31	j
Ficedula crypta	Vaurie's Flycatcher	24	h
Ficedula cyanomelana[2]	Blue-and-White Flycatcher	24	h
Ficedula dumetoria	Orange-breasted Flycatcher	19 21 55	g h
Ficedula harterti	Hartert's Flycatcher	32	j
Ficedula henrici	Damar Flycatcher	63	i
Ficedula hodgsonii	Slaty-backed Flycatcher	55	g h
Ficedula hyperythra	White-fronted Blue	15 17 18 19 21 22 55	f g h
Ficedula hypoleuca	Pied Flycatcher	1 8	b c
Ficedula monileger	White-gorgetted Flycatcher	15 18 19 55	f g h
Ficedula mugimaki	Black-and-Orange Flycatcher	1 17 19 21 55	b g h
Ficedula narcissina	Black-and-Yellow Flycatcher	1 17 19 21 22 55	b g h
Ficedula nigrorufa	Black-and-Rufous Flycatcher	15	f
Ficedula parva	Red-breasted Flycatcher	1 17 55	b g h
Ficedula platenae	Palawan Flycatcher	22	h
Ficedula rufigula	Red-throated Flycatcher	27	h
Ficedula sapphira	Sapphire Flycatcher	15 17 18 55	f g
Ficedula solitaria	Rufous-browed Flycatcher	18 19 55	f
Ficedula superciliaris	White-browed Blue Flycatcher	1 15 17 18 55	b f g
Ficedula timorensis	Timor Flycatcher	32	j
Ficedula tricolor	Slaty Blue Flycatcher	1 17 55	b g
Ficedula westermanni	Little Pied Blue Flycatcher	15 17 18 19 21 55	f h g
Ficedula zanthpygia	Yellow-rumped Flycatcher	1 17 55	
Niltava banumas	Hill Blue Niltava	17 17 18 19 21 55	f g h
Niltava caerulata	Large-billed Niltava	19 21	h
Niltava concreta	White-tailed Niltava	15 18 19 21	f h
Niltava davida	Fukien Niltava	17 55	g h
Niltava grandis	Large Niltava	15 17 18 19 55	f g h
Niltava hainana	Hainan Niltava	17 18 55	g h
Niltava herioti	Blue-breasted Niltava	22	h
Niltava hodgsoni[3]	Pygmy Niltava	1 15 17 18 19 21 55	b f g h
Niltava hoevelli	Celebes Niltava	27	h
Niltava hyacinthina	Hyacinthine Niltava	32	j
Niltava macgrigoriae	Small Niltava	15 17 18	f g h
Niltava pallipes	White-bellied Niltava	15	f
Niltava poliogenys	Brooks's Niltava	15 18	f g
Niltava rubeculoides	Blue-throated Niltava	1 15 17 18 55	b f g h
Niltava ruecki	Rueck's Niltava	19 55	h
Niltava rufigastra	Mangrove Niltava	19 21 22	h
Niltava sanfordi	Sanford's Niltava	27	h
Niltava sundara	Rufous-bellied Niltava	15 17 18 19 55	f g h
Niltava superba	Bornean Niltava	19	h
Niltava tickelliae	Tickell's Niltava	15 17 18 55	f g
Niltava turcosa	Malaysian Niltava	19 21 55	h
Niltava unicolor	Pale Niltava	15 17 18 19 21 55	f g h
Niltava vivida	Vivid Niltava	15 17 18 55	f g h
Muscicapa adusta	Dusky Flycatcher	8	c
Muscicapa albicaudata	Nilgiri Flycatcher	15	f
Muscicapa aquatica	Swamp Flycatcher	8	c

132

Scientific Name	Common Name	Source Codes	Region Codes
MUSCICAPIDAE · MUSCICAPINAE · OLD WORLD FLYCATCHERS *contd.*			
Muscicapa bohmi	Böhm's Flycatcher	8	c
Muscicapa caerulescens	Ashy Flycatcher	8	c
Muscicapa cassini	Cassin's Gray Flycatcher	8	c
Muscicapa comitata	Dusky-Blue Flycatcher	8	c
Muscicapa epulata	Little Gray Flycatcher	8	c
Muscicapa ferruginea	Ferruginous Flycatcher	15 17 18 21 22 55	f g h
Muscicapa gambagae	Gambaga Spotted Flycatcher	8	c
Muscicapa griseigularis	Gray-throated Flycatcher	8	c
Muscicapa griseisticta	Gray-spotted Flycatcher	1 17 22 35 55	b g h j
Muscicapa indigo	Indigo Flycatcher	19 21	h
Muscicapa infuscata[4]	African Sooty Flycatcher	9	c
Muscicapa latirostris	Brown Flycatcher	1 15 18 21 55	b f g h
Muscicapa lendu	Lendu Flycatcher	8	c
Muscicapa muttui	Brown-breasted Flycatcher	15 17 18 55	f g h
Muscicapa olivascens	Olivaceous Flycatcher	8	c
Muscicapa parva	Red-breasted Flycatcher	1 17 55	b g h
Muscicapa panayensis	Philippine Verditer Flycatcher	22	h
Muscicapa segregata	Sumba Flycatcher	63	j
Muscicapa seth-smithi	Yellow-footed Flycatcher	8	c
Muscicapa sibirica	Sooty Flycatcher	1 15 17 18 21 55	b f g h
Muscicapa sordida	Dusky Blue Flycatcher	15	f
Muscicapa striata	Spotted Flycatcher	1 8 15 17	b c f g
Muscicapa tessmanni	Tessmann's Flycatcher	8	c
Muscicapa thalassina	Verditer Flycatcher	1 15 17 18 19 21 55	b f g h
Muscicapa ussheri	Ussher's Dusky Flycatcher	8	c
Humblotia flavirostris	Humblot's Flycatcher	14	c
Newtonia amphichroa	Dark Newtonia	10	c
Newtonia archboldi	Archbold's Newtonia	10	c
Newtonia brunneicauda	Common Newtonia	10	c
Newtonia fanovanae	Fanovana Newtonia	10	c
Myioparus plumbeus	Gray Tit-Flycatcher	8	c
Microeca brunneicauda	Brown-tailed Microeca	36	i
Microeca flavigaster	Leomon-breasted Microeca	35 36	i j
Microeca flavovirescens	Olive Microcca	35	j
Microeca griseoceps	Yellow-footed Microeca	35 36	i j
Microeca hemixantha	Tenimber Microeca	63	j
Microeca leucophaea	Australian Brown Flycatcher	36	i
Microeca papuana	Pauan Microeca	35	j
Eopsaltria australis	Southern Yellow Robin	35	j
Eopsaltria crissogularis	Western Yellow Robin	36	i
Eopsaltria flaviventris	Yellow-bellied Robin	38	k
Eopsaltria georgiana	White-breasted Robin	36	i
Tregellasia capito	Pale Yellow Robin	36	i
Tregellasia leucops	White-faced Robin	35 36	i j
Petroica archboldi	Rock Robin-Flycatcher	36	i
Petroica australis	Robin-Flycatcher	37	i
Petroica bivittata	Forest Robin-Flycatcher	35	j
Petroica cucullata	Hooded Robin-Flycatcher	36	i
Petroica goodenovii	Red-capped Robin-Flycatcher	36	i
Petroica macrocephala	Tomtit	37	i
Petroica multicolor	Scarlet Robin-Flycatcher	36 38	i k
Petroica phoenicea	Flame Robin-Flycatcher	36	i
Petroica rodinogaster	Pink Robin-Flycatcher	36	i
Petroica rosea	Rose Robin-Flycatcher	36	i
Petroica traversi	Chatham Island Robin-Flycatcher	37 53	i

Scientific Name	Common Name	Source Codes	Region Codes

Scientific Name	Common Name	Source Codes	Region Codes
Petroica vittata	Dusky Robin-Flycatcher	36	i
Culicicapa ceylonensis	Gray-headed Flycatcher	15 17 18 19 21 55	f g h
Culicicapa helianthea	Citrine Canary Flycatcher	22	h

MUSCICAPIDAE · RHIPIDURINAE · FANTAIL FLYCATCHERS

38 species recorded

Scientific Name	Common Name	Source Codes	Region Codes
Rhipidura albicollis	White-throated Fantail Flycatcher	15 17 18 19 21 55	f g h
Rhipidura albogularis	White-spotted Fantail Flycatcher	15	f
Rhipidura albolimbata	Friendly Fantail	35	j
Rhipidura atra	Black Fantail	35	j
Rhipidura aureola	White-browed Fantail Flycatcher	15 17 18 55	f g
Rhipidura brachyrhyncha	Dimorphic Rufous Fantail	35	j
Rhipidura cockerelli	Cockerell's Fantail	38	k
Rhipidura cyaniceps	Blue-headed Fantail	22	h
Rhipidura dahli	Island Fantail	34	j
Rhipidura dedemi	Tenimber Fantail	31	j
Rhipidura drownei	Mountain Fantail	38	k
Rhipidura euryura	White-bellied Fantail	19	h
Rhipidura fulginosa	Gray Fantail	35 36 37 38	i j k
Rhipidura hyperthra	Chestnut-bellied Fantail	35	j
Rhipidura hypoxantha	Yellow-bellied Fantail Flycatcher	1 15 17 18 55	b f g
Rhipidura javanica	Pied Fantail Flycatcher	18 19 21 22 55	g h
Rhipidura lepida	Palau Fantail	47	j
Rhipidura leucophrys	Willie Wagtail	35 36 38	i j k
Rhipidura leucothorax	White-breasted Thicket Fantail	35	j
Rhipidura maculipectus	Black Thicket Fantail	35	j
Rhipidura malaitae	Malaita Fantail	38	k
Rhipidura matthiae	St. Matthias Fantail	47	
Rhipidura nebulosa	Samoan Fantail	38	k
Rhipidura nigrocinnamomea	Black-and-Cinnamon Fantail	22	h
Rhipidura opistherythra	Red-backed Fantail Flycatcher	47	j
Rhipidura perlata	Spotted Fantail Flycatcher	19 21	g h
Rhipidura personata	Kandavu Fantail	38	k
Rhipidura phoenicura	Red-tailed Fantail	19	h
Rhipidura rennelliana	Rennell Fantail	38	k
Rhipidura rufidorsa	Gray-breasted Rufous Fantail	35	j
Rhipidura rufifrons	Rufous-fronted Fantail	35 36 38	i j k
Rhipidura rufiventris	White-throated Fantail	35	j
Rhipidura spilodera	Spotted Fantail	38	k
Rhipidura superciliaris	Blue Fantail	22	h
Rhipidura superflua	Moluccan Fantail	31	j
Rhipidura teijsmanni	Celebes Fantail Flycatcher	27 31	h j
Rhipidura tenebrosa	Dusky Fantail	38	k
Rhipidura threnothorax	Sooty Thicket Fantail	35	j

Scientific Name	Common Name	Source Codes	Region Codes

MUSCICAPIDAE · MONARCHINAE · MONARCH FLYCATCHERS 133 species
recorded

Hyliota australis	Mashona Flycatcher	8	c
Hyliota flavigaster	Yellow-bellied Flycatcher	8	c
Hyliota violacea	Violet-backed Flycatcher	8	c
Megabyas flammulata	Shrike Flycatcher	8	c
Pseudobias wardi	Ward's Flycatcher	10	c
Bias musicus	Black-and-White Flycatcher	8	c
Batis capensis	Cape Flycatcher	8	c
Batis diops	Ruwenzori Puff-Back Flycatcher	9	c
Batis fratrum	Woodward's Puff-Back Flycatcher	8	c
Batis margaritae	Boulton's Puff-Back Flycatcher	9	c
Batis minima	Western Gray-headed Puff-Back Flycatcher	8	c
Batis minor	Black-headed Puff-Back Flycatcher	8	c
Batis minulla	Angola Puff-Back Flycatcher	8	c
Batis mixta	Puff-Back Flycatcher	9	c
Batis molitor	Chin-Spot Puff-Back Flycatcher	8	c
Batis orientalis	Gray-headed Puff-Back Flycatcher	8	c
Batis perkeo	Pygmy Puff-Back Flycatcher	8	c
Batis poensis	Fernando Po Puff-Back Flycatcher	9	c
Batis pririt	Pririt Puff-Back Flycatcher	8	c
Batis senegalensis	Senegal Puff-Back Flycatcher	8	c
Batis soror	Paler Chin-Spot Puff-Back Flycatcher	8	c
Platysteira albifrons	White-fronted Wattle-Eye	8	c
Platysteira blissetti	Blissett's Wattle-Eye	8	c
Platysteira castanea	Chestnut Wattle-Eye	8	c
Platysteira concreta	Chestnut-bellied Wattle-Eye	8	c
Platysteira cyanea	Wattle-Eye	8	c
Platysteira peltata	Black-throated Wattle-Eye	8	c
Platysteira tonsa	White-spotted Wattle-Eye	8	c
Stenostira scita	Fairy Flycatcher	8	c
Erythrocercus holochlorus	Little Yellow Flycatcher	8	c
Erythrocercus livingstonei	Livingstone's Flycatcher	8	c
Erythrocercus mccalli	Chestnut-capped Flycatcher	8	c
Trochocercus albicauda[1]	White-tailed Blue Monarch	8	c
Trochocercus albiventris	White-bellied Crested Flycatcher	8	c
Trochocercus albonotatus	White-tailed Crested Flycatcher	8	c
Trochocercus cyanomelas	Cape Crested Flycatcher	8	c
Trochocercus longicauda	Blue Flycatcher	8	c
Trochocercus nigromitratus	Black-crowned Crested Flycatcher	8	c
Trochocercus nitens	Blue-headed Crested Flycatcher	8	c
Terpsiphone atrocaudata	Black Paradise Flycatcher	1 17 19 22 55	b g h
Terpsiphone atrochalybeia	Sao Thome Paradise Flycatcher	8	c
Terpsiphone batesi	Bates's Paradise Flycatcher	8	c
Terpsiphone bourbonniensis	Mascarene Paradise Flycatcher	14	c
Terpsiphone cinnamomea	Rufous Paradise Flycatcher	22	h
Terpsiphone corvina	Seychelles Paradise Flycatcher	14 53	c

Scientific Name	Common Name	Source Codes	Region Codes
MUSCICAPIDAE · MONARCHINAE · MONARCH FLYCATCHERS *contd.*			
Terpsiphone cyanescens	Blue Paradise Flycatcher	22 24	h
Terpsiphone mutata	Madagascar Paradise Flycatcher	10	c
Terpsiphone paradisi	Asian Paradise Flycatcher	1 15 17 18 19 21 55	b f g h
Terpsiphone rufiventer	Red-bellied Paradise Flycatcher	8	c
Terpsiphone rufocinerea	Rufous-vented Paradise Flycatcher	9	c
Terpsiphone viridis	African Paradise Flycatcher	8	c
Peltops blainvillii	Lowland Peltops Flycatcher	35	j
Peltops montanus	Mountain Peltops Flycatcher	35	j
Clytorhynchus hamlini	Rennell Shrikebill	38	k
Clytorhynchus nigrogularis	Black-faced Shrikebill	38	k
Clytorhynchus pachycephaloides	Southern Shrikebill	38	k
Clytorhynchus vitiensis	Fiji Shrikebill	38	k
Metabolus rugensis	Truk Monarch	38	k
Myiagra albiventris	Samoan Broadbill	38	k
Myiagra atra	Black Myiagra Flycatcher	35	j
Myiagra azureocapilla	Blue-crested Broadbill	38	k
Myiagra caledonica	New Hebrides Broadbill	38	k
Myiagra cyanoleuca	Satin Myiagra Flycatcher	35 36 37	i j
Myiagra ferrocyanea	Solomons Broadbill Flycatcher	38	k
Myiagra galeata	Helmet Flycatcher	31	j
Myiagra inquieta[2]	Restless Flycatcher	35 36	i j
Myiagra oceanica	Micronesian Broadbill	38	k
Myiagra rubecula	Leaden Flycatcher	35 36	i j
Myiagra ruficollis	Broad-billed Myiagra Flycatcher	35 36	i j
Myiagra vanikorensis	Vanikoro Broadbill	38	k
Monarcha alecto[3]	Shining Monarch Flycatcher	35 36	i j
Monarcha axillaris	Black Monarch Flycatcher	35	j
Monarcha azurea	Black-naped Monarch Flycatcher	15 17 18 19 21 22 55	f g h
Monarcha barbata[4]	Pied Monarch Flycatcher	38	k
Monarcha brehmii	Biak Monarch Flycatcher	35	j
Monarcha castaneiventris[5]	Chestnut-bellied Monarch	38	k
Monarcha chrysomela	Black-and-Yellow Monarch Flycatcher	35	j
Monarcha cinerascens	Islet Monarch	35 38	j k
Monarcha coelestis	Celestial Blue Monarch	22	h
Monarcha frater[6]	Black-winged Monarch Flycatcher	35 36	i j
Monarcha godeffroyi	Yap Island Monarch	38	k
Monarcha guttula	Spot-Wing Monarch Flycatcher	35	j
Monarcha hebetior	Dull Monarch Flycatcher	34	j
Monarcha helenae	Short-crested Blue Monarch	22	h
Monarcha infelix	Admiralty Island Monarch Flycatcher	65	j
Monarcha julianae	Kofiau Monarch Flycatcher	35	j
Monarcha leucotis	White-eared Flycatcher	36	i
Monarcha leucurus	Kei Monarch Flycatcher	65	j
Monarcha manadensis	Black-and-White Monarch Flycatcher	35	j
Monarcha melanopsis	Gray-winged Monarch Flycatcher	35 36	i j

Scientific Name	Common Name	Source Codes	Region Codes

Scientific Name	Common Name	Source Codes	Region Codes
Monarcha menkei	Menke's Monarch Flycatcher	65	j
Monarcha mundus	Tenimber Monarch Flycatcher	47	j
Monarcha pileatus	Tufted Monarch Flycatcher	31	j
Monarcha puella	Moluccan Monarch Flycatcher	29 31	h j
Monarcha pyrrhoptera	Chestnut-winged Monarch	18 19 21 55	g h
Monarcha rubiensis	Rufous Monarch Flycatcher	35	j
Monarcha sacerdotum	Mees's Monarch Flycatcher	70	h
Monarcha sericeus	New Hebrides Monarch Flycatcher		
Monarcha takatsukasae	Tinian Island Monarch	38 53	k
Monarcha trivirgatus	Spectacled Monarch Flycatcher	35 36	i j
Monarcha velata	Maroon-breasted Monarch	18 19 21 55	g h
Monarcha verticalis	New Britain Pied Monarch	34	j
Arses kaupi	Australian Pied Flycatcher	36	i
Arses lorealis	Frill-necked Flycatcher	36	i
Arses telescophthalmus	Frilled Flycatcher	35 36	i j
Monachella mulleriana	River Flycatcher	35	j
Poecilodryas albonotata	Black-throated Flycatcher	35	j
Poecilodryas brachyura	White-breasted Flycatcher	35	j
Poecilodryas hypoleuca	Black-and-White Flycatcher	35	j
Poecilodryas placens	Olive-Yellow Flycatcher	35	j
Poecilodryas pulverulenta[7]	Mangrove Flycatcher	35 36	i j
Poecilodryas superciliosa[8]	White-browed Robin	36	i
Peneothello bimaculatus	White-rumped Thicket-Flycatcher	35	j
Peneothello cryptoleucus	Gray Thicket-Flycatcher	35	j
Peneothello cyanus	Slaty Thicket-Flycatcher	35	j
Peneothello sigillatus	White-winged Thicket-Flycatcher	35	j
Heteromyias albispecularis	Ground Thicket-Flycatcher	35	j
Heteromyias cinereifrons	Gray-headed Thicket-Flycatcher	36	i
Mayrornis lessoni	White-tipped Slaty Flycatcher	38	k
Mayrornis schistaceus	Slaty Flycatcher	38	k
Mayrornis versicolor	Versicolor Flycatcher	38	k
Neolalage banksiana	Buff-bellied Flycatcher	38	k
Chasiempis sandwichensis	Elepaio	3	k
Pomarea dimidiata	Rarotonga Flycatcher	39	k
Pomarea mendozae[9]	Marquesas Flycatcher	39	k
Pomarea nigra	Tahiti Flycatcher	39 53	k
Pomarea whitneyi	Fatuhiva Flycatcher	39	k
Pachycephalopsis hattamensis	Green Thicket-Flycatcher	35	j
Pachycephalopsis poliosoma	White-throated Thicket-Flycatcher	35	j

MUSCICAPIDAE · PACHYCEPHALINAE · WHISTLERS, SHRIKE-THRUSHES
48 species recorded

Scientific Name	Common Name	Source Codes	Region Codes
Eulacestoma nigropectus	Wattled Shrike-Tit	35	j
Falcunculus frontatus[1]	Shrike-Tit	36	i
Oreoica gutturalis	Crested Bellbird	36	i
Pachycare flavogrisea	Golden-faced Pachycare	35	j
Rhagologus leucostigma	Mottled Whistler	35	j
Hylocitrea bonensis	Celebes Mountain Whistler	27	h
Pachycephala aurea	Yellow-backed Whistler	35	j

137

Scientific Name	Common Name	Source Codes	Region Codes

MUSCICAPIDAE · PACHYCEPHALINAE · WHISTLERS, SHRIKE-THRUSHES *contd.*

Scientific Name	Common Name	Source Codes	Region Codes
Pachycephala caledonica	New Caledonian Whistler	38	k
Pachycephala cinerea[2]	Mangrove Whistler	15 18 19 21 55	f g h
Pachycephala flavifrons	Samoan Whistler	38	k
Pachycephala hyperythra	Rufous-breasted Whistler	35	j
Pachycephala hypoxantha	Bornean Mountain Whistler	19 21	h
Pachycephala implicata	Mountain Whistler	38	k
Pachycephala inornata	Gilbert Whistler	36	i
Pachycephala lanioides	White-breasted Whistler	36	i
Pachycephala lorentzi	Lorentz's Whistler	35	j
Pachycephala meyeri	Vogelkop Whistler	35	j
Pachycephala modesta	Brown-backed Whistler	35	j
Pachycephala nudigula	Sunda Whistler	32	j
Pachycephala olivacea	Olive Whistler	36	i
Pachycephala orpheus	Timor Whistler	32	j
Pachycephala pectoralis[3]	Golden Whistler	19 35 36 38	f i j k
Pachycephala phaionota	Island Whistler	35	j
Pachycephala philippinensis	Yellow-bellied Whistler	22	h
Pachycephala raveni	Celebes Whistler	27	h
Pachycephala rufinucha	Rufous-naped Whistler	35	j
Pachycephala rufiventris[4]	Rufous Whistler	35 36 38	i j k
Pachycephala rufogularis	Red-throated Whistler	36	i
Pachycephala schlegelii	Schlegel's Whistler	35	j
Pachycephala simplex[5]	Brown Whistler	36	i j
Pachycephala soror	Sclater's Whistler	35	j
Pachycephala sulfuriventer	Yellow-bellied Whistler	27	h
Pachycephala tenebrosa	Sooty Whistler	35	j k
Colluricincla boweri	Bower Shrike-Thrush	36	i
Colluricincla brunnea	Brown Shrike-Thrush	36	i
Colluricincla harmonica	Gray Shrike-Thrush	35 36	i j
Colluricincla megarhyncha[6]	Rufous Shrike-Thrush	36	i j
Colluricincla parvula	Little Shrike-Thrush	36	i
Colluricincla rufiventris	Western Shrike-Thrush	36	i
Colluricincla woodwardi	Brown-breasted Shrike-Thrush	36	i
Pitohui cristatus	Crested Pitohui	35	j
Pitohui dichrous	Black-headed Pitohui	35	j
Pitohui ferrugineus	Rusty Pitohui	35	j
Pitohui incertus	Mottle-Breast Pitohui	35	j
Pitohui kirhocephalus	Variable Pitohui	35	j
Pitohui nigrescens	Black Pitohui	35	j
Pitohui tenebrosus	Palau Pitohui	47	k
Turnagra capensis	Piopio	37 53	i

AEGITHALIDAE · LONG-TAILED TITS   7 species recorded

Scientific Name	Common Name	Source Codes	Region Codes
Aegithalos caudatus	Long-tailed Tit	1 17	b g
Aegithalos concinnus	Red-headed Long-tailed Tit	1 15 17 18 55	b g
Aegithalos fuliginosus[1]	Sooty Long-tailed Tit	1 17	b g
Aegithalos iouschistos	Blyth's Long-tailed Tit	1 15 17 18	b g
Aegithalos leucogenys	White-cheeked Long-tailed Tit	1 15	b h
Psaltria exilis	Pygmy Tit	19	h
Psaltriparus minimus[2]	Common Bushtit	3 4	a e

Scientific Name	Common Name	Source Codes	Region Codes

REMIZIDAE · PENDULINE TITS 9 species recorded

Scientific Name	Common Name	Source Codes	Region Codes
Remiz caroli[1]	African Penduline Tit	8	c
Remiz flavifrons	Forest Penduline Tit	8	c
Remiz minutus	Cape Penduline Tit	8	c
Remiz musculus	Mouse-colored Penduline Tit	8	c
Remiz parvulus	Yellow Penduline Tit	8	c
Remiz pendulinus	Penduline Tit	1 15 17	b f g
Remiz punctifrons	Cappoc Tit	1 8	b c
Auriparus flaviceps	Verdin	3	a
Cephalopyrus flammiceps	Fire-capped Tit	1 15 17 55	b f g

PARIDAE · TYPICAL TITS, TITMICE 46 species recorded

Scientific Name	Common Name	Source Codes	Region Codes
Parus afer	Gray Tit	8	c
Parus albiventris	White-breasted Tit	8	c
Parus amabilis	Palawan Tit	22	h
Parus ater	Coal Tit	1 15 17 18	b f g
Parus atricapillus	Black-capped Chickadee	3	a
Parus bicolor[1]	Tufted Titmouse	3 4	a e
Parus bokharensis	Turkestan Tit	1	b
Parus caeruleus	Blue Tit	1	b
Parus carolinensis	Carolina Chickadee	3	a
Parus cinctus	Siberian Tit	1 3	a b
Parus cristatus	Crested Tit	1	b
Parus cyanus	Azure Tit	1 15 17	b f g
Parus davidi	Pere David's Tit	1 17	b g
Parus dichrous	Brown Crested Tit	1 15 17 18	b f g
Parus elegans	Elegant Titmouse	22	h
Parus fasciiventer	Stripe-breasted Tit	8	c
Parus fringillinus	Red-throated Tit	8	c
Parus funereus	Dusky Tit	8	c
Parus gambeli	Mountain Chickadee	3 4	a e
Parus griseiventris	Northern Gray Tit	8	c
Parus holsti	Formosan Yellow Tit	17	g
Parus hudsonicus	Boreal Chickadee	3	a
Parus inornatus	Plain Titmouse	3 4	a e
Parus leucomelas	Black Tit	8	c
Parus leuconotus	White-backed Black Tit	8	c
Parus lugubris	Sombre Tit	1	b
Parus major	Great Tit	1 15 17 18 19 21 55	b f g h
Parus melanolophus	Vigor's Black Crested Tit	1 15	b f
Parus modestus	Yellow-browed Tit	15 18	f h
Parus montanus	Willow Tit	1 17	b g
Parus monticolus	Green-backed Tit	1 15 17 18 55	b f g
Parus niger	Southern Black Tit	8	c
Parus nuchalis	White-winged Black Tit	15	f
Parus palustris	Marsh Tit	1 15 17 18	b f g
Parus rubidiventris	Black-crested Tit	1 15 17 18	b f g
Parus rufescens	Chestnut-backed Chickadee	3	a
Parus rufiventris	Cinnamon-breasted Tit	8	c
Parus sclateri	Mexican Chickadee	3 4	a e
Parus semilarvatus	White-fronted Titmouse	22	h
Parus superciliosus	White-browed Tit	1 17	b g

Scientific Name	Common Name	Source Codes	Region Codes

PARIDAE · TYPICAL TITS, TITMICE *contd.*

Scientific Name	Common Name	Source Codes	Region Codes
Parus varius	Varied Tit	1 3 17	b g k
Parus venustulus	Yellow-bellied Tit	1 17	b g
Parus wollweberi	Bridled Titmouse	3 4	a e
Parus xanthogenys[2]	Black-spotted Yellow Tit	15 17 18 55	f g
Melanochlora sultanea	Sultan Tit	15 17 18 19 55	f g h
Sylviparus modestus	Yellow-browed Tit	1 17 18 55	b g

SITTIDAE · NUTHATCHES   21 species recorded

Scientific Name	Common Name	Source Codes	Region Codes
Sitta azurea	Azure Nuthatch	19	h
Sitta canadensis	Red-breasted Nuthatch	3 4	a e
Sitta carolinensis	White-breasted Nuthatch	3 4	a e
Sitta castanea	Chestnut-breasted Nuthatch	15	f
Sitta europaea[1]	Eurasian Nuthatch	1 15 17 18 55	b f g
Sitta formosa	Beautiful Nuthatch	15 18 55	f h
Sitta frontalis[2]	Velvet-fronted Nuthatch	15 17 18 19 21 22 55	f g h
Sitta himalayensis[3]	White-tailed Nuthatch	1 15 17 18 55	b f g
Sitta kruperi	Krüper's Nuthatch	1	b
Sitta leucopsis	White-cheeked Nuthatch	1 15 17	b f g
Sitta magna	Giant Nuthatch	17 18 55	g
Sitta neumayer	Neumayer's Rock Nuthatch	1	b
Sitta pusilla[4]	Brown-headed Nuthatch	3 4 5	a e
Sitta tephronota	Rock Nuthatch	1 15	b f
Sitta villosa	Black-headed Nuthatch	1 17	b g
Sitta whiteheadi	Corsican Nuthatch	1	b
Sitta yunnanensis	Yunnan Nuthatch	1	b
Neositta chrysoptera[5]	Australian Sittella	36	i
Neositta papuensis	Papuan Sittella	35	j
Daphoenositta miranda	Pink-faced Nuthatch	35	j
Tichodroma murina	Wall Creeper	1 15 17	b f g

CERTHIIDAE · TREE-CREEPERS   6 species recorded

Scientific Name	Common Name	Source Codes	Region Codes
Certhia brachydactyla	Short-toed Tree-Creeper	1	b
Certhia discolor	Brown-throated Tree-Creeper	1 15 17 18 55	b f g
Certhia familiaris	Common Tree-Creeper	1 3 4 15 17 18	a b e f g
Certhia himalayana	Himalayan Tree-Creeper	1 15 17 18	b f g
Certhia nipalensis	Stoliczka's Tree-Creeper	1 15 18	b f g
Salpornis spilonota	Spotted Creeper	8 15	c f

RHABDORNITHIDAE · PHILIPPINE CREEPERS   2 species recorded

Scientific Name	Common Name	Source Codes	Region Codes
Rhabdornis inornatus	Plain-headed Creeper	22	k
Rhabdornis mystacalis	Striped-headed Creeper	22	k

140

Scientific Name	Common Name	Source Codes	Region Codes

CLIMACTERIDAE · AUSTRALIAN TREE-CREEPERS   6 species recorded

Scientific Name	Common Name	Source Codes	Region Codes
Climacteris affinis	White-browed Tree-Creeper	36	i
Climacteris erythrops	Red-browed Tree-Creeper	36	i
Climacteris leucophaea[1]	White-throated Tree-Creeper	35 36	i j
Climacteris melanura[2]	Black-tailed Tree-Creeper	36	i
Climacteris picumnus[3]	Brown Tree-Creeper	36	i
Climacteris rufa	Rufous Tree-Creeper	36	i

DICAEIDAE · FLOWERPECKERS   58 species recorded

Scientific Name	Common Name	Source Codes	Region Codes
Melanocharis arfakiana	Obscure Berrypecker	35	j
Melanocharis longicauda	Mid-Mountain Berrypecker	35	j
Melanocharis nigra	Black Berrypecker	35	j
Melanocharis striativentris	Streaked Berrypecker	35	j
Melanocharis versteri	Fan-tailed Berrypecker	35	j
Rhamphocharis crassirostris	Spotted Berrypecker	35	j
Prionochilus maculatus[1]	Yellow-throated Flowerpecker	18 19 21 55	g h
Prionochilus olivaceus	Olive-backed Flowerpecker	22 23	h
Prionochilus percussus	Crimson-breasted Flowerpecker	18 19 21 55	g h
Prionochilus plateni[2]	Palawan Yellow-rumped Flowerpecker	22	h
Prionochilus thoracicus	Scarlet-breasted Flowerpecker	19 21 55	g h
Prionochilus xanthopygius	Yellow-rumped Flowerpecker	19 21	h
Dicaeum aeruginosum	Fairy Flowerpecker	24	h
Dicaeum aeneum	Midget Flowerpecker	38	k
Dicaeum agile[3]	Thick-billed Flowerpecker	15 18 19 21 55	f g h
Dicaeum annae	Anna's Flowerpecker	33	j
Dicaeum anthonyi	Yellow-crowned Flowerpecker	22	h
Dicaeum aureolimbatum	Golden-edged Flowerpecker	47	h
Dicaeum australe	Philippine Flowerpecker	23 24	h
Dicaeum bicolor	Bicolored Flowerpecker	22	h
Dicaeum celebicum	Black-sided Flowerpecker	21	h
Dicaeum chrysorrheum	Yellow-vented Flowerpecker	15 17 18 19 21 55	f g h
Dicaeum concolor	Plain Flowerpecker	15 17 18 19 21 55	f g h
Dicaeum cruentatum	Scarlet-backed Flowerpecker	15 17 18 19 21 55	f g h
Dicaeum erythrorhynchos	Tickell's Flowerpecker	15 18	f g
Dicaeum erythrothorax	Reddish Flowerpecker	31	j
Dicaeum everetti	Brown-backed Flowerpecker	55	g h
Dicaeum eximium	Bismarck Flowerpecker	26 34	j
Dicaeum hirundinaceum	Mistletoe Flowerpecker	35 36	i j
Dicaeum hypoleucum	White-bellied Flowerpecker	22	h
Dicaeum igniferum	Rusty Flowerpecker	33	j
Dicaeum ignipectus	Fire-breasted Flowerpecker	1 15 17 18 19 22 55	b f g h
Dicaeum maugei	Mauge's Flowerpecker	32	j
Dicaeum melanoxanthum	Yellow-bellied Flowerpecker	1 15 17 18 55	b f g h
Dicaeum monticolum	Bornean Fire-breasted Flowerpecker	19	h
Dicaeum nehrkorni	Nehrkorn's Flowerpecker	27	h
Dicaeum nigrilore	Olive-capped Flowerpecker	22	h
Dicaeum pectorale[4]	Olive-crowned Flowerpecker	35	j
Dicaeum proprium	Gray-breasted Flowerpecker	24	h
Dicaeum pygmaeum	Pygmy Flowerpecker	22	h
Dicaeum quadricolor	Four-colored Flowerpecker	22	h

141

Scientific Name	Common Name	Source Codes	Region Codes

Scientific Name	Common Name	Source Codes	Region Codes
Dicaeum retrocinctum	Mindoro Flowerpecker	22	h
Dicaeum sanguinolentum[5]	Javan Fire-breasted Flowerpecker	19	h
Dicaeum trigonostigma	Orange-bellied Flowerpecker	15 18 19 21 22 55	f g h
Dicaeum tristrami	San Cristobal Midget	38	k
Dicaeum trochileum	Scarlet-headed Flowerpecker	19 21	h
Dicaeum vincens	Legge's Flowerpecker	15	f
Dicaeum vulneratum	Moluccan Flowerpecker	31	j
Oreocharis arfaki[6]	Tit-Berrypecker	35	j
Paramythia montium[6]	Crested Berrypecker	35	j
Pardalotus melanocephalus	Black-headed Pardalote	36	i
Pardalotus ornatus	Red-tipped Pardalote	36	i
Pardalotus punctatus	Spotted Pardalote	36	i
Pardalotus quadragintus	Forty-spotted Pardalote	36	i
Pardalotus rubricatus	Red-browed Pardalote	36	i
Pardalotus striatus	Yellow-tipped Pardalote	36	i
Pardalotus substriatus	Striated Pardalote	36	i
Pardalotus xanthopygus	Yellow-tailed Pardalote	36	i

NECTARINIIDAE · SUNBIRDS   118 species recorded

Scientific Name	Common Name	Source Codes	Region Codes
Anthreptes anchietae	Anchieta's Sunbird	8	c
Anthreptes aurantium	Violet-tailed Sunbird	8	c
Anthreptes collaris	Collared Sunbird	8	c
Anthreptes fraseri	Scarlet-tufted Sunbird	8	c
Anthreptes gabonicus	Mouse-Brown Sunbird	8	c
Anthreptes longuemarei	Violet-backed Sunbird	8	c
Anthreptes malacensis	Brown-throated Sunbird	18 19 21 22 55	g h
Anthreptes metallicus[1]	Bronzed Pygmy Sunbird	9	c
Anthreptes neglectus	Uluguru Violet-backed Sunbird	8	c
Anthreptes orientalis	Eastern Violet-backed Sunbird	8	c
Anthreptes pallidigaster	Amani Sunbird	8	c
Anthreptes platura	Pygmy Sunbird	1 8	b c
Anthreptes pujoli	Pujoli Sunbird	8	c
Anthreptes rectirostris	Green Sunbird	8	c
Anthreptes reichenowi	Plain-backed Sunbird	8	c
Anthreptes rhodolaema	Rufous-throated Sunbird	18 19 21 55	g h
Anthreptes rubritorques[2]	Banded Green Sunbird	9	c
Anthreptes simplex	Plain-colored Sunbird	18 19 21 55	g h
Anthreptes singalensis	Ruby-cheeked Sunbird	15 17 18 19 21 55	f g h
Hypogramma hypogrammica	Blue-naped Sunbird	17 18 19 21 55	g h
Nectarinia adelberti	Buff-throated Sunbird	8	c
Nectarinia afra	Greater Double-collared Sunbird	8	c
Nectarinia alinae	Blue-headed Sunbird	8	c
Nectarinia amethystina	Amethyst Sunbird	8	c
Nectarinia asiatica	Purple Sunbird	1 15 18 55	b f
Nectarinia balfouri	Socotra Sunbird	8	c
Nectarinia bannermani	Bannerman's Sunbird	8	c
Nectarinia batesi	Bates's Sunbird	8	c
Nectarinia bifasciata	Purple-banded Sunbird	8	c
Nectarinia bocagii	Bocage's Sunbird	8	c
Nectarinia bouvieri	Orange-tufted Sunbird	8	c
Nectarinia buettikoferi	Sumba Sunbird	32	j

Scientific Name	Common Name	Source Codes	Region Codes
NECTARINIIDAE · SUNBIRDS contd.			
Nectarinia chalcostetha	Macklot's Sunbird	18 19 21 55	g h
Nectarinia chalybea	Southern Double-collared Sunbird	8	c
Nectarinia chloropygia	Olive-bellied Sunbird	8	c
Nectarinia coccinigastra	Splendid Sunbird	8	c
Nectarinia comorensis	Anjouan Sunbird	14	c
Nectarinia congensis	Black-bellied Sunbird	8	c
Nectarinia coquerelli	Mayotte Yellow-bellied Sunbird	14	c
Nectarinia cuprea	Copper Sunbird	8	c
Nectarinia cyanolaema	Blue-throated Brown Sunbird	8	c
Nectarinia dussumieri	Seychelles Sunbird	14	c
Nectarinia erythroceria	Red-chested Sunbird	8	c
Nectarinia famosa	Malachite Sunbird	8	c
Nectarinia fuliginosa	Carmelite Sunbird	8	c
Nectarinia fusca	Dusky Sunbird	8	c
Nectarinia habessinica	Shining Sunbird	8	c
Nectarinia hartlaubii	Principe Island Sunbird	8	c
Nectarinia humbloti	Humblot's Sunbird	14	c
Nectarinia hunteri[3]	Hunter's Sunbird	8	c
Nectarinia johannae	Scarlet-tufted Malachite Sunbird	8	c
Nectarinia johnstoni	Johnston's Malachite Sunbird	9	c
Nectarinia jugularis[4]	Yellow-breasted Sunbird	15 17 18 19 21 22 35 38 55	f g h j k
Nectarinia kilimensis	Bronze Sunbird	8	c
Nectarinia lotenia	Loten's Sunbird	15	f
Nectarinia loveridgei	Loveridge's Sunbird	8	c
Nectarinia mariquensis	Mariqua Sunbird	8	c
Nectarinia mediocris	Eastern Double-collared Sunbird	8	c
Nectarinia minima	Small Sunbird	15	f
Nectarinia minulla	Tiny Sunbird	8	c
Nectarinia moreaui[5]	Moreau's Sunbird	9	c
Nectarinia nectarinoides	Smaller Black-bellied Sunbird	8	c
Nectarinia neergardi	Neergard's Sunbird	8	c
Nectarinia newtonii	Sao Thome Yellow-breasted Sunbird	8	c
Nectarinia notata	Pemba Violet-breasted Sunbird	8 10	c
Nectarinia olivacea	Olive Sunbird	8	c
Nectarinia oritis	Green-headed Sunbird	8	c
Nectarinia osea	Orange-tufted Sunbird	1 8	b c
Nectarinia oustaleti	Angola White-bellied Sunbird	8	c
Nectarinia pembae	Violet-breasted Sunbird	9	c
Nectarinia preussi	Preuss's Double-collared Sunbird	8	c
Nectarinia pulchella	Beautiful Sunbird	1 8	b c
Nectarinia purpureiventris	Purple-breasted Sunbird	8	c
Nectarinia regia	Regal Sunbird	8	c
Nectarinia reichenbachii	Reichenbach's Sunbird	8	c
Nectarinia reichenowi	Golden-winged Sunbird	8	c
Nectarinia rockefelleri	Rockefeller's Sunbird	8	c
Nectarinia rubescens	Green-throated Sunbird	8	c
Nectarinia seimundi	Little Green Sunbird	8	c
Nectarinia senegalensis	Scarlet-chested Sunbird	8	c
Nectarinia shelleyi	Shelley's Double-collared Sunbird	8	c

Scientific Name	Common Name	Source Codes	Region Codes

Scientific Name	Common Name	Source Codes	Region Codes
Nectarinia souimanga	Souimanga Sunbird	10 14	c
Nectarinia sperata	Van Hesselt's Sunbird	15 18 19 21 22 55	f g h
Nectarinia superba	Superb Sunbird	8	c
Nectarinia tacazze	Tacazze Sunbird	8	c
Nectarinia talatala	White-bellied Sunbird	8	c
Nectarinia thomensis	Sao Thome Giant Sunbird	8	c
Nectarinia tsavoensis[6]	Tsavo Purple-banded Sunbird	8	c
Nectarinia ursulae	Ursula's Sunbird	8	c
Nectarinia venusta	Variable Sunbird	8	c
Nectarinia veroxii	Mouse-colored Sunbird	8	c
Nectarinia verticalis	Olive-backed Sunbird	8	c
Nectarinia violacea	Orange-breasted Sunbird	8	c
Nectarinia zeylonica	Purple-rumped Sunbird	15 18	f g
Aethopyga boltoni	Apo Sunbird	22	h
Aethopyga christinae	Fork-tailed Sunbird	17 55	g
Aethopyga duyvenbodei	Sanghir Sunbird	47	h
Aethopyga eximia	Kuhl's Sunbird	19	h
Aethopyga flagrans	Flaming Sunbird	22	h
Aethopyga gouldiae	Mrs. Gould's Sunbird	1 15 17 18 55	b f g
Aethopyga ignicauda	Fire-tailed Sunbird	1 15 17 18	b f g
Aethopyga mystacalis	Scarlet Sunbird	19 21	h
Aethopyga nipalensis	Green-tailed Sunbird	1 15 17 18 55	b f g
Aethopyga primigenia	Hachisuka's Sunbird	23 24	h
Aethopyga pulcherrima	Mountain Sunbird	22	h
Aethopyga saturata	Black-breasted Sunbird	15 17 18 19 55	f g h
Aethopyga shelleyi	Lovely Sunbird	22	h
Aethopyga siparaja	Yellow-backed Sunbird	15 17 18 19 21 22 55	f g h
Arachnothera affinis	Gray-breasted Spider Hunter	18 19 21 55	g h
Arachnothera chrysogenys	Lesser Yellow-eared Spider Hunter	18 19 21	h
Arachnothera clarae[7]	Naked-faced Spider Hunter	23	h
Arachnothera crassirostris	Thick-billed Spider Hunter	19 21 55	g h
Arachnothera everetti	Everett's Spider Hunter	47	h
Arachnothera flavigaster	Greater Yellow-eared Spider Hunter	19 21 35 55	g h j
Arachnothera juliae	Whitehead's Spider Hunter	19 21	h
Arachnothera longirostris	Little Spider Hunter	15 17 18 19 21 22 55	f g h
Arachnothera magna	Streaked Spider Hunter	15 17 18 19 55	f g h
Arachnothera robusta	Long-billed Spider Hunter	19 21	g h

ZOSTEROPIDAE · WHITE-EYES   79 species recorded

Scientific Name	Common Name	Source Codes	Region Codes
Zosterops abyssinica[1]	White-breasted White-Eye	8	c
Zosterops albogularis	Norfolk Island White-Eye	47	i
Zosterops atricapilla	Black-capped White-Eye	19 21	h
Zosterops atriceps	Moluccan White-Eye	31	j
Zosterops atrifrons[2]	White-fronted White-Eye	27	h j
Zosterops bourbonica	Mascarene Gray White-Eye	14	c
Zosterops buruensis	Buru White-Eye	31	j
Zosterops ceylonensis	Ceylon White-Eye	15	f
Zosterops chloris[3]	Mangrove White-Eye	21 35 36	h i j
Zosterops cinerea	Gray-Brown White-Eye	38	k
Zosterops consobrinorum	Peninsular White-Eye	27	h

144

Scientific Name	Common Name	Source Codes	Region Codes

ZOSTEROPIDAE · WHITE-EYES *contd.*

Scientific Name	Common Name	Source Codes	Region Codes
Zosterops conspicillata	Bridled White-Eye	38	k
Zosterops erythropleura	Chestnut-flanked White-Eye	1 17 18 55	b g
Zosterops everetti[4]	Everett's White-Eye	21 55	g h
Zosterops explorator	Layard's White-Eye	38	k
Zosterops ficedulina	Principe White-Eye	8	c
Zosterops flava	Javan White-Eye	21	h
Zosterops flavifrons	Yellow White-Eye	38	k
Zosterops fuscicapilla	Yellow-bellied Mountain White-Eye	35	j
Zosterops grayi	Kei Island White-Eye	47	
Zosterops griseotincta	Louisiades White-Eye	35 38	j k
Zosterops griseovirescens	Annobon White-Eye	8	c
Zosterops inornata	Large Lifu White-Eye	38	k
Zosterops japonica	Japanese White-Eye	1 3 17 18 22 55	b g h k
Zosterops kuehni	Kuehn's White-Eye	31	j
Zosterops lateralis	Gray-breasted Silver-Eye	36 37 38	i k
Zosterops lutea	Mangrove White-Eye	19 36	h i
Zosterops luteirostris	Gizo White-Eye		
Zosterops maderaspatanus	Mascarene White-Eye	10	c
Zosterops mayottensis[5]	Chestnut-flanked White-Eye	14	c
Zosterops metcalfei	Yellow-throated White-Eye	38	k
Zosterops minuta	Small Lifu White-Eye	38	k
Zosterops modesta	Seychelles Gray White-Eye	14	c
Zosterops montana[6]	Mountain White-Eye	19 22	h j
Zosterops mouroniensis	Mount Karthala Green White-Eye	14	c
Zosterops murphyi	Kulambangra Mountain White-Eye	38	k
Zosterops mysorensis	Biak White-Eye	35	j
Zosterops natalis	Christmas Island White-Eye	14	c
Zosterops nigrorum	Philippine Yellow White-Eye	22	h
Zosterops novaeguineae	New Guinea Mountain White-Eye	35	j
Zosterops olivacea	Mascarene Olive White-Eye	14	c
Zosterops pallida	Pale White-Eye	8	c
Zosterops palpebrosa[7]	Oriental White-Eye	1 15 17 18 19 21 22 35 55	b f g h j
Zosterops poliogastra	Yellow-bellied White-Eye	9	c
Zosterops rendovae	Central Solomons' White-Eye	38	k
Zosterops rennelliana	Rennell White-Eye	38	k
Zosterops salvadorii	Engano White-Eye	47	k
Zosterops samoensis	Samoan White-Eye	38	k
Zosterops sanctaecrucis	Santa Cruz White-Eye	38	k
Zosterops senegalensis	African Yellow White-Eye	8	c
Zosterops stresemanni	Malaita White-Eye	38	k
Zosterops ugiensis	Gray-throated White-Eye	38	k
Zosterops vaughani	Pemba White-Eye	8	c
Zosterops vellavella	Vellavella White-Eye	47	k
Zosterops virens	Green White-Eye	8	c
Zosterops wallacei	Wallace's White-Eye	32	j
Zosterops xanthochroa	Green-backed White-Eye	38	k
Woodfordia lacertosa	Sanford's White-Eye	38	k
Woodfordia superciliosa	Woodford's White-Eye	38	k
Rukia longirostra[8]	Large Ponape White-Eye	38 53	k
Rukia oleaginea	Large Yap White-Eye	38	k
Rukia palauensis	Large Palau White-Eye	38	k
Rukia ruki	Large Truk White-Eye	38 53	k

145

Scientific Name	Common Name	Source Codes	Region Codes

ZOSTEROPIDAE · WHITE-EYES *contd.*

Scientific Name	Common Name	Source Codes	Region Codes
Tephrozosterops stalkeri	Stalker's White-Eye	47	
Madanga ruficollis	Madanga White-Eye	31	j
Lophozosterops dohertyi[9]	Doherty's White-Eye	33	j
Lophozosterops goodfellowi	Goodfellow's White-Eye	22	h
Lophozosterops javanica	Javan Gray-throated White-Eye	19 20	h
Lophozosterops pinaiae	Ceram White-Eye	31	j
Lophozosterops squamiceps[10]	Pygmy Gray White-Eye	19 29	h
Lophozosterops superciliaris	Sunda White-Eye	33	j
Oculocincta squamifrons	Pygmy White-Eye	21	h
Heleia crassirostris[11]	Large-billed White-Eye	33	j
Heleia muelleri	Mueller's White-Eye	47	h
Chlorocharis emiliae	Olive Black-Eye	19 21	h
Hypocryptadius cinnamomeus	Cinnamon White-Eye	22	h
Speirops brunnea	Fernando Po Speirops	8	c
Speirops leucophaea	Principe Speirops	8	c
Speirops lugubris	Black-capped Speirops	8	c

EPTHIANURIDAE · AUSTRALIAN CHATS 5 species recorded

Scientific Name	Common Name	Source Codes	Region Codes
Epthianura albifrons	White-fronted Chat	36	i
Epthianura aurifrons	Orange Chat	36	i
Epthianura crocea	Yellow Chat	36	i
Epthianura tricolor	Crimson Chat	36	i
Ashbyia lovensis	Gibber-bird	36	i

MELIPHAGIDAE · HONEYEATERS 169 species recorded

Scientific Name	Common Name	Source Codes	Region Codes
Timeliopsis fulvigula	Mountain Straight-billed Honeyeater	35	j
Timeliopsis griseigula	Lowland Straight-billed Honeyeater	35	j
Melilestes bougainvillei[1]	Solomon Island Honeyeater	47	k
Melilestes megarhynchus	Long-billed Honeyeater	35	j
Toxorhamphus novaeguineae	Yellow-billed Longbill	35	j
Toxorhamphus poliopterus	Slaty-chinned Longbill	35	j
Oedistoma iliolophum[2]	Dark-crested Honeyeater	47	j
Oedistoma pygmaeum	Pygmy Honeyeater	35	j
Glycichaera fallax[3]	White-eyed Honeyeater	35 36	i j
Lichmera alboauricularis	White-eared Honeyeater	35	j
Lichmera argenturis	Plain Olive Honeyeater	35	j
Lichmera cockerelli	Cockerell's Honeyeater	47	i
Lichmera deningeri	Deninger's Honeyeater	31	j
Lichmera flavicans	Vieillot's Honeyeater	32	j
Lichmera incana	Silver-eared Honeyeater	38	k
Lichmera indistincta	Brown Honeyeater	19 35 36	h i j
Lichmera lombokia	Lombok Honeyeater	33	j
Lichmera monticola	Ceram Honeyeater	31	j
Lichmera notabilis	Wetar Honeyeater	47	h
Lichmera squamata	Scaled Honeyeater	31	j
Myzomela adolphinae	Mountain Red-headed Myzomela	35	j
Myzomela albigula	White-chinned Myzomela	35	j

Scientific Name	Common Name	Source Codes	Region Codes
MELIPHAGIDAE · HONEYEATERS *contd.*			
Myzomela blasii	Blas's Honeyeater	31	j
Myzomela cardinalis	Cardinal Honeyeater	38	k
Myzomela chermesina	Rotuma Honeyeater	27	h
Myzomela cineracea	Bismarck Honeyeater	47	g
Myzomela cruentata	Red Myzomela	35	j
Myzomela eichhorni	Eichhorn's Honeyeater	38	k
Myzomela eques	Red-Spot Myzomela	35	j
Myzomela erythrocephala	Red-headed Honeyeater	35 36	i j
Myzomela erythromelas	New Britain Honeyeater	34	j
Myzomela jugularis	Orange-breasted Honeyeater	38	k
Myzomela kuehni	Rothschild's Honeyeater	47	
Myzomela lafargei	Small Solomon Islands Honeyeater	38	k
Myzomela malaite	Malaite Honeyeater	36	i k
Myzomela melanocephala	Black-headed Myzomela	40	k
Myzomela nigrita	Black Honeyeater	35 36 38	i j k
Myzomela obscura	Dusky Honeyeater	35 36	i j
Myzomela pulchella	Dainty Honeyeater	47	g
Myzomela rosenbergii	Black-and-Red Honeyeater	35	j
Myzomela sanguinolenta[4]	Scarlet Honeyeater	36	i
Myzomela sclateri	Sclater's Myzomela	35	j
Myzomela tristrami	Tristram's Myzomela	47	k
Myzomela vulnerata	Timor Honeyeater	32	j
Certhionyx niger	Dark Honeyeater		
Certhionyx variegatus	Pied Honeyeater	36	i
Meliphaga albilineata	White-lined Honeyeater	36	i
Meliphaga albonotata	White-marked Meliphaga	35	j
Meliphaga analoga	Mimic Meliphaga	35	j
Meliphaga aruensis	Puff-backed Meliphaga	35	j
Meliphaga cassidix	Helmeted Honeyeater	36	i
Meliphaga chrysops	Yellow-faced Honeyeater	36	i
Meliphaga cratitia	Purple-gaped Honeyeater	36	i
Meliphaga fasciogularis	Mangrove Honeyeater	36	i
Meliphaga flava	Yellow Honeyeater	36	i
Meliphaga flavicollis	Yellow-throated Honeyeater	36	i
Meliphaga flavirictus	Yellow-gaped Meliphaga	35	j
Meliphaga flaviventer	Tawny-breasted Honeyeater	36	i
Meliphaga frenata	Bridled Honeyeater	36	i
Meliphaga fusca[5]	Fuscous Honeyeater	36	i j
Meliphaga gracilis	Slender-billed Meliphaga	35 36	i j
Meliphaga inexpectata[6]	Guadalcanal Honeyeater	38	k
Meliphaga keartlandi	Gray-headed Honeyeater	36	i
Meliphaga leucotis	White-eared Meliphaga	36	i
Meliphaga lewini	Lewin's Honeyeater	36	i j
Meliphaga macleayana	Macleay's Honeyeater	36	i
Meliphaga melanops	Yellow-tufted Honeyeater	36	i
Meliphaga mimikae	Large Spot-breasted Meliphaga	35	j
Meliphaga montana	White-eared Mountain Meliphaga	35	j
Meliphaga notata	Lesser Lewin's Honeyeater	36	i
Meliphaga obscura	Obscure Honeyeater	35	j
Meliphaga orientalis	Small Spot-breasted Meliphaga	35	j
Meliphaga ornata[7]	Yellow-plumed Honeyeater	36	i
Meliphaga penicillata	White-plumed Honeyeater	36	i
Meliphaga plumula	Yellow-fronted Honeyeater	36	i
Meliphaga polygramma[8]	Spotted Xanthotis	35	j
Meliphaga reticulata	Reticulated Honeyeater	32	j

Scientific Name	Common Name	Source Codes	Region Codes

MELIPHAGIDAE · HONEYEATERS *contd.*

Scientific Name	Common Name	Source Codes	Region Codes
Meliphaga subfrenatus	Black-throated Honeyeater	35 47	j
Meliphaga unicolor	White-gaped Honeyeater	36	i
Meliphaga versicolor	Varied Honeyeater	36	i
Meliphaga vicina	Louisiades Meliphaga	35	j
Meliphaga virescens	Singing Honeyeater	35 36	i j
Oreornis chrysogenys	Orange-cheeked Honeyeater	35	j
Foulehaio carunculata[7]	Wattled Honeyeater	38	k
Foulehaio provocator	Kandavu Honeyeater	38	k
Cleptornis marchei	Golden Honeyeater	38	k
Apalopteron familiare	Bonin Islands Honeyeater	1	b
Melithreptus affinis	Black-headed Honeyeater	36	i
Melithreptus albogularis	White-throated Honeyeater	35 36	i j
Melithreptus brevirostris	Brown-headed Honeyeater	36	i
Melithreptus gularis	Black-chinned Honeyeater	36	i
Melithreptus laetior	Golden-backed Honeyeater	36	i
Melithreptus lunatus	White-naped Honeyeater	36	i
Melithreptus validirostris	Strong-billed Honeyeater	36	i
Entomyzon cyanotis	Blue-faced Honeyeater	35 36	i j
Notiomystis cincta	Stitchbird	37 53	i
Pycnopygius cinereus	Gray Honeyeater	35	j
Pycnopygius ixoides	Olive-Brown Honeyeater	35	j
Pycnopygius stictocephalus	Streak-capped Honeyeater	35	j
Philemon albitorques	Admiralty Island Friar Bird	36	i j
Philemon argenticeps	Silver-crowned Friar Bird	36	i
Philemon brassi	Brass's Friar Bird	35	j
Philemon buceroides[9]	Noisy Friar Bird	32	j
Philemon citreogularis	Yellow-throated Friar Bird	35 36	i j
Philemon cockerelli[10]	White-streaked Friar Bird	36	i
Philemon corniculatus	Bald Friar Bird	35 36	i j
Philemon diemenensis	New Caledonian Friar Bird	38	k
Philemon eichornii	Helmeted Friar Bird	36	i k
Philemon fuscicapillus	Moluccan Friar Bird	31	j
Philemon gilolensis	Gililo Friar Bird	29	h
Philemon inornatus	Timor Friar Bird	32	j
Philemon meyeri	Meyer's Friar Bird	35	j
Philemon moluccensis	Moluccan Friar Bird	31	j
Philemon novaeguineae[11]	Leatherhead	35	j
Philemon subcorniculatus	Ceram Friar Bird	31	j
Ptiloprora erythropleura	Red-sided Streaked Honeyeater	35	j
Ptiloprora guisei	Red-backed Honeyeater	35	j
Ptiloprora meekiana	Meek's Streaked Honeyeater	35	j
Ptiloprora perstriata	Black-backed Streaked Honeyeater	35	j
Ptiloprora plumbea	Leaden Honeyeater	35	j
Melidectes belfordi[12]	Belford's Honeyeater	35	j
Melidectes fuscus	Sooty Honeyeater	35	j
Melidectes leucostephes	White-fronted Melidectes	35	j
Melidectes nouhuysi	Short-bearded Honeyeater	35	j
Melidectes ochromelas	Mid-Mountain Honeyeater	35	j
Melidectes princeps	Long-bearded Honeyeater	35	j
Melidectes torquatus	Cinnamon-breasted Wattle Bird	35	j
Melidectes whitemanensis[13]	Whiteman Mountains Honeyeater	49	j
Melipotes ater	Huon Melipotes	35	j
Melipotes fumigatus	Common Melipotes	35	j
Melipotes gymnops	Arfak Melipotes	35	j

Scientific Name	Common Name	Source Codes	Region Codes

Scientific Name	Common Name	Source Codes	Region Codes
Myza celebensis	Mever's Myza	??	h
Myza sarasinorum	Wiglesworth's Myza	29	h
Meliarchus sclateri	San Cristobal Honeyeater	38	k
Gymnomyza aubryana	Crow Honeyeater	38	k
Gymnomyza samoensis	Mao	38	k
Gymnomyza viridis	Giant Forest Honeyeater	38	k
Moho braccatus	Ooaa	3 53	k
Chaetoptila angustipluma	Kioea	3	k
Phylidonyris albifrons[14]	White-fronted Honeyeater	36	i
Phylidonyris melanops	Tawny-crowned Honeyeater	36	i
Phylidonyris nigra	White-cheeked Honeyeater	36	i
Phylidonyris notabilis	White-bellied Honeyeater	38	k
Phylidonyris novaehollandiae	Yellow-winged Honeyeater	36	i
Phylidonyris pyrrhoptera	Crescent Honeyeater	36	i
Phylidonyris undulata	Barred Honeyeater	38	k
Ramsayornis fasciatus	Bar-breasted Honeyeater	36	i
Ramsayornis modestus[14]	Brown-backed Honeyeater	35 36	i j
Plectorhyncha lanceolata	Striped Honeyeater	36	i
Conopophila albogularis[15]	Rufous-banded Honeyeater	35 36	i j
Conopophila picta	Painted Honeyeater	36	i
Conopophila rufogularis	Rufous-throated Honeyeater	36	i
Conopophila whitei	White's Gray Honeyeater	36	i
Xanthomiza phrygia	Regent Honeyeater	36	i
Cissomela pectoralis	Banded Honeyeater	36	i
Acanthorhynchus superciliosus	Western Spinebill	36	i
Acanthorhynchus tenuirostris	Eastern Spinebill	36	i
Manorina flavigula	Yellow-throated Miner	36	i
Manorina melanocephala[16]	Noisy Miner	36	i
Manorina melanophrys	Bellminer	36	i
Manorina melanotis	Dusky Miner	36	i
Anthornis melanura	Bellbird	37	i
Anthochaera carunculata	Red Wattle-Bird	36 37	i
Anthochaera chrysoptera	Little Wattle-Bird	36	i
Anthochaera paradoxa	Yellow Wattle-Bird	36	i
Anthochaera rufogularis[17]	Spiny-cheeked Honeyeater	36	i
Prosthemadera novaeseelandiae	Tui	37	i
Promerops cafer	Sugarbird	8	c
Promerops gurneyi	Gurney's Sugarbird	9	c

EMBERIZIDAE · EMBERIZINAE · BUNTINGS, AMERICAN SPARROWS
281 species recorded

Scientific Name	Common Name	Source Codes	Region Codes
Melophus lathami	Crested Bunting	15 17 18 55	f g
Latoucheornis siemsseni	Chinese Blue Bunting	17	g
Emberiza aureola	Yellow-breasted Bunting	1 15 17 18 19 55	b f g h
Emberiza bruniceps	Red-headed Bunting	1 15 17	b f g
Emberiza buchanani	Gray-necked Bunting	1 15 17	b f g
Emberiza cabanisi	Cabanis's Bunting	8	c
Emberiza caesia	Cretzschmar's Bunting	1 8	b c
Emberiza calandra	Corn Bunting	1 15 17	b f g
Emberiza capensis	Southern Rock Bunting	8	c
Emberiza chrysophrys	Yellow-browed Bunting	1 17	b g
Emberiza cia	Rock Bunting	1 15 17 18	b f g
Emberiza cineracea	Ashy-headed Bunting	1 8	b c
Emberiza cioides	Long-tailed Bunting	1 17	b g

Scientific Name	Common Name	Source Codes	Region Codes

EMBERIZIDAE · EMBERIZINAE · BUNTINGS, AMERICAN SPARROWS *contd.*

Scientific Name	Common Name	Source Codes	Region Codes
Emberiza cirlus	Cirl Bunting	1 37	b i
Emberiza citrinella	Yellowhammer	1 17 37	b g i
Emberiza elegans	Yellow-throated Bunting	1 17 18	b g
Emberiza flaviventris	Golden-breasted Bunting	8	c
Emberiza forbesi	Brown-rumped Bunting	8	c
Emberiza fucata	Gray-hooded Bunting	1 15 17 18 55	b f g
Emberiza hortulana	Ortolan Bunting	1 8 15 17	b c f g
Emberiza impetuana	Pale Rock Bunting	8	c
Emberiza jankowskii	Jankowski's Bunting	1 17	b g
Emberiza koslowi	Kozlov's Bunting	1 17	b g
Emberiza leucocephala	Pine Bunting	1 15 17	b f g
Emberiza melanocephala	Black-headed Bunting	1 15 17	b f g
Emberiza pallasi	Pallas's Reed Bunting	1 17	b g
Emberiza poliopleura	Somali Golden-breasted Bunting	8	c
Emberiza pusilla	Little Bunting	1 15 17 18 19 21 22 55	b f g h
Emberiza rustica	Rustic Bunting	1 3 17	a b g
Emberiza rutila	Chestnut Bunting	1 15 17 18 55	b f g
Emberiza schoeniclus	Reed Bunting	1 15 17	b f g
Emberiza socotrana	Socotra Mountain Bunting	8	c
Emberiza spodocephala	Black-faced Bunting	1 15 17 18 22 55	b f g h
Emberiza stewarti	White-capped Bunting	1 15	b f
Emberiza striolata	Striped Bunting	1 8 15	b c f
Emberiza sulphurata	Japanese Yellow Bunting	1 17 22 55	b g h
Emberiza tahapisi	Cinnamon-breasted Rock Bunting	8	c
Emberiza tristrami	Tristram's Bunting	1 17 18 55	b g
Emberiza variabilis	Gray Bunting	1 17	b g
Emberiza yessoensis	Far-Eastern Reed Bunting	1 17	b g
Calcarius lapponicus	Lapland Longspur	1 3 17	a b g
Calcarius mccownii[1]	McCown's Longspur	3 4	a e
Calcarius ornatus	Chestnut-collared Longspur	3 4	a e
Calcarius pictus	Smith's Longspur	3	a
Plectrophenax nivalis[2]	Snow Bunting	1 3 17	a b g
Calamospiza melanocorys	Lark Bunting	3 4	a e
Zonotrichia albicollis[3]	White-throated Sparrow	3 4	a e
Zonotrichia atricapilla	Golden-crowned Sparrow	3 4	a e
Zonotrichia capensis	Rufous-collared Sparrow	4 5 6	d e
Zonotrichia georgiana	Swamp Sparrow	3 4	a e
Zonotrichia iliaca	Fox Sparrow	3 4	a e
Zonotrichia leucophrys	White-crowned Sparrow	3 4	a e
Zonotrichia lincolni	Lincoln's Sparrow	3 4	a e
Zonotrichia melodia	Song Sparrow	3 4	a e
Zonotrichia querula	Harris's Sparrow	3	a
Junco caniceps	Gray-headed Junco	3 4	a e
Junco hyemalis[4]	Slate-colored Junco	3 4	a e
Junco phaeonotus[5]	Dark-eyed Junco	3 4	a e
Junco vulcani	Yellow-eyed Junco	4	e
Myospiza aurifrons	Yellow-browed Sparrow	6	d
Myospiza humeralis	Grassland Sparrow	6	d
Xenospiza baileyi	Sierra Madre Sparrow	4	e
Ammodramus bairdii[6]	Baird's Sparrow	3 4	a e
Ammodramus henslowii	Henslow's Sparrow	3	a
Ammodramus sandwichensis	Savannah Sparrow	3 4 6	a e
Ammodramus savannarum	Grasshopper Sparrow	3 4 5 6	a d e
Ammospiza caudacutus	Sharp-tailed Sparrow	3	a

150

Scientific Name	Common Name	Source Codes	Region Codes

EMBERIZIDAE · EMBERIZINAE · BUNTINGS, AMERICAN SPARROWS *contd.*

Scientific Name	Common Name	Source Codes	Region Codes
Ammospiza leconteii	Le Conte's Sparrow	3	a
Ammospiza maritima[7]	Seaside Sparrow	3	a
Spizella arborea	Tree Sparrow	3	a
Spizella atrogularis	Black-chinned Sparrow	3 4	a e
Spizella breweri	Brewer's Sparrow	3 4	a e
Spizella pallida	Clay-colored Sparrow	3 4	a e
Spizella passerina	Chipping Sparrow	3 4	a e
Spizella pusilla[8]	Field Sparrow	3 4	a e
Pooecetes gramineus	Vesper Sparrow	3 4	a e
Chondestes grammacus	Lark Sparrow	3 4	a e
Amphispiza belli	Sage Sparrow	3 4	a e
Amphispiza bilineata	Black-throated Sparrow	3 4	a e
Aimophila aestivalis	Bachman's Sparrow	3	a
Aimophila botterii[9]	Botteri's Sparrow	3 4	a e
Aimophila carpalis	Rufous-winged Sparrow	3 4	a e
Aimophila cassinii	Cassin's Sparrow	3 4	a e
Aimophila humeralis	Black-chested Sparrow	4	e
Aimophila mystacalis	Bridled Sparrow	4	e
Aimophila notosticta	Oaxaca Sparrow	4	e
Aimophila quinquestriata	Five-striped Sparrow	4	e
Aimophila rufescens	Rusty Sparrow	4	e
Aimophila ruficauda	Stripe-headed Sparrow	4	e
Aimophila ruficeps	Rufous-crowned Sparrow	3 4	a e
Aimophila stolzmanni[10]	Tumbes Sparrow	6	d
Aimophila strigiceps	Stripe-capped Sparrow	6	d
Aimophila sumichrasti	Cinnamon-tailed Sparrow	4	e
Torreornis inexpectata	Zapata Sparrow	5	c
Oriturus superciliosus	Striped Sparrow	4	e
Phrygilus alaudinus	Band-tailed Sierra-Finch	6	d
Phrygilus atriceps	Black-hooded Sierra-Finch	6	d
Phrygilus carbonarius	Carbonated Sierra-Finch	6	d
Phrygilus dorsalis	Red-backed Sierra-Finch	6	d
Phrygilus erythronotus	White-throated Sierra-Finch	6	d
Phrygilus fructiceti	Mourning Sierra-Finch	6	d
Phrygilus gayi	Gray-hooded Sierra-Finch	6	d
Phrygilus patagonicus	Patagonian Sierra-Finch	6	d
Phrygilus plebejus	Ash-breasted Sierra-Finch	6	d
Phrygilus unicolor	Plumbeous Sierra-Finch	6	d
Melanodera melanodera	Black-throated Finch	6	d
Melanodera xanthogramma	Yellow-bridled Finch	6	d
Haplospiza rustica	Slaty Finch	6	d
Haplospiza unicolor	Uniform Finch	6	d
Acanthidops bairdii	Peg-billed Finch	4	e
Lophospingus griseocristatus	Gray-crested Finch	6	d
Lophospingus pusillus	Black-crested Finch	6	d
Donacospiza albifrons	Long-tailed Reed-Finch	6	d
Rowettia goughensis	Gough Bunting	11	c
Nesospiza acunhae	Tristan Finch	11 53	c
Nesospiza wilkinsi	Tristan Grosbeak	11 53	c
Diuca diuca	Common Diuca-Finch	6	d
Diuca speculifera	White-winged Diuca-Finch	6	d
Idiopsar brachyurus	Short-tailed Finch	6	d
Piezorhina cinerea	Cinereous Finch	6	d
Xenospingus concolor	Slender-billed Finch	6	d
Incaspiza laeta	Buff-bridled Inca-Finch	6	d
Incaspiza ortizi	Gray-winged Inca-Finch	6	d
Incaspiza personata	Rufous-backed Inca-Finch	6	d

Scientific Name	Common Name	Source Codes	Region Codes

EMBERIZIDAE · EMBERIZINAE · BUNTINGS, AMERICAN SPARROWS *contd.*

Scientific Name	Common Name	Source Codes	Region Codes
Incaspiza pulchra	Great Inca-Finch	6	d
Incaspiza watkinsi	Little Inca-Finch	6	d
Poospiza alticola	Plain-tailed Warbling-Finch	6	d
Poospiza baeri[11]	Tucuman Mountain-Finch	6	d
Poospiza boliviana	Bolivian Warbling-Finch	6	d
Poospiza caesar	Chestnut-breasted Mountain-Finch	6	d
Poospiza cinerea	Cinereous Warbling-Finch	6	d
Poospiza erythrophrys	Rusty-browed Warbling-Finch	6	d
Poospiza garleppi	Cochabamba Mountain-Finch	6	d
Poospiza hispaniolensis	Collared Warbling-Finch	6	d
Poospiza hypochondria	Rufous-sided Warbling-Finch	6	d
Poospiza lateralis	Red-rumped Warbling-Finch	6	d
Poospiza melanoleuca	Black-capped Warbling-Finch	6	d
Poospiza nigrorufa	Black-and-Rufous Warbling-Finch	6	d
Poospiza ornata	Cinnamon Warbling-Finch	6	d
Poospiza rubecula	Rufous-breasted Warbling-Finch	6	d
Poospiza thoracica	Bay-chested Warbling-Finch	6	d
Poospiza torquata	Ringed Warbling-Finch	6	d
Sicalis auriventris	Greater Yellow-Finch	6	d
Sicalis citrina	Stripe-tailed Yellow-Finch	6	d
Sicalis columbiana	Orange-fronted Yellow-Finch	6	d
Sicalis flaveola	Saffron Finch	4 5 6	d e
Sicalis lebruni	Patagonian Yellow-Finch	6	d
Sicalis lutea	Puna Yellow-Finch	6	d
Sicalis luteocephala	Citron-headed Yellow-Finch	6	d
Sicalis luteola	Grassland Yellow-Finch	4 5 6	d e
Sicalis olivascens	Greenish Yellow-Finch	6	d
Sicalis raimondii	Raimondi's Yellow-Finch	6	d
Sicalis taczanowskii[12]	Sulphur-throated Finch	6	d
Sicalis urppygialis	Bright-rumped Yellow-Finch	6	d
Emberizoides herbicola	Wedge-tailed Grass-Finch	4 6	d e
Emberizoides ypiranganus	Lesser Grass-Finch	6	d
Embernagra longicauda	Buff-throated Pampa-Finch	6	d
Embernagra platensis	Great Pampa-Finch	6	d
Volatinia jacarina	Blue-Black Grassquit	4 5 6	d e
Sporophila albogularis	White-throated Seedeater	6	d
Sporophila americana[13]	Variable Seedeater	6	d
Sporophila ardesiaca	Dubois's Seedeater	6	d
Sporophila bouvreuil	Capped Seedeater	6	d
Sporophila caerulescens	Double-collared Seedeater	6	d
Sporophila castaneiventris	Chestnut-bellied Seedeater	6	d
Sporophila cinnamomea	Chestnut Seedeater	6	d
Sporophila collaris	Rusty-collared Seedeater	6	d
Sporophila falcirostris	Temminck's Seedeater	6	d
Sporophila frontalis	Buffy-fronted Seedeater	6	d
Sporophila hypochroma	Rufous-rumped Seedeater	6	d
Sporophila insulata	Tumaco Seedeater	6	d
Sporophila intermedia	Gray Seedeater	6	d
Sporophila leucoptera	White-bellied Seedeater	6	d
Sporophila lineola	Lined Seedeater	6	d
Sporophila luctuosa	Black-and-White Seedeater	6	d
Sporophila melanogaster	Black-bellied Seedeater	6	d
Sporophila minuta	Ruddy-breasted Seedeater	4 6	d e

152

Scientific Name	Common Name	Source Codes	Region Codes

EMBERIZIDAE · EMBERIZINAE · BUNTINGS, AMERICAN SPARROWS *contd.*

Scientific Name	Common Name	Source Codes	Region Codes
Sporophila nigricollis	Yellow-bellied Seedeater	4 5 6	d e
Sporophila nigrorufa	Black-and-Tawny Seedeater	6	d
Sporophila obscura	Dull-colored Seedeater	6	d
Sporophila palustris	Marsh Seedeater	6	d
Sporophila peruviana	Parrot-billed Seedeater	6	d
Sporophila plumbea	Plumbeous Seedeater	6	d
Sporophila ruficollis	Dark-throated Seedeater	6	d
Sporophila schistacea	Slate-colored Seedeater	4 6	d e
Sporophila simplex	Drab Seedeater	6	d
Sporophila telasco	Chestnut-throated Seedeater	6	d
Sporophila torqueola	White-collared Seedeater	3 4	a e
Oryzoborus angolensis	Lesser Seed-Finch	4 6	d e
Oryzoborus crassirostris	Large-billed Seed-Finch	4 6	d e
Amaurospiza concolor	Blue Seedeater	4 6	d e
Amaurospiza moesta[14]	Blackish-Blue Seedeater	4 6	d e
Melopyrrha nigra	Cuban Bullfinch	5	d
Dolospingus fringilloides	White-naped Seedeater	6	d
Catamenia analis	Band-tailed Seedeater	6	d
Catamenia homochroa	Paramo Seedeater	6	d
Catamenia inornata	Plain-colored Seedeater	6	d
Tiaris bicolor	Black-faced Grassquit	3 5 6	a d e
Tiaris canora	Melodious Grassquit	3 5	a e
Tiaris fuliginosa	Sooty Grassquit	6	d
Tiaris olivacea	Yellow-faced Grassquit	4 5 6	d e
Loxipasser anoxanthus	Yellow-shouldered Grassquit	5	e
Loxigilla noctis	Lesser Antillean Bullfinch	5	e
Loxigilla portoricensis	Puerto Rican Bullfinch	5	e
Loxigilla violacea	Greater Antillean Bullfinch	5	e
Melanospiza richardsoni	St. Lucia Black Finch	5	e
Geospiza conirostris	Large Cactus Ground Finch	46	d
Geospiza difficilis	Sharp-billed Ground Finch	46	d
Geospiza fortis	Medium Ground Finch	46	d
Geospiza fuliginosa	Small Ground Finch	46	d
Geospiza magnirostris	Large Ground Finch	46	d
Geospiza scandens	Cactus Ground Finch	46	d
Camarhynchus crassirostris	Vegetarian Tree-Finch	46	d
Camarhynchus heliobates	Mangrove-Finch	46	d
Camarhynchus pallidus	Woodpecker-Finch	46	d
Camarhynchus parvulus	Small Tree-Finch	46	d
Camarhynchus pauper	Charles Tree-Finch	46	d
Camarhynchus psittacula	Large Tree-Finch	46	d
Certhidea olivacea	Warbler-Finch	46	d
Pinaroloxias inornata	Cocos Island Finch	4	e
Pipilo aberti	Abert's Towhee	3 4	a e
Pipilo albicollis	White-throated Towhee	4	e
Pipilo chlorura[15]	Green-tailed Towhee	3 4	a e
Pipilo erythrophthalmus[16]	Rufous-sided Towhee	3	a e
Pipilo fuscus	Brown Towhee	3 4	a e
Pipilo ocai	Collared Towhee	4	e
Pipilo socorroensis	Olive-backed Towhee	4	e
Melozone biarcuatim	Chiapas Sparrow	47	e
Melozone kieneri	Rusty-crowned Ground-Sparrow	4	e
Melozone leucotis	White-eared Ground-Sparrow	4	e
Arremon abeillei	Black-capped Sparrow	6	d
Arremon aurantiirostris	Orange-billed Sparrow	4 6	d e
Arremon flavirostris	Saffron-billed Sparrow	6	d

153

Scientific Name	Common Name	Source Codes	Region Codes

EMBERIZIDAE · EMBERIZINAE · BUNTINGS, AMERICAN SPARROWS *contd.*

Scientific Name	Common Name	Source Codes		Region Codes	
Arremon schlegeli	Golden-winged Sparrow	6		d	
Arremon taciturnus	Pectoral Sparrow	6		d	
Arremonops conirostris	Black-striped Sparrow	4	6	d	e
Arremonops rufivirgata	Olive Sparrow	3	4	a	e
Arremonops tocuyensis	Tocuyo Sparrow	6		d	
Atlapetes albiceps	White-headed Brush-Finch	6		d	
Atlapetes albinucha	White-naped Brush-Finch	4		e	
Atlapetes albofrenatus	Moustached Brush-Finch	6		d	
Atlapetes atricapillus	Black-headed Brush-Finch	4	6	d	e
Atlapetes brunneinucha[17]	Chestnut-capped Brush-Finch	4	6	d	e
Atlapetes citrinellus	Yellow-striped Brush-Finch	6		d	
Atlapetes flaviceps	Olive-headed Brush-Finch	6		d	
Atlapetes fulviceps	Fulvous-headed Brush-Finch	6		d	
Atlapetes fuscoolivaceus	Dusky-headed Brush-Finch	6		d	
Atlapetes gutturalis	Yellow-throated Brush-Finch	4	6	d	e
Atlapetes leucopis	White-rimmed Brush-Finch	6		d	
Atlapetes leucopterus	White-winged Brush-Finch	6		d	
Atlapetes melanocephalus	Santa Marta Brush-Finch	6		d	
Atlapetes nationi	Rusty-bellied Brush-Finch	6		d	
Atlapetes pallidiceps	Pale-headed Brush-Finch	6		d	
Atlapetes pallidinucha	Pale-naped Brush-Finch	6		d	
Atlapetes personatus	Tepui Brush-Finch	6		d	
Atlapetes pileatus	Rufous-capped Brush-Finch	4		e	
Atlapetes rufigenis	Rufous-eared Brush-Finch	6		d	
Atlapetes rufinucha	Rufous-naped Brush-Finch	6		d	
Atlapetes schistaceus	Slaty Brush-Finch	6		d	
Atlapetes seebohmi	Bay-crowned Brush-Finch	6		d	
Atlapetes semirufus	Ochre-breasted Brush-Finch	6		d	
Atlapetes torquatus[18]	Stripe-headed Brush-Finch	4	6	d	e
Atlapetes tricolor	Tricolored Brush-Finch	6		d	
Pezopetes capitalis	Large-footed Finch	4		e	
Oreothraupis arremonops	Tanager-Finch	6		d	
Pselliophorus luteoviridis	Yellow-Green Finch	4		e	
Pselliophorus tibialis	Yellow-thighed Finch	4		e	
Lysurus castaneiceps[19]	Olive Finch	6		d	
Urothraupis stolzmanni	Black-backed Bush-Tanager	6		d	
Charitospiza eucosma	Coal-crested Finch	6		d	
Coryphaspiza melanotis	Black-masked Finch	6		d	
Saltatricula multicolor	Many-colored Chaco-Finch	6		d	
Gubernatrix cristata	Yellow Cardinal	6		d	
Coryphospingus cucullatus	Red-crested Finch	6		d	
Coryphospingus pileatus	Pileated Finch	6		d	
Rhodospingus cruentus	Crimson Finch	6		d	
Paroaria baeri	Crimson-fronted Cardinal	6		d	
Paroaria capitata	Yellow-billed Cardinal	6		d	
Paroaria coronata[20]	Red-crested Cardinal	3	6	d	k
Paroaria dominicana	Red-cowled Cardinal	6		d	
Paroaria gularis	Red-capped Cardinal	6		d	

EMBERIZIDAE · CATAMBLYRHYNCHINAE · PLUSH-CAPPED FINCH
1 species recorded

Catamblyrhynchus diadema	Plush-capped Finch	6	d

154

Scientific Name	Common Name	Source Codes	Region Codes

EMBERIZIDAE · CARDINALINAE · CARDINAL-GROSBEAKS 37 species recorded

Scientific Name	Common Name	Source Codes	Region Codes
Spiza americana	Dickcissel	3 4 5 6	a d e
Pheucticus aureoventris	Black-backed Grosbeak	6	d
Pheucticus chrysopeplus[1]	Yellow Grosbeak	4 6	d e
Pheucticus ludovicianus	Rose-breasted Grosbeak	3 4 5 6	a d e
Pheucticus melanocephalus	Black-headed Grosbeak	3 4	a e
Cardinalis cardinalis[2]	Cardinal	3 4	a e
Cardinalis phoeniceus	Vermilion Cardinal	6	d
Cardinalis sinuata[3]	Pyrrhuloxia	3 4	a e
Caryothraustes canadensis[4]	Yellow-Green Grosbeak	4 6	d e
Caryothraustes humeralis	Yellow-shouldered Grosbeak	6	d
Rhodothraupis celaeno	Crimson-collared Grosbeak	4	e
Periporphyrus erythromelas	Red-and-Black Grosbeak	6	d
Pitylus grossus[5]	Slate-colored Grosbeak	4 6	d e
Saltator albicollis	Streaked Saltator	4 5 6	d e
Saltator atriceps	Black-headed Saltator	4	e
Saltator atricollis	Black-throated Saltator	6	d
Saltator atripennis	Black-winged Saltator	6	d
Saltator aurantiirostris[6]	Golden-billed Saltator	6	d
Saltator cinctus	Masked Saltator	6	d
Saltator coerulescens	Grayish Saltator	4 6	d e
Saltator maxillosus	Thick-billed Saltator	6	d
Saltator maximus	Buff-throated Saltator	4 6	d e
Saltator orenocensis	Orinocan Saltator	6	d
Saltator rufiventris	Rufous-bellied Saltator	6	d
Saltator similis	Green-winged Saltator	6	d
Passerina amoena[1]	Lazuli Bunting	3 4	a e
Passerina brissonii	Ultramarine Grosbeak	6	d
Passerina caerulea	Blue Grosbeak	3 4 5	a e
Passerina caerulescens	Blue Finch	6	d
Passerina ciris	Painted Bunting	3 4 5	a e
Passerina cyanea	Indigo Bunting	3 4 5	a e
Passerina cyanoides	Blue-Black Grosbeak	4 6	d e
Passerina glaucocaerulea	Indigo Grosbeak	6	d
Passerina leclancherii	Orange-breasted Bunting	4	e
Passerina parellina	Blue Bunting	4	e
Passerina rositae	Rose-bellied Bunting	4	e
Passerina versicolor	Varied Bunting	3 4	a e

EMBERIZIDAE · THRAUPINAE · TANAGERS, HONEYCREEPERS
233 species recorded

Scientific Name	Common Name	Source Codes	Region Codes
Orchesticus abeillei	Brown Tanager	6	d
Schistochlamys melanopis	Black-faced Tanager	6	d
Schistochlamys ruficapillus	Cinnamon Tanager	6	d
Neothraupis fasciata	White-banded Tanager	6	d
Cypsnagra hirundinacea	White-rumped Tanager	6	d
Conothraupis mesoleuca	Cone-billed Tanager	6	d
Conothraupis speculigera	Black-and-White Tanager	6	d
Lamprospiza melanoleuca	Red-billed Pied Tanager	6	d
Cissopis leveriana	Magpie-Tanager	6	d
Chlorornis riefferii	Grass-Green Tanager	6	d
Compsothraupis loricata[1]	Scarlet-throated Tanager	6	d
Sericossypha albocristata	White-capped Tanager	6	d
Nesospingus speculiferus	Puerto Rican Tanager	5	e

155

Scientific Name	Common Name	Source Codes	Region Codes

EMBERIZIDAE · THRAUPINAE · TANAGERS, HONEYCREEPERS *contd.*

Scientific Name	Common Name	Source Codes		Region Codes	
Chlorospingus canigularis	Ash-throated Bush-Tanager	4	6	d	e
Chlorospingus flavigularis[2]	Yellow-throated Bush-Tanager	4	6	d	e
Chlorospingus flavovirens	Yellow-Green Bush-Tanager	6		d	
Chlorospingus inornatus	Mount Pirri Bush-Tanager	4		e	
Chlorospingus ophthalmicus	Common Bush-Tanager	4	6	d	e
Chlorospingus parvirostris	Short-billed Bush-Tanager	6		d	
Chlorospingus pileatus	Sooty-capped Bush-Tanager	4		e	
Chlorospingus semifuscus	Dusky-bellied Bush-Tanager	6		d	
Chlorospingus zeledoni[3]	Volcano Bush-Tanager	4		e	
Cnemoscopus rubrirostris	Gray-hooded Bush-Tanager	6		d	
Hemispingus atropileus	Black-capped Hemispingus	6		d	
Hemispingus frontalis	Oleaginous Hemispingus	6		d	
Hemispingus goeringi	Slaty-backed Hemispingus	6		d	
Hemispingus melanotis	Black-eared Hemispingus	6		d	
Hemispingus reyi	Gray-capped Hemispingus	6		d	
Hemispingus superciliaris	Superciliaried Hemispingus	6		d	
Hemispingus trifasciatus	Three-striped Hemispingus	6		d	
Hemispingus verticalis	Black-headed Hemispingus	6		d	
Hemispingus xanthophthalmus	Drab Hemispingus	6		d	
Pyrrhocoma ruficeps	Chestnut-headed Tanager	6		d	
Thlypopsis fulviceps	Fulvous-headed Tanager	6		d	
Thlypopsis inornata	Buff-bellied Tanager	6		d	
Thlypopsis ornata	Rufous-chested Tanager	6		d	
Thlypopsis pectoralis	Brown-flanked Tanager	6		d	
Thlypopsis ruficeps	Rust-and-Yellow Tanager	6		d	
Thlypopsis soridida	Orange-headed Tanager	6		d	
Hemithraupis flavicollis	Yellow-backed Tanager	4	6	d	e
Hemithraupis guira	Guira Tanager	6		d	
Hemithaurus ruficapilla	Rufous-headed Tanager	6		d	
Chrysothlypis chrysomelas	Black-and-Yellow Tanager	4		e	
Chrysothlypis salmoni[4]	Scarlet-and-White Tanager	6		d	
Nemosia pileata	Hooded Tanager	6		d	
Phaenicophilus palmarum	Black-crowned Palm Tanager	5		e	
Phaenicophilus poliocephalus	Gray-crowned Palm Tanager	5		e	
Calyptophilus frugivorus	Chat-Tanager	5		e	
Rhodinocicla rosea	Rose-breasted Thrush-Tanager	4	6	d	e
Mitrospingus cassinii	Dusky-faced Tanager	4	6	d	e
Mitrospingus oleangineus	Olive-backed Tanager	6		d	
Chlorothraupis carmioli	Carmiol's Tanager	4	6	d	e
Chlorothraupis olivacea	Lemon-browed Tanager	4	6	d	e
Chlorothraupis stolzmanni	Ochre-breasted Tanager	6		d	
Orthogonys chloricterus	Olive-Green Tanager	6		d	
Eucometis penicillata	Gray-headed Tanager	4	6	d	e
Lanio aurantius[5]	Black-throated Shrike-Tanager	4		e	
Lanio fulvus	Fulvous Shrike-Tanager	6		d	
Lanio versicolor	White-winged Shrike-Tanager	6		d	
Creurgops dentata	Slaty Tanager	6		d	
Creurgops verticalis	Rufous-crested Tanager	6		d	
Heterospingus rubrifrons	Sulphur-rumped Tanager	4		e	
Heterospingus xanthopygius	Scarlet-browed Tanager	6		d	
Tachyphonus coronatus	Ruby-crowned Tanager	6		d	
Tachyphonus cristatus	Flame-crested Tanager	6		d	
Tachyphonus delatrii	Tawny-crested Tanager	4	6	d	e
Tachyphonus luctuosus	White-shouldered Tanager	4	6	d	e
Tachyphonus nattereri	Natterer's Tanager	6		d	
Tachyphonus phoenicius	Red-shouldered Tanager	6		d	
Tachyphonus rufiventer	Yellow-crested Tanager	6		d	

156

Scientific Name	Common Name	Source Codes	Region Codes

Scientific Name	Common Name	Source Codes	Region Codes
Tachyphonus rufus	White-lined Tanager	4 6	d e
Tachyphonus surinamus	Fulvous-crested Tanager	6	d
Trichothraupis melanops	Black-goggled Tanager	6	d
Habia cristata	Crested Ant-Tanager	6	d
Habia gutturalis[6]	Red-throated Ant-Tanager	6	d
Habia rubica	Red-crowned Ant-Tanager	4 6	d e
Piranga bidentata	Flame-colored Tanager	4	e
Piranga erythrocephala	Red-headed Tanager	4	e
Piranga flava	Hepatic Tanager	3 4 6	a d e
Piranga leucoptera	White-winged Tanager	4 6	d e
Piranga ludoviciana	Western Tanager	3 4	a e
Piranga olivacea	Scarlet Tanager	3 4 5 6	a d e
Piranga roseogularis	Rose-throated Tanager	4	e
Piranga rubra	Summer Tanager	3 4 5 6	a d e
Piranga rubriceps	Red-hooded Tanager	6	d
Calochaetes coccineus	Vermilion Tanager	6	d
Ramphocelus bresilius	Brazilian Tanager	6	d
Ramphocelus carbo	Silver-beaked Tanager	6	d
Ramphocelus dimidiatus	Crimson-backed Tanager	4 6	d e
Ramphocelus flammigerus	Flame-rumped Tanager	6	d
Ramphocelus icteronotus	Yellow-rumped Tanager	4 6	d e
Ramphocelus melanogaster	Black-bellied Tanager	6	d
Ramphocelus nigrogularis	Masked Crimson Tanager	6	d
Ramphocelus passerinii	Scarlet-rumped Tanager	4	e
Ramphocelus sanguinolenta	Crimson-collared Tanager	4	e
Spindalis zena	Stripe-headed Tanager	4 5	e
Thraupis abbas	Yellow-winged Tanager	4	e
Thraupis bonariensis	Blue-and-Yellow Tanager	6	d
Thraupis cyanocephala	Blue-capped Tanager	6	d
Thraupis cyanoptera	Azure-shouldered Tanager	6	d
Thraupis episcopus	Blue-Gray Tanager	4 6	d e
Thraupis ornata	Golden-chevroned Tanager	6	d
Thraupis palmarum	Palm Tanager	4 6	d e
Thraupis sayaca	Sayaca Tanager	6	d
Cyanicterus cyanicterus	Blue-backed Tanager	6	d
Buthraupis arcaei[7]	Blue-and-Gold Tanager	4	e
Buthraupis aureocincta	Gold-ringed Tanager	6	d
Buthraupis edwardsi	Moss-backed Tanager	6	d
Buthraupis eximia	Black-chested Mountain-Tanager	6	d
Buthraupis melanochlamys	Black-and-Gold Tanager	6	d
Buthraupis montana	Hooded Mountain-Tanager	6	d
Buthraupis rothschildi	Golden-chested Tanager	6	d
Buthraupis wetmorei	Masked Mountain-Tanager	6	d
Wetmorethraupis sterrohopteron	Orange-throated Tanager	6	d
Anisognathus flavinuchus	Blue-winged Mountain-Tanager	6	d
Anisognathus igniventris	Scarlet-bellied Mountain-Tanager	6	d
Anisognathus lacrymosus[8]	Lacrimose Mountain-Tanager	6	d
Anisognathus notabilis	Black-chinned Mountain-Tanager	6	d
Stephanophorus diadematus	Diademed Tanager	6	d
Iridosornis analis	Yellow-throated Tanager	6	d
Iridosornis jelskii	Golden-collared Tanager	6	d
Iridosornis porphyrocephala	Purplish-mantled Tanager	6	d
Iridosornis rufivertex[9]	Golden-crowned Tanager	6	d

157

Scientific Name	Common Name	Source Codes	Region Codes
EMBERIZIDAE · THRAUPINAE · TANAGERS, HONEYCREEPERS *contd.*			
Dubusia taeniata	Buff-breasted Mountain-Tanager	6	d
Delothraupis castaneoventris[10]	Chestnut-bellied Mountain-Tanager	6	d
Pipraeidea melanonota	Fawn-breasted Tanager	6	d
Euphonia affinis[11]	Scrub Euphonia	4	e
Euphonia anneae	Tawny-capped Euphonia	4 6	d e
Euphonia cayennensis	Golden-sided Euphonia	6	d
Euphonia chalybea	Green-throated Euphonia	6	d
Euphonia chlorotica	Purple-throated Euphonia	6	d
Euphonia chrysopasta	Golden-bellied Euphonia	6	d
Euphonia concinna	Velvet-fronted Euphonia	6	d
Euphonia finschi	Finsch's Euphonia	6	d
Euphonia fulvicrissa	Fulvous-vented Euphonia	4 6	d e
Euphonia gouldi	Olive-backed Euphonia	4	e
Euphonia hirundinacea[12]	Yellow-throated Euphonia	4 47	e
Euphonia imitans	Spot-crowned Euphonia	4	e
Euphonia jamaica	Jamaican Euphonia	5	e
Euphonia laniirostris	Thick-billed Euphonia	4 6	d e
Euphonia luteicapilla	Yellow-crowned Euphonia	4	e
Euphonia mesochrysa	Bronze-Green Euphonia	6	d
Euphonia minuta	White-vented Euphonia	4 6	d e
Euphonia musica[13]	Blue-hooded Euphonia	4 5 6	d e
Euphonia pectoralis	Chestnut-bellied Euphonia	6	d
Euphonia plumbea	Plumbeous Euphonia	6	d
Euphonia rufiventris	Rufous-bellied Euphonia	6	d
Euphonia saturata	Orange-crowned Euphonia	6	d
Euphonia trinitatis	Trinidad Euphonia	6	d
Euphonia violacea	Violaceous Euphonia	6	d
Euphonia xanthogaster	Orange-bellied Euphonia	4 6	d e
Chlorophonia cyanea	Blue-naped Chlorophonia	6	d
Chlorophonia flavirostris	Yellow-collared Chlorophonia	6	d
Chlorophonia occipitalis[14]	Blue-crowned Chlorophonia	4	e
Chlorophonia pyrrhophrys	Chestnut-breasted Chlorophonia	6	d
Chlorochrysa calliparaea	Orange-eared Tanager	6	d
Chlorochrysa nitidissima	Multicolored Tanager	6	d
Chlorochrysa phoenicotis	Glistening-Green Tanager	6	d
Tangara argyrofenges	Green-throated Tanager	6	d
Tangara arthus	Golden Tanager	6	d
Tangara cabanisi	Azure-rumped Tanager	4	e
Tangara callophrys	Opal-crowned Tanager	6	d
Tangara cayana	Burnished-Buff Tanager	6	d
Tangara chilensis	Paradise Tanager	6	d
Tangara chrysotis	Golden-eared Tanager	6	d
Tangara cucullata	Hooded Tanager	5	e
Tangara cuanicollis	Blue-necked Tanager	6	d
Tangara cyanocephala	Red-necked Tanager	6	d
Tangara cyanoptera	Black-headed Tanager	6	d
Tangara cyanotis	Blue-browed Tanager	6	d
Tangara cyanoventris	Gilt-edged Tanager	6	d
Tangara desmaresti	Brassy-breasted Tanager	6	d
Tangara dowii[15]	Spangle-cheeked Tanager	4	e
Tangara fastuosa	Seven-colored Tanager	6	d
Tangara florida	Emerald Tanager	4 6	d e
Tangara guttata[16]	Speckled Tanager	6	d e
Tangara gyrola	Bay-headed Tanager	4 6	d e

158

Scientific Name	Common Name	Source Codes	Region Codes

EMBERIZIDAE ' THRAUPINAE ' TANAGERS, HONEYCREEPERS *contd.*

Scientific Name	Common Name	Source Codes	Region Codes
Tangara heinei	Black-capped Tanager	6	d
Tangara icterocephala	Silver-throated Tanager	4 6	d e
Tangara inornata	Plain-colored Tanager	4 6	d e
Tangara johannae	Blue-whiskered Tanager	6	d
Tangara labradorides	Metallic-Green Tanager	6	d
Tangara larvata	Golden-masked Tanager	4	e
Tangara lavinia	Rufous-winged Tanager	4 6	d e
Tangara mexicana	Turquoise Tanager	6	d
Tangara nigrocincta	Masked Tanager	6	d
Tangara nigroviridis	Beryl-spangled Tanager	6	d
Tangara palmeri	Gray-and-Gold Tanager	4 6	d e
Tangara parzudakii	Flame-faced Tanager	6	d
Tangara peruviana	Black-backed Tanager	6	d
Tangara preciosa	Chestnut-backed Tanager	6	d
Tangara pulcherrima	Golden-collared Honeycreeper	6	d
Tangara punctata	Spotted Tanager	6	d
Tangara ruficervix	Golden-naped Tanager	6	d
Tangara rufigenis	Rufous-cheeked Tanager	6	d
Tangara rufigula	Rufous-throated Tanager	6	d
Tangara schrankii	Green-and-Gold Tanager	6	d
Tangara seledon	Green-headed Tanager	6	d
Tangara varia	Dotted Tanager	6	d
Tangara vassorii	Blue-and-Black Tanager	6	d
Tangara velia	Opal-rumped Tanager	6	d
Tangara viridicollis	Silvery Tanager	6	d
Tangara vitriolina	Scrub Tanager	6	d
Tangara xanthocephala	Saffron-crowned Tanager	6	d
Tangara xanthogastra	Yellow-bellied Tanager	6	d
Dacnis albiventris	White-bellied Dacnis	6	d
Dacnis berlepschi	Scarlet-breasted Dacnis	6	d
Dacnis cayana	Blue Dacnis	4 6	d e
Dacnis flaviventer	Yellow-bellied Dacnis	6	d
Dacnis hartlaubi[17]	Turquoise Dacnis-Tanager	6	d
Dacnis lineata	Black-faced Dacnis	6	d
Dacnis nigripes	Black-legged Dacnis	6	d
Dacnis venusta	Scarlet-thighed Dacnis	4 6	d e
Dacnis viguieri	Viridian Dacnis	4 6	d e
Chlorophanes spiza	Green Honeycreeper	4 6	d e
Cyanerpes caeruleus	Purple Honeycreeper	6	d
Cyanerpes cyaneus	Red-legged Honeycreeper	4 5 6	d e
Cyanerpes lucidus	Shining Honeycreeper	4 6	d e
Cyanerpes nitidus	Short-billed Honeycreeper	6	d
Xenodacnis parina	Tit-like Dacnis	6	d
Oreomanes fraseri	Giant Conebill	6	d
Diglossa albilatera	White-sided Flower-Piercer	6	d
Diglossa baritula	Slaty Flower-Piercer	4 6	d e
Diglossa caerulescens	Bluish Flower-Piercer	6	d
Diglossa carbonaria	Carbonated Flower-Piercer	6	d
Diglossa cyanea	Masked Flower-Piercer	6	d
Diglossa duidae	Scaled Flower-Piercer	6	d
Diglossa glauca	Deep-blue Flower-Piercer	6	d
Diglossa indigotica	Indigo Flower-Piercer	6	d
Diglossa lafresnayii	Glossy Flower-Piercer	6	d
Diglossa major	Greater Flower-Piercer	6	d
Diglossa venezuelensis	Venezuelan Flower-Piercer	6	d
Euneornis campestris	Orangequit	5	e

159

Scientific Name	Common Name	Source Codes	Region Codes

EMBERIZIDAE · TERSINAE · SWALLOW-TANAGER 1 species recorded

Tersina viridis	Swallow-Tanager	4 6	d e

PARULIDAE · WOOD WARBLERS 120 species recorded

Scientific Name	Common Name	Source Codes	Region Codes
Mniotilta varia	Black-and-White Warbler	3 4 5 6	a d e
Vermivora bachmanii	Bachman's Warbler	3 5 53	a e
Vermivora celata	Orange-crowned Warbler	3 4	a e
Vermivora chrysoptera	Golden-winged Warbler	3 4 5 6	a d e
Vermivora crissalis	Colima Warbler	3 4	a e
Vermivora gutturalis	Flame-throated Warbler	4	e
Vermivora luciae	Lucy's Warbler	3 4	a e
Vermivora peregrina	Tennessee Warbler	3 4 5 6	a d e
Vermivora pinus	Blue-winged Warbler	3 4 5	a e
Vermivora ruficapilla	Nashville Warbler	3 4	a e
Vermivora superciliosa	Crescent-chested Warbler	4	e
Vermivora virginiae	Virginia's Warbler	3 4	a e
Parula americana	Northern Parula	3 4 5 6	a d e
Parula pitiayumi	Tropical Parula	3 4 6	a d e
Dendroica adelaidae	Adelaide's Warbler	5	e
Dendroica angelae	Elfin Woods Warbler	7	e
Dendroica caerulescens	Black-throated Blue Warbler	3 4 5	a e
Dendroica castanea	Bay-breasted Warbler	3 4 5 6	a d e
Dendroica cerulea	Cerulean Warbler	3 4 5 6	a d e
Dendroica chrysoparia[1]	Golden-cheeked Warbler	3 4 53	a e
Dendroica coronata[2]	Yellow-rumped Warbler	3 4 5	a e
Dendroica discolor	Prairie Warbler	3 4 5	a e
Dendroica dominica	Yellow-throated Warbler	3 4 5	a e
Dendroica fusca	Blackburnian Warbler	3 4 5 6	a d e
Dendroica graciae	Grace's Warbler	3 4	a e
Dendroica kirtlandii	Kirtland's Warbler	3 5 53	a e
Dendroica magnolia	Magnolia Warbler	3 4 5	a e
Dendroica nigrescens	Black-throated Gray Warbler	3 4	a e
Dendroica occidentalis	Hermit Warbler	3 4	a e
Dendroica palmarum	Palm Warbler	3 4 5	a e
Dendroica pensylvanica	Chestnut-sided Warbler	3 4 5	a e
Dendroica petechia	Yellow Warbler	3 4 5 6	a d e
Dendroica pharetra	Arrow-headed Warbler	5	e
Dendroica pinus	Pine Warbler	3 4 5	a e
Dendroica pityophila	Olive-capped Warbler	5	e
Dendroica plumbea	Plumbeous Warbler	5	e
Dendroica striata[3]	Blackpoll Warbler	3 5 6	a d e
Dendroica tigrina	Cape May Warbler	3 4 5	a e
Dendroica townsendi	Townsend's Warbler	3 4	a e
Dendroica virens	Black-throated Green Warbler	3 4 5	a e
Dendroica vitellina[4]	Vitelline Warbler	5	e
Catharopeza bishopi	Whistling Warbler	5	e
Setophaga ruticilla[5]	American Redstart	3 4 5 6	a d e
Seiurus aurocapillus	Ovenbird	3 4 5 6	a d e
Seiurus motacilla	Louisiana Waterthrush	3 4 5 6	a d e
Seiurus noveboracensis	Northern Waterthrush	3 4 5 6	a d e
Helmitheros swainsonii	Swainson's Warbler	3 4 5	a e
Helmitheros vermivorus	Worm-eating Warbler	3 4 5	a e
Protonotaria citrea	Prothonotary Warbler	3 4 5 6	a d e
Geothlypis aequinoctialis[6]	Masked Yellowthroat	6	d

Scientific Name	Common Name	Source Codes	Region Codes

Scientific Name	Common Name	Source Codes	Region Codes
Geothlypis agilis	Connecticut Warbler	3 5 6	a d
Geothlypis formosus	Kentucky Warbler	3 4 5 6	a d e
Geothlypis nelsoni	Hooded Yellowthroat	4	e
Geothlypis philadelphia[7]	Mourning Warbler	3 4 6	a d e
Geothlypis poliocephala[8]	Gray-crowned Yellowthroat	3 4	a e
Geothlypis rostrata	Bahama Yellowthroat	5	e
Geothlypis semiflava	Olive-crowned Yellowthroat	4 6	d e
Geothlypis speciosa	Black-polled Yellowthroat	4	e
Geothlypis trichas[9]	Common Yellowthroat	3 4 5	a e
Microligea palustris	Ground Warbler	5	e
Teretistris fernandinae	Yellow-headed Warbler	5	e
Teretistris fornsi	Oriente Warbler	5	e
Leucopeza semperi	Semper's Warbler	5 53	c
Wilsonia canadensis	Canada Warbler	3 4 6	a d e
Wilsonia citrina	Hooded Warbler	3 4 5	a e
Wilsonia pusilla	Wilson's Warbler	3 4	a e
Cardellina rubrifrons	Red-faced Warbler	3 4	a e
Ergaticus ruber	Red Warbler	4	e
Ergaticus versicolor	Pink-headed Warbler	4	e
Myioborus albifacies	White-faced Redstart	6	d
Myioborus albifrons	White-fronted Redstart	6	d
Myioborus brunniceps	Brown-capped Redstart	6	d
Myioborus cardonai	Saffron-breasted Redstart	6	d
Myioborus flavivertex	Yellow-crowned Redstart	6	d
Myioborus melanocephalus	Spectacled Redstart	6	d
Myioborus miniatus	Slate-throated Redstart	4 6	d e
Myioborus ornatus	Golden-fronted Redstart	6	d
Myioborus pariae	Yellow-faced Redstart	6	d
Myioborus pictus	Painted Redstart	3 4	a e
Myioborus torquatus	Collared Redstart	4	e
Euthlypis lachrymosa	Fan-tailed Warbler	4	e
Basileuterus basilicus	Santa Marta Warbler	6	d
Basileuterus belli	Golden-browed Warbler	4	e
Basileuterus bivittatus	Two-banded Warbler	6	d
Basileuterus chrysogaster	Golden-bellied Warbler	6	d
Basileuterus cinereicollis	Gray-throated Warbler	6	d
Basileuterus conspicillatus[10]	White-lored Warbler	47	d
Basileuterus coronatus	Russet-crowned Warbler	6	d
Basileuterus culicivorus	Golden-crowned Warbler	4 6	d e
Basileuterus flaveolus	Flavescent Warbler	6	d
Basileuterus fraseri	Gray-and-Gold Warbler	6	d
Basileuterus griseiceps	Gray-headed Warbler	6	d
Basileuterus hypoleucus	White-bellied Warbler	6	d
Basileuterus leucoblepharus	White-browed Warbler	6	d
Basileuterus leucophrys	White-striped Warbler	6	d
Basileuterus luteoviridis	Citrine Warbler	6	d
Basileuterus melanogenys	Black-cheeked Warbler	4	e
Basileuterus nigrocristatus	Black-crested Warbler	6	d
Basileuterus rufifrons[11]	Rufous-capped Warbler	4	e
Basileuterus signatus	Pale-legged Warbler	6	d
Basileuterus trifasciatus	Three-banded Warbler	6	d
Basileuterus tristriatus	Three-striped Warbler	4 6	d e
Basileuterus rivularis[12]	River Warbler	4 6	d e
Peucedramus taeniatus	Olive Warbler	3	a
Xenoligea montana	White-winged Warbler	5	e
Granatellus pelzelni[13]	Rose-breasted Chat	6	d
Granatellus sallaei	Gray-throated Chat	4	e

Scientific Name	Common Name	Source Codes	Region Codes

PARULIDAE · WOOD WARBLERS *contd.*

Scientific Name	Common Name	Source Codes	Region Codes
Granatellus venustus[14]	Red-breasted Chat	4	e
Icteria virens	Yellow-breasted Chat	3 4	a e
Conirostrum albifrons	Capped Conebill	6	d
Conirostrum bicolor	Bicolored Conebill	6	d
Conirostrum cinereum	Cinereous Conebill	6	d
Conirostrum ferrugineiventre	White-browed Conebill	6	d
Conirostrum leucogenys	White-eared Conebill	4 6	d e
Conirostrum margaritae	Pearly-breasted Conebill	6	d
Conirostrum rufum	Rufous-browed Conebill	6	d
Conirostrum sitticolor	Blue-backed Conebill	6	d
Conirostrum speciosum	Chestnut-vented Conebill	6	d
Conirostrum tamarugensis	Johnson's Warbler	72	d
Coereba flaveola	Bananaquit	3 4 5 6	a d e

DREPANIDIDAE · HAWAIIAN HONEYCREEPERS 15 species recorded

Scientific Name	Common Name	Source Codes	Region Codes
Himatione sanguinea	Apapane	3	k
Palmeria dolei	Crested Honeycreeper	3 53	k
Vestiaria coccinea	Iiwi	3 53	k
Viridonia parva	Anianiau	3 53	k
Viridonia virens	Amakihi	3 53	k
Hemignathus lucidus	Nukupuu	3	k
Hemignathus obscurus	Akialoa	3 53	k
Hemignathus wilsoni	Akiapolaau	3 53	k
Loxops coccinea	Akepa	3	k
Paroreomyza maculata	Hawaiian Creeper	3 53	k
Pseudonestor xanthophrys	Pseudonestor	3 53	k
Psittirostra psittacea	Ou	3 53	k
Loxioides bailleui	Palila	3 53	k
Loxioides cantans	Laysan Finch	3 53	k
Loxioides flaviceps[1]	Lesser Koa Finch	3	k

VIREONIDAE · VIREOS, SHRIKE-VIREOS, PEPPER SHRIKES 39 species recorded

Scientific Name	Common Name	Source Codes	Region Codes
Cyclarhis gujanensis	Rufous-browed Pepper Shrike	4 6	d e
Cyclarhis nigrirostris	Black-billed Pepper Shrike	6	d
Vireo altiloquus	Black-whiskered Vireo	3 4 5 6	a d e
Vireo atricapilla	Black-capped Vireo	3 4	a e
Vireo bairdi	Cozumel Vireo	4	e
Vireo bellii	Bell's Vireo	3 4	a e
Vireo brevipennis[1]	Slaty Vireo	4	e
Vireo carmioli	Yellow-winged Vireo	4	e
Vireo flavifrons	Yellow-throated Vireo	3 4 5 6	a d e
Vireo gilvus[2]	Warbling Vireo	3 4 6	a d e
Vireo griseus[3]	White-eyed Vireo	3 4 5	a e
Vireo huttoni	Hutton's Vireo	3 4	a e
Vireo hypochryseus	Golden Vireo	4	e
Vireo latimeri	Puerto Rican Vireo	5	e
Vireo magister	Yucatan Vireo	4 5	c
Vireo nanus	Flat-billed Vireo	5	e
Vireo nelsoni	Dwarf Vireo	4	e
Vireo olivaceus[4]	Red-eyed Vireo	3 4 5 6	a d e
Vireo osburni	Blue Mountain Vireo	5	e

Scientific Name	Common Name	Source Codes	Region Codes

Scientific Name	Common Name	Source Codes	Region Codes
Vireo pallens	Mangrove Vireo	4	e
Vireo philadelphicus	Philadelphia Vireo	3 4	a e
Vireo solitarius	Solitary Vireo	3 4 5	a e
Vireo vicinior	Gray Vireo	3 4	a e
Vireolanius leucotis[5]	Slaty-capped Shrike-Vireo	6	d
Vireolanius melitophrys	Chestnut-sided Shrike-Vireo	4	e
Vireolanius pulchellus[5]	Green Shrike-Vireo	4 6	d e
Hylophilus aurantifrons	Golden-fronted Greenlet	4 6	d e
Hylophilus brunneiceps	Brown-headed Greenlet	6	d
Hylophilus decurtatus[6]	Gray-headed Greenlet	4	e
Hylophilus flavipes[7]	Scrub Greenlet	4 6	d e
Hylophilus hypoxanthus	Dusky-capped Greenlet	6	d
Hylophilus muscicapinus	Buff-chested Greenlet	6	d
Hylophilus ochraceiceps	Tawny-crowned Greenlet	4 6	d e
Hylophilus pectoralis	Ashy-headed Greenlet	6	d
Hylophilus poicilotis	Rufous-crowned Greenlet	6	d
Hylophilus sclateri	Tepui Greenlet	6	d
Hylophilus semibrunneus	Rufous-naped Greenlet	6	d
Hylophilus semicinereus	Gray-chested Greenlet	6	d
Hylophilus thoracicus	Lemon-chested Greenlet	6	d

ICTERIDAE · BLACKBIRDS, TROUPIALS 92 species recorded

Scientific Name	Common Name	Source Codes	Region Codes
Psarocolius angustifrons[1]	Russet-backed Oropendola	6	d
Psarocolius atrovirens	Dusky-Green Oropendola	6	d
Psarocolius bifasciatus	Para Oropendola	6	d
Psarocolius cassini	Chestnut-mantled Oropendola	6	d
Psarocolius decumanus	Crested Oropendola	4 6	d e
Psarocolius guatimozinus	Black Oropendola	4 6	d e
Psarocolius latirostris	Band-tailed Oropendola	6	d
Psarocolius montezuma	Montezuma Oropendola	4	e
Psarocolius oseryi	Casqued Oropendola	6	d
Psarocolius viridis	Green Oropendola	6	d
Psarocolius wagleri	Chestnut-headed Oropendola	4 6	d e
Psarocolius yuracares	Olive Oropendola	6	d
Cacicus cela	Yellow-rumped Cacique	4 6	d e
Cacicus chrysopterus	Golden-winged Cacique	6	d
Cacicus haemorrhous	Red-rumped Cacique	6	d
Cacicus holosericeus	Yellow-billed Cacique	4 6	d
Cacicus koepckeae	Selva Cacique	6	d
Cacicus leucorhamphus[2]	Mountain Cacique	6	d
Cacicus melanicterus[3]	Yellow-winged Cacique	4	e
Cacicus sclateri	Ecuadorean Black Cacique	6	d
Cacicus solitarius	Solitary Black Cacique	6	d
Cacicus uropygialis	Scarlet-rumped Cacique	4 6	d e
Icterus auratus	Orange Oriole	4	e
Icterus auricapillus	Orange-crowned Oriole	4 6	d e
Icterus bonana[4]	Martinique Oriole	5	e
Icterus cayanensis[5]	Epaulet Oriole	6	d
Icterus chrysater	Yellow-backed Oriole	4 6	d e
Icterus cucullatus	Hooded Oriole	3 4	a e
Icterus dominicensis[6]	Black-cowled Oriole	5	e
Icterus galbula[7]	Northern Oriole	3 4 5 6	a d e
Icterus graceannae	White-edged Oriole	6	d

163

Scientific Name	Common Name	Source Codes	Region Codes
ICTERIDAE · BLACKBIRDS, TROUPIALS *contd.*			
Icterus graduacauda	Black-headed Oriole	3 4	a e
Icterus gularis	Lichtenstein's Oriole	3 4	a e
Icterus icterus	Troupial	5 6	d e
Icterus laudabilis	St. Lucia Oriole	5	e
Icterus leucopteryx	Jamaican Oriole	5	e
Icterus maculialatus	Bar-winged Oriole	4	e
Icterus mesomelas	Yellow-tailed Oriole	4 6	d e
Icterus nigrogularis	Yellow Oriole	4 6	d e
Icterus oberi[4]	Montserrat Oriole	5	e
Icterus parisorum	Scott's Oriole	3 4	a e
Icterus pectoralis	Spotted-breasted Oriole	3 4	a e
Icterus pustulatus[8]	Scarlet-headed Oriole	3 4	a e
Icterus spurius[9]	Orchard Oriole	3 4 5 6	a d e
Icterus wagleri	Black-vented Oriole	4	e
Nesopsar nigerrimus	Jamaican Blackbird	5	e
Gymnomystax mexicanus	Oriole Blackbird	6	d
Xanthocephalus xanthocephalus	Yellow-headed Blackbird	3 4	a e
Xanthopsar flavus	Saffron-cowled Blackbird	6	d
Agelaius cyanopus	Unicolored Blackbird	6	d
Agelaius humeralis	Tawny-shouldered Blackbird	3 5	a e
Agelaius icterocephalus	Yellow-hooded Blackbird	6	d
Agelaius phoenicus	Red-winged Blackbird	3 4 5	a e
Agelaius ruficapillus	Chestnut-capped Blackbird	6	d
Agelaius thilius	Yellow-winged Blackbird	6	d
Agelaius tricolor	Tricolored Blackbird	3 4	a e
Agelaius xanthomus	Yellow-shouldered Blackbird	5	e
Agelaius xanthophthalmus	Pale-eyed Blackbird	6	d
Leistes militaris	Red-breasted Blackbird	4 6	d e
Sturnella bellicosa[10]	Peruvian Red-breasted Meadowlark	6	d
Sturnella defilippi	Lesser Red-breasted Meadowlark	6	d
Sturnella loyca	Long-tailed Meadowlark	6	d
Sturnella magna	Eastern Meadowlark	3 4 5 6	a d
Sturnella neglecta	Western Meadowlark	3 4	a e
Pseudoleistes guirahuro	Yellow-rumped Marshbird	6	d
Pseudoleistes virescens	Brown-and-Yellow Marshbird	6	d
Amblyramphus holosericeus	Scarlet-headed Blackbird	6	d
Hypopyrrhus pyrohypogaster	Red-bellied Grackle	6	d
Curaeus curaeus	Austral Blackbird	6	d
Curaeus forbesi	Forbes's Blackbird	6	d
Gnorimopsar chopi	Chopi Blackbird	6	d
Oreopsar bolivianus	Bolivian Blackbird	6	d
Lampropsar tanagrinus	Velvet-fronted Grackle	6	d
Macroagelaius imthurni[11]	Golden-tufted Grackle	6	d
Macroagelaius subalaris	Mountain Grackle	6	d
Dives atroviolaceus	Cuban Blackbird	5	e
Dives dives[12]	Melodious Blackbird	4	e
Quiscalus lugubris	Carib Grackle	5 6	d e
Quiscalus major	Boat-tailed Grackle	47	a
Quiscalus mexicanus[13]	Great-tailed Grackle	3 4 6	a d e
Quiscalus nicaraguensis[13]	Nicaraguan Grackle	4	e
Quiscalus niger	Greater Antillean Grackle	5	e
Quiscalus quiscula	Common Grackle	3 4	a e
Euphagus carolinus	Rusty Blackbird	3 4	a e
Euphagus cyanocephalus	Brewer's Blackbird	3 4	a e
Molothrus aeneus[14, 15]	Bronzed Cowbird	3 4 6	a d e

164

Scientific Name	Common Name	Source Codes	Region Codes

ICTERIDAE BLACKBIRDS, TROUPIALS contd.

Scientific Name	Common Name	Source Codes	Region Codes
Molothrus ater	Brown-headed Cowbird	3 4	a e
Molothrus badius	Bay-winged Cowbird	6	d
Molothrus bonariensis	Shiny Cowbird	4 5 6	d e
Molothrus rufoaxillaris	Screaming Cowbird	6	d
Scaphidura oryzivora	Giant Cowbird	4 6	d e
Dolichonyx oryzivorus	Bobolink	3 4 5 6	a d e

FRINGILLIDAE · FRINGILLINAE · OLD WORLD SEED EATERS 3 species recorded

Scientific Name	Common Name	Source Codes	Region Codes
Fringilla coelebs	Chaffinch	1 8 15 37	b c f i
Fringilla montifringilla	Brambling	1 3 15 17 22	a b f g h
Fringilla teydea	Canary Islands Chaffinch	1	b

FRINGILLIDAE · CARDUELINAE · GOLDFINCHES AND ALLIES 122 species recorded

Scientific Name	Common Name	Source Codes	Region Codes
Serinus alario	Black-head Canary	8	c
Serinus albogularis	White-throated Seed-eater	8	c
Serinus atrogularis	Black-throated Canary	8	c
Serinus burtoni	Grosbeak Seed-eater	8	c
Serinus canaria	Canary	1 3	b k
Serinus canicollis	Yellow-crowned Canary	8	c
Serinus capistratus	Black-faced Canary	8	c
Serinus citrinella	Citril Finch	1	b
Serinus citrinelloides	African Citril	8	c
Serinus citrinipectus	Lemon-breasted Canary	8	c
Serinus donaldsoni	Grosbeak Canary	8	c
Serinus dorsostriatus	White-bellied Canary	8	c
Serinus estherae[1]	Malay Goldfinch	19	h
Serinus flavigula	Yellow-throated Seed-eater	8	c
Serinus flaviventris	Yellow Canary	8	c
Serinus gularis	Streaky-headed Seed-eater	8	c
Serinus koliensis	Koli Canary	8	c
Serinus leucopterus	White-winged Seed-eater	8	c
Serinus leucopygius	White-rumped Seed-eater	1 8	b c
Serinus menachensis	Yemeni Seed-eater	8	c
Serinus mennelli	Black-eared Seed-eater	8	c
Serinus mozambicus	Yellow-fronted Canary	8	c
Serinus nigriceps	Black-headed Serin	8	c
Serinus pusillus	Gold-fronted Serin	1 15 17	b f g
Serinus reichardi	Reichard's Seed-eater	8	c
Serinus rufobrunneus	West African Island Seed-eater	8	c
Serinus scotops	Forest Canary	8	c
Serinus serinus	Serin	1	b
Serinus striolatus	Streaky Seed-eater	8	c
Serinus sulphuratus	Brimstone Canary	8	c
Serinus symondsi	Symond's Cape Siskin	9	c
Serinus syriacus	Syrian Serin	1	b
Serinus thibetana[1]	Tibetan Siskin	1 15 17 18	b f g
Serinus totta	Cape Siskin	8	c
Serinus tristriatus	Brown-rumped Seed-eater	8	c
Neospiza concolor	Sao Thome Grosbeak	8	c
Linurgus olivaceus	Oriole-Finch	8	c

165

Scientific Name	Common Name	Source Codes	Region Codes
FRINGILLIDAE · CARDUELINAE · GOLDFINCHES AND ALLIES *contd.*			
Rhynchostruthus socotranus	Golden-winged Grosbeak	8	c
Carduelis ambigua[2]	Oustalet's Black-headed Greenfinch	1 17 55	b g
Carduelis atratus	Black Siskin	6	d
Carduelis atriceps	Black-capped Siskin	4	e
Carduelis barbatus	Black-chinned Siskin	6	d
Carduelis carduelis[3]	Eurasian Goldfinch	1 3 15 17 37	a b f g i
Carduelis chloris	Greenfinch	1 37	b i
Carduelis crassirostris	Thick-billed Siskin	6	d
Carduelis cucullatus	Red Siskin	6	d
Carduelis dominicensis	Antillean Siskin	5	e
Carduelis lawrencei	Lawrence's Goldfinch	3 4	a e
Carduelis magellanicus	Hooded Siskin	6	d
Carduelis notatus	Black-headed Siskin	4	e
Carduelis olivaceus	Olivaceous Siskin	6	d
Carduelis pinus	Pine Siskin	3 4	a e
Carduelis psaltria	Lesser Goldfinch	3 4 5 6	a d e
Carduelis siemiradzkii	Saffron Siskin	6	d
Carduelis sinica	Oriental Greenfinch	1 17	b g
Carduelis spinescens	Andean Siskin	6	d
Carduelis spinoides	Black-headed Greenfinch	1 15 17 18 55	b f g
Carduelis spinus	Eurasian Siskin	1 17 22	b g h
Carduelis tristis	American Goldfinch	3 4	a e
Carduelis uropygialis	Yellow-rumped Siskin	6	d
Carduelis xanthogaster	Yellow-bellied Siskin	4 6	d e
Carduelis yarrellii	Yellow-faced Siskin	6	d
Acanthis cannabina	Linnet	1 15 17	b f g
Acanthis flammea	Redpoll	1 3 17 37	a b g i
Acanthis flavirostris	Twite	1 15 17	b f g
Acanthis hornemanni	Hoary Redpoll	1 3 17	a b g
Acanthis johannis	Warsangli Linnet	8	c
Acanthis yemenensis	Yemeni Linnet	8	c
Leucosticte arctoa[4]	Rosy Finch	1 3 17	a b g
Leucosticte brandti	Brandt's Rosy Finch	1 15 17	b f g
Leucosticte nemoricola	Hodgson's Rosy Finch	1 15 17 18	b f g
Callacanthis burtoni	Red-browed Finch	1	b
Rhodopechys githaginea	Trumpeter Finch	1 8 15 17	b c f g
Rhodopechys mongolica	Mongolian Trumpeter Finch	1 15	b f
Rhodopechys obsoleta	Desert Finch	1 15 17	b f g
Rhodopechys sanguinea	Crimson-winged Finch	1 15 17	b f g
Uragus sibiricus	Long-tailed Rosefinch	1 17	b g
Urocynchramus pylzowi	Przevalski's Rosefinch	1 17	b g
Carpodacus cassinii	Cassin's Finch	3 4	a e
Carpodacus edwardsii	Large Rosefinch	1 15 17 18	b f g
Carpodacus eos	Stresemann's Rosefinch	1 17 55	b g
Carpodacus erythrinus	Scarlet Grosbeak	1 15 17 18	b f g h
Carpodacus mexicanus	House Finch	3 4	a e
Carpodacus nipalensis	Dark Rosefinch	1 15 17 18 55	b f g
Carpodacus pulcherrimus	Beautiful Rosefinch	1 15 17	b f g
Carpodacus puniceus	Red-breasted Rosefinch	1 15 17	b f g
Carpodacus purpureus	Purple Finch	3 4	a e
Carpodacus rhodochlamys	Red-mantled Rosefinch	1 15 17	b f g
Carpodacus rhodochrous	Pink-browed Rosefinch	1 15	b f
Carpodacus rhodopeplus[5]	Spotted Rosefinch	1 15 17 18	b f g
Carpodacus roborowskii[6]	Roborowski's Rosefinch	1	b
Carpodacus roseus	Pallas's Rosefinch	1 17	b g
Carpodacus rubescens	Blanford's Rosefinch	1 15 17	b f g

166

Scientific Name	Common Name	Source Codes	Region Codes

FRINGILLIDAE · CARDUELINAE · GOLDFINCHES AND ALLIES *contd.*

Scientific Name	Common Name	Source Codes	Region Codes
Carpodacus rubicilla	Great Rosefinch	1 15 17	b f g
Carpodacus rubicilloides	Streaked Great Rosefinch	1 15 17	b f g
Carpodacus synoicus	Sinai Rosefinch	1 17	b g
Carpodacus thura	Mlle Thura's Rosefinch	1 15 17	b f g
Carpodacus trifasciatus	Three-banded Rosefinch	1 15 17	b f g
Carpodacus vinaceus	Vinaceous Rosefinch	1 17 18	b g
Chaunoproctus ferreorostris	Bonin Islands Grosbeak	1	b
Pinicola enucleator	Pine Grosbeak	1 3 17	a b g
Pinicola subhimachala[7]	Red-headed Finch	1 15 17 18	b f g
Haematospiza sipahi	Scarlet Finch	1 15 17 18 55	b f g
Loxia curvirostra	Red Crossbill	1 3 4 15 17 18 22 55	a b e f g h
Loxia leucoptera	White-winged Crossbill	1 3 5 17	a b e g
Loxia pytopsittacus	Parrot Crossbill	1	b
Pyrrhula aurantiaca	Orange Bullfinch	1 15	b f
Pyrrhula erythaca	Beavan's Bullfinch	1 15 17 18	b f g h
Pyrrhula erythrocephala	Red-headed Bullfinch	1 15 17	b f g
Pyrrhula leucogenys	Philippine Bullfinch	22	h
Pyrrhula nipalensis	Brown Bullfinch	1 15 17 18 19 55	b f g h
Pyrrhula pyrrhula[8]	Bullfinch	1 3 17	a b g
Coccothraustes abeillei[9]	Hooded Grosbeak	4	e
Coccothraustes affinis	Allied Grosbeak	1 15 17 18	b f g
Coccothraustes carnipes	White-winged Grosbeak	1 15 17 18	b f g
Coccothraustes coccothraustes	Hawfinch	1 3 15 17	a b f g
Coccothraustes icterioides	Black-and-Yellow Grosbeak	1 15	b f
Coccothraustes melanozanthos	Spotted-wing Grosbeak	1 15 17 18 55	b f g
Coccothraustes migratorius	Black-tailed Hawfinch	1 17 18 55	b g
Coccothraustes personatus	Masked Hawfinch	1 17	b g
Coccothraustes vespertina	Evening Grosbeak	3 4	a e
Pyrrhoplectes epauletta	Gold-headed Finch	1 15 17 18	b f g

ESTRILDIDAE · WAXBILLS   124 species recorded

Scientific Name	Common Name	Source Codes	Region Codes
Parmoptila jamesoni[1]	Red-fronted Ant-Pecker	9	c
Parmoptila woodhousei	Flower-Pecker Weaver-Finch	8	c
Nigrita bicolor	Chestnut-breasted Negro-Finch	8	c
Nigrita canicapilla	Gray-headed Negro-Finch	8	c
Nigrita fusconota	White-breasted Negro-Finch	8	c
Nigrita luteifrons	Pale-fronted Negro-Finch	8	c
Nesocharis ansorgei	White-collared Olive-Weaver	8	c
Nesocharis capistrata	White-cheeked Olive-Weaver	8	c
Nesocharis shelleyi	Little Olive-Weaver	9	c
Pytilia afra	Orange-winged Pytilia	8	c
Pytilia hypogrammica	Yellow-winged Pytilia	8	c
Pytilia melba	Green-winged Pytilia	8	c
Pytilia phoenicoptera	Red-winged Pytilia	8	c
Mandigoa nitidulus	Green-backed Twin-Spot	8	c
Cryptospiza jacksoni	Dusky Crimson-Wing	8	c
Cryptospiza reichenovii	Red-faced Crimson-Wing	8	c
Cryptospiza salvadorii	Abyssinian Crimson-Wing	8	c
Cryptospiza shelleyi	Shelley's Crimson-Wing	8	c
Pirenestes minor	Nyasa Seedcracker	9	c
Pirenestes ostrinus	Black-bellied Seedcracker	8	c
Pirenestes sanguineus	Crimson Seedcracker	9	c
Spermophaga haematina	Blue-billed Weaver	8	c
Spermophaga poliogenys	Grant's Blue-Bill	8	c

Scientific Name	Common Name	Source Codes	Region Codes

ESTRILDIDAE · WAXBILLS *contd.*

Scientific Name	Common Name	Source Codes	Region Codes
Spermophaga ruficapilla	Red-headed Blue-Bill	8	c
Euchystospiza cinereovinacea	Dusky Twin-Spot	8	c
Euchystospiza dybowskii	Dybowski's Twin-Spot	8	c
Clytospiza monteiri	Brown Twin-Spot	8	c
Hypargos margaritatus	Rosy Twin-Spot	8	c
Hypargos niveoguttatus	Peter's Twin-Spot	8	c
Lagonosticta landanae	Landana Firefinch	8	c
Lagonosticta larvata	Black-faced Firefinch	9	c
Lagonosticta nitidula	Brown Firefinch	9	c
Lagonosticta rara	Black-bellied Firefinch	8	c
Lagonosticta rhodopareia	Jameson's Firefinch	8	c
Lagonosticta rubricata	African Firefinch	8	c
Lagonosticta rufopicta	Bar-breasted Firefinch	8	c
Lagonosticta senegala	Red-billed Firefinch	8	c
Uraeginthus angolensis	Angolan Cordon-Bleu	8	c
Uraeginthus bengalus	Red-cheeked Cordon-Bleu	8	c
Uraeginthus cyanocephala	Blue-capped Cordon-Bleu	8	c
Uraeginthus granatina	Violet-eared Cordon-Bleu	8	c
Uraeginthus ianthinogaster	Purple Grenadier	8	c
Estrilda astrild	Waxbill	8 38	c k
Estrilda atricapilla	Black-headed Waxbill	8	c
Estrilda caerulescens	Bluish Waxbill	8	c
Estrilda erythronotos	Black-cheeked Waxbill	8	c
Estrilda melanotis	Yellow-bellied Waxbill	8	c
Estrilda melpoda	Orange-cheeked Waxbill	5 8	e c
Estrilda nigriloris	Black-lored Waxbill	8	c
Estrilda nonnula	Black-crowned Waxbill	8	c
Estrilda paludicola	Fawn-breasted Waxbill	8	c
Estrilda perreini	Lavender Waxbill	8	c
Estrilda poliopareia	Gray-cheeked Waxbill	8	c
Estrilda rhodopyga	Crimson-rumped Waxbill	8	c
Estrilda thomensis	Neumann's Waxbill	8	c
Estrilda troglodytes	Black-rumped Waxbill	8	c
Aegintha temporalis	Red-browed Finch	36	i k
Amandava amandava	Red Avadavat	3 15 17 18 19 22 55	f g h k
Amandava formosa	Green Avadavat	15	f
Amandava subflava	Zebra Waxbill	8	c
Ortygospiza atricollis	Black-chinned Quail-Finch	8	c
Ortygospiza fuscocrissa	Dark Quail-Finch	8	c
Ortygospiza gabonensis	Gabon Quail-Finch	8	c
Ortygospiza locustella	Locust-Finch	8	c
Emblema bella[2]	Beautiful Firetail	36	i
Emblema guttata	Diamond-Firetail	36	i
Emblema oculata	Red-eared Firetail	47	i
Emblema picta	Painted Finch	36	i
Oreostruthus fuliginosus	Crimson-sided Mountain Finch	35	j
Neochmia phaeton	Crimson Finch	36	i
Neochmia ruficauda	Star Finch	36	i
Poephia acuticauda	Long-tailed Finch	36	i
Poephila bichenovii	Banded Finch	36	i
Poephila cincta	Black-throated Finch	36	i
Poephila guttata	Zebra Finch	36	i j
Poephila personata	Masked Finch	36	i
Erythrura coloria	Mindinao Parrot-Finch	24	g
Erythrura cyanovirens	Red-headed Parrot-Finch	38	j k
Erythrura hyperythra	Green-tailed Parrot-Finch	19 21 22 55	g h

Scientific Name	Common Name	Source Codes	Region Codes

Scientific Name	Common Name	Source Codes	Region Codes
Erythrura kleinschmidti	Pink-billed Parrot-Finch	38	k
Erythrura papuana	Papuan Parrot-Finch	35	j
Erythrura prasina	Long-tailed Munia	18 19 21 55	g h
Erythrura psittacea	Red-throated Parrot-Finch	38	h
Erythrura trichroa	Blue-faced Parrot-Finch	35 36 38	i j k
Erythrura viridifacies	Green-faced Parrot-Finch	22	h
Erythrura tricolor	Timor Parrot-Finch	32	j
Chloebia gouldiae	Gouldian Finch	36	i
Aidemosyne modesta	Plum-headed Finch	36	i
Lonchura bicolor	Black-and-White Mannikin	8	c
Lonchura caniceps	Gray-headed Mannikin	35	j
Lonchura castaneothorax	Chestnut-breasted Mannikin	35 36	i j
Lonchura cucullata	Bronze Mannikin	5 8	e c
Lonchura flaviprymna	Yellow-tailed Finch	36	i
Lonchura forbesi	New Ireland Finch	47	
Lonchura fringilloides	Magpie Mannikin	8	c
Lonchura fuscans	Dusky Mannikin	19 21	h
Lonchura grandis	Great-billed Mannikin	35	j
Lonchura griseicapilla	Gray-headed Silver-Bill	8	c
Lonchura hunsteini[3]	New Hanover Mannikin	47	h
Lonchura kelaarti	Jerdon's Mannikin	15	f
Lonchura leucogastra	White-breasted Mannikin	18 19 21 22 55	g h
Lonchura leucogastroides	Javanese Mannikin	19 55	g h
Lonchura leucosticta	White-spotted Mannikin	35	j
Lonchura maja	Pale-headed Mannikin	19 55	g h
Lonchura malabarica	White-throated Munia	8 15	c f
Lonchura malacca[4]	Black-headed Munia	15 17 18 19 21 22 55	f g h
Lonchura melaena	New Britain Mannikin	34	j
Lonchura molucca	Moluccan Mannikin	31	g
Lonchura montana	Snow Mountain Mannikin	35	j
Lonchura monticola	Alpine Mannikin	35	j
Lonchura nana[5]	Madagascar Mannikin	10	c
Lonchura nevermanni	White-crowned Mannikin	35	j
Lonchura pallida	Pale Sunda Munia	47	j
Lonchura pectoralis[6]	Pictorella Finch	36	i
Lonchura punctulata	Spotted Munia	3 14 15 17 18 19 22 55	c f g h k
Lonchura quinticolor	Sunda Munia	32	j
Lonchura spectabilis	New Britain Mannikin	35	j
Lonchura striata	White-rumped Munia	15 17 18 19 55	f g h
Lonchura stygia	Black Mannikin	35	j
Lonchura teerinki	Grand Valley Mannikin	35	j
Lonchura tristissima	Streak-headed Mannikin	35	j
Lonchura vana	Arfak Mannikin	35	j
Padda fuscata	Timor Sparrow	32	j
Padda oryzivora	Java Sparrow	14 17 19 21 22 55	c g h
Amadina erythrocephala	Red-headed Finch	8	c
Amadina fasciata	Cut-Throat	8	c

PLOCEIDAE · VIDUINAE · PARASITIC VIDUINES 9 species recorded

Scientific Name	Common Name	Source Codes	Region Codes
Vidua chalybeata[1]	Indigo-Bird	8	c
Vidua fischeri	Fischer's Whydah	8	c
Vidua funerea[2]	Dusky Indigo-Bird	9	c
Vidua hypocherina	Steel-Blue Whydah	8	c

169

Scientific Name	Common Name	Source Codes	Region Codes
PLOCEIDAE · VIDUINAE · PARASITIC VIDUINES contd.			
Vidua macroura	Pin-tailed Whydah	8	c
Vidua obtusa[3]	Angolan Paradise Whydah	9	c
Vidua orientalis[4]	Broad-tailed Paradise Whydah	8	c
Vidua paradisea	Paradise Whydah	8	c
Vidua regia	Shaft-tailed Whydah	8	c

PLOCEIDAE · PLOCEINAE · WEAVERS, SPARROWS 141 species recorded

Scientific Name	Common Name	Source Codes	Region Codes
Bubalornis albirostris	Buffalo-Weaver	8	c
Bubalornis niger[1]	Red-billed Buffalo-Weaver	9	c
Dinemellia dinemelli	White-headed Buffalo-Weaver	8	c
Plocepasser donaldsoni	Donaldson Smith's Sparrow-Weaver	8	c
Plocepasser mahali	Stripe-breasted Sparrow-Weaver	8	c
Plocepasser rufoscapularis	Rufous-backed Sparrow-Weaver	8	c
Plocepasser superciliosus	Chestnut-crowned Sparrow-Weaver	8	c
Histurgops ruficauda	Rufous-tailed Weaver	8	c
Pseudonigrita arnaudi	Gray-headed Social Weaver	8	c
Pseudonigrita cabanisi	Black-capped Social Weaver	8	c
Philetairus socius	Social Weaver	8	c
Passer ammodendri	Saxaul Sparrow	1 17	b g
Passer castanopterus	Somali Sparrow	8	c
Passer domesticus	House Sparrow	1 3 4 5 8 15 17 18 37	a b c e f g i
Passer eminibey	Chestnut Sparrow	8	c
Passer euchlorus	Arabian Golden Sparrow	9	c
Passer flaveolus	Pegu House Sparrow	18 55	g h
Passer gongonensis[2]	Parrot-billed Sparrow	9	c
Passer griseus	Gray-headed Sparrow	1 8	b c
Passer hispaniolensis	Spanish Sparrow	1 8 15 17	b c f g
Passer iagoensis	Rufous-backed Sparrow	1 8	b c
Passer luteus	Golden Sparrow	1 8	b c
Passer melanurus	Cape Sparrow	9	c
Passer moabiticus	Dead Sea Sparrow	1	b
Passer montanus	Tree Sparrow	1 3 15 17 18 19 22 55	a b f g h
Passer pyrrhonotus	Sind Jungle Sparrow	1 15	b f
Passer rutilans	Cinnamon Sparrow	1 15 17 18 55	b f g
Passer simplex	Desert Sparrow	1 8	b c
Passer suahelicus[3]	Swahili Sparrow	9	c
Passer swainsonii	Swainson's Sparrow	9	c
Petronia brachydactyla	Pale Rock Sparrow	1 8	b c
Petronia dentata	Bush Petronia	8	c
Petronia petronia	Rock Sparrow	1 15 17	b f g
Petronia pyrgita[4]	Yellow-spotted Petronia	9	c
Petronia superciliaris	Yellow-throated Petronia	8	c
Petronia xanthocollis	Yellow-throated Sparrow	1 8 15	b c f
Montifringilla adamsi	Adams's Snow Finch	1 15 17	b f g
Montifringilla blanfordi	Blanford's Snow Finch	1 15 17	b f g
Montifringilla davidiana	Père David's Snow Finch	1 15 17	b f g
Montifringilla nivalis	Snow Finch	1 15 17	b f g
Montifringilla ruficollis	Red-necked Snow Finch	1 15 17	b f g
Montifringilla taczanowskii	White-rumped Snow Finch	1 15 17	b f g

170

Scientific Name	Common Name	Source Codes	Region Codes

PLOCEIDAE · PLOCEINAE · WEAVERS, SPARROWS *contd.*

Scientific Name	Common Name	Source Codes	Region Codes
Montifringilla theresae	Theresa's Snow Finch	1	b
Sporopipes frontalis	Speckle-fronted Weaver	8	c
Sporopipes squamifrons	Scaly-fronted Weaver	8	c
Amblyospiza albifrons	Grosbeak Weaver	8	c
Ploceus albinucha	White-naped Black Weaver	8	c
Ploceus alienus	Strange Weaver	8	c
Ploceus angolensis	Bar-winged Weaver	8	c
Ploceus aurantius	Orange Weaver	8	c
Ploceus aureonucha	Golden-naped Weaver	8	c
Ploceus badius	Cinnamon Weaver	8	c
Ploceus baglafecht	Baglafecht Weaver	8	c
Ploceus bannermani	Bannerman's Weaver	8	c
Ploceus batesi	Bates's Weaver	8	c
Ploceus benghalensis	Black-throated Weaver Bird	15	f
Ploceus bertrandi	Bertram's Weaver	8	c
Ploceus bicolor	Dark-backed Weaver	8	c
Ploceus bojeri	Golden Palm-Weaver	8	c
Ploceus capensis	Cape Weaver	8	c
Ploceus castaneiceps	Taveta Golden Weaver	8	c
Ploceus castanops	Northern Brown-throated Weaver	8	c
Ploceus cucullatus	Black-headed Weaver	5 8	c e
Ploceus dichrocephalus	Jubaland Weaver	8	c
Ploceus dorsomaculatus	Yellow-capped Weaver	8	c
Ploceus flavipes	Yellow-footed Weaver	8	c
Ploceus galbula	Ruppell's Weaver	8	c
Ploceus golandi	Clarke's Weaver	8	c
Ploceus grandis	Giant Weaver	8	c
Ploceus heuglini	Heuglin's Masked Weaver	8	c
Ploceus hypoxanthus	Golden Weaver	18 19 55	g h
Ploceus insignis	Brown-capped Weaver	8	c
Ploceus intermedius	Masked Weaver	8	c
Ploceus jacksoni	Golden-backed Weaver	8	c
Ploceus luteolus	Little Weaver	8	c
Ploceus manyar	Streaked Weaver	15 17 18 19 55	f g h
Ploceus megarhynchus	Finn's Baya	15	f
Ploceus melanocephalus	Yellow-backed Weaver	8	c
Ploceus melanogaster	Black Mountain-Weaver	8	c
Ploceus nelicourvi	Nelicourvi Weaver	10	c
Ploceus nigerrimus	Vieillot's Black Weaver	8	c
Ploceus nigricollis	Black-necked Weaver	8	c
Ploceus nigrimentum	Angola Weaver	8	c
Ploceus ocularis	Spectacled Weaver	8	c
Ploceus olivaceiceps	Olive-headed Golden Weaver	8	c
Ploceus pelzelni	Slender-billed Weaver	8	c
Ploceus philippinus	Baya Weaver	15 17 18 19 55	f g h
Ploceus preussi	Golden-backed Weaver	8	c
Ploceus princeps	Principe Golden Weaver	8	c
Ploceus rubiginosus	Chestnut Weaver	8	c
Ploceus sakalava	Sakalava Weaver	10	c
Ploceus spekei	Speke's Weaver	8	c
Ploceus spekeoides	Fox's Weaver	8	c
Ploceus stthomae	Sao Thome Weaver	8	c
Ploecus subaureus	Olive-headed Golden Weaver	8	c
Ploceus subpersonatus	Western Golden Weaver	8	c
Ploceus superciliosus	Compact Weaver	8	c
Ploceus taeniopterus	Northern Masked Weaver	8	c

Scientific Name	Common Name	Source Codes	Region Codes

PLOCEIDAE · PLOCEINAE · WEAVERS, SPARROWS *contd.*

Scientific Name	Common Name	Source Codes	Region Codes
Ploceus temporalis	Angolan Weaver	9	c
Ploceus tricolor	Yello w-mantled Weaver	8	c
Ploceus velatus	Vitelline Masked Weaver	8	c
Ploceus weynsi	Weyns's Weaver	8	c
Ploceus xanthops	Holub's Golden Weaver	8	c
Ploceus xanthopterus	Southern Brown-throated Weaver	8	c
Malimbus cassini	Cassin's Malimbe	8	c
Malimbus coronatus	Red-crowned Malimbe	8	c
Malimbus erythrogaster	Red-bellied Malimbe	8	c
Malimbus ibadanensis	Ibadan Malimbe	8 49	c
Malimbus malimbicus	Crested Malimbe	8	c
Malimbus nitens	Blue-billed Malimbe	8	c
Malimbus racheliae	Rachel's Malimbe	8	c
Malimbus rubriceps	Red-headed Weaver	8	c
Malimbus rubricollis	Red-headed Malimbe	8	c
Malimbus scutatus	Red-vented Malimbe	8	c
Quelea anomala	Bob-tailed Weaver	9	c
Quelea cardinalis	Cardinal Quelea	8	c
Quelea erythrops	Red-headed Quelea	8	c
Quelea quelea	Red-billed Quelea	8	c
Foudia aldabrana	Aldabra Fody	14	c
Foudia eminentissimo	Red Forest Fody	10	c
Foudia madagascariensis	Madagascar Fody	10	c
Foudia rubra	Mauritius Fody	14	c
Foudia seychellarum	Seychelles Fody	14 53	c
Euplectes afer	Yellow-crowned Bishop	8	c
Euplectes albonotatus	White-winged Widow-Bird	8	c
Euplectes anomalus	Anomalous Bishop	8	c
Euplectes ardens	Red-collared Widow-Bird	8	c
Euplectes aureus	Golden-backed Bishop	8	c
Euplectes axillaris	Fan-tailed Widow-Bird	8	c
Euplectes capensis	Yellow Bishop	8	c
Euplectes diadematus	Fire-fronted Bishop	8	c
Euplectes franciscanus	West African Red Bishop	9	c
Euplectes gierowii	Black Bishop	8	c
Euplectes hartlaubi	Marsh Widow-Bird	8	c
Euplectes hordeaceus	Black-winged Red Bishop	8	c
Euplectes jacksoni	Jackson's Widow-Bird	8	c
Euplectes macrourus	Yellow-shouldered Widow-Bird	8	c
Euplectes nigroventris	Black-vented Widow-Bird	8	c
Euplectes orix	Red Bishop	8	c
Euplectes progne	Long-tailed Widow-Bird	8	c
Anomalospiza imberbis	Parasitic Weaver	8	c

STURNIDAE · STARLINGS 106 species recorded

Scientific Name	Common Name	Source Codes	Region Codes
Aplonis atrifuscus	Samoan Starling	38	k
Aplonis brunneocapillus	White-eyed Starling	38	k
Aplonis cantoroides[1]	Little Starling	35 38	j k
Aplonis cinerascens	Cook Island Starling	43	k
Aplonis corvinus	Kusaie Mountain Starling	38	k
Aplonis feadensis[2]	Atoll Starling	38	k
Aplonis fusca	Lord Howe Island Starling	47	i

172

Scientific Name	Common Name	Source Codes	Region Codes
STURNIDAE · STARLINGS contd.			
Aplonis grandis[3]	Brown-winged Starling	38	k
Aplonis magna	Long-tailed Starling	35	j
Aplonis metallicus	Colonial Starling	35 36 38	i j k
Aplonis minor	Lesser Glossy Starling	19 22	h
Aplonis mysolensis	Moluccan Starling	35	j
Aplonis mystacea	Grant's Starling	35	j
Aplonis opacus	Micronesian Starling	38	k
Aplonis panayensis	Glossy Starling	15 18 19 21 22 55	f g h
Aplonis pelzelni	Ponape Mountain Starling	38	k
Aplonis santovestris	Mountain Starling	38	k
Aplonis striatus	Striped Glossy Starling	38	k
Aplonis tabuensis	Polynesian Starling	38	k
Aplonis zelandicus	Rusty-winged Starling	38	k
Poeoptera kenricki	Kenrick's Starling	9	c
Poeoptera lugubris	Narrow-tailed Starling	8	c
Poeoptera stuhlmanni	Stuhlmann's Starling	8	c
Grafisia torquata	White-collared Starling	8	c
Onycognathus albirostris	White-billed Starling	8	c
Onycognathus blythii	Somali Chestnut-winged Starling	8	c
Onycognathus frater	Socotra Chestnut-winged Starling	8	c
Onycognathus fulgidus	Chestnut-winged Starling	8	c
Onycognathus morio	Red-winged Starling	8	c
Onycognathus nabouroup	Pale-winged Starling	8	c
Onycognathus salvadorii	Bristle-crowned Starling	8	c
Onycognathus tenuirostris	Thin-billed Chestnut-winged Starling	8	c
Onycognathus tristramii	Tristram's Starling	1	b
Onycognathus walleri	Waller's Chestnut-winged Starling	8	c
Lamprotornis acuticaudus	Wedge-tailed Glossy Starling	8	c
Lamprotornis australis	Burchell's Glossy Starling	8	c
Lamprotornis caudatus	Long-tailed Glossy Starling	8	c
Lamprotornis chalcurus	Short-tailed Glossy Starling	8	c
Lamprotornis chalybaeus	Blue-eared Glossy Starling	8	c
Lamprotornis chloropterus	Swainson's Glossy Starling	8	c
Lamprotornis corruscus	Black-breasted Glossy Starling	8	c
Lamprotornis cupreocauda	Copper-tailed Glossy Starling	8	c
Lamprotornis iris	Emerald Starling	8	c
Lamprotornis mevesii	Meves's Long-tailed Glossy Starling	9	c
Lamprotornis nitens	Red-shouldered Glossy Starling	8	c
Lamprotornis ornatus	Principe Glossy Starling	8	c
Lamprotornis purpureiceps	Purple-headed Glossy Starling	8	c
Lamprotornis purpureus	Purple Glossy Starling	8	c
Lamprotornis purpuropterus	Rüppell's Long-tailed Glossy Starling	9	c
Lamprotornis splendidus	Splendid Glossy Starling	8	c
Cinnyricinclus femoralis	Abbot's Starling	8	c
Cinnyricinclus leucogaster	Violet-backed Starling	8	c
Cinnyricinclus sharpii	Sharpe's Starling	8	c
Speculipastor bicolor	Magpie Starling	8	c
Neocichla gutturalis	White-winged Babbling Starling	8	c
Spreo albicapillus	White-crowned Starling	8	c
Spreo bicolor[4]	Pied Starling	8	c

Scientific Name	Common Name	Source Codes	Region Codes

STURNIDAE · STARLINGS contd.·

Scientific Name	Common Name	Source Codes	Region Codes
Spreo fischeri	Fischer's Starling	8	c
Spreo hildebrandti	Hildebrandt's Starling	8	c
Spreo pulcher	Chestnut-bellied Starling	8	c
Spreo regius	Golden-breasted Starling	8	c
Spreo shelleyi[5]	Shelley's Starling	8	c
Spreo superbus	Superb Starling	8	c
Spreo unicolor	Ashy Starling	8	c
Saroglossa aurata	Madagascar Starling	10	c
Saroglossa spiloptera	Spotted-winged Starling	15 18 55	f g
Creatophora cinerea	Wattled Starling	8	c
Sturnus burmannicus	Jerdon's Starling	18 55	g
Sturnus cineraceus	Gray Starling	1 17 18 22 55	b g h
Sturnus contra	Pied Starling	15 17 18 19 55	f g h
Sturnus erythropygius	White-headed Starling	15	f
Sturnus malabaricus	Gray-headed Starling	15 17 18 55	f g
Sturnus melanopterus	Black-winged Starling	19	h
Sturnus nigricollis	Black-collared Starling	17 18 55	g
Sturnus pagodarum	Brahminy Starling	1 15	b f
Sturnus philippensis	Red-cheeked Starling	1 17 19 21 22	b g h
Sturnus roseus	Rose-colored Starling	1 15 17	b f g
Sturnus senex	Ceylon White-headed Starling	15	f
Sturnus sericeus	Silky Starling	17 22 55	g h
Sturnus sinensis	Gray-backed Starling	15 17 18 19 22 55	f g h
Sturnus sturninus	Daurian Starling	1 15 17 18 19 21 55	b f g h
Sturnus unicolor	Spotless Starling	1	b
Sturnus vulgaris	Common Starling	1 3 4 5 8 15 17 18 37 55	a b c e f g h i
Leucopsar rothschildi	Rothschild's Myna	19 53	h
Acridotheres albocinctus	Collared Myna	15 17 18	f g
Acridotheres cristatellus	Crested Myna	3 17 18 22 55	a g h
Acridotheres fuscus[6]	Jungle Myna	15 17 18 19 55	f g h
Acridotheres ginginianus	Bank Myna	15	f
Acridotheres grandis[7]	Great Myna	20 47	f h
Acridotheres tristis	Common Myna	1 3 8 10 15 17 18 19 37 38 55	b c f g h i k
Mino anais[8]	Golden-breasted Myna	35	j
Mino coronatus	Golden-crested Myna	15 18 55	f g
Mino dumonti	Yellow-faced Myna	35 38	j k
Basilornis celebensis	Celebes Starling	27 31	h j
Basilornis corythaix	Moluccan Starling	31	j
Basilornis galeatus	Sula Starling	31	j
Basilornis miranda	Mount Apo Myna	22	h
Streptocitta albertinae	Albertina's Starling	31	j
Streptocitta albicollis[9]	New Caledonian Starling	29	h
Sarcops calvus	Bald Starling	22	h
Gracula ptilogenys	Ceylon Myna	15	f
Gracula religiosa[10]	Hill Myna	15 17 18 19 21 55	f g h
Enodes erythrophrys	Celebes Enodes Starling	27	h
Scissirostrum dubium	Grosbeak Starling	29	h
Buphagus africanus	Yellow-billed Oxpecker	8	c
Buphagus erythrorhynchus	Red-billed Oxpecker	8	c

174

Scientific Name	Common Name	Source Codes	Region Codes

ORIOLIDAE · OLD WORLD ORIOLES, FOREST ORIOLES 28 species recorded

Scientific Name	Common Name	Source Codes	Region Codes
Oriolus albiloris	White-lored Oriole	22	h
Oriolus auratus	African Golden Oriole	8	c
Oriolus bouroensis	Buru Oriole	31	j
Oriolus brachyrhynchus	Western Black-headed Oriole	8	c
Oriolus chinensis[1]	Black-naped Oriole	1 15 17 18 19 21 22 55	b f g h
Oriolus chlorocephalus	Green-headed Oriole	8	c
Oriolus crassirostris	Sao Thome Oriole	8	c
Oriolus cruentus	Crimson-breasted Oriole	19 21	h
Oriolus flavocinctus	Green Oriole	35 36	i j
Oriolus forsteni	Forsten's Oriole	31	j
Oriolus hosii	Black Oriole	19 21	h
Oriolus isabellae	Isabella Oriole	22	h
Oriolus larvatus	Eastern Black-headed Oriole	8	c
Oriolus mellianus	Mell's Maroon Oriole	17 55	g
Oriolus monacha	Black-headed Forest Oriole	8	c
Oriolus nigripennis	Black-winged Oriole	8	c
Oriolus oriolus	Golden Oriole	1 8 15 17	b c f g
Oriolus phaeochromus	Ruddy Oriole	31	j
Oriolus sagittatus	White-bellied Oriole	35 36	i j
Oriolus szalayi	Brown Oriole	35	j
Oriolus traillii	Maroon Oriole	15 17 18 55	f g
Oriolus viridifuscus	Dark Oriole	32	j
Oriolus xanthonotus	Dark-throated Oriole	18 19 21 22 55	g h
Oriolus xanthornus	Black-headed Oriole	15 17 18 19 21 55	f g h
Sphecotheres flaviventris	Yellow Figbird	36	i
Sphecotheres hypoleucus	Wetar Figbird	31	j
Sphecotheres vieilloti	Figbird	35 36	i j
Sphecotheres viridis	Timor Figbird	31	j

DICRURIDAE · DRONGOS 20 species recorded

Scientific Name	Common Name	Source Codes	Region Codes
Chaetorhynchus papuensis	Mountain Drongo	35	j
Dicrurus megarhynchus	New Ireland Drongo	47	i
Dicrurus adsimilis	Fork-tailed Drongo	8 15	c f
Dicrurus aeneus	Bronzed Drongo	15 17 18 19 21 55	f g h
Dicrurus aldabranus	Aldabra Drongo	14	c
Dicrurus andamanensis	Andaman Drongo	15	f
Dicrurus annectens	Crow-billed Drongo	15 17 18 19 21 55	f g h
Dicrurus atripennis	Shining Drongo	8	c
Dicrurus balicassius	Balicassiao	22	h
Dicrurus caerulescens	White-bellied Drongo	15	f
Dicrurus forficatus	Crested Drongo	10	c
Dicrurus fuscipennis	Grand Comoro Drongo	14	c
Dicrurus hottentottus[1]	Hair-crested Drongo	1 15 17 18 19 21 22 35 36 38	b f g h i j k
Dicrurus leucophaeus	Ashy Drongo	1 15 17 18 19 21 55	b f g h
Dicrurus ludwigii	Square-tailed Drongo	8	c
Dicrurus macrocercus	Black Drongo	1 17 18 19 55	b g h
Dicrurus montanus	Celebes Mountain Drongo	27	h
Dicrurus paradiseus	Greater Racket-tailed Drongo	15 17 18 19 21 55	b g h
Dicrurus remifer	Lesser Racket-tailed Drongo	15 17 18 19 55	b g h
Dicrurus waldeni	Mayotte Drongo	14	c

175

Scientific Name	Common Name	Source Codes	Region Codes

CALLAEIDAE · WATTLEBIRDS, HUIAS, SADDLEBACKS 3 species recorded

Callaeas cinerea	Kokako	37 53	i
Creadion carunculatus	Saddleback	37 53	i
Heteralocha acutirostris	Huia	37	i

GRALLINIDAE · MAGPIE LARKS, CHOUGHS, MUDNEST BUILDERS 4 species recorded

Grallina bruijni[1]	Torrent-Lark	35	j
Grallina cyanoleuca	Magpie-Lark	3 36	i k
Corcorax melanorhamphos	White-winged Chough	36	i
Struthidea cinerea	Apostle-Bird	36	i

ARTAMIDAE · WOOD-SWALLOWS 10 species recorded

Artamus cinereus	Black-faced Wood-Swallow	35 36	i j
Artamus cyanopterus	Dusky Wood-Swallow	36	i
Artamus fuscus	Ashy Swallow-Shrike	15 17 18 55	f g
Artamus insignis	Bismarck Wood-Swallow	34	j
Artamus leucorhynchus	White-breasted Wood-Swallow	15 19 21 22 35 36 38	f h i j k
Artamus maximus	Greater Wood-Swallow	35	j
Artamus minor	Little Wood-Swallow	36	i
Artamus monachus	White-backed Wood-Swallow	29	h j
Artamus personatus	Masked Wood-Swallow	36	i
Artamus superciliosus	White-browed Wood-Swallow	36	i

CRATICIDAE · BELL MAGPIES, AUSTRALIAN BUTCHERBIRDS 11 species recorded

Cracticus cassicus	Black-headed Butcherbird	35	j
Cracticus louisiadensis	Louisiade Butcherbird	35	j
Cracticus mentalis	White-throated Butcherbird	35 36	i j
Cracticus nigrogularis	Pied Butcherbird	36	i
Cracticus quoyi	Black Butcherbird	35 36	i j
Cracticus torquatus[1]	Gray Butcherbird	36	i
Gymnorhina tibicen[2]	Black-backed Magpie	35 36 37 40	i j k
Strepera arguta	Clinking Currawong	36	i
Strepera fuliginosa	Black Currawong	36	i
Strepera graculina	Pied Currawong	36	i
Strepera versicolor	Gray Currawong	36	i

PTILONORHYNCHIDAE · BOWERBIRDS 17 species recorded

Ailuroedus buccoides	White-eared Catbird	35	j
Ailuroedus crassirostris[1]	Green Catbird	35 36	i j
Scenopoeetes dentirostris	Tooth-billed Bowerbird	36	i
Archboldia papuensis	Archbold's Bowerbird	35	j
Amblyornis flavifrons	Yellow-fronted Bowerbird	35	j

176

Scientific Name	Common Name	Source Codes	Region Codes

PTILONORHYNCHIDAE · BOWERBIRDS *contd.*

Scientific Name	Common Name	Source Codes	Region Codes
Amblyornis inornatus	Gardener Bowerbird	35	j
Amblyornis macgregoriae	MacGregor's Bowerbird	35	j
Amblyornis subalaris	Striped Bowerbird	35	j
Prionodura newtoniana	Golden Bowerbird	36	i
Sericulus aureus[2]	New Guinea Golden Bowerbird	35	j
Sericulus bakeri	Beck's Bowerbird	35	j
Sericulus chrysocephalus	Regent Bowerbird	36	i
Ptilonorhynchus violaceus	Satin Bowerbird	36	i
Chlamydera cerviniventris	Fawn-breasted Bowerbird	35 36	i j
Chlamydera lauterbachi	Yellow-breasted Bowerbird	35	j
Chlamydera maculata[3]	Spotted Bowerbird	36	i
Chlamydera nuchalis	Great Bowerbird	36	i

PARADISAEIDAE · BIRDS OF PARADISE 40 species recorded

Scientific Name	Common Name	Source Codes	Region Codes
Loria loriae	Loria's Bird of Paradise	35	j
Loboparadisea sericea	Yellow-breasted Bird of Paradise	35	j
Cnemophilus macgregorii	Multi-crested Bird of Paradise	35	j
Macgregoria pulchra	MacGregor's Bird of Paradise	35	j
Lycocorax pyrrhopterus	Brown-winged Bird of Paradise	29 31	h j
Manucodia ater	Glossy-mantled Manucode	35	j
Manucodia chalybatus	Green-breasted Manucode	35	j
Manucodia comrii	Curl-breasted Manucode	35	j
Manucodia jobiensis	Jobi Manucode	35	j
Phonygammus keraudrenii	Trumpet Bird	35 36	i j
Ptiloris magnificus	Magnificent Rifle-Bird	35 36	i j
Ptiloris paradiseus	Paradise Rifle-Bird	36	i
Ptiloris victoriae	Victoria Rifle-Bird	36	i
Semioptera wallacii	Standard-winged Bird of Paradise	29 31	h j
Seleucides melanoleuca	Twelve-wired Bird of Paradise	35	j
Paradigalla carunculata[1]	Long-tailed Paradigalla	35	j
Drepanornis albertisii	Black-billed Sicklebill Bird of Paradise	35	j
Drepanornis bruijnii	White-billed Sicklebill Bird of Paradise	35	j
Epimachus fastuosus	Black Sickle-billed Bird of Paradise	35	j
Epimachus mayeri	Brown Sickle-billed Bird of Paradise	35	j
Astrapia mayeri	Ribbon-tailed Astrapia	35	j
Astrapia nigra	Arfak Astrapia	35	j
Astrapia rothschildi	Huon Astrapia	35	j
Astrapia splendidissima	Splendid Astrapia	35	j
Astrapia stephaniae	Princess Stephania Astrapia	35	j
Lophorina superba	Superb Bird of Paradise	35	j
Parotia carolae	Queen Carola's Parotia	35	j
Parotia lawesi	Lawes's Six-wired Parotia	35	j
Parotia sefilata	Arfak Six-wired Parotia	35	j
Parotia wahnesi	Wahnes's Six-wired Parotia	35	j
Pteridophora alberti	King of Saxony Bird of Paradise	35	j
Cicinnurus regius	King Bird of Paradise	35	j

Scientific Name	Common Name	Source Codes	Region Codes

PARADISAEIDAE · BIRDS OF PARADISE *contd.*

Scientific Name	Common Name	Source Codes	Region Codes
Diphyllodes magnificus	Magnificent Bird of Paradise	35	j
Diphyllodes respublica	Waigeu Bird of Paradise	35	j
Paradisaea apoda[2]	Greater Bird of Paradise	35	j
Paradisaea decora	Goldie's Bird of Paradise	35	j
Paradisaea guilielmi	Emperor of Germany's Bird of Paradise	35	j
Paradisaea minor	Lesser Bird of Paradise	35	j
Paradisaea rubra	Red Bird of Paradise	35	j
Paradisaea rudolphi	Blue Bird of Paradise	35	j

CORVIDAE · CROWS, MAGPIES, JAYS, RAVENS 103 species recorded

Scientific Name	Common Name	Source Codes	Region Codes
Platylophus galericulatus	Crested Malay Jay	18 19 21 55	g h
Platysmurus leucopterus	Black-crested Magpie	18 19 21 55	g h
Gymnorhinus cyanocephalus	Piñon Jay	3 4	a e
Cyanocitta cristata	Blue Jay	3	a
Cyanocitta stelleri	Steller's Jay	3 4	a e
Aphelocoma coerulescens	Scrub Jay	3 4	a e
Aphelocoma ultramarina	Mexican Jay	3 4	a e
Aphelocoma unicolor	Unicolored Jay	4	e
Cyanolyca argenticula	Silvery-throated Jay	4	e
Cyanolyca cucullata	Azure-hooded Jay	4	e
Cyanolyca mirabilis	White-throated Jay	4	e
Cyanolyca nana	Dwarf Jay	4	e
Cyanolyca pulchra	Beautiful Jay	6	d
Cyanolyca pumilo	Black-throated Jay	4	e
Cyanolyca viridicyana[1]	Collared Jay	6	d
Cissilopha beecheii	Purplish-backed Jay	4	e
Cissilopha melanocyanea	Bushy-crested Jay	4	e
Cissilopha sanblasiana	Black-and-Blue Jay	3 4	a e
Cyanocorax affinis	Black-chested Jay	4 6	d e
Cyanocorax caeruleus	Azure Jay	6	d
Cyanocorax cayanus	Cayenne Jay	6	d
Cyanocorax chrysops[2]	Plush-crested Jay	6	d
Cyanocorax cristatellus	Curl-crested Jay	6	d
Cyanocorax cyanomelas	Purplish Jay	6	d
Cyanocorax dickeyi	Tufted Jay	4	e
Cyanocorax heilprini	Azure-naped Jay	6	d
Cyanocorax mystacalis	White-tailed Jay	6	d
Cyanocorax violaceus	Violaceous Jay	6	d
Cyanocorax yncas	Green Jay	3 4 6	a d e
Psilorhinus morio	Brown Jay	4	e
Calocitta formosa[3]	Magpie-Jay	4	e
Garrulus glandarius	Eurasian Jay	1 15 17 18 55	b f g
Garrulus lanceolatus	Eurasian Black-throated Jay	1 15	b f
Garrulus lidthi	Lidth's Jay	1	b
Perisoreus canadensis	Gray Jay	3	a
Perisoreus infaustus	Siberian Jay	1 17	b g
Perisoreus internigrans	Szechwan Gray Jay	1 17	b g
Urocissa caerulea[4]	Formosan Blue Magpie	17	g
Urocissa erythrorhyncha	Red-billed Blue Magpie	1 15 17 18 55	b f g h
Urocissa flavirostris	Yellow-billed Blue Magpie	1 15 17 18 55	b f g h
Urocissa ornata	Ceylon Magpie	15	f
Urocissa whiteheadi	Whitehead's Blue Magpie	17 55	g
Cissa chinensis	Green Magpie	15 17 18 19 21 55	f g h

178

Scientific Name	Common Name	Source Codes	Region Codes
CORVIDAE · CROWS, MAGPIES, JAYS, RAVENS contd.			
Cissa thalassina	Short-tailed Green Magpie	17 19 21 55	g h
Cyanopica cyanus	Azure-winged Magpie	1 17	b g
Dendrocitta bayleyi	Andaman Treepie	15	f
Dendrocitta formosae[5]	Gray Treepie	15 55	f g h
Dendrocitta frontalis	Black-browed Treepie	15 55	f g
Dendrocitta leucogastra	Southern Treepie	15	f
Dendrocitta occipitalis	Malaysian Treepie	19 21	h
Dendrocitta vagabunda	Indian Treepie	15 55	f g
Crypsirina cucullata	Hooded Racket-tailed Treepie	18	g
Crypsirina temia	Bronzed Treepie	18 19 55	g h
Temnurus temnurus[6]	Racket-tailed Treepie	17 55	g
Pica nuttalli	Yellow-billed Magpie	3	a
Pica pica	Common Magpie	1 8 15 17 18 55	a b c f g
Zavattariornis stresemanni	Stresemann's Bush-Crow	8	c
Podoces biddulphi	Biddulph's Ground Jay	1 17	b g
Podoces hendersoni	Henderson's Ground Jay	1 17	b g
Podoces panderi	Pander's Ground Jay	1	b
Podoces pleskei	Pleske's Ground Jay	1	b
Pseudopodoces humilis	Hume's Ground Jay	1 15 17	b f g
Nucifraga caryocatactes	Nutcracker	1 15 17 18	b f g
Nucifraga columbiana	Clark's Nutcracker	3 4	a e
Pyrrhocorax graculus	Alpine Chough	1 15 17	b f g
Pyrrhocorax pyrrhocorax	Red-billed Chough	1 8 15 17	b c f g
Ptilostomus afer	Piapiac	8	c
Corvus albicollis[7]	African White-necked Raven	8	c
Corvus albus	Pied Crow	8 10	c
Corvus bennetti	Small-billed Crow	30	i
Corvus brachyrhynchos[8]	Common Crow	3 4	a e
Corvus capensis	Black Crow	8	c
Corvus corax	Raven	1 3 4 15 17	a b e f g
Corvus corone	Carrion Crow	1 15 17 55	b f g
Corvus coronoides	Australian Raven	36	i
Corvus crassirostris	Thick-billed Raven	8	c
Corvus cryptoleucus	White-necked Raven	3 4	a e
Corvus dauricus	Daurian Jackdaw	1	b
Corvus enca	Little Crow	19 21 22	h
Corvus florensis	Flores Crow	32	j
Corvus frugilegus	Rook	1 15 17 37	b f g i
Corvus fuscicapillus	Brown-headed Crow	35	j
Corvus imparatus	Mexican Crow	4	e
Corvus jamaicensis	Jamaican Crow	5	e
Corvus kubaryi	Guam Crow	38	k
Corvus leucognaphalus	White-necked Crow	5	e
Corvus macrorhynchos	Jungle Crow	1 15 17 18 19 21 22	b f g h
Corvus mellori	South Australian Raven	49	i
Corvus monedula	Jackdaw	1 15 17	b f g
Corvus moneduloides	New Caledonian Crow	38	k
Corvus nasicus	Cuban Crow	5	e
Corvus orru	Australian Crow	35 36	i j
Corvus ossifragus	Fish Crow	3	a
Corvus palmarum	Palm Crow	5	e
Corvus rhipidurus	Fan-tailed Raven	1 8	b c
Corvus ruficollis	Brown-necked Raven	1 8	b c
Corvus splendens	House Crow	1 8 15 17 18 19 55	b c f g h
Corvus torquatus	Collared Crow	1 17 55	b g

Scientific Name	Common Name	Source Codes	Region Codes
CORVIDAE · CROWS, MAGPIES, JAYS, RAVENS contd.			
Corvus tristis[9]	Gray Crow	35	j
Corvus tropicus	Hawaiian Crow	3 53	k
Corvus typicus[10]	Celebes Crow	27	h
Corvus validus	Moluccan Crow	31	j
Corvus woodfordi	White-billed Crow	38	k

Notes

181

Notes

9 CICONIIDAE . STORKS

1 Includes *C. boyciana*

2 Replaces *Sphenorhynchus, Dissoura* and includes *C. stormi*

9 THRESKIORNITHIDAE . IBISES, SPOONBILLS

1 May be conspecific with *T. aethiopicus*
2 Replaces *Carphibis*
3 May be conspecific with *P. papillosa*
4 Replaces *Thaumatibis*
5 Commonly called Waldrapp
6 Replaces *Lampribis, Hagedashia*
7 Replaces *Guara*
8 May be conspecific with *P. chichi*
9 Replaces *Ajaia, Platibis*

10 PHOENICOPTERIDAE . FLAMINGOS

1 Includes *P. chilensis, roseus*

10 ANATIDAE . DUCKS, GEESE, SWANS

1 Includes *C. bewickii*
2 Includes *C. buccinator*
3 Replaces *Chen, Philacte*
4 Includes *A. hyperborea*
5 Replaces *Casarca*
6 Replaces *Mareca, Amazonetta, Salvadorina*
7 Includes *A. aucklandia*
8 Syn. with *A. punctata*
9 Includes *A. laysanensis, wyvilliana, fulvigula, diazi, oustaleti*
10 Includes *A. puna*
11 Replaces *Lampronetta*
12 Replaces *Nyroca*
13 Includes *S. sylvia*
14 Includes *M. deglandi*
15 Replaces *Lophodytes*

13 CATHARTIDAE . NEW WORLD VULTURES

1 Replaces *Gymnogyps*

13 ACCIPITRIDAE . HAWKS, OLD WORLD VULTURES, HARRIERS

1 Replaces *Chelictinia*
2 Replaces *Helicolestes*
3 Replaces *Necrosyrtes*
4 Replaces *Pseudogyps*
5 Replaces *Torgos*
6 Includes *C. beaudouini, pectoralis, ferox*
7 Includes *P. typus*
8 Includes *C. spilonotus, approximans, ranivorus*
9 Includes *A. butleri*
10 Includes *A. erythrauchen*
11 Syn. with *A. imitator*
12 Includes *A. griseogularis*
13 Includes *A. nana*
14 Replaces *Uroeatus*
15 Includes *A. hastata*
16 Includes *A. nipalensis*
17 Includes *S. limnaetus*

18 FALCONIDAE . FALCONS, CARACARAS

1 Includes *P. cheriway, lutosus*
2 Replaces *Neohierax*
3 Includes *M. horsfieldi*
4 Ripley treats *F. jugger* and *F. cherrug* as ssp. of *F. biarmicus*
5 Includes *F. altaicus*
6 Includes *F. albigularis*
7 Includes *F. amurensis*

19 MEGAPODIIDAE . MEGAPODES

1 Includes *M. reinwardti*

2 Replaces *Eulipoa*

182

19 CRACIDAE . CURASOWS, GUANS, CHACHALACAS

1 Sometimes treated as ssp. of *O. garrula*
2 Sometimes treated as ssp. of *O. retula*
3 Includes *O. guttata* and *superciliaris*
4 Includes *O. wagleri*
5 Sometimes treated as ssp. of *P. argyrotis*
6 Sometimes treated as ssp. of *P. jacquacu*
7 Replaces *Pipile*
8 Includes *A. cujubi*

20 TETRAONIDAE . GROUSE

1 Replaces *Canachites, Falcipennis*
2 Replaces *Tetrastes*
3 Includes *T. pallidicinctus*
4 Replaces *Pedioecetes*

20 PHASIANIDAE . QUAILS, PHEASANTS, PEACOCKS

1 Includes *C. leucopogon*
2 May be conspecific with *C. virginianus*
3 Syn. with *F. ochropectus*
4 Replaces *Excalfactoria* and includes *adansoni*
5 May be ssp. of *C. coturnix*
6 Includes *P. argoondah*
7 Replaces *Tropicoperdix* and may be conspecific with *A. charltoni*
8 Replaces *Lobiophasis*
9 Includes *Lirufa*
10 Includes *P. schleiermacheri*

24 NUMIDIDAE . GUINEAFOWL

1 May be conspecific with *N. meleagris*

25 GRUIDAE . CRANES

1 Replaces *Bugeranus*

25 RALLIDAE . RAILS, COOTS, GALLINULES

1 Includes *T. lafresnayanus*
2 Some believe these to be ssp. of *R. leucospila*
3 Includes *N. poecilopterus*
4 Replaces *Mentocrex*
5 Replaces *Crecopsis*
6 Includes *L. albigularis*
7 Known from one specimen as is *Aphanolimnas monasa* (Kusaie Rail)
8 Includes *S. lynesi*
9 Includes *P. madagascariensis, melanotus, poliocephalus*
10 Some use *Porphyrio*
11 Includes *F. ardesiaca*

28 OTIDIDAE . BUSTARDS

1 Replaces *Choriotis* and may be conspecific with *A. arabs*
2 Includes *E. savilei* and replaces *Lophitis*
3 Includes *E. rupelli*

29 JACANIDAE . JACANAS

1 Includes *J. jacana*

29 HAEMATOPODIDAE . OYSTERCATCHERS

1 Includes *H. moquini*

29 CHARADRIIDAE . PLOVERS, DOTTERELS

1 Replaces *Erythrogonys*
2 May be conspecific with *C. alexandrinus*
3 Replaces *Eupoda*
4 Syn. with *Pluvialis obscurus*
5 May be conspecific with *C. asiaticus*

31 SCOLOPACIDAE . SNIPE, WOODCOCK, SANDPIPERS
1 May be conspecific with *T.*
  hypoleucos
2 Replaces *Capella*
3 Replaces *Philohela*
4 Replaces *Crocethia*

33 RECURVIROSTRIDAE . AVOCETS, STILTS
1 Mayr and Short consider
  Himantopus to include *H.*
  himantopus, melanurus, mexicanus,
  ceylonensis, leucocephalus,
  knudseni, novaezelandiae and
  meridionalis
2 Includes *Himantopus mexicanus*
3 Includes *R. leucocephalus*
  novaezealandiae

34 GLAREOLIDAE . PRATINCOLES, COURSERS
1 Replaces *Rhinopticus*
2 Replaces *Stiltia*
3 May be conspecific with *G. pratincola*

35 LARIDAE . GULLS, TERNS
1 Replaces *Xema, Pagophila,*
  Leucophaeus, Rhodostethia, Rissa
2 Includes *S. melanogaster*
3 Includes *A. minutus*

37 ALCIDAE . AUKS, AUKLETS, MURRES
1 Replaces *Endomychura*
2 Includes *B. craveri*

38 COLUMBIDAE . PIGEONS, DOVES
1 Includes *C. sjöstedi* and *thomensis*
2 May be ssp. of *C. trocaz*
3 May be syn. of *C. norfolciensis*
4 Includes *C. iriditorgues*
5 Replaces *Nesoenas*
6 Includes *S. hypopyrrha*
7 Replaces *Geohaps, Lophophaps*
8 Replaces *Histriophaps*
9 Replaces *Columbigallina*
10 Replaces *Scardafella* and includes
  C. inca
11 Includes *C. buckleyi*
12 Includes *G. criniger, keayi, menagei,*
  platenae
13 Includes *G. kubaryi*
14 Replaces *Sphenurus*
15 Includes *T. calva, de la landii,*
  pembaensis, s. thomae
16 Replaces *Megaloprepia*

43 PSITTACIDAE . LORY, LORIKEETS, PARROTS, PARROTLETS
1 Some put into genus *Eos*
2 Replaces *Psitteuteles*
3 Replaces *Domicella*
4 Includes *L. tibialis*
5 Sometimes treated as conspecific
  with *C. sanguinea*
6 Sometimes treated as ssp. of *C.*
  galerita
7 Includes *T. heterus*
8 Peters treats as ssp. of *P. krameri*
9 Includes *P. finschii*
10 *P. intermedia* treated as hybrid
  of *P. himalayana* and *P.*
  cyanocephala
11 De Schauensee puts into genus *Ara*
12 Includes *A. caninde*
13 De Schauensee treats as ssp. *A.*
  solstitialis
14 De Schauensee treats as ssp. *A.*
  solstitialis
15 Includes *A. astec*
16 Includes *P. berlepschi*
17 De Schauensee treats as ssp. of *P.*
  haematotis
18 De Schauensee treats as ssp. of *A.*
  brasilianus. Forshaw gives it species
  status and includes in it *A.*
  rhodocorytha

184

50 CUCULIDAE . CUCKOOS, ROADRUNNERS, ANIS

1 Replaces *Chalcites*
2 Replaces *Misocalius*
3 May be conspecific with *C. americanus*
4 Replaces *Hyetornis*
5 Includes *S. longirostris*

6 Includes *M. viulloti*
7 Replaces *Rhamphococcyx*
8 Replaces *Lepidogrammus*
9 Replaces *Taccucua*
10 Replaces *Rhopodytes*
11 Replaces *Cochlothraustes*

52 STRIGIDAE . TYPICAL OWLS

1 Includes *O. vinaceus*
2 Includes *O. whiteheadi*
3 May be ssp. of *O. scops* unless *O. sunia* is recognized in which case it might be ssp. of *O. sunia*
4 Includes *O. insularis*

5 Includes *O. hartlaubi* and *senegalensis*
6 May be extinct
7 Includes *G. nanum* and *jardini*
8 Includes *G. castaneum*
9 Includes *N. spilonota* and *spilocephala*
10 Replaces *Speotyto*

56 CAPRIMULGIDAE . GOATSUCKERS, NIGHTJARS

1 Syn. with *S. brewsteri*
2 Includes *C. monticolus*

3 Disagreement exists about the status of this species
4 May be conspecific with *C. carolinensis*

57 HEMIPROCNIDAE . CRESTED SWIFTS

1 Includes *H. coronata*

57 APODIDAE . SWIFTS

1 Includes *C. maxima*
2 Includes *H. cochinchinensis*
3 Replaces *Streptoprocne*
4 Includes *C. rothschildi*

5 Replaces *Mernsia, Zoonavena*
6 Replaces *Micropanyptila*
7 Replaces *Reinarda*
8 Syn. with *C. batasiensis*

64 TROGONIDAE . TROGONS

1 Includes *P. auriceps*

2 Replaces *Heterotrogon*

65 ALCEDINIDAE . KINGFISHERS

1 Syn. with *D. gigas*

2 Includes *H. albicilla*

67 MEROPIDAE . BEE-EATERS

1 Replaces *Bombylonax*
2 Includes *M. bullockoides*

3 Includes *N. nubicoides*

68 CORACIIDAE . ROLLERS

1 Includes *E. pacificus*

69 PHOENICULIDAE . WOOD-HOOPOES

1 Replaces *Scoptelus, Rhinopomastus*

2 Some consider ssp. of *P. damarensis*

69 BUCEROTIDAE . HORNBILLS

1 Replaces *Tropicranus*
2 Replaces *Rhyticeros*
3 Includes *A. corrugatus*

4 Includes *A. narcondami*
5 Replaces *Acerus*

70 BUCCONIDAE . PUFFBIRDS

1 Includes *N. frontalis*

Notes

71 CAPITONIDAE . BARBETS
1 Replaces *Tricholaema*
2 Includes *L. chaplini*

72 INDICATORIDAE . HONEYGUIDES
1 Includes *I. conirostris*

72 RAMPHASTIDAE . TOUCANS
1 Includes *A. caeruleogularis*
2 Includes *P. frantzii*
3 Includes *P. inscriptus*
4 Replaces *Baillonius*
5 Includes *R. brevis*
6 May be ssp. of *R. vitellinus*

73 PICIDAE . WOODPECKERS, PICULETS
1 Includes *P. pallidus*
2 Includes *P. leucogaster*
3 Includes *C. cafer, chrysoides*
4 Replaces *Nesoceleus*
5 Includes *P. callopterus*
6 Includes *P. xanthopygaeus*
7 Replaces *Lichtensteinipicus*
8 Replaces *Centurus*
9 Includes *M. hoffmanni, uropygialis*
10 Replaces *Asyndesmus*
11 Includes *M. pygmaeus*
12 See Mayr and Short
13 Replaces *Dendrocopos*
14 Replaces *Hypopicus*
15 Includes *D. arizonae*

77 EURYLAIMIDAE . BROADBILLS
1 Includes *S. rubropygius*

79 FURNARIIDAE . OVENBIRDS
1 See de Schauensee, *The Species of Birds of South America*

88 PITTIDAE . PITTAS
1 Includes *P. megarhyncha*
2 Includes *P. mackloti*

89 TYRANNIDAE . TYRANT FLYCATCHERS
1 Includes *P. nana, dubius*
2 See Mayr and Short
3 Gooders includes *M. solitarius*
4 These genera placed in Cotingidae by Eisenmann
5 Includes *C. lugubris*
6 Includes *C. richardsonii*
7 Includes *M. sulphurpygius*
8 Includes *O. mexicanus*
9 Includes *O. olivaceum*
10 Includes *Perissotriccus atricapillus*
11 May be conspecific with *E. obscura*

95 PIPRIDAE . MANAKINS
1 Includes *M. aurantiacus, cerritus*

96 COTINGIDAE . COTINGAS, COCKS-OF-THE-ROCK, BECARDS
1 May be conspecific with *C. natterii*
2 Replaces *Zaratornis, Doliornis*
3 Includes *P. lubomirskii, jacunda* and *pulch*
4 Replaces *Platypsaris*

98 ALAUDIDAE . LARKS
1 Replaces *Certhilauda*
2 Replaces *Heteromirafra*
3 Includes *C. brachydactyla*
4 Replaces *Eremalauda*
5 Includes *C. somalica*
6 Replaces *Pseudalaemon*

100   HIRUNDINIDAE . SWALLOWS, MARTINS
1 Replaces *Iridoprocne*   3 Includes *H. javanica*
2 Replaces *Ptyonoprogne, Cecropsis*

101   MOTACILLIDAE . WAGTAILS, PIPITS
1 Some use *Motacilla*   3 Includes *A. pelopus*
2 Includes *A. australis, richardi*   4 Includes *A. petrusus*

102   CAMPEPHAGIDAE . CUCKOO-SHRIKES
1 Replaces *Edolisoma*   4 Peters treats as ssp. of *C. phoenicea*
2 Includes *C. robusta*   5 Includes *P. igneus*
3 Peters treats as ssp. of *C. lobata*

104   PYCNONOTIDAE . BULBULS
1 Lumped with *Pycnonotus* in Peters 4 Replaces *Bernieria*
2 Includes *P. xanthopygos*   5 Includes *N. gularis*
3 Includes *P. hypochloris*   6 Includes *H. castanotus*

107   LANIIDAE . SHRIKES
1 Peters considers ssp. of *L.*   4 Replaces *Telophorus*
  ferrugineus   5 Peters considers ssp. of *M. blanchoti*
2 Peters considers ssp. of *L. barbarus* 6 Includes *L. newtoni*
3 Peters considers ssp. of *L. fulleborni* 7 Syn. with *L. excubitorius*

109   CINCLIDAE . DIPPERS
1 Includes *C. schultzi*

109   TROGLODYTIDAE . WRENS
1 Includes *C. chiapensis*   8 Includes *T. leucopogon*
2 Includes *C. albo-brunneus*   9 Includes *T. musculus, tanneri,*
3 Replaces *Telmatodytes*   *brunneicollis*
4 Includes *T. spadix*   10 Replaces *Thryochilus*
5 Includes *T. zeledoni*   11 Includes *T. rufocileatus, ochraceus*
6 May be ssp. of *T. rufalbus*   12 Includes *C. phaeocephalus*
7 Includes *T. castaneus, semibadius*

110   MIMIDAE . THRASHERS, MOCKINGBIRDS
1 Replaces *Melanoptila*   3 Replaces *Oreoscoptes*
2 Includes *M. gilvus*   4 Replaces *Allenia*

111   PRUNELLIDAE . ACCENTORS
1 Peters considers a ssp. of *P.*
  ocularis

111   TURDINAE . THRUSHES, WREN-THRUSHES
1 Replaces *Erythropygia*   8 Replaces *Thamnolaea*
2 White uses *Erithacus*   9 Includes *Thamnolaea coronata*
3 Replaces *Tarsiger*   10 Peters considers as ssp. of *O. oenanthe*
4 Peters considers part of *Cossypha* 11 Syn. with *Thamnolaea leucocephala*
5 Replaces *Dessornis*   12 Includes *M. gularis*
6 Includes *M. melanops, coloratus* 13 African *Zoothera* lumped in *Turdus*
7 Replaces *Stizorhina*   14 Includes *T. helleri, menachensis, ludoviciae*

15 Includes *T. assimilis*
16 Includes *T. hortulorum*
17 Syn. with *Zoothera guttata*
18 Includes *T. hauxwelli, obsoletus*
19 Includes *Zoothera crossleyi*

20 Includes *T. plebejus*
21 Replaces *T. musicus*
22 Peters considers ssp. of *T. olivaceus*
23 Includes *T. infuscatus*

117 ORTHONYCHINAE . LOGRUNNERS
1 Replaces *Ptilorrhoa*

117 TIMALIINAE . BABBLERS, WREN-TIT
1 Peters considers as ssp. of *P. erythrogenys*
2 Includes *P. basilanica*
3 Includes *N. rufipectus*
4 Peters considers as ssp. of *T. plebejus*
5 Peters considers as ssp. of *T. melanops*
6 Includes *G. morrisonianus*
7 Includes *G. jerdoni*
8 Includes *G. poecilorhynchus*
9 Includes *G. nuchalis*
10 Includes *G. gularis*
11 Includes *G. courtoisi*
12 Includes *G. bieti*
13 Includes *H. desgodsini*
14 Replaces *Minla castaniceps*
15 Includes *Y. humilis*

122 PARADOXORNITHINAE . PARROTBILLS, SUTHORAS
1 Includes *P. poliotis, verreauxi*

122 SYLVIINAE . OLD WORLD WARBLERS
1 Includes *R. rufiventris*
2 Possibly conspecific with *P. schistaceigula*
3 Possibly conspecific with *P. plumbea*
4 Includes *C. canturians*
5 Replaces *Phragmaticola*
6 Replaces *Lusciniola*
7 Includes *P. ricketti*
8 African *Seicercus* lumped with *Phylloscopus*
9 Replaces *Seicercus*
10 Includes *R. satrapa*
11 Hall and Moreau use *Spiloptila*

129 MALURINAE . WREN-WARBLERS
1 Includes *M. leuconotus*
2 Includes *A. modestus*

130 ACANTHIZINAE . AUSTRALASIAN WARBLERS
1 Includes *D. longirostris*
2 Includes *A. castaneiventris*
3 Includes *M. albicilla*
4 Includes *C. campestris, isabellinus, montanellus*
5 Gooders lists *G. inornata*
6 Includes *S. minimus*
7 Replaces *Trichocichla*
8 Includes *Trichocichla rufa*

131 MUSCICAPINAE . OLD WORLD FLYCATCHERS
1 Not in Vaurie's monograph
2 Replaces *Cyanoptila*
3 Replaces *Muscicapella*
4 Replaces *Artomyias* and syn. with *A. fuliginosa*

135 MONARCHINAE . MONARCH FLYCATCHERS
1 Replaces *Tchitrea*
2 Replaces *Seisura*
3 Replaces *Drymophila, Hypothymis, Philentoma*
4 Includes *M. browni* and *vidua*
5 Includes *M. erythrosticta, richardsii*
6 Includes *M. canescens, everetti*
7 Replaces *Peneonanthe*
8 Includes *P. cerviniventris*
9 Includes *P. iphis*

188

137   PACHYCEPHALINAE . WHISTLERS, SHRIKE-THRUSH
1 Includes *F. leucogaster, whitei*   4 Includes *P. monacha*
2 Includes *P. whiteheadi*   5 Includes *P. griseiceps*
3 Includes *P. melanops*   6 Replaces *Myiolestes*

138   AEGITHALIDAE . LONG-TAILED TITS
1 Includes *A. niveogularis*   2 Includes *P. melanotis*

139   REMIZIDAE . PENDULINE TITS
1 Includes *Anthoscopus sylviella*

139   PARIDAE . TYPICAL TITS, TITMICE
1 Includes *P. atricristatus*   2 Includes *P. spilonotus*

140   SITTIDAE . NUTHATCHES
1 Includes *S. nagaensis, castanea*   4 Includes *S. pygmea*
2 Includes *S. solangei*   5 Includes *N. striata, pileata, leucoptera,*
3 Includes *S. victoriae*   *leucocephala*

141   CLIMACTERIDAE . AUSTRALIAN TREE-CREEPERS
1 Includes *C. minor, placens*   3 Includes *C. melanota*
2 Includes *C. wellsi*

141   DICAEIDAE . FLOWERPECKERS
1 Replaces *Anaimos*   4 Includes *D. geelvinkianum, nitidum*
2 Includes *Anaimos johannae*   5 Includes *D. wilheminae*
3 Includes *D. obsoletum*   6 Might be bulbuls

142   NECTARINIIDAE . SUNBIRDS
1 Peters considers as ssp. of *A*   4 Includes *N. frenata*
   platurus   5 Peters considers as ssp. of *N. loveridge*
2 Peters considers as ssp. of *A.*   6 Peters considers as possible ssp. of *N.*
   rectirostris   *bifasciata*
3 Peters considers as ssp. of *N.*   7 Includes *A. philippinensis*
   senegalensis

144   ZOSTEROPIDAE . WHITE-EYES
1 Replaces *Malacirops*   7 Includes *Z. siamensis*
2 Includes *Z. minor, meeki*   8 Syn. with *R. sanfordi*
3 Includes *Z. albiventris*   9 Replaces *Apoia*
4 Includes *Z. parvus*   10 Replaces *Pseudozosterops squamiceps*
5 Includes *Z. semiflava*   11 Replaces *Pseudozosterops*
6 Includes *Z. chlorates*

146   MELIPHAGIDAE . HONEYEATERS
1 Syn. with *Meliphaga bougainvillei*   10 Replaces *Trichodere*
2 Syn. with *Toxorhamphus iliophus*   11 Includes *P. yorki*
3 Includes *G. claudi*   12 Includes *M. foersteri*
4 Includes *M. chloroptera*   13 Replaces *Vosea*
5 Includes *M. flavescens*   14 Replaces *Glyciphila* (Part)
6 Replaces *Guadalcanaria*   15 Replaces *Grantiella, Lacustroica*
7 Replaces *Ptilotis*   16 Replaces *Myzantha*
8 Replaces *Xanthosis*   17 Replaces *Acanthagenys*
9 Includes *P. gordoni*

Notes

149 EMBERIZINAE . BUNTINGS, AMERICAN SPARROWS

1 Replaces *Rhynchophanes*
2 Includes *P. hyperboreus*
3 Replaces *Melospiza, Passerella*
4 Includes *J. aikeni, oreganus, insularis*
5 Includes *J. bairdi, alticola*
6 Replaces *Passerculus, Passerherbulus*
7 Includes *A. mirabilis, princeps, nigrescens*
8 Includes *S. wortheni*
9 Includes *A. petenica*
10 Replaces *Rhynchospiza*
11 Replaces *Compsospiza*
12 Replaces *Gnathospiza*
13 Includes *S. aurita*
14 Includes *A. relicta*
15 Replaces *Chlorura*
16 Includes *P. macronyx, maculatus*
17 Includes *A. apertus*
18 Includes *A. virenticeps, assimilis*
19 Includes *L. crassirostris*
20 Includes *P. cristata*

155 CARDINALINAE . CARDINAL-GROSBEAKS

1 Includes *P. tibialis*
2 Replaces *Richmondena*
3 Replaces *Pyrrhuloxia*
4 Includes *C. poliogaster*
5 Includes *P. fulginosus*
6 Includes *S. nigriceps*
7 Replaces *Cyanocompsa, Guiraca, Porphyrospiza*

155 THRAUPINAE . TANAGERS, HONEYCREEPERS

1 Replaces *Sericossypha*
2 Includes *C. tacarcunae*
3 May be a ssp. of *C. pileatus*
4 Replaces *Erythrothlypis*
5 Includes *L. leucothorax*
6 Includes *H. atrimaxillaris, fuscicauda*
7 Replaces *Bangsia*
8 Includes *A. melanogenys*
9 Includes *I. reinhardti*
10 Syn. with *Dubusia castaneoventris*
11 Includes *E. godmani*
12 Replaces *E. lauta*
13 Includes *E. elegantissima*
14 Includes *C. callophrys*
15 Includes *T. chrysophrys*
16 Includes *T. fucosa*
17 Replaces *Pseudodacnis*

160 PARULIDAE . WOOD WARBLERS

1 May be ssp. of *D. virens*
2 Includes *D. auduboni*
3 Includes *D. breviunguis*
4 *D. vitellina* considered ssp. of *D. discolor* by Peters, but as good species by Mayr and Short
5 Includes *S. picta*
6 Includes *G. chiriquensis*
7 Includes *G. tolmei*
8 Replaces *Chamaethlypis*
9 Includes *G. chapalensis, beldingi, flavovelata*
10 Most, other than Peters, treat as ssp. of *B. cinereicollis*
11 Includes *B. delatrii*
12 Includes *B. fulvicauda*
13 According to Peters, 'probably not a parulid'
14 Includes *G. francescae*

162 DREPANIDIDAE . HAWAIIAN HONEYCREEPERS

1 Status uncertain

162 VIREONIDAE . VIREOS, SHRIKE-VIREOS, PEPPER SHRIKES

1 Replaces *Neochloe*
2 Includes *V. leucophrys*
3 Includes *V. perquisitor, caribeus, crassirostris, gundlachi, modestus*
4 Includes *V. flavoviridis*
5 Replaces *Smaragdolanius*
6 Includes *H. minor*
7 Includes *H. olivaceus*

190

163 ICTERIDAE . BLACKBIRDS, TROUPIALS

1 Replaces *Clypicterus, Gymnostinops, Ocyalus, Zarhynchos*
2 Includes *C. chrysonotus*
3 Replaces *Cassiculus*
4 May be conspecific with *I. dominicensis*
5 Includes *I. chrysocephalus*
6 Includes *I. prosthemelas*
7 Includes *I. bullocki*
8 Includes *I. graysoni, sclateri*
9 Includes *I. fuertesi*
10 The genus *Sturnella* follows de Schauensee
11 Peters uncertain whether a good species
12 Includes *D. warszewiczi*
13 Replaces *Cassidix*
14 Replaces *Tangavius*
15 Syn. with *M. armenti*

165 CARDUELINAE . GOLDFINCHES AND ALLIES

1 Replaces *Carduelis*
2 Replaces *Spinus*
3 Includes *C. caniceps*
4 Includes *L. atrata, australis, tephrocotis*
5 Includes *C. verreauxi*
6 Replaces *Kozlowia*
7 Replaces *Propyrrhula*
8 Includes *P. griseiventris*
9 Replaces *Euphona, Hesperiphona, Mycerobas*

167 ESTRILDIDAE . WAXBILLS

1 Peters treats as ssp. of *P. woodhousei*
2 Replaces *Zonaeginthus*
3 Includes *L. nigerrima*
4 Includes *L. ferruginosa*
5 Replaces *Spermestes*
6 Replaces *Heteromunia*

169 VIDUINAE . PARASITIC VIDUINES

1 Includes *V. ultramurina, centralis, nigeriae, camerunensis, wilsoni, funerea* and replaces *Hypochera*
2 Includes *V. purpurescens, nigerrima, amauropteryx, codringtoni*
3 Peters considers as ssp. of *V. orientalis*
4 Includes *V. aucupum, toguensis, interjecta*

170 PLOCEINAE . WEAVERS, SPARROWS

1 Peters considers as ssp. of *B. albirostris*
2 Peters considers as ssp. of *P. griseus*
3 Replaces *Penthetria*
4 Peters considers as ssp. of *P. xanthocollis*

172 STURNIDAE . STARLINGS

1 Includes *A. crassa*
2 Includes *A. insularis*
3 Includes *A. dichroa*
4 Replaces *Cosmopsarus*
5 Peters considers as ssp. of *S. hildebrandti*
6 Includes *A. javanicus*
7 Not in Ripley
8 Replaces *Ampliceps*
9 Includes *S. torquata*
10 Includes *G. venerata*

175 ORIOLIDAE . OLD WORLD ORIOLES, FOREST ORIOLES

1 Includes *O. tenuirostris*

175 DICRURIDAE . DRONGOS

1 Includes *D. bracteus*

176 GRALLINIDAE . MAGPIE-LARKS, CHOUGHS, MUDNEST BUILDERS
1 Replaces *Pomareopsis*

176 CRACTICIDAE . BELL MAGPIES, AUSTRALIAN BUTCHER-BIRDS
1 Includes *C. argenteus*   2 Includes *G. dorsalis, hypoleuca*

176 PTILONORHYNCHIDAE . BOWERBIRDS
1 Includes *A. melanotis*   3 Includes *C. guttata*
2 Replaces *Xanthomelus*

177 PARADISAEIDAE . BIRDS OF PARADISE
1 Includes *P. brevicauda*   2 Includes *P. raggiana*

178 CORVIDAE . CROWS, MAGPIES, JAYS, RAVENS
1 Includes *C. turcosa*   6 Syn. with *Crypsirina temnura*
2 Includes *C. cyanopogon*   7 Includes *C. cryptoleucus*
3 Peters suggests that a ssp. *C. f.*   8 Includes *C. caurinus*
  collei may be a full species   9 Replaces *Gymnocorvus*
4 Replaces *Kitta*   10 Replaces *Nesocorax*
5 May be conspecific with *D.*
  occipitalis

Source Codes

PALEARCTIC REGION
1. Vaurie, Charles. *The Birds of the Palearctic Fauna*. Volume 1: *Passeriformes*.
2. Vaurie, Charles. *The Birds of the Palearctic Fauna*. Volume 2. *Non-Passeriformes*.

NEARCTIC REGION
3. *The A.O.U. Checklist of North American Birds*.

NEOTROPICAL REGION
4. Eisenmann, Eugene. The Species of Middle American Birds.
5. Bond, J. *Birds of the West Indies*.
6. de Schauensee, R. M. *A Guide to the Birds of South America*.
7. Kepler, C. B. & Parkes, K. C. A New Species of Warbler (Parulidae) from Puerto Rico.

ETHIOPIAN REGION
8. White, C. M. N. A Check List of the Ethiopian Muscicapidae (Sylviinae).
   White, C. M. N. *A Revised Check List of African Broadbills, Pittas, Larks, Swallows, Wagtails and Pipits*.
   White, C. M. N. *A Revised Check List of African Shrikes, Orioles, Drongos, Starlings, Crows, Waxwings, Cuckoo-Shrikes, Bulbuls, Accentors, Thrushes and Babblers*.
   White, C. M. N. *A Revised Check List of African Flycatchers, Tits, Tree Creepers, Sunbirds, White-eyes, Honey Eaters, Buntings, Finches, Weavers and Waxbills*.
   White, C. M. N. *A Revised Check List of African Non-Passerine Birds*.
9. Hall, B. P. & Moreau, R. E. *An Atlas of Speciation in African Passerine Birds*.
10. Rand, A. L. The Distribution and Habits of Madagascar Birds.
11. Hagen, Y. Birds of Tristan da Cunha.
12. Elliott, H. F. I. A Contribution to the Ornithology of the Tristan da Cunha Group.
13. Farkas, T. *Monticola bensoni*, A New Species from Southwestern Madagascar.
14. Watson, G. E., Zusi, R. L. & Stover, R. E. *Preliminary Field Guide to the Birds of the Indian Ocean*.

ORIENTAL REGION
15. Ripley, S. D. *A Synopsis of the Birds of India and Pakistan*.
16. Cheng, Tso-Hsin. *A Distributional List of Chinese Birds. Part 1: Non-Passeriformes*.
17. Cheng, Tso-Hsin. *A Distributional List of Chinese Birds. Part 2: Passeriformes*.
18. Smythies, B. *The Birds of Burma*.
19. Delacour, J. *Birds of Malaysia*.
20. Hoogerwerf, A. Distribution of Birds in Java.
21. Smythies, B. *The Birds of Borneo*.
22. Delacour, J. & Mayr, E. *Birds of the Philippines*.
23. de Schauensee, R. M. & du Pont, J. E. Birds from the Philippine Islands.
24. du Pont, J. E. *Philippine Birds*.
25. Ripley, S. D. & Rabor, D. S. New Birds from Palawan and Culion Islands.
26. Salomonsen, F. Some Birds from Dyaul Island.
27. Stresemann, E. Die Vogel von Celebes.
28. Ripley, S. D. Notes on a Collection of Birds from Northern Celebes.
29. Kuroda, N. On a Collection of Birds from Celebes and Halmahera.
30. Kuroda, N. A Collection of Birds from Halmahera and North Celebes.

Source Codes

AUSTRALASIAN REGION

31. van Bemmel, A. C. V. A Faunal List of the Birds of the Moluccan Islands.
32. Mayr, E. The Birds of Timor and Sumba.
33. Rensch, B. Die Vogelwelt von Lombock, Sumbawa und Flores.
34. Gilliard, E. T. & Lecroy, M. Results of the 1958-1959 Gilliard New Britain Expedition.
35. Rand, A. L. & Gilliard, E. T. *Handbook of New Guinea Birds.*
36. Slater, P. *A Field Guide to Australian Birds: Non-Passerines.*
    Royal Australasian Ornithologists' Union. *The Official Checklist of the Birds of Australia. (Passerine)*
37. Falla, R. A., Sibson, R. B. & Turbott, E. G. *A Field Guide to the Birds of New Zealand.*
    Ornithological Society of New Zealand, Inc. *Annotated Checklist of the Birds of New Zealand.*

PACIFIC OCEAN ISLANDS

38. Mayr, E. *Birds of the Southwest Pacific.*
39. Baker, R. H. The Avifauna of Micronesia.
40. Cain, A.J. & Galbraith, I.C.J. Field Notes on Birds of the Eastern Solomon Islands.
41. King, J. E. Some Observations on the Birds of Tahiti and the Marquesas Islands.
42. Amerson, Jr., A. B. Ornithology of the Marshall and Gilbert Islands.
43. Wilson, S. B. Birds of Tahiti and the Society Group.
44. Morrison, J. P. E. Notes on the Birds of Raroia.
45. Williams, G. R. Birds of the Pitcairn Islands.
46. Swarth, H. The Avifauna of the Galapagos Islands.

MISCELLANEOUS

47. Peters, J. L. et al. *Checklist of Birds of the World.*
48. Gooders, J. ed. *Birds of the World.*
49. Mayr, E. New Species of Birds Described from 1956 to 1965.
50. Brown, L. & Amadon, D. *Eagles, Hawks and Falcons of the World.*
51. Grossman, M. L. & Hamlet, J. *Birds of Prey of the World* (Owls only).
52. Goodwin, D., *Pigeons and Doves of the World.*
53. Fisher, J., Simon, N., & Vincent, J., *The Red Book, Wildlife in Danger.*
54. von Boetticher, H., Papageien.
55. King, B., Woodcock, M. W. & Dickinson, E. C. *A Field Guide to the Birds of South-East Asia.*
56. Mayr, E. & Short, L. L. *Species Taxa of North American Birds.*
57. Bryan, E. H. Notes on the Geography and Natural History of Wake Island.
58. Watson, G. E. et al. *Birds of the Antarctic and Subantarctic.*
59. Watson, G. E. *Sea Birds of the Tropical Atlantic Ocean.*
60. Delacour, J. & Amadon, D. *Curassows and Related Birds*
61. Voous, K. H. List of Recent Holarctic Bird Species.
62. Burton, J. A. *Owls of the World.*
63. Vaurie, Charles. A Generic Revision of Flycatchers of the Tribe Muscicapini.
64. Forshaw, J. M. & Cooper, W. *Parrots of the World*
65. Mayr, E. Notes on the Birds of Northern Melanesia.
66. Collins, 1972. Cont. Sci. Los Angeles Nat. Hist. Mus., No. **229**, p. 4.
67. Progogine, 1972. Bull. Brit. Ornith. Club. **92**(5), p. 138.
68. Farkas, Ostrich, Suppl. **9**, p. 85.
69. Forbes-Watson, 1970. Bull. Brit. Ornith. Club. **90**(6), p. 146.
70. Mees, 1973. Zool. Meded. **46**(12), p. 179.
71. Favaloro & McEvey, 1968. Mem. Nat. Mus. Vict., **28**, p. 1.
72. Johnson & Millie, 1972. *Supplement to the Birds of Chile.*

Bibliography

ALEXANDER, W. B. (1954). *Birds of the Ocean*. New York, Putnam.

AMERSON, JR., A. B. (1969). Ornithology of the Marshall and Gilbert Islands. *Atoll Research Bulletin* **127**:1-348.

A. O. U. (1957). *The A.O.U. Checklist of North American Birds*. Baltimore, A.O.U.

AUSTIN, JR., O. L. (1961). *Birds of the World*. New York, Golden Press.

AUSTIN, JR., O. L. (1971). *Families of Birds*. New York, Golden Press.

BAKER, R. H. (1951). The Avifauna of Micronesia. *Univ. Kansas Publ. Mus. Nat. Hist.* **3**:1-359.

BIERMAN, W. H. & VOOUS, K. H. (1950). *Birds Observed and Collected During Whaling Expeditions of the* William Barendsz *in the Antarctic, 1946-1947 and 1947-1948*. Leiden, Brill.

BOND, J. (1971). *Birds of the West Indies*. London, Collins.

BRATTSTROM, B. H. & HOWELL, T. R. (1956). The Birds of the Revilla Gigedo Islands, Mexico. *Condor* **58**:107-20.

BROWN, L. & AMADON, D. (1968). *Eagles, Hawkes and Falcons of the World*. New York, McGraw-Hill, 2 vols.

BRYAN, JR., E. H. (1959). Notes on the Geography and Natural History of Wake Island. *Atoll Research Bulletin* **66**:1-22.

BURLAND, J. C. (1964). Some Notes on the Bird Life of Palmerston Atoll. *Notornis* **XI**:145-54.

BURTON, J. A. (1973). *Owls of the World*. New York, Dutton.

CAIN, A. J. & GALBRAITH, I. C. J. (1956). Field Notes on Birds of the Eastern Solomon Islands. *Ibis* **98**:100-34 and 262-95.

CAYLEY, N. W. (1969). *What Bird Is That?* Sydney, Angus and Robertson.

CHENG, TSO-HSIN (1955). *A Distributional List of Chinese Birds. Part 1: Non-Passeriformes*. Peking, Academica Sinica.

CHENG, TSO-HSIN (1958). *A Distributional List of Chinese Birds. Part II: Passeriformes*. Peking, Academica Sinica.

CHILD, P. (1960). Birds of the Gilbert and Ellice Islands Colony. *Atoll Research Bulletin*. **74**:1-38.

CLAPP, R. B. & SIBLEY, F. C. (1966). Notes on the Birds of Tutuila, American Samoa. *Notornis* **XIII**:157-64.

CLAPP, R. B. & SIBLEY, F. C. (1967). New Records of Birds from the Phoenix and Line Islands. *Ibis* **109**:132-5.

COMMONWEALTH SCIENTIFIC & INDUSTRIAL RESEARCH ORGANIZATION. (1969). An Index of Australian Bird Names. *Division of Wildlife Research Technical Paper No. 20*.

DEIGNAN, H. G. (1963). *Checklist of The Birds of Thailand*. Washington, D.C., Smithsonian Institution.

DELACOUR, J. & GREENWAY, JR., J. C. (1941). Commentaires, Additions et Modifications à la Liste des Oiseaux de l'Indochine Française. *L'Oiseau* **11** (Special): I-XXI.

DELACOUR, J. & MAYR, E. (1946). *Birds of the Philippines*. New York, Macmillan.

DELACOUR, J. (1947). *Birds of Malaysia*. New York, Hamilton.

Bibliography

DELACOUR, J. (1951). Commentaires, Modifications et Additions à la Liste des Oiseaux de l'Indochine Française (II). *L'Oiseau* **21**:1-32, 81-119.

DELACOUR, J. (1951). *The Pheasants of the World.* London, Country Life.

DELACOUR, J. & JABOUILLE, P. (1960). Liste des Oiseaux de l'Indochine Française, Complétée et Mise à Jour. *L'Oiseau* **10**:89-220.

DELACOUR, J. & Amadon, D. (1973). *Curassows and Related Birds.* New York, American Museum of Natural History.

DE SCHAUENSEE, R. M. & DU PONT, J. E. (1962). Birds from the Philippine Islands. *Proc. Acad. Nat. Sci. Phil.* **114**:149-73.

DE SCHAUENSEE, R. M. (1966). *The Species of Birds of South America.* Philadelphia Acad. Nat. Sci. Phil.

DE SCHAUENSEE, R. M. (1970). *A Guide to the Birds of South America.* Wynnewood, Pa., Livingston.

DOWNES, M. C., et al. (1959). *The Birds of Heard Island.* Melbourne, Antarctic Division, Dept. of Ext. Aff.

DU PONT, J. E. (1971). *Philippine Birds.* Greenville, Delaware, Museum of Natural History.

EISENMANN, EUGENE. (1955). The Species of Middle American Birds. *Trans. Lin. Soc. N.Y.* **7**:128 pp.

ELLIOTT, H. F. I. (1957). A Contribution to the Ornithology of the Tristan da Cunha Group. *Ibis* **99**:545-55.

FALLA, R. A., SIBSON, R. B. & TURBOTT, E. G. (1970). *A Field Guide to the Birds of New Zealand.* London, Collins.

FARKAS, T. (1971). *Monticola bensoni,* A New Species from Southwestern Madagascar. *Ostrich* **42**: Supp. **9**:83-90.

FISHER, J. & PETERSON, R. T. (1964). *The World of Birds.* Garden City, N.Y. Doubleday.

FISHER, J., SIMON, N. & VINCENT, J. (1969). *The Red Book, Wildlife in Danger.* London, Collins.

FORSHAW, J. M. & COOPER, W. (1973). *Parrots of the World.* New York, Doubleday.

GALLAGHER, M. D. (1960). Bird Notes from Christmas Island, Pacific Ocean. *Ibis* **102**:489-502.

GILLIARD, E. T. (1965). *Living Birds of the World.* London, Hamilton.

GILLIARD, E. T. & LECROY, M. (1967). Results of the 1958-1959 Gilliard New Britain Expedition: 4. Annotated List of the Birds of the Whiteman Mountains, New Britain. *Bull. Amer. Mus. Nat. Hist.* **135**:1-213.

GOODERS, J. ed. (1969-1971). *Birds of the World.* London, IPC Magazines Ltd.

GOODWIN, D. (1967). *Pigeons and Doves of the World.* London, British Museum (Nat. Hist.).

GREENWAY, JR., J. C. (1967). *Extinct and Vanishing Birds of the World.* New York, Dover.

GROSSMAN, M. L. & HAMLET, J. (1964). *Birds of Prey of the World.* New York, Potter.

HAGEN, Y. (1952). Birds of Tristan da Cunha. *Results of the Norwegian Scientific Expedition 1938-1939.* No. 20. Oslo, Dybwad.

HALL, B. P. & MOREAU, R. E. (1970). *An Atlas of Speciation in African Passerine Birds.* London, British Museum (Nat. Hist.).

HAYDOCK, E. L. (1954). A Survey of the Birds of St. Helena Island. *Ostrich* **25**:62-75.

196

HILL, R. (1967). *Australian Birds*. New York, Funk & Wagnalls.

HOOGERWERF, A. (1948). Distribution of Birds in Java. *Treubia* 19:116 27.

KEARST, A. (1961). Bird Speciation on the Australian Continent. *Bull. Mus. Comp. Zool.* **123**(8):305-495.

KEPLER, C. B. & PARKES, K. C. (1972). A New Species of Warbler (Parulidae) from Puerto Rico. *Auk* **89**:1-18.

KING, B., WOODCOCK, M. W. & DICKINSON, E. C. *A Field Guide to the Birds of South-East Asia*. London, Collins.

KING, J. E. (1958). Some Observations on the Birds of Tahiti and the Marquesas Islands. *The Elepaio* **19**:14-17.

KING, W. B. (1967). *Seabirds of the Tropical Pacific Ocean*, Washington, Smithsonian Institution.

KIRBY, Jr., H. (1925). The Birds of Fanning Island, Central Pacific Ocean. *Condor* **27**:194-6.

KURODA, N. (1938). A Collection of Birds from Halmahera and North Celebes. *Tori* **10**:376-93.

KURODA, N. (1953-1957). On a Collection of Birds from Celebes and Halmahera. *Misc. Rep. Yam. Inst.* **3**:98-111; **4**:156-73; **5**:206-19; **9**:352-60; **10**:389-98.

LEKAGUL, B. (n.d.). *Bird Guide of Thailand*. Bangkok, Association for the Conservation of Wildlife.

LLOYD, G. & LLOYD, D. (1971). *Birds of Prey*. New York, Bantam.

MAYR, E. & SERVENTY, D. L. (1944). The Number of Australian Bird Species. *Emu*, **44**:33-40.

MAYR, E. (1944). The Birds of Timor and Sumba. *Bull. Amer. Mus. Nat. Hist.* **83**: 123-94.

MAYR, E. (1945). *Birds of the Southwest Pacific*. New York, Macmillan.

MAYR, E. (1946). The Number of Species of Birds. *Auk* **63**:64-9.

MAYR, E. & AMADON, D. (1951). A Classification of Recent Birds. *Am. Mus. Nov.* **1496**:1-42.

MAYR, E. (1957). New Species of Birds Described from 1941 to 1955. *J. Orn.* **98**:22-35.

MAYR, E. (1965). Classification, Identification and Sequence of Genera and Species. *L' Ois. et la Rev. Fr. d'Ornith.* **35**:(Special) 90-5.

MAYR, E. & SHORT, L.L. (1970). *Species Taxa of North American Birds*. Cambridge, Mass., Nuttall Ornithological Club Publication No. 9.

MAYR, E. (1971). New Species of Birds Described from 1956 to 1965. *J. Orn.* **112**: 302-16.

MOREAU, R. E. (1960). Conspectus and Classification of the Ploceine Weaver-birds. Part 2. The Group A Ploceinae. *Ibis*, **102**:443-71.

MORGAN, B. & MORGAN, J. (1965). Some Notes on Birds of the Fiji Islands. *Notornis* **XII**:158-68.

MORRISON, J. P. E. (1954). Notes on the Birds of Raroia. *Atoll Research Bulletin No.* 34.

National Geographic Atlas of the World. (1963). Edited by M. B. Grosvenor. Washington, D.C., National Geographic Society.

OLROG, C. CHR. (1959). *Las Aves Argentinas, Una Guia de Campo*. Tucuman, Instituto "Miguel Lillo".

OLROG, C. CHR. (1968). *Las Aves Sudamericanas, Una Guia de Campo*, Tomo Prim. Tucuman, Fundacion-Instituto "Miguel Lillo".

197

Bibliography

Ornithological Society of New Zealand, Inc. (1970). *Annotated Checklist of the Birds of New Zealand*. Wellington, Reed; for the Society.

PEARSON, A. J. (1962). Field Notes on the Birds of Ocean Island and Nauru During 1961. *Ibis* **104**:421-4.

PETERS, J. L., et al. (1931-1970). *Checklist of Birds of the World*. Cambridge, Mass., Harvard University Press, 13 (of 15) vols. to 1972.

RAND, A. L. (1936). The Distribution and Habits of Madagascar Birds. *Bull. Amer. Mus. Nat. Hist.* **72**:143-499.

RAND, A. L. & GILLIARD, E. T. (1967). *Handbook of New Guinea Birds*. London, Weidenfeld and Nicolson.

REILLY, JR., E. M. (1968). *The Audubon Illustrated Handbook of American Birds*. New York, McGraw-Hill.

RENSCH, B. (1931). Die Vogelwelt von Lombock, Sumbawa und Flores. *Mitt. Zool. Mus. Berl.* **17**:451-637.

RIPLEY, S. D. (1941). Notes on a Collection of Birds from Northern Celebes. *Occ. Pap. Bos. Soc. Nat. Hist.* **8**:343-58.

RIPLEY, S. D. (1961). *A Synopsis of the Birds of India and Pakistan*. Bombay, Bombay National History Society.

RIPLEY, S. D. & RABOR, D. S. (1962). New Birds from Palawan and Culion Islands. *Yale Peab. Mus. Nat. Hist.*, *Postilla* **73**:1-16.

ROYAL AUSTRALASIAN ORNITHOLOGISTS' UNION. (1926). *The Official Checklist of the Birds of Australia*. Melbourne, Green.

SALOMONSEN, F. (1964). Some Birds from Dyaul Island. *Biol. Skr. Dansk. Vid. Selsk* **14**:1-38.

SCOTT, P. (1968). *A Coloured Key to the Wildfowl of the World*. London, The Wildfowl Trust.

SLATER, P. (1971). *A Field Guide to Australian Birds: Non-Passerines*. Wynnewood, Pa., Livingston.

SMYTHIES, B. (1953). *The Birds of Burma*. Edinburgh, Oliver & Boyd.

SMYTHIES, B. (1960). *The Birds of Borneo*. Edinburgh, Oliver & Boyd.

SORENSEN, J. H. (1964). Birds of the Kermadec Islands. *Notornis* **XI**:69-81.

STAGER, K. E. (1964). The Birds of Clipperton Island, Eastern Pacific. *Condor* **66**:357-61.

STRESEMANN, E. (1939-1941). Die Vogel von Celebes. *J. Orn.* **87**:299-425; **88**:1-135, 389-487; **89**:1-102.

SWARTH, H. (1931). The Avifauna of the Galapagos Islands. *Oc. Pap. Cal. Acad. Sci.* **18**:1-299.

URBAN, E. K. & BROWN, L. H. (1971). *A Checklist of the Birds of Ethiopia*. Addis Ababa, Haile Selassie I University Press.

VAN BEMMEL, A. C. V. (1948). A Faunal List of the Birds of the Moluccan Islands. *Treubia*. **19**:323-402.

VAURIE, CHARLES (1953). A Generic Revision of Flycatchers of the Tribe Musicapini. *Bull. A.M.N.H.* **100**:457-538.

VAURIE, CHARLES (1959). *The Birds of the Palearctic Fauna. Volume 1: Passeriformes*. London, Witherby.

VAURIE, CHARLES (1965). *The Birds of the Palearctic Fauna. Volume 2: Non-Passeriformes*. London, Witherby.

VON BOETTICHER, H. (1959). Papageien. *Neue Brehm-Buch* **229**:3-116.

VOOS, K. H. (1973). List of Recent Holarctic Bird Species, Non-Passerines. *Ibis.* **115**:612-638.

WATSON, G. E., ZUSI, R. L., STOVER, R. E. (1963). *Preliminary Field Guide to the Birds of the Indian Ocean.* Washington, Smithsonian Institution.

WATSON, G. E. (1966). *Sea Birds of the Tropical Atlantic Ocean.* Washington, Smithsonian Institution.

WATSON, G. E., et al. (1971). *Birds of the Antarctic and Subantartic.* Antarctic Map Folio Series, Folio 14. New York, American Geographical Society.

WETMORE, A. (1960). A Classification for the Birds of the World. *Smithsonian Misc. Coll.* **139**(11):1-37.

WHITE, C. M. N. (1960/62). A Check List of the Ethiopian Muscicapidae (Sylviinae). Pts. I and II. *Occ. Pap. Nat. Mus. Sci. Rhod.* **24B**:399-430; **26B**:653-738.

WHITE, C. M. N. (1961). *A Revised Check List of African Broadbills, Pittas, Larks, Swallows, Wagtails and Pipits.* Lusaka, Government Printer.

WHITE, C. M. N. (1962). *A Revised Check List of African Shrikes, Orioles, Drongos, Starlings, Crows, Waxwings, Cuckoo-Shrikes, Bulbuls, Accentors, Thrushes and Babblers.* Lusaka, Government Printer.

WHITE, C. M. N. (1963). *A Revised Check List of African Flycatchers, Tits, Tree Creepers, Sunbirds, White-eyes, Honey Eaters, Buntings, Finches, Weavers and Waxbills.* Lusaka, Government Printer.

WHITE, C. M. N. (1965). *A Revised Check List of African Non-Passerine Birds.* Lusaka, Government Printer.

WILDASH, P. (1968). *Birds of South Vietnam.* Rutland, Vt., Tuttle.

WILLIAMS, G. R. (1960). Birds of the Pitcairn Islands. *Ibis* **102**:58-70.

WILSON, E. (1968). *Birds of the Antarctic.* New York, Humanities Press.

WILSON, S. B. (1907). Birds of Tahiti and the Society Group. *Ibis* (*9th*) **3**:373-79.

Index of generic names

Index of Generic Names

203

Index of Generic Names

Index of English names

208

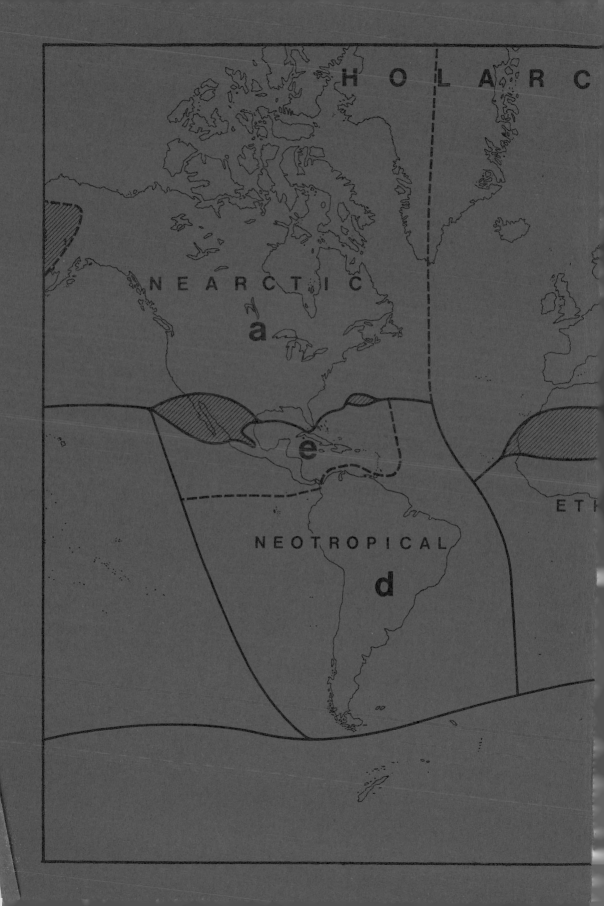